Religious Disagreement and Pluralism

Religious Disagreement and Pluralism

Edited by

MATTHEW A. BENTON AND
JONATHAN L. KVANVIG

OXFORD
UNIVERSITY PRESS

OXFORD
UNIVERSITY PRESS

Great Clarendon Street, Oxford, OX2 6DP,
United Kingdom

Oxford University Press is a department of the University of Oxford.
It furthers the University's objective of excellence in research, scholarship,
and education by publishing worldwide. Oxford is a registered trade mark of
Oxford University Press in the UK and in certain other countries

Published in the United States of America by Oxford University Press
198 Madison Avenue, New York, NY 10016, United States of America

British Library Cataloguing in Publication Data
Data available

Library of Congress Control Number: 2021938233

ISBN 978-0-19-884986-5

DOI: 10.1093/oso/9780198849865.001.0001

Printed and bound in the UK by
TJ Books Limited

Links to third party websites are provided by Oxford in good faith and
for information only. Oxford disclaims any responsibility for the materials
contained in any third party website referenced in this work.

Contents

Acknowledgments   vii
List of Contributors   ix

1. Disagreement and Religion: Problems and Prospects   1
   Matthew A. Benton

2. Disagreement, Testimony, and Religious Understanding   41
   Laura Frances Callahan

3. How Confident Should the Religious Believer Be in the
   Face of Religious Pluralism?   65
   Sanford C. Goldberg

4. Religious Disagreement Is Not Unique   91
   Margaret Greta Turnbull

5. Is There Something Special About Religious Disagreement?   108
   Richard Feldman

6. Transformative Experience and the Problem of Religious
   Disagreement   127
   Joshua Blanchard and L.A. Paul

7. The Apologist's Dilemma   142
   Nathan L. King

8. Rationalist Resistance to Disagreement-Motivated Religious
   Skepticism   180
   John Pittard

9. How to Be an Inclusivist   217
   Jonathan L. Kvanvig

10. The Loyalty of Religious Disagreement   238
    Katherine Dormandy

11. Democracy of the Dead? The Relevance of Majority
    Opinion in Theology   271
    Isaac Choi

Index   289

Acknowledgments

The editors gratefully acknowledge the early input of Ted A. Warfield, who helped conceive of this volume, selected and invited several of the contributors, and began work in co-editing it. We would also like to thank Michael Bergmann for helpful advice during the middle stages of this project.

We are also grateful to Peter Momtchiloff at Oxford University Press, and for the advice of anonymous reviewers for the Press.

Work on this volume was also supported by a Faculty Research and Scholarship Grant from Seattle Pacific University, 2018–2019.

List of Contributors

Matthew A. Benton is Associate Professor of Philosophy, Seattle Pacific University

Joshua Blanchard is Visiting Assistant Professor of Philosophy, Oakland University

Laura Frances Callahan is Assistant Professor of Philosophy, University of Notre Dame

Isaac Choi is Assistant Professor of Philosophy, George Fox University

Katherine Dormandy is Professor of Philosophy, Department of Christian Philosophy, University of Innsbruck

Richard Feldman is University Professor of Philosophy, University of Rochester

Sanford C. Goldberg is Chester D. Tripp Professor in the Humanities, Northwestern University

Nathan L. King is Professor of Philosophy, Whitworth University

Jonathan L. Kvanvig is Professor of Philosophy, Washington University in St. Louis

L.A. Paul is Millstone Family Professor of Philosophy and Cognitive Science, Yale University

John Pittard is Associate Professor of Philosophy of Religion, Yale Divinity School

Margaret Greta Turnbull is Assistant Professor of Philosophy, Gonzaga University

List of Contributors

1

Disagreement and Religion

Problems and Prospects

Matthew A. Benton

Disagreements over religion are common, entrenched, and often bitter. Harmful sectarian and internecine conflict, when taken to extremes, often results in war and terrorism. Even when less violent, such pervasive disagreements can nevertheless afflict social groups and family relationships. Understanding the social and political contexts of such events is a task for historians and sociologists. Evaluating the religious divisions themselves is a task for theologians and scholars of religion.

Philosophers, on the other hand, focus largely on conceptual and normative issues emerging from what sorts of disagreements there are, and what differences they might make to what an individual should, or should not, believe. Such disagreements over religion offer a lens on how to think about distinctive epistemological issues, such as the nature and weight of evidence when it comes to religious topics; the rationality of belief or religious practices; the epistemological import of understanding; the value of epistemic humility given an awareness of religious diversity; whether testimony is an adequate basis for believing anything related to religion; and whether knowledge in some religious domain is possible given widespread disagreement.

Religious devotion, of course, consists in more than simply cognitive commitments of the sort labeled by doxastic concepts like *belief, faith*, or *credence* (subjective probability, as studied by formal epistemology). But epistemologists in philosophy have attended largely to the doxastic terrain because cognitive commitments are thought in some sense to ground the rationality of deciding to engage, or continue in, the practices associated with a religion (or in the case of non-belief, refraining from such commitments grounds the rationality of abstaining from practicing any particular religion at all). So we shall focus largely on the broad family of doxastic notions often captured by the label of "belief," where this most often refers to outright belief of the sort which, if true and other conditions hold, could count as knowledge; but we

Matthew A. Benton, *Disagreement and Religion: Problems and Prospects* In: *Religious Disagreement and Pluralism.* Edited by: Matthew A. Benton and Jonathan L. Kvanvig, Oxford University Press. © Matthew A. Benton 2021. DOI: 10.1093/oso/9780198849865.003.0001

shall sometimes also consider credence, understanding, and where relevant, faith.[1]

This chapter aims to provide a map of the contemporary landscape on disagreement, detailing both the conceptual and normative issues in play in mainstream analytic epistemology, and how these have (and have not) translated into the domain of religious diversity and disagreement.[2] In section 1 we examine several sorts of disagreement, and consider in detail some epistemological issues on which many philosophers have recently focused: in particular, what range of attitudes a body of evidence can support, understanding higher-order evidence, and thinking about who counts as an epistemic "peer." In section 2 we will turn to how some of these questions surface when considering disagreements over religion, including debates over the nature of evidence and truth in religion, epistemic humility, concerns about irrelevant influences and about divine hiddenness, and arguments over exclusivism, inclusivism, and pluralism.[3] Finally, section 3 offers a brief summary of the contributors' essays in this volume.

1. Epistemology and Disagreement

Philosophers thinking about the epistemology of disagreement[4] have tended to approach the matter by asking when, if ever, learning about a specific sort of disagreement with one's belief ought to lead one to revise that belief (for example, by dropping the belief and suspending judgment on the matter; or, if one began with merely a high credence as opposed to an outright belief, by lowering one's credence). For it seems that in a great range of cases, encountering such a disagreement puts pressure on you to at least become less confident that you, as opposed to your disagreer, are getting things right. That is, it can seem that the only rational option for you is to concede that you may be getting it wrong, and to modulate your conviction so as to be

---

[1] A large literature has recently emerged examining the nature of faith, including whether it must involve a cognitive propositional commitment. See, e.g., Audi 2011, Buchak 2012 and Buchak 2014a; Howard-Snyder 2016, Kvanvig 2018; and Rice, McKaughn, and Howard-Snyder 2017 (including the several essays in that issue). For a helpful overview, see Buchak 2014b. Related issues are raised by the philosophy literature on trust: see e.g., Faulkner and Simpson 2017 for a selection.

[2] Related issues arise with the domain of moral disagreement; though we cannot consider them here, see Mackie 1977, Chap. 1, Audi 2014, Vavova 2014, and Rowland 2017.

[3] Some parts of these sections borrow from, or expand on, material in Benton 2019.

[4] See especially the collections Feldman and Warfield 2010, Christensen and Lackey 2013, and Machuca 2013. For overviews, see Christensen 2009, Frances and Matheson 2018, and Ferrari and Pedersen 2019.

conciliatory toward your interlocutor. For example, imagine that you and a friend go out to dinner. You both agree to split the check evenly, adding a 20 percent tip. You both look at the bill, and each mentally calculate your share. You confidently conclude that each owes $43, whereas your friend concludes that each of you owe $48. How should you respond?[5]

If you supposed yourself to be typically better at such mental calculations, you might insist that your friend recalculate while you maintain confidence in your result. (Or vice versa if you think your friend is likely to be better at such calculations.) But suppose that, prior to this dinner check disagreement, you regarded your friend as being about as good as you at mental math; and suppose that you regarded your memory and cognitive functioning (and how much you've had to drink) as being about equal. If you had regarded them in these ways as your *peer* with respect to mental calculation on this occasion, it would be in part because you had no reasons *independent* of the current disagreement over how much each owes to think that you rather than they would conclude correctly. But if so, it can seem highly irrational for you now to prioritize your answer as correct and insist that they must have made a mistake. For from your perspective, you were each as likely as the other to have made a mistake. So if you're rational, you will probably lower your confidence that you each owe $43, since either (or both) of you may have made a mistake;[6] and it's because you've reduced your confidence that you would then recalculate. This seems all the more appropriate when you imagine how you would feel if you came to learn instead that your dinner friend had *agreed* with your conclusion: you would no doubt become, if only slightly, more confident that you had gotten it right.

More generally, when we regard our interlocutors as being our peers—as well-informed as we are, and of similar intelligence (and not joking with us)— then learning that they disagree, particularly when we are working with the same evidence, ought to lead us each to suspend judgment and reassess. Similar results apply when we move from full *belief, disbelief,* and *suspension* of belief, to finer-grained doxastic states like degrees of belief or subjective probabilities, sometimes called *credences:*[7] if you have a 0.9 credence that it will rain in Seattle today, whereas I have only 0.3 credence that it will rain in Seattle

[5] See Christensen 2007, 193 and 2009, 757 for such cases.

[6] Similar cases can be given about perceptual judgments rather than mental reasoning (Feldman 2006, 223, and 2007, 207–208), for example, that you and your friend each see the end of a horse race, from nearly identical viewing points, but you disagree about which horse won (Kelly 2010, 113).

[7] Credences are thought of as a measure of "partial" belief. Credences in a proposition p are given by real numbers from 0 (complete certainty in p's falsity) to 1 (complete certainty in p's truth), where 0.5 amounts to being indifferent, p being as likely as not. Axioms of the probability calculus provide

today, and we both updated only on evidence from (what we regard as) equally reliable sources about the weather, you will likely lower your credence from 0.9 (and I will likely raise mine from 0.3).[8] And this seems like the most rational thing for each of us to do.

Both of the above cases are framed from the first-person perspective, imagining yourself as one of the participants: from that perspective, it seems that you each should reduce your confidence (or drop your belief altogether) and reconsider. But return to the dinner check-splitting case, and take a neutral third-person perspective: someone else observing us might arrive at a different judgment about what we each should do. They might insist that if the correct answer was that we each owe $48, then strictly speaking, only you, and not your friend, should reduce your confidence (and recalculate), since your friend in fact got it right. Perhaps then there is a sense in which the person, if any, who was accurate in their assessment has the right to remain steadfast in their belief. But recall that from the accurate party's perspective, their disagreer was as likely as they themselves were to have made a mistake; for a crucial feature of the case is that they have no *independent* reason, outside their handling of the evidence, to think that they are indeed accurate rather than inaccurate on this occasion. It would seem dubiously obstinate for them to insist that, even though they regard you as a mental math peer, you and not they should recalculate because, in fact, you each owe $48; for the disagreement itself, given that you are peers, seems to call into question whether you each owe that amount. Perhaps then rationality requires that in cases of disagreement between those we regard as peers, we ought to be conciliatory by shifting our confidence away from our initial conclusion, and toward our peer's. The normative principles according to which we ought to do this vary among those who endorse such *Conciliationism*. For example, according to an early view, one must grant "equal weight" to one's peer's opinion as one would to one's own, and doing so requires that each reduce one's confidence, perhaps even suspend judgment or move to 0.5 credence, when one first learns of such disagreements.[9] Such a view might recommend that in such cases, one must "split the difference" between a peer's credence and one's own.

---

constraints on such credences; formal epistemologists argue over principles of probabilistic reasoning, particularly how to model appropriate updates to one's credences, given new evidence. For overviews, see Weisberg 2019, and Hájek and Staffel 2021.

[8] Hereafter, unless otherwise stated, I shall use "belief" as a catch-all to refer to both full and partial belief, such that "lowering" one's confidence can mean either dropping one's full belief in favor of suspending judgment, or reducing one's credence.

[9] See Elga 2007, Christensen 2007, King 2012, Cohen 2013, and Matheson 2014 and 2015 for discussion.

1.1 Uniqueness and Permissivism

Many philosophers claim that implicit in such Conciliationist views is the idea that a given set of evidence supports, at most, only one doxastic response, such as belief, or a particular credence.[10] Consider the principle *Uniqueness*:

Uniqueness   Given one's total evidence there is, at most, one unique rational doxastic attitude that one can take to any proposition.[11]

If Uniqueness (or something comparable) is true, then when two peers handle the same evidence and end up disagreeing on the conclusion, at least one of them has mistakenly arrived at an irrational doxastic attitude. The one who has formed the irrational attitude should revise their view; but on the assumption that each peer has no independent reason to think themselves the irrational one, each will, given Uniqueness, likely feel conciliatory pressure in the above cases.

Thus some philosophers argue that Uniqueness helps explain such conciliatory pressure. But if Uniqueness is false, there is room for thinking that there could sometimes be reasonable disagreements, even among peers who have the same evidence. Denying Uniqueness amounts to endorsing a permissive view of what rationality requires, such that one's evidence may rationally support more than one doxastic position. But there are different ways of departing from Uniqueness. One might be what Roger White (2005) calls a *radical* permissivist, by thinking that, at least in some circumstances, one's total evidence can permit either believing that p or believing that $\neg p$. But arguably, if rationality could be that permissive (even if only in perhaps rare circumstances), then people with identical evidence could sometimes reasonably disagree, since that evidence can reasonably support believing either way. Yet in those cases at least, believing a particular way can seem arbitrary and not directed at the truth. Such a radical permissiveness would also, paradoxically, suggest that each of the disagreers could rightly think that the other reasonably evaluated the evidence, even though each will presumably still regard their own assessment of the evidence as reasonable and correct.[12]

---

[10] However, Christensen 2016 argues that Conciliationism can be motivated even without Uniqueness.

[11] White 2005, 445, and Feldman 2007, 205. For a detailed overview of ensuing debate, see Kopec and Titelbaum 2016.

[12] See Schoenfield 2014, 200–202 for discussion of similar worries.

Less controversially, one might be a *moderate* permissivist by denying this radical view yet insisting that, at least in some circumstances, one's total evidence can permit, say, either believing that *p* or suspending judgment on *p*. More moderate still would be a view that denies each of the above concerning outright belief and withholding belief, but allows that in some circumstances, one's evidence at least makes rational a (perhaps small) range of credences (e.g., Schoenfield 2014 and 2018).[13] Each of these permissivist approaches offers a kind of pluralism about the sorts of doxastic response that a set of evidence supports.

Notice however that for any such permissivist view, it is desirable that the view be able to offer an account of under what circumstances, or with respect to which domains, we can expect the permissivism to hold, and why. When exactly might a set of evidence in and of itself permit more than one doxastic response, or a range of credences? What domains, if not idealized cases of peers doing mental math for splitting a dinner check, may allow for reasonable disagreement over one's conclusion? In addition, permissivist approaches need to explain how, if rationality is permissive (when it is), it remains a guide to the truth: for if rationality permits a range of doxastic responses on some matter, some rational believers will be less accurate than others[14] (e.g., Horowitz 2019).

1.2 Higher-Order Evidence

Perhaps any conciliatory pressure when learning of a peer's differing response may be explained by the suggestion that learning, for the first time, of a peer disagreement provides you with *new* evidence, higher-order evidence. Evidence which bears directly on the truth of a proposition *p* may be called first-order evidence, whereas higher-order evidence is indirect in its bearing on *p*: it may reveal something about the character of the first-order evidence, or about how well you evaluated the first-order evidence. So according to this line of thought, in cases of disagreement, although the initial (first-order)

---

[13] Note that in the empirical sciences, it is standard practice to offer confidence intervals along with predictions, where the disciplinary methodologies have some guidelines for how to produce such intervals, given the data and the hypotheses under examination. One way to think about such confidence intervals is to allow that the data (evidence) in question permit a range of credences in the prediction.

[14] Or, on a credence-accuracy framework, some subjects' credences will be scored as further from the truth, which will presumably (eventually) yield undesirable practical results owing to their credences being less than fully accurate. For a substantial study, see Pettigrew 2018.

evidence on which you arrived at your conclusion seems to you to support, say, p, learning that your peer with comparable evidence concluded instead that p is false ($\neg p$) can give you higher-order evidence that you wrongly evaluated the initial, first-order evidence.[15]

For example, Richard Feldman insisted that learning of a peer's reaching a different conclusion, on the basis of the same evidence, amounts to evidence against one's own conclusion because "evidence that there is evidence for p is evidence for p" (Feldman 2006, 223; 2007, 208).[16] Such a principle makes sense of the idea that learning about peers disagreeing gives me a new sort of evidence for their conclusion. For it says that discovering that a peer concludes differently on the basis of the same evidence E provides me with new higher-order evidence that I have misconstrued what E supports. More specifically, Feldman recently argues for:

EEE3 If S has evidence, E1, supporting the proposition that there is someone who has evidence that supports p, then S has some evidence, E2, that supports p (2014, 292).

EEE3 could explain why we ought to reduce our confidence in such situations. For if learning about the relevant disagreement provides me with additional evidence against what I had concluded, then respecting this new evidence plausibly requires that I adjust my confidence downward in light of it.

However, EEE3, as a universal principle, cannot be correct. Suppose that your friend Joe is to guess which one of three objects you are about to put into an empty box: an apple, a ball, or some cheese. Out of his sight, you put in the apple; so you know that there is an apple in the box, but he does not. You then tell Joe that it isn't a ball in the box. Given what Joe knows about the setup, your testimony provides Joe with some evidence there is cheese in the box, because Joe's learning that it's not a ball raises the probability for Joe that it's cheese in the box. This is because when Joe learns that of the three possibilities, it isn't a ball, the probability for him that it is cheese in the box goes up (as does the probability for him that it is an apple). As the antecedent of EEE3 has it, you have evidence (E1) that there is someone (namely Joe) who has evidence which supports (p) that there is cheese in the box. But E1 does not raise the probability for you that there is cheese in the box, because you know there is

---

[15] For helpful discussion of the relation between first-order and higher-order evidence, see Kvanvig 2014, Chaps. 4 and 5.

[16] But see Fitelson 2012 for a swift refutation of this slogan, which also casts doubt on Feldman's EEE3, considered below.

no cheese in the box. So your knowing E1 is not, for you, evidence (E2) which supports the hypothesis (*p*) that there is cheese inside. (If it were, then by merely telling Joe that what you put in the box is not a ball, you would thereby have acquired some startling evidence that you *didn't* put in an apple. But that's absurd.) So EEE3 is false.[17]

So precise principles about evidence such as Uniqueness, or about the relation of higher-order to first-order evidence, can seem problematic. Another way to think about why disagreements often induce us, when they do, to lower our confidence is that they raise the possibility that the route by which we arrived at our belief may not be reliably related to that belief's being true. Looked at in this way, disagreements bear a similarity to certain debunking arguments which explicitly offer a genealogical account of the causal origins of one's beliefs whose causal paths do not include the truth of what is believed; so if one nevertheless believes a truth, such debunking arguments suggest, it is largely a matter of luck.[18] But disagreements raise such doubt implicitly, without offering any genealogy, since they merely reveal that one of the disagreeing parties must be arriving at their beliefs by a less than ideal route. Once such a doubt is raised, many think that one can typically address the doubt only by having (or finding) some independent grounds for thinking that one's belief forming methods are indeed the sort that would reliably lead to true beliefs. Moreover, large scale disagreements such as those found among religious groups, along with the demographic distributions of them, can

[17] Note that Feldman's replies to anticipated objections to EEE3 (2014, 296–299) don't apply to this case. For example, it won't do to say that EEE3 stands because you have some evidence E2 which, *for Joe*, supports *p*; for EEE3 is supposed to be about how S's having evidence of someone else's evidence provides evidential support *for S*. Sometimes Feldman replies to objections by noting that S still has evidence, even though it is defeated (such that it is indeed evidence for someone else, who doesn't have the defeater). But in our above case, what proposition would serve as the defeater for you? For the relevant propositions are: (E1) that there is someone, Joe, who has evidence that there is cheese in the box, (E2) that you told him that there is not a ball in the box, (*p*) that there is cheese in the box, and (*r*), known only to you, that there is (only) an apple in the box. But given what is salient in this case, knowing *r* amounts to knowing the conjunction of (*q*) there is an apple in the box and (¬*p*) there is not cheese in the box. So if one wants to claim that you indeed have evidence for *p*, that there is cheese in the box, but which is nevertheless defeated, it is defeated by your knowledge that ¬*p*, that there is not cheese in the box. But this is highly unorthodox: for most epistemologists, having rebutting evidence defeats one's knowledge, rather than one's knowledge "defeating" a rebutting defeater. (Note, if one takes this unorthodox road, the more general question looms: what distinguishes cases of knowledge in the presence of such defeaters, from cases where the defeater robs one of knowledge?) It seems better then to abandon such talk and just admit that in this case you really don't "have" evidence for *p*; and this is because you know that *p* is false. (For a related case where knowledge precludes defeat, see Benton 2016, §4, cf. also Kelly 2013, 45. For helpful discussion on providing and having evidence, see Anderson 2018.)

[18] For recent debate in epistemology over how problematic debunking considerations are, see White 2010, Vavova 2018, and Srinivasan 2015, 2019.

suggest how susceptible many people are to the ways that beliefs pattern among social groups (more on this in section 2.2).

A common way of construing how disagreement accomplishes its epistemic work is to appeal explicitly to the notion of an epistemic *defeater*, which is supposed to defeat the justification one might need in order to know, or even acceptably believe, one's views. Perhaps some disagreements provide one with a defeater even if not by providing one with counterevidence or even with higher-order evidence concerning *p* itself; and such defeaters, it would seem, can make it rationally mandatory to revise one's belief. Perhaps then in the dinner case, learning that your peer reached a different conclusion defeats whatever it was from your own calculating which justified believing your own conclusion (and realizing the force of this defeater, you rightly reconsider). Thinking about larger scale disagreements, Sanford Goldberg (2013b, 2014, and 2015) argues that when the peer disagreements are known to be *systematic*, this presents one with a defeater for the justification one might have for one's belief. Systematic disagreements are (i) widespread, (ii) entrenched, and (iii) non-localized, that is, they involve many related matters rather than the dispute being only over a particular local proposition. Such defeaters are not easily dispensed with (for example, by defeating them with some other evidence which would defeat the defeater), because these disagreements induce the concern that even those who believe truly are, again, somehow lucky to arrive at the truth. Given this, systematic disagreements can seem to rob one's beliefs of justification.[19] Whether this is plausible, however, will depend on an array of details: Do such disagreements still defeat when someone carefully arrives at one's view while fully understanding the systematic nature of the disagreements in question (such as in philosophy, or in religion)? Does defeat only occur when the disagreements lead a subject to take seriously the prospect that they've misevaluated the evidence, or does the fact of such disagreements make it the case that one *ought* to take this seriously, whether or not one does so?[20] What if, in particular, one's view predicts or explains why there would be systematic disagreements of the sort in question? Would that be enough to render the defeater inert?

The main idea considered thus far is that learning of disagreements, particularly when they are with peers who seem to have the same or

---

[19] Though widely used in epistemology, the viability of knowledge defeat in epistemology has come under challenge: see Lasonen-Aarnio 2010 and 2014, Greco 2010, Chap. 10, Hawthorne and Srinivasan 2013, and Baker-Hytch and Benton 2015. See also fn.17.

[20] This would be a special kind, a *normative* defeater. See Lackey 2018, 45 and 198ff., Goldberg 2016 and 2017, and Benton 2016 for concerns.

comparable evidence, generates pressure to revise or weaken our opinion; and Conciliationists argue that this pressure reflects something important about epistemic rationality. Yet it is difficult to formulate well-motivated principles which express the normative idea underlying why we ought to revise when it seems that we should. Moreover, some have criticized Conciliationism on a number of grounds which are worth exploring.

1.3 When I Think About You, I Trust Myself

Insofar as some Conciliationists have aimed to offer a universal principle of rationality which would cover all the relevant cases, a common objection is that Conciliationism is self-undermining: if it is true, then we should not be very confident of it, for when applied to itself, it says we should lower our confidence in it. This is because many philosophers, who presumably regard each other as peers and consider all the same arguments, disagree over the truth of Conciliationism. At the very least, by the (unrestricted) Conciliationist's lights, such a Conciliationist should not be very confident of their own view.[21] Even worse, a philosopher inclined toward Conciliationism thus has reasons from peer disagreement to become not very confident in *any* of their philosophical views, given the presence of capable philosophers who disagree with them (see Goldberg 2013a). Similar thoughts apply to equal weight views of Conciliationism: to accept such an equal weight view, given philosophers who disagree, one has to "inconsistently both be very confident that it is true and not very confident that it is true" (Weatherson 2013, 55).

Thomas Kelly (2005, 2010, and 2011) raises several concerns for versions of Conciliationism, even for idealized cases. One worry is that deferring to one's peer by reducing one's confidence can look like an illicit double-counting of the evidence. Suppose we each begin with the same evidence set E bearing on whether p, and after evaluating E, we share our findings: I conclude that p whereas you conclude that $\neg p$. If I treat your contrary belief, reached from *your* evaluation of E, as an added reason to believe $\neg p$, then I've allowed E to have additional evidential weight (processed through you) beyond the weight I've already given it. And somewhat awkwardly, in doing this, I would be treating the fact that you believe $\neg p$ on the basis of E, as a reason for me to believe $\neg p$, even though you wouldn't yourself regard your believing that $\neg p$ as

---

[21] See Elga 2010, cf. Pittard 2015b and 2020 for a way out.

an additional reason—on top of E—for believing ¬p (Kelly 2005, 187ff.). But it would be illicit for you to use the fact that you believe ¬p on the basis of E as *further* reason, on top of E, to believe ¬p: it would seem like a sort of bootstrapping[22] to use your own belief in this way to increase your confidence in what you believe.[23] Yet if it would be problematic for you to use your belief that ¬p in this way, why should it be okay for me to use your belief to increase my confidence in ¬p?

Another worry, at least for Equal Weight versions of Conciliationism which assume Uniqueness, is that doing what they advise can lead one *away* from the rational attitude required by Uniqueness. Suppose there is a fact about the degree to which evidence E supports p, namely, that it makes p 0.8 probable, and that we each only have E bearing on p. Upon evaluating E, suppose that your credence in p is, quite rightly, 0.8, whereas I botch it, quite unreasonably arriving at a credence of 0.2. In such a case you got it exactly right, fulfilling the uniquely rational doxastic attitude given E. But when we discuss E and our conflicting credences over p, the Equal Weight view requires that you must, to be rational, split the difference with me and we must both then be 0.5 confident in p. But to do this would be for you to *depart* from the uniquely rational attitude toward p given E. Thus the Equal Weight view results in making the original E irrelevant to the bearing of our new evidence (which includes E but also includes the facts about what credences we had reached upon consulting E) on p; the actual evidence E bearing on p gets completely swamped by psychological facts about what the two of us believe (Kelly 2010, 123–124). What is more, the Equal Weight view arguably cannot be spelled out in a plausible way in a Bayesian framework while also capturing all the intuitions of the cases marshaled in its support, unless it disrespects some of the very principles which motivated it (Lasonen-Aarnio 2013).[24]

Concerns like these have led some philosophers to argue that often enough, when encountering some peer disagreements, one can nevertheless rationally

---

[22] See Weisberg 2012.

[23] Indeed, this consideration is part of why Conciliationists oppose a view on which one can remain steadfast in one's belief in the face of such a disagreement: for it would beg the question against one's disagreeing peer to reason, "Well, you believe that ¬p, but E supports p (as I believe), so clearly, your belief is mistaken." However, Lasonen-Aarnio 2015 argues against the idea that learning of others' opinions may function as higher-order evidence for one, whereas learning of one's own cannot: "it is at best implausible and at worst incoherent to allow evidence about the (present) doxastic states of others to have a certain kind of epistemic import, but not to allow evidence about one's own (present) states to have that kind of import" (269–270).

[24] Lasonen-Aarnio 2013 argues that it is subject to a trilemma: it violates intuitively correct updates (conditionalization), it imposes implausible restrictions on prior credence functions, or it is non-substantive. What is worse, she argues that any blanket view of disagreement is subject to a similar worry.

remain *steadfast* in one's belief. Such views insist that the facts about who reasoned correctly, or best evaluated the evidence, or gets (closest to) the truth, play a role in who may rationally maintain their belief, for what is rational here is not simply a matter of judging who is most likely to be in epistemic error from the internal, first-person perspective.[25] On Kelly's "total evidence" view, for example, parties to such disagreements must take into account both the first-order evidence on which they each initially arrived at their conclusions, as well as the higher-order evidence gained from learning about the disagreement. But in some cases it may be that the first-order evidence is strong enough to allow one party, who assessed it correctly in fact, to maintain their belief, even if they lose a bit of confidence. On this view, whether it is reasonable for one party to remain steadfastly in their belief is not separable from whether they are getting it most right (Kelly 2013, 35).[26]

Even more strongly, Hawthorne and Srinivasan (2013) argue for a knowledge disagreement norm, on which "one should be 'conciliatory' in the face of disagreement—that is, give up one's belief that *p* and trust one's disagreeing interlocutor that not-*p*—just in case so trusting would lead one to know that not-*p*," whereas "one should be 'dogmatic' in the face of disagreement—that is, dismiss one's interlocutor and continue to believe *p*—if one knows that *p*" (2013, 12). Such a view supposes that even in many disclosed disagreements, one of the parties can, in some cases at least, count as knowing their conclusion, despite the standard assumption made by most philosophers above, that such disagreements change each party's evidence, or at least defeat one's justification or knowledge.[27] Even if one takes on their (controversial) view that one party's knowledge might survive in a context of disagreement, Hawthorne and Srinivasan also accept that knowing is not always transparent to the knower,[28] and thus their proposed knowledge disagreement norm is not, as they acknowledge, perfectly operationalizable (2013, 15ff.). This aspect of

---

[25] See van Inwagen 2010, Hawthorne and Srinivasan 2013, Kelly 2010 and 2013, Weatherson 2013, and Titelbaum 2015, esp. 282ff.

[26] There are, of course, lots of cases where one quite reasonably is unmoved by a disagreement, such as when confronting a conspiracy theorist (see Kelly 2013, 40–46, discussing a Holocaust denier; or compare someone who denies climate change; etc.). But in such cases, it is far more plausible to judge that they have not considered all of the evidence, or have unreasonably discounted much of it. So these tend to be uninteresting cases of non-peer disagreement.

[27] Hawthorne and Srinivasan 2013, 21–25 are unimpressed by the extant work arguing for easy knowledge defeat. Cf. also fn.19 above.

[28] Using Williamson's terminology (2000, Chap. 4): where a condition C is *luminous* just in case whenever one is in C, one is in a position to know one is in C, whereas C is *absence-luminous* just in case whenever one is not in C, one is in a position to know that one is not in C; and a condition is *transparent* just in case it is both luminous and absence-luminous. Williamson (Chap. 4) argues against the luminosity of knowledge, and of mental states more generally.

their view will dissatisfy those who expect from a norm of what one ought to do that one be well-positioned to discern, and to carry out, what the norm requires in a given situation.[29]

Some may worry that any non-Conciliationist view will sanction a problematic stance of dogmatism in the face of disagreement, and that such a stance contributes to the phenomenon of *belief polarization*.[30] When people with incompatible views are presented with mixed evidence bearing on those views, people tend to interpret the evidence in such a way that minimizes the evidence against their own view while allowing the evidence for their view to increase their confidence in it (and it may be that certain sorts of cherished domains, such as politics, morality, or religion, lend themselves more easily to the evidence looking rather mixed). Such responses exacerbate the extent of the disagreement, as each side hardens in their commitments. Approaches to peer disagreement which permit Steadfast responses might be objected to on the grounds that they seem to give cover to each side of a disagreement: inasmuch as each party treats their own side with partiality in their handling of the evidence, or avoids proper engagement with the contrary evidence when it is encountered, they are to that extent fostering belief polarization by irrational means. Arguably, however, what best explains the occurrence of belief polarization is not some normative view (such as Steadfastness), nor (in some cases) confirmation bias, but rather the fact that people tend to devote more cognitive effort to scrutinizing heavily the evidence which does not comport well with their own view, so as to explain it in other ways (Kelly 2008).[31] Doing so means that one assesses the counterevidence against a broader background of alternative hypotheses, and thus it has a smaller evidential effect for the party which disagrees; whereas each party will tend to spend less time and effort scrutinizing the evidence which supports their view (Kelly 2008). It is possible for such attentive scrutiny to be the result of epistemic humility in one's own view, if such differential treatment manifests a respect for opposing positions. And a habit of closer scrutiny of the counter-evidence is obviously compatible with the spirit of Conciliationism, should one

---

[29] Astute readers will notice that the debate between Conciliationists and (some forms of) Steadfasters mimics the broader rivalry between internalists and externalists in epistemology. Looked at another way, the former seems to prioritize avoiding error, whereas the latter prioritizes believing the truth (in terms of William James' twin epistemic goals: James 1912, 17). I leave it to readers to draw out any significant ramifications of such parallels.

[30] See Lord, Ross, and Lepper 1979, and Kelly 2008.

[31] For those who want to conclude that such a practice is unreasonable, Kelly 2008, 624, notes that the empirical sciences proceed in just this way.

allow that counterevidence to reduce one's confidence in one's view (even if such reduction is muted in part by the mixed nature of the evidence).

We have so far explored in some detail the concepts at play in recent work on the epistemology of disagreement, including grounds for offering, or questioning, normative principles which have been proposed about what one should do when learning about different sorts of disagreement. Let us now turn to disagreement over religion.

2. Disagreement over Religion

Many of the central questions raised above were originally posed by philosophers who had their eye on the significance of religious disagreement (especially Gutting 1982; Alston 1988; Hick 1988, 1989, and 1997; van Inwagen 1994, 41–46, and van Inwagen 1996, 139; Plantinga 1995; Rosen 2001, 83–87).[32]

Religion is a controversial domain: religions distinguish themselves by making various claims about the supernatural, humanity, and how to live. Even among religious adherents who share certain core religious commitments, there remains much disagreement between sects or denominations, and even within narrow denominations, over doctrine, worship, spirituality, the afterlife, religious or spiritual leadership, and so on. Insofar as it is possible to demarcate major religions in terms of their core traditions, texts, and doctrinal agreements, we may call disagreements between those within a religion *intra-religious* disagreements. More central to our purposes are disagreements between major religions, such as disagreements over the nature of the divine or the supernatural, what sacred texts are divinely inspired or otherwise canonical, how God or the supernatural has manifested itself in historical events, who counts as a prophet or divine messenger, how to practice spirituality, and so on. Such differences distinguish, say, Islam from Christianity, each of these from Buddhism or Hinduism, and so on. This is *inter-religious* disagreement. But of course, contributing to the overall diversity concerning religion are the many non-religious or irreligious, particularly atheists, who think that nearly all positive claims (at least about the existence of the supernatural) are false. This we may call *extra-religious* disagreement.

[32] For overviews of the issues applied to religious disagreement, see King 2008, Basinger 2015, Pittard 2015a, and King and Kelly 2017. For in-depth discussions, see the collections Kraft and Basinger 2016, and Meister 2011, as well as the monographs Kraft 2012, Axtell 2018, De Cruz 2019, and especially Pittard 2020, which is state of the art.

For simplicity's sake, we shall begin by focusing on the basic positions of the theist, atheist, and agnostic (one who has not yet decided what to believe).[33] Later we will consider how questions about disagreement surface related to inter-religious disagreement.

One swift application of the ideas from the last section is to suggest that the fact of extra-religious disagreement puts conciliatory pressure on any theist (or other religious view such as non-theist Hinduism), and on any naturalistic atheist, to reduce their confidence in their view. Even if we allow that there will be varying sorts of experiences and evidence, and that not everyone will count as one's "peer," the sheer numbers of those who disagree with one's own stance on religion ought to give one pause that one is getting it right.[34] Looked at this way, widespread extra-religious disagreement looks like it supports the agnostic who insists we should suspend judgment on what stance on religion is correct, and continue to examine all such worldviews.[35] But when considering whether such agnosticism is justified, someone weighing up atheism versus a broadly religious worldview (theistic or otherwise) might insist that it also matters that the broadly religious outlook manifests large scale *agreements*, against the atheist, about the nature of ultimate reality and the life most worth living. Indeed, one might argue that this feature of extra-religious disagreement blunts any apparent pressure to be agnostic, and it could even provide some weight in favor of a broadly religious worldview[36] (we shall consider this in more detail when we look at common consent arguments later). Looked at this way, it is unclear that Conciliationist considerations should automatically push one toward agnosticism. But if so, what of the choice between atheism and a religious worldview? Presumably, one should sincerely assess any available arguments and evidence.

However, complicating matters are concerns about what counts as evidence in the religious domain; whether some forms of evidence are more probative than others; and whether one must grant more weight to public or shared

---

[33] By "theist" I mean to be as broad as possible: someone who thinks that an extremely powerful, extremely knowledgeable, and extremely benevolent being exists. By "atheist" I mean one who thinks ultimate reality is at bottom just the physical, natural world, and there are no spiritual truths or practices worthy of our attention. Given these labels, a non-theistic Hindu or Buddhist, for example, would be religious but not count as an atheist (nor a theist).

[34] However, see White 2018 for a challenge to the idea that *if* there is an epistemological problem of the diversity of opinion, it only gets worse in a larger universe with more diversity.

[35] This is roughly the position Feldman 2006, 212–213, lands upon, which, he acknowledges, is a challenge to his preference for atheism.

[36] Imagine we find that nine people independently agree on *p*, but those nine disagree on more specific claims *q, r, s, . . .*, each of which entail *p*; whereas we find 1 person who thinks that ¬*p*, and thus disagrees with the nine. We are unlikely to be moved by an argument to the effect that, because those nine disagree over the more specific claims *q, r, s, . . .*, we should suspend judgment on *p*.

evidence.[37] In epistemology more generally, the main methods of belief formation (or sources of evidence, if you like) are perception, testimony, and reasoning (arguments). But reasoning from arguments is typically thought to be more trustworthy when they involve premises or experiences which are universally available or involve shared common ground. Thus philosophical arguments such as the cosmological or fine-tuning arguments, or arguments from evil and suffering, often present themselves as publicly available and neutral reasoning about, say, whether there is a theistic God. By contrast, those who appeal to religious experience (Alston 1991 and Swinburne 2004, Ch. 13) as a kind of perceptual evidence for God's existence typically conceive of such evidence as inherently private. Even though religious experience, as with sensory experience, seems to provide a sort of direct evidence (as opposed to indirect grounds offered by reasoning or testimony), some argue that with religious experience at least, its private nature weakens any epistemic support it might give to the would-be believer.[38]

Testimony from trusted individuals can form another kind of ground for belief (or disbelief), and social epistemologists have debated the conditions under which we can acquire knowledge purely on the basis of another's say-so.[39] Perhaps we can even consider the testimony of, or from within, an entire tradition (cf. Zagzebski 2012; MacIntyre 1988). When it comes to testimony about religion or the existence of the supernatural, there are questions about whether testimonial grounds could justify religious belief; yet some have argued about that such testimony can appropriately ground religious beliefs even in the midst of religious diversity (Baker-Hytch 2018). But the epistemic force of such testimony may depend whether the testifier functions as an authority or as a kind of expert advisor (see Lackey 2018). Moreover, most reflective individuals will weigh the value of these distinct sources—arguments, testimony, and religious experience, one's own or others'—in very different ways. This confers on such sources the problem of how best to appraise these kinds of evidence, particularly when there is such great variation in peoples' exposure to, and their relative evaluations of, such evidence.

Finally, and relatedly, there is plausibly no dispute-independent standard of the epistemic credentials by which one might be judged one's epistemic "peer":

---

[37] For a broader introduction to issues of knowledge and skepticism in religious epistemology, see Dunaway and Hawthorne 2017. For recent insights and new directions, see Benton, Hawthorne, and Rabinowitz 2018.

[38] Where its inherent privacy results in its untestability; for this worry, see Martin 1952 and 1959; see Alston 1991, 209–111 for a reply. Cf. also James 1994 [1902], 460–462, who argued that some mystical experiences could provide strong evidence to their subjects, but not to anyone else.

[39] For a recent sampling, see Lackey and Sosa 2006; Lackey 2008; and Goldberg 2010.

for example, philosophically minded atheists may think that only one's capacity for intellectual reasoning matters, whereas certain religious views may claim, say, that purity of heart or selfless love for others is a precondition of learning the truth about God or the supernatural (see Pittard 2015a, section 4). How would one decide which view, if either, is more correct? Or, to take another example, what do we make of someone (perhaps a close friend) who claims to have had a vivid and mystical religious experience, and on this basis converts to a religious life? Those who have not had such a religious experience, yet are sympathetic to religion, might now regard this friend as an epistemic expert of a kind, whose testimony should be given strong weight. Whereas a religious skeptic will likely rule out such an experience, if really had, as easily explained on other psychological or naturalistic grounds; given this, the skeptic may insist that such experiences should not count as evidence for religious claims at all. Thus, even if there were consensus on what kind of evidence in the religious domain is most probative, there is no dispute-neutral way of assessing which epistemic credentials one must have in order to properly assess that evidence.[40]

2.1 What Does Religious Disagreement Reveal?

So it appears that disagreement over religion, whether extra-religious or inter-religious, is something of an intractable problem: Whether investigating the extra-religious dispute over whether to entertain a religious worldview at all, or evaluating inter-religious disagreements in order to choose between religions, sincere inquirers should examine as much of the arguments and evidence as they can. And yet deciding what counts as strong evidence, or determining how to evaluate different (possibly conflicting) sources, are tasks fraught with difficulty.

Some take the fact of such intractable disagreements to offer us a lesson or two about religious reality. One natural approach sides with the sensibilities of Conciliationism, and suggests that such disagreement (or learning that it is widespread and entrenched) provides the religious believer with a defeater of their justification, which at best downgrades how confident they should be of their own religious view, and at worst, provides an argument for religious

---

[40] This problem may extend to proposals on which what matters isn't having the same evidence, but rather that one should judge another a peer when they are (roughly) as justified, given their evidence, in holding their religious beliefs: see Lackey 2014.

skepticism.[41] But if the former, such that one should be less confident, the result should be more humility and respectful tolerance for other religions.[42] Yet we shall consider three stronger applications of such ideas, those found in debunking arguments, an argument from divine hiddenness, and an argument for pluralism about religious truth.

2.2 Debunking and Irrelevant Influences

Some argue that the demographic distributions of religious disagreement provide a debunking argument against religious belief, for it seems as though we are strongly influenced to believe what those around us also believe. Thus, the worry goes, what we end up believing seems highly contingent, depending largely on the society and culture in which were raised. But such correlations look like they hold whether or not the beliefs are true. Thus, religious diversity, in the patterns we find it, raises the concern that if one's religious beliefs are largely correct, this is somehow a matter of luck (recall our discussion from section 1.2).

This observation is not new. The medieval Muslim theologian al-Ghazālī (ca. 1058–1111) acknowledged this concern:

> As I drew near the age of adolescence the bonds of mere authority (*taqlīd*) ceased to hold me and inherited beliefs lost their grip upon me, for I saw that Christian youths always grew up to be Christians, Jewish youths to be Jews, and Muslim youths to be Muslims.   (Watt 1994, 19)

Similarly, Descartes (1596–1650), in *Discourse on the Method*, noted:

> I thought, too, how the same man, with the same mind, if brought up from infancy among the French or Germans, develops otherwise than he would if he had always lived among the Chinese or cannibals; and how, even in our fashions of dress, the very thing that pleased us ten years ago, and will perhaps please us again ten years hence, now strikes us as extravagant and

---

[41] See Feldman 2006, 212–213, cited above, as well as Bogardus 2013a, Bergmann 2015 and 2017, and King 2016, who also assess how the argument to skepticism might be resisted. Contrast Thurow 2012, who argues that extra-religious disagreement, given the equal weight view, can provide evidence *for* theism, when deployed in a Bayesian framework.

[42] See especially Quinn 2006, Chaps. 13 and 14, and Quinn 2002, 533–537 (excerpts reprinted in Kraft and Basinger 2016).

ridiculous. Thus it is custom and example that persuade us, rather than any certain knowledge.   (Descartes 1985, 119; AT 16[43])

Note that these arguments depend upon the fact of religious diversity, and the ways such traditions manifest themselves globally (though similar concerns have been raised about other views, including views in philosophy[44]). If we instead learned of a global environment where there was great religious diversity but sociological facts about religious adherence did not reveal such tight clustering with the culture in which one was raised, it would be much harder to raise this debunking worry.

Why might we think of such socio-cultural forces as being *irrelevant* influences when it comes to religious commitment? After all, we find similar such tight clustering in other domains: for it is also a sociological fact that Parisians tend to know what the Eiffel Tower is and exactly where it is located, whereas those raised in Bangladesh may not even have such beliefs. So what about religious beliefs and their diversity, exactly, makes them vulnerable to the objection that there are irrelevant influences in play? Katia Vavova (2018, 136) argues that we should understand an irrelevant influence as follows:

An irrelevant influence (factor) for me with respect to my belief that *p* is one that (a) has influenced my belief that *p*, and (b) does not bear on the truth of *p*.

Thus an important difference between the tight clustering of beliefs about the Eiffel Tower among Parisians, and the non-beliefs (or even false beliefs) of others is one we can make sense of given the truth that the Eiffel Tower is in Paris, and so Parisians are mostly likely to know about it. But with religious diversity, there appears to be little reason to suppose that the socio-demographic clustering of religious commitments can be easily explained by which religion might be true; rather, it looks more plausible that we are likely to adopt the dominant religious perspectives of our upbringing, whether or not they are true. (Notice that parallel considerations apply to one who might've been raised in a largely secular environment, so this is plausibly

---

[43] See also J.S. Mill 1975 [1859], Chap. 2: "And the world, to each individual, means the part of it with which he comes in contact; his party, his sect, his church, his class of society . . . Nor is his faith in this collective authority at all shaken by his being aware that other ages, countries, sects, churches, classes, and parties have thought, and even now think, the exact reverse. . . . it never troubles him that mere accident has decided which of these numerous worlds is the object of his reliance, and that the same causes which make him a Churchman in London, would have made him a Buddhist or a Confucian in [Beijing]."

[44] See White 2010; see also Korman 2014 on related concerns about perception.

not only a problem for religious adherents.) It's not just that had you been raised elsewhere and formed your beliefs in comparable ways (in part by learning from those around you), you easily might have believed falsely;[45] it's rather that, without any other guide to what is true of religion, forming one's beliefs in these ways looks arbitrary, guided primarily by what dominates one's communal context.[46]

Importantly, however, the mere fact of religious diversity need not require one to conclude that contingent facts about one's social and cultural upbringing count as an irrelevant influence. In order for such facts to be an irrelevant influence, they must not bear on the truth of the matter (Vavova's clause (b)). But we will properly judge that such facts of upbringing do not satisfy (b) only when we have examined carefully what the truth of religion is, or, having made such investigations, found them inconclusive. So such factors will only look to be irrelevant to the truth for one who lacks any independent grounds for thinking that their religious outlook is more correct than the alternatives. If it is possible to study religious worldviews other than one's own and satisfy oneself that the best evidence and arguments support a particular religious outlook, one may then argue that demographic facts about one's upbringing are not playing a large casual role in what one believes. Indeed, it would be precisely in virtue of such honest study that one would be guided by an assessment of what seems most true, rather than complacently believing what is most comfortable given one's upbringing.[47] Similarly for one who, having investigated the matter, converts to a new religious perspective from whatever outlook with which one was raised: the mere fact of changing one's view after having examined its merits suggests that one has not been merely swayed by what is familiar and communally accepted.[48]

---

[45] If so, then epistemologists would say your belief forming methods are unsafe, and safe methods are arguably required in order to know (e.g., Sosa 1999; Williamson 2000, 123ff.). However, see Bogardus 2013b for the idea that one sometimes could have knowledge even with unsafe belief (religious belief or otherwise).

[46] For more on such concerns, see Axtell 2018, and De Cruz 2019, Chap. 2.

[47] Sometimes the irrelevant influences worrier about religious belief seems to assume that most people whose beliefs largely conform to the worldview with which they were raised have not subjected their beliefs to any honest scrutiny nor explored much of the evidence. But if we learned instead that a majority of people in a given society have, in fact, critically evaluated the evidence or arguments over their worldview during their lives (even though the majority of them continue to hold roughly those same beliefs), it would be unclear whether the irrelevant influences concern still has much force.

[48] Note that the pursuit of the truth through such investigation seems crucial here; one who converts purely to enter into a marriage, for example, still seems subject to the irrelevant influences objection.

2.3 Divine Hiddenness

A different sort of argument, due to J.L. Schellenberg (1993, 2015), draws on (extra-) religious disagreement in order to conclude that there can be no God, at least of the Christian, perhaps broader monotheist, sort.[49] Not all people seem to have experiences of God, nor are all exposed to comparable reasoning or testimony about God; but even when they have some of this evidence, many find the evidence mixed, and thus they do not believe that there is a God. So there appear to be many who are not culpable in resisting the evidence, but simply find it inconclusive. So if there is a God, God is in this sense "hidden" from some. Yet this can seem contrary to what we would expect if God is loving and wants to be in personal relationship with everyone. As Schellenberg argues (in its most succinct form):

(1) There are people who are capable of relating personally to God but who, through no fault of their own, fail to believe that God exists. ("non-resistant" non-believers)

(2) If there is a personal God of love, then there are (would be) no such people.

(3) So: There is no personal God of love.

This argument depends on the existence of disagreement (or at least, non-agreement) over theism, but only requires there to be some who are "non-resistant" in their unbelief: Schellenberg's argument would presumably extend to a scenario where all religious adherents practiced only *one* religion, but where there remained some who sincerely find the evidence or arguments for it lacking. For Schellenberg then, the possibility of reasonable non-belief somehow demonstrates the non-existence of (a certain sort of) God.

Much has been written about this style of argument from divine "hiddenness."[50] And for many theists, it can be easy to challenge both of its premises. But at its heart it asks why, if there is a God, would there not be agreement on that matter? Indeed, more significantly, why would there be such *diverse* views about religion and the nature of the supernatural, particularly if there is a divine being that desires us to know or practice the right religion?[51]

---

[49] McGinnis 2015 argues that it would not be an argument against medieval Islamic understandings of God, which are not personal and relational in the relevant senses.

[50] For some recent work, see Green and Stump 2015, Anderson 2017, Rea 2018.

[51] See Marsh and Marsh 2016. See also Nathan King's contribution to this volume, for how issues of hiddenness contribute to what he calls the "apologist's dilemma."

Notice, however, in light of the social demographic patterns adverted to in the last section, that we already have at hand some (perhaps incomplete) sociological explanations of why fairly entrenched patterns of religious diversity might persist. Additionally, because theistic worldviews normally have built into them an account of why there is extra-religious disagreement, it is unclear that there is a significant further explanatory burden for them here.[52]

2.4 Exclusivism, Inclusivism, Pluralism

Concerns about the epistemological upshots of such diversity often invoke additional issues such as how much is at stake for those whose religious views (or lack thereof) are getting things wrong—do matters of salvation or an afterlife, or enlightenment, or nirvana, depend on practicing the right religion? (Or worse, is punishment on offer for those who do not believe or practice the right religion?) Once these questions are raised, it can seem all the more important that one believe and practice the true religion.

Normally people assume that, if there is a religious or supernatural reality, some particular religion is the correct (or most true) one (an assumption we have made up until now). Thus one's religious beliefs will be true or false, and one religion's claims will presumably most approximate the truth, even if it makes some false claims. And if there is one religion whose tenets are true or mostly true, then the tenets of other, differing religions are to varying degrees false insofar as their tenets are untrue.[53] Of course, for some religions, believing some of these truths might be crucial to one's salvation or end state as redeemed, enlightened, and so on. So it is common to distinguish between *exclusivist* religions which only grant redemption to the believers or practitioners of the one (most) true religion, and *inclusivist* religions (or interpretations of them) which insist on there being a single (most) true religion, but do not insist that only the believers or practitioners of that religion, during their earthly lives, will be redeemed.[54]

---

[52] See, for example, Dumsday 2012a and 2012b, and Baker-Hytch 2016.

[53] Note that, even given their distinct tenets, the common commitments of various religions mean that some of their overlapping claims might be true: for example, if there is exactly one divine being, who created the universe, the monotheistic religions (such as Judaism, Christianity, and Islam) all agree in this truth. But if Christianity, say, is true, then Judaism's and Islam's denial of many specific Christian claims (such as that Jesus is God incarnate) would mean that these denials are false.

[54] Inclusivist positions are prominent in Judaism (the Noahide Laws or *Brit Noah* extend salvation to those who follow seven commandments; cf. Gen. 2:16 and 9:4–6). They are also found in Islam (Qur'an, 2:256; 2:62; 32:7; see also Khalil 2012); and in Christianity (at least on a straightforward interpretation of Paul's letter to the Romans, Chap. 11; cf. also Matt. 7:21–23, and 25:31–46). The

One might ask, however, whether the great range of religious diversity, both intra-religious and inter-religious, provides support for a different meta-theory of how one's own religious view relates to the others. John Hick (1989) contends that such diversity supports a *pluralism* on which a divine being of some kind is the revelatory source of all religions, but where the revelatory process necessarily involves cultural reception which influences how different groups adopt and interpret religious claims. Thus we have different religious perspectives such as Hinduism, Buddhism, Judaism, Christianity, and Islam (among many others) which are geographically and historically situated such that the dominant cultural concepts and social priorities end up influencing how each understands the divine. Thus Hick's approach can easily explain the demographic patterns of religious commitment. In addition, he can appeal to the widespread agreement among such religions about morality and the spiritual life, insisting that in their essentials, they converge on a common ethic and orientation to a transcendent reality outside ourselves. Looked at one way, Hick's line can seem correct: a pluralist picture, where each religious tradition is accurately (if incompletely) referring to some core features of supernatural reality while also reflecting varying cultural concepts, can appear to be a better explanation of religious diversity than a particularist exclusivism (or an inclusivism) on which only one religion is the most accurate account of the supernatural. In this sense then, the sorts of religious diversity we find globally are evidence for pluralism (call this *abductive pluralism*, because it offers a best-explanation account of why we find the patterns of religious diversity). But on the assumption that this pluralist picture is correct, it raises many further questions. One question is in virtue of what it would be rational commit to, or to practice, any particular religion. Another question is why, if pluralism is correct, it is rarely a part of the doctrine of so many religions. For while many religious traditions are inclusivist or otherwise tolerate respectful dissent, almost no major religion embraces the idea that it is just as true (namely, not very true) as all the other major religions. Thus if abductive pluralism gains some support from the fact of religious diversity, it also seems at a loss to explain why so few religions have been tolerant enough to allow for such a pluralistic diversity.

However, Hick's articulation of his view is complicated by the places in which he appears to go anti-realist about religious truth, insisting that

---

twentieth century Catholic theologian Karl Rahner popularized an inclusivism with his view (unfortunately named) that there can be "anonymous Christians" (1976, 283). For more in-depth discussion, see Jonathan Kvanvig, Chapter 9, in this volume, "How to Be an Inclusivist."

religions' claims about ultimate reality do not conflict logically, and are neither true nor false: they are instead merely "mythologically true" such that they "tend to evoke an appropriate dispositional attitude" for those who endorse them (Hick 1989, 348); and "what are called conflicting truth-claims ... do not in fact conflict, because they are claims about different human awarenesses of the divine" (Hick 2001). But this *anti-realist pluralism*, in my view, loses any explanatory advantages its abductive cousin might have held, because it is not in the business of offering a meta-theory on which all such religions are on a par; nor can it plausibly contend that there is inherent value in any core agreement over an ethical or spiritual life. Finally, an anti-realist pluralism has fewer resources to offer a soteriological story on which genuine practitioners of all religions (or at least the major ones?) will be redeemed or saved or be granted a good afterlife; nor can such an anti-realism plausibly claim that such religions even guarantee redemptive transformation in *this* life. For if religions' varying claims about ultimate reality or how to live are "neither true nor false," how can religions make good on promises to redeem us from our flaws, let alone deliver some sort of salvation or (good) afterlife?

Alvin Plantinga (1995) argues forcefully that the fact of religious diversity, and the pluralist's handling of it, need not make a religious exclusivist suspect that their own religious beliefs suffer from any irrationality or epistemic defect, or that maintaining such an exclusivism need involve intellectual arrogance or imperialism. Yet Plantinga allows that acknowledging the diversity of religious perspectives could (though might not) defeat the knowledge which the believer might otherwise have had in the absence of such acknowledgment (1995, 214–215), particularly if it leads one to the irrelevant influences worry that one believes as one does largely due to the religious culture into which one was born. In this way, knowing more about diversity may lead to less religious knowledge, at least in the short run. Yet again, much will depend on the method by which one gained such knowledge (if knowledge it is) in the first place. If one has in fact gained knowledge of theism, say, by direct acquaintance with the truth of theism (either by apprehending the soundness of an ontological proof, or by perceptual acquaintance with God), it is entirely unclear why acknowledging disagreement must undermine that knowledge.[55]

Notice that exclusivists, as well as some inclusivists, will presumably care about the considerations favoring Conciliationism in the face of realized

---

[55] Cf. Bogardus 2013a for similar points. *Mutatis mutandis* if theism is false and it's possible to know, by "seeing" directly, that theism is false: acknowledging disagreement from theists might not dislodge the atheist's knowledge. For discussion of how secure such knowledge might be (either the atheist's or theist's, depending on which is true), see Benton, Hawthorne, and Isaacs 2016, esp. §12.

religious disagreement, for they will suppose that it can matter a great deal that one believes or follows the one (or most) true religion. To that extent then, following Conciliationist advice might be thought to aid one in (eventually) reaching the truth. By contrast, pluralists might be less moved by Conciliationist motivations, and may well find Steadfast views appealing insofar as they offer some support to the idea that it can be rational to stick with one's current religious worldview (if one practices a major religion): for at least on an abductive pluralism, any inter-religious disagreements we find between world religions belie the common agreement they have underneath it all, and so learning of such religious diversity should do little to make one less confident of one's own specific religious tradition. (It is far less clear what an anti-realist pluralist would make of either the Conciliationist or Steadfast lines of argument; in what follows, I shall mainly have in mind the abductive pluralist.)

Motivations for (abductive) pluralism can seem structurally analogous to an argument aimed at cutting through some problems of inter-religious disagreement.[56] Common consent arguments,[57] in their most modest versions, appeal to the large number of people who believe that p, and then suggest that this common consent can at least provide significant evidence for p. While our focus so far has been on religious disagreement, the common consent arguer aims to capitalize on the widespread popularity—both currently and historically—of theism,[58] in order to claim that, while not decisive, this fact is at least some evidence in favor of theism. Whereas the pluralist might argue in similar ways that the broadly popular and near universal acceptance of some transcendental religious reality is some reason to think it is real. While treating common consent as evidence for theism (or religion in its broadest sense) might seem initially implausible, notice that more generally, broad agreement (even if not unanimous consensus) that p arrived at independently provides some evidence in favor of p. It does so because the truth of p can figure in the best explanation of how broad agreement would have been reached, at least if there are other plausible assumptions about how so many would have arrived at the belief that p.[59] However, where people reach agreement that p in dependent fashion (such that their reaching the same

---

[56] It is unclear whether they provide any solace in the face of extra-religious disagreement, namely between atheists, agnostics, and religious (theistic or non-theistic).

[57] See Kelly 2011, Zagzebski 2012, 185ff., and Matheson 2021.

[58] At least a strong supermajority. Kelly 2011, 146, n.18 cites one sociologist (whose avowed goal is to show that non-belief is more prevalent than typically thought) who estimates that around 88 percent of the global population is theist.

[59] See Kelly 2011 for thoughtful discussion.

conclusion is due to collaboration or external pressure), most will deny that broad agreement is evidence for *p*. Note also that *dis*agreement over *p*, if reached independently, can (if there are sufficiently many on each side) provide reason to suspend judgment: for those who found themselves confident that *p* (or that not-*p*), independently reached disagreement offers higher-order evidence that one misjudged the initial evidence. But disagreement similarly loses its force if one learns that such disagreement arose in *dependent* fashion.[60] So common consent arguers for theism will need to make the case for enough independence among those in broad agreement that theism is true.

3. Contributions to This Volume

The contributors to this volume take up a number of the issues raised above relating religious diversity and disagreement to epistemological issues. In many cases they also pose fascinating new questions about, and offer intriguing answers on, how to theorize about religious truth, religious understanding, and decisions over religious or non-religious worldviews.

Laura Frances Callahan, in Chapter 2 of this volume ("Disagreement, Testimony, and Religious Understanding"), maintains that questions about appropriate responses to religious disagreement are related to questions about appropriate responses to religious testimony. Callahan argues that if it is appropriate to alter one's credence in a religious proposition on the basis of encountering a disagreeing peer, it is also appropriate to alter one's credence in a religious proposition on the basis of encountering a testifier who is at least as competent and informed as oneself, when one is antecedently unopinionated on the matter at hand. However, recent literature on moral testimony should give us pause, in assuming that it is generally appropriate to alter one's credences in religious propositions purely on the basis of encountering putatively trustworthy testifiers. Callahan suggests that, in many religious cases as in many moral cases, there is distinctive value or importance in acquiring not merely knowledge but understanding. The distinctive importance of understanding in the religious and moral domains generates a reason not to engage in doxastic practices that threaten or disincentivize understanding in these

---

[60] Suppose one learns that ten people believe that *p*, while ten believe that not-*p*. But one also learns that their beliefs were formed by each telling the next, one by one, what they believe, and they were lined up in such a way that the next listener was always inclined to distrust and believe the negation of what their informant told them. In such a set-up, the existence of such a balanced disagreement would not lead one to revise one's belief, if one believed that *p* (or if one believed that not-*p*).

domains—such as changing one's doxastic attitudes purely on the authority of another's testimony. She claims that it is often inappropriate to adjust one's credence in a religious proposition purely on the basis of encountering a testifier, no matter how competent and well-informed. This suggests that it may often also be inappropriate to adjust one's credence on the basis of religious disagreement, for the reason that in so doing one would threaten or disincentivize religious understanding.

In Chapter 3 of this volume ("How Confident Should the Religious Believer Be in the Face of Religious Pluralism?"), Sanford C. Goldberg defends various arguments from religious diversity or disagreement which purport to support skepticism regarding justified (or rational) religious belief. Goldberg explores the prospects for resisting these sorts of argument. He notes that those who would resist can (i) downgrade their disagreeing interlocutor(s), (ii) appeal to epistemic permissivism, (iii) argue that the believer is no worse off, epistemically speaking, than the atheist or agnostic non-believer, or (iv) argue that the principles that convict the faithful of irrationality overreach, and would establish a more widespread skepticism about rational belief. After presenting what Goldberg regards as the best version of the argument from diversity or disagreement, he then argues that any believer who hopes for truth will not get much solace from any of these responses.

Margaret Greta Turnbull, in Chapter 4 ("Religious Disagreement Is Not Unique"), argues against a common approach taken by some epistemologists, who insist that religious disagreement is distinctive from other sorts of disagreements, and that this distinction changes whether religious disagreements demand a conciliatory response. More specifically, these epistemologists have argued that religious disagreement has special features which make it possible for theists to resist conciliatory arguments according to which they must adjust their religious beliefs in response to finding that peers disagree with them. Turnbull considers the three most prominent features which are claimed to make religious disagreement distinct: religious evidence, evaluative standards in religious contexts, and religious transformative experience. She argues that these three features fail to distinguish religious disagreement in the ways that others have thought. However, she also shows that the view that religious disagreement is not a unique form of disagreement makes religious disagreement *less*, rather than more, worrisome to the theist who would prefer to rationally remain steadfast in her religious beliefs.

In a similar spirit, Richard Feldman argues in Chapter 5 ("Is there Something Special About Religious Disagreement?"), that there is nothing special about *disagreement* as compared with other cases of mixed evidence, and further, that there are no principles governing *religious* disagreements that differ from those governing other disagreements. Rather, in all such scenarios and for all domains, including religious matters, one should endeavor to follow the evidence. Feldman thinks that what is typical about such contexts is that they typically provide circumstances wherein one should be conciliatory toward those who disagree by reducing one's confidence, because learning about others who disagree tends to shift the weight of one's evidence, even if only slightly, away from what one already believes. Yet he examines how complicated it might be to discern such evidential pressure, particularly when it bears on one's fundamental or "core" religious beliefs. Along the way he considers how religious experiences, along with the recognition that others have not had such experiences, may figure in what sorts of evidence one has with respect to religious matters.

Joshua Blanchard and L.A. Paul, in Chapter 6 ("Transformative Experience and the Problem of Religious Disagreement"), take up the issue of how religious diversity affects the decision over whether to adopt a particular religious worldview, given that such a conversion can transform who one becomes. Religious pluralism presents religious believers, agnostics, and skeptics alike with an epistemological problem: How can confidence in any religious claims (including their negations) be epistemically justified? There seem to be rational, well-informed adherents among a variety of mutually incompatible religious and non-religious perspectives, and so the problem of peer disagreement inevitably arises in the religious domain. Blanchard and Paul show that the transformative nature of religious experience and identity poses more than just this traditional, epistemic problem of religious belief. In encountering one another, believers, agnostics, and skeptics confront not just different beliefs, but different *ways of being a person.* To transition between religious belief and skepticism is not just to adopt a different set of beliefs, but to transform into a different version of oneself. They argue that the transformative nature of religious identity intensifies the problem of pluralism by adding a new dimension to religious disagreement, for there are principled reasons to think we can lack epistemic and affective access to potential religious, agnostic, or skeptical selves. In addition, Blanchard and Paul reflect on the relationship between the transformative problem of religious pluralism and the more traditional question about which religious beliefs are true.

Nathan L. King, in Chapter 7 ("The Apologist's Dilemma"), considers the position of the theistic apologist. Such a person seeks to provide rational arguments for her belief that God exists. In today's intellectual milieu, she must do so with a keen awareness of religious diversity and disagreement.

However, in an intellectual setting that calls for epistemic humility, the apologist faces a dilemma concerning the rational force she takes her arguments to have. This dilemma concerns the Uniqueness Thesis—roughly, the idea that for a given body of evidence, E, precisely one doxastic attitude toward E is epistemically rational. Should the apologist embrace Uniqueness or not? There appear to be pitfalls either way. If the apologist embraces Uniqueness, then she seems committed to the claim that those who reject her arguments are irrational—a result that can seem arrogant and overbearing. This might seem to suggest that the apologist should deny Uniqueness and instead embrace the idea that rationality is permissive: for some bodies of evidence, E, more than one doxastic response to E can be rational. However, King points out that adopting this position appears to come at a cost: it seems to commit the apologist to the claim that even in the face of her apologetic arguments, someone might be rational in not embracing theism. That is, despite her arguments, rational non-belief occurs. Inasmuch as the latter claim is a key premise in atheistic arguments from divine hiddenness, denying the Uniqueness Thesis seems to raise the specter of atheism. In sum, this is the Apologist's Dilemma: either embrace Uniqueness at the cost of losing humble apologetics, or deny Uniqueness at the cost of skirting atheism. King aims to further articulate this Dilemma and explore possible responses to it.

In Chapter 8 ("Rationalist Resistance to Disagreement-Motivated Religious Skepticism"), John Pittard considers the question: When is it reasonable to maintain confident religious (or irreligious) belief in the face of systematic religious disagreement? Pittard argues that the answer to this question depends in large measure on the scope of what may be called *partisan justification*: roughly, a subject has partisan justification for her belief that *p* when she is reasonable in having a degree of confidence for *p* that exceeds an impartial estimate of her cognitive reliability on the matter. He considers a number of different views on the nature and scope of partisan justification, and defends a rationalist account according to which partisan justification is grounded in rational insight and is not available in disagreements with acknowledged rational parity. Pittard then explores some implications of this rationalist account for religious belief. One such implication is that "reformed epistemology,"[61] which deemphasizes the role that *rational insight* and *rational assessment* play in the formation and justification of religious

---

[61] See especially Plantinga 2000, Alston 1991, and Wolterstorff 2010 (esp. Chaps. 8, 11, and 12). For an overview, see McNabb 2019.

belief, does not have the resources to adequately defend religious belief in the face of skeptical worries raised by religious disagreement.

Jonathan Kvanvig, in Chapter 9 ("How to Be an Inclusivist"), examines in detail a meta-theory of the relationship between religious truth and salvation or redemption. Inclusivism is designed to be a middle position between Exclusivism and Pluralism, but current formulations suffer from limitations. First, Karl Rahner's own version of the view is put in Christian terms, but if the view is supposed to be metatheoretic, it needs a formulation that is neutral as to the truth of any particular religion. Second, attempts to generate such neutrality run into the difficulty of being unable delineate exactly what distinguishes this middle position from fully relativistic Pluralism. The solution to both problems, Kvanvig argues, is to adopt a broader understanding of faith, one that is not centrally cognitive, one which explains why faith is a generic virtue in any context, and one which gives a way of distinguishing Inclusivism from its alternatives. The key element of Kvanvig's proposal is that, if faith is not centrally cognitive, there is nothing about this attitude that makes an appeal to it a partisan one with respect to the universe of faiths. That result allows a religion-neutral metatheoretic stance that can nonetheless avoid Pluralism by allowing the redemptive value of a religion to be located in the one true religion, as Rahner maintained, but without implying that the story of salvation appeals to cognitive attitudes constitutive of saving faith.

In Chapter 10 ("The Loyalty of Religious Disagreement"), Katherine Dormandy argues that religious disagreement, like disagreement in science, stands to deliver important epistemic benefits.[62] But within religious communities, engaging with others who disagree tends to be frowned upon. A salient reason for this is that, whereas scientists should be neutral toward the topics they discuss, theistic believers, it is thought, should be loyal to God; and religious disagreement, they claim, is disloyal. For if one is a religious theist, engaging with disagreement often involves discussion with people who believe more negatively about God than you do, putting you at risk of forming negative beliefs yourself. And forming negative beliefs about someone (in certain sorts of relationships), or even being open to doing so, is disloyal. A loyal person, says the objector, should instead exhibit *doxastic partiality*, doing their best to believe positively about the other party even at the cost of accuracy. Dormandy discusses two arguments from doxastic partiality that

---

[62] Extending arguments developed in Dormandy 2018a, 2018b, 2020.

aim to show that religious disagreement is typically disloyal. She argues that *even given* doxastic partiality, religious disagreement is not typically disloyal, and can in fact be loyal. But she also argues that doxastic partiality is false. A superior form of loyalty, she argues, is *epistemically oriented*, namely, concerned with knowing the other party as they really are. This opens up new ways in which religious disagreement not only is not disloyal to God but can be loyal.

Finally, Isaac Choi, in Chapter 11 ("Democracy of the Dead? The Relevance of Majority Opinion in Theology"), explores how to think about indicators of expertise and discernment of the truth in theological doctrines, particularly given intra-religious disagreement both diachronically and synchronically. Should Christians prefer the majority opinion in Christian theology, whether it be the majority opinion over the history of the church (as in G.K. Chesterton's "democracy of the dead") or the majority opinion of contemporary theologians? Choi argues that because of the vast differences in accessible evidence between past and present-day theologians, diachronic majority opinion is problematic. In the synchronic case, ignorance of minority arguments, biases, selection effects, and the difficulty to deciding who gets to vote present many opportunities for majorities to be wrong. Finally, Choi considers whether a Christian doctrine of the internal testimony of the Holy Spirit can rescue the democracy of the dead, but he concludes that given the gentle way God might correct people, diachronic majority opinion, apart from belief in a very basic set of truths, is not epistemically bolstered by the Spirit.[63]

References

Alston, William P. 1988. "Religious Diversity and Perceptual Knowledge of God." *Faith and Philosophy* 5: 433–448.

Alston, William P. 1991. *Perceiving God: The Epistemology of Religious Experience.* Ithaca, NY: Cornell University Press.

Anderson, Charity. 2017. "Divine Hiddenness: Defeated Evidence." *Royal Institute of Philosophy Supplements* 81: 119–132.

Anderson, Charity. 2018. "On Providing Evidence." *Episteme* 15: 245–260.

Audi, Robert. 2011. *Rationality and Religious Commitment.* Oxford: Oxford University Press.

---

[63] Many thanks to Jonathan Kvanvig, John Pittard, Patrick McDonald, Rebekah Rice, and Leland Saunders for helpful feedback on this chapter.

Audi, Robert. 2014. "Normative Disagreement as a Challenge to Moral Philosophy and Philosophical Theology." In Michael Bergmann and Patrick Kain (eds.), *Challenges to Moral and Religious Belief: Disagreement and Evolution*, 61–79. Oxford: Oxford University Press.

Axtell, Guy. 2018. *Problems of Religious Luck: Assessing the Limits of Reasonable Religious Disagreement*. Lanham, MD: Lexington Books.

Baker-Hytch, Max. 2016. "Mutual Epistemic Dependence and the Demographic Divine Hiddenness Problem." *Religious Studies* 52: 375–394.

Baker-Hytch, Max. 2018. "Testimony Amidst Diversity." In Matthew A. Benton, John Hawthorne, and Dani Rabinowitz (eds.), *Knowledge, Belief, and God: New Insights in Religious Epistemology*, 183–202. Oxford: Oxford University Press.

Baker-Hytch, Max and Matthew A. Benton. 2015. "Defeatism Defeated." *Philosophical Perspectives* 29: 40–66.

Basinger, David. 2015. "Religious Diversity (Pluralism)." In Edward N. Zalta (ed.), *The Stanford Encyclopedia of Philosophy*. https://plato.stanford.edu/entries/religious-pluralism/

Benton, Matthew A. 2016. "Knowledge and Evidence You Should Have Had." *Episteme* 13: 471–479.

Benton, Matthew A. 2019. "Religious Diversity and Disagreement." In Miranda Fricker, Peter Graham, David Henderson, and Nikolaj J.L.L. Pedersen (eds.), *The Routledge Handbook of Social Epistemology*, 185–195. London: Routledge.

Benton, Matthew A., John Hawthorne, and Yoaav Isaacs. 2016. "Evil and Evidence." *Oxford Studies in Philosophy of Religion* 7: 1–31.

Benton, Matthew A., John Hawthorne, and Dani Rabinowitz (eds.). 2018. *Knowledge, Belief, and God: New Insights in Religious Epistemology*. Oxford: Oxford University Press.

Bergmann, Michael. 2015. "Religious Disagreement and Rational Demotion." *Oxford Studies in Philosophy of Religion* 6: 21–57.

Bergmann, Michael. 2017. "Religious Disagreement and Epistemic Intuitions." *Royal Institute of Philosophy Supplements* 81: 19–43.

Bogardus, Tomas. 2013a. "Disagreeing with the (Religious) Skeptic." *International Journal for Philosophy of Religion* 74: 5–17.

Bogardus, Tomas. 2013b. "The Problem of Contingency for Religious Belief." *Faith and Philosophy* 30: 371–392.

Buchak, Lara. 2012. "Can it Be Rational to Have Faith?" In Jake Chandler and Victoria S. Harrison (eds.), *Probability in the Philosophy of Religion*, 225–247. Oxford: Oxford University Press.

Buchak, Lara. 2014a. "Rational Faith and Justified Belief." In Laura Frances Callahan and Timothy O'Connor (eds.), *Religious Faith and Intellectual Virtue*, 49–73. Oxford: Oxford University Press.

Buchak, Lara. 2014b. "Reason and Faith." In William J. Abraham and Frederick D. Aquino (eds.), *The Oxford Handbook of the Epistemology of Theology*, 46–63. Oxford: Oxford University Press.

Christensen, David. 2007. "Epistemology of Disagreement: The Good News." *The Philosophical Review* 116: 187–217.

Christensen, David. 2009. "Disagreement as Evidence: The Epistemology of Controversy." *Philosophy Compass* 4: 756–767.

Christensen, David. 2016. "Conciliation, Uniqueness, and Rational Toxicity." *Noûs* 50: 584–603.

Christensen, David and Jennifer Lackey (eds.). 2013. *The Epistemology of Disagreement: New Essays*. Oxford: Oxford University Press.

Cohen, Stewart. 2013. "A Defense of the (Almost) Equal Weight View." In David Christensen and Jennifer Lackey (eds.), *The Epistemology of Disagreement: New Essays*, 98–117. Oxford: Oxford University Press.

De Cruz, Helen. 2019. *Religious Disagreement*. Cambridge Elements in Philosophy of Religion. Cambridge: Cambridge University Press.

Descartes, René. 1985. *The Philosophical Writings of Descartes*, John Cottingham, Robert Stoothoff, and Dugald Murdoch (eds.), volume 1. Cambridge: Cambridge University Press.

Dormandy, Katherine. 2018a. "Disagreement from the Religious Margins." *Res Philosophica* 95: 371–395.

Dormandy, Katherine. 2018b. "Resolving Religious Disagreements: Evidence and Bias." *Faith and Philosophy* 35: 56–83.

Dormandy, Katherine. 2020. "The Epistemic Benefits of Religious Disagreement." *Religious Studies* 56: 390–408.

Dumsday, Travis. 2012a. "Divine Hiddenness and Creaturely Resentment." *International Journal for Philosophy of Religion* 72: 41–51.

Dumsday, Travis. 2012b. "Divine Hiddenness as Divine Mercy." *Religious Studies* 48: 183–198.

Dunaway, Billy and John Hawthorne. 2017. "Scepticism." In William J. Abraham and Frederick D. Aquino (eds.), *The Oxford Handbook of the Epistemology of Theology*, 290–308. Oxford: Oxford University Press.

Elga, Adam. 2007. "Reflection and Disagreement." *Noûs* 48: 478–502.

Elga, Adam. 2010. "How to Disagree about How to Disagree." In Richard Feldman and Ted A. Warfield (eds.), *Disagreement*, 175–186. Oxford: Oxford University Press.

Faulkner, Paul and Thomas Simpson (eds.). 2017. *The Philosophy of Trust.* Oxford: Oxford University Press.

Feldman, Richard. 2006. "Epistemological Puzzles about Disagreement." In Stephen Hetherington (ed.), *Epistemology Futures*, 216–236. Oxford: Oxford University Press.

Feldman, Richard. 2007. "Reasonable Religious Disagreements." In Louise Antony (ed.), *Philosophers without Gods*, 194–214. Oxford: Oxford University Press.

Feldman, Richard. 2014. "Evidence of Evidence is Evidence." In Jonathan Matheson and Rico Vitz (eds.), *The Ethics of Belief*, 284–300. Oxford: Oxford University Press.

Feldman, Richard and Ted A. Warfield (eds.). 2010. *Disagreement.* Oxford: Oxford University Press.

Ferrari, Filippo and Nikolaj J.L.L. Pedersen. 2019. "Epistemic Peer Disagreement." In Miranda Fricker, Peter Graham, David Henderson, and Nikolaj J.L.L. Pedersen (eds.), *The Routledge Handbook of Social Epistemology*, 174–184. London: Routledge.

Fitelson, Branden. 2012. "Evidence of Evidence is Not (Necessarily) Evidence." *Analysis* 72: 85–88.

Frances, Bryan and Jonathan Matheson. 2018. "Disagreement." In Edward N. Zalta (ed.), *The Stanford Encyclopedia of Philosophy*. https://plato.stanford.edu/entries/disagreement/

Goldberg, Sanford C. 2010. *Relying on Others: An Essay in Epistemology.* Oxford: Oxford University Press.

Goldberg, Sanford. 2013a. "Defending Philosophy in the Face of Systematic Disagreement." In Diego E. Machuca (ed.), *Disagreement and Skepticism*, 277–294. New York: Routledge.

Goldberg, Sanford C. 2013b. "Disagreement, Defeat, and Assertion." In David Christensen and Jennifer Lackey (eds.), *The Epistemology of Disagreement: New Essays*, 167–189. Oxford: Oxford University Press.

Goldberg, Sanford C. 2014. "Does Externalist Epistemology Rationalize Religious Commitment?" In Laura Frances Callahan and Timothy O'Connor (eds.), *Religious Faith and Intellectual Virtue*, 279–298. Oxford: Oxford University Press.

Goldberg, Sanford C. 2015. *Assertion: On the Philosophical Significance of Assertoric Speech.* Oxford: Oxford University Press.

Goldberg, Sanford C. 2016. "On the Epistemic Significance of Evidence You Should Have Had." *Episteme* 13: 449–470.

Goldberg, Sanford C. 2017. "Should Have Known." *Synthese* 194: 2863–2894.

Greco, John. 2010. *Achieving Knowledge.* Cambridge: Cambridge University Press.

Green, Adam and Eleonore Stump (eds.). 2015. *Hidden Divinity and Religious Belief: New Perspectives*. Cambridge: Cambridge University Press.

Gutting, Gary. 1982. *Religious Belief and Religious Skepticism*. Notre Dame, IN: University of Notre Dame Press.

Hájek, Alan and Julia Staffel. 2021. "Subjective Probability and its Dynamics." In Markus Knauff and Wolfgang Spohn (eds.), *MIT Handbook of Rationality*. Cambridge, MA: MIT Press.

Hawthorne, John and Amia Srinivasan. 2013. "Disagreement Without Transparency: Some Bleak Thoughts." In David Christensen and Jennifer Lackey (eds.), *The Epistemology of Disagreement: New Essays*, 9–30. Oxford: Oxford University Press.

Hick, John. 1988. "Religious Pluralism and Salvation." *Faith and Philosophy* 5: 365–377.

Hick, John. 1989. *An Interpretation of Religion: Human Responses to the Transcendent*. New Haven: Yale University Press. 2nd edition, 2004.

Hick, John. 1997. "The Epistemological Challenge of Religious Pluralism." *Faith and Philosophy* 14: 277–286.

Hick, John. 2001. "Is Christianity the Only True Religion, or One among Others?" http://www.johnhick.org.uk/jsite/index.php/articles-by-john-hick/16-is-christianity-the-onlytrue-religion-or-one-among-others/

Horowitz, Sophie. 2019. "The Truth Problem for Permissivism." *Journal of Philosophy* 116: 237–262.

Howard-Snyder, Daniel. 2016. "Does Faith Entail Belief?" *Faith and Philosophy* 33: 142–162.

James, William. 1912. *The Will to Believe, and Other Essays in Popular Philosophy*. New York: Longmans, Green, and Co.

James, William. 1994 [1902]. *The Varieties of Religious Experience*. New York: The Modern Library.

Kelly, Thomas. 2005. "The Epistemic Significance of Disagreement." In Tamar Szabó Gendler and John Hawthorne (eds.), *Oxford Studies in Epistemology*, volume 1, 167–196. Oxford: Clarendon Press.

Kelly, Thomas. 2008. "Disagreement, Dogmatism, and Belief Polarization." *Journal of Philosophy* 105: 611–633.

Kelly, Thomas. 2010. "Peer Disagreement and Higher-Order Evidence." In Richard Feldman and Ted A. Warfield (eds.), *Disagreement*, 111–176. Oxford: Oxford University Press.

Kelly, Thomas. 2011. "Consensus Gentium: Reflections on the 'Common Consent' Argument for the Existence of God." In Kelly James Clark and Raymond

J. VanArragon (eds.), *Evidence and Religious Belief*, 135–156. Oxford: Oxford University Press.

Kelly, Thomas. 2013. "Disagreement and the Burdens of Judgment." In David Christensen and Jennifer Lackey (eds.), *The Epistemology of Disagreement: New Essays*, 31–53. Oxford: Oxford University Press.

Khalil, Mohammad Hassan. 2012. *Islam and the Fate of Others: The Salvation Question*. Oxford: Oxford University Press.

King, Nathan L. 2008. "Religious Diversity and its Challenges to Religious Belief." *Philosophy Compass* 3: 830–853.

King, Nathan L. 2012. "Disagreement: What's the Problem? Or, a Good Peer is Hard to Find." *Philosophy and Phenomenological Research* 85: 249–272.

King, Nathan L. 2016. "Religious Skepticism and Higher-Order Evidence." *Oxford Studies in Philosophy of Religion* 7: 126–156.

King, Nathan L. and Thomas Kelly. 2017. "Disagreement and the Epistemology of Theology." In William J. Abraham and Frederick D. Aquino (eds.), *The Oxford Handbook of the Epistemology of Theology*, 309–324. Oxford: Oxford University Press.

Kopec, Matthew and Michael G. Titelbaum. 2016. "The Uniqueness Thesis." *Philosophy Compass* 11: 189–200.

Korman, Daniel Z. 2014. "Debunking Perceptual Beliefs about Ordinary Objects." *Philosophers' Imprint* 14: 1–21.

Kraft, James. 2012. *The Epistemology of Religious Disagreement: A Better Understanding*. New York: Palgrave MacMillan.

Kraft, James and David Basinger (eds.). 2016. *Religious Tolerance through Humility: Thinking with Philip Quinn*. London: Routledge.

Kvanvig, Jonathan L. 2014. *Rationality and Reflection: How to Think About What to Think*. Oxford: Oxford University Press.

Kvanvig, Jonathan L. 2018. *Faith and Humility*. Oxford: Oxford University Press.

Lackey, Jennifer. 2008. *Learning from Words: Testimony as a Source of Knowledge*. Oxford: Oxford University Press.

Lackey, Jennifer. 2014. "Taking Religious Disagreement Seriously." In Laura Frances Callahan and Timothy O'Connor (eds.), *Religious Faith and Intellectual Virtue*, 299–316. Oxford: Oxford University Press.

Lackey, Jennifer. 2018. "Experts and Peer Disagreement." In Matthew A. Benton, John Hawthorne, and Dani Rabinowitz (eds.), *Knowledge, Belief, and God: New Insights in Religious Epistemology*, 228–245. Oxford: Oxford University Press.

Lackey, Jennifer and Ernest Sosa (eds.). 2006. *The Epistemology of Testimony*. Oxford: Clarendon Press.

Lasonen-Aarnio, Maria. 2010. "Unreasonable Knowledge." *Philosophical Perspectives* 24: 1–21.

Lasonen-Aarnio, Maria. 2013. "Disagreement and Evidential Attenuation." *Noûs* 47: 767–794.

Lasonen-Aarnio, Maria. 2014. "Higher-Order Evidence and the Limits of Defeat." *Philosophy and Phenomenological Research* 88: 314–345.

Lasonen-Aarnio, Maria. 2015. " 'I'm onto Something!' Learning about the World by Learning What I Think about It." *Analytic Philosophy* 56: 267–297.

Lord, Charles G., Lee Ross, and Mark R. Lepper. 1979. "Biased Assimilation and Attitude Polarization: The effects of prior theories on subsequently considered evidence." *Journal of Personality and Social Psychology* 37: 2098–2109.

Machuca, Diego E. (ed.). 2013. *Disagreement and Skepticism*. New York: Routledge.

MacIntyre, Alasdair. 1988. *Whose Justice? Which Rationality?* Notre Dame, IN: University of Notre Dame Press.

Mackie, J.L. 1977. *Ethics: Inventing Right and Wrong*. New York: Penguin.

Marsh, Jason and Jon Marsh. 2016. "The Explanatory Challenge of Religious Diversity." In Helen De Cruz and Ryan Nichols (eds.), *Advances in Religion, Cognitive Science, and Experimental Philosophy*, 61–83. London: Bloomsbury Academic.

Martin, C.B. 1952. "A Religious Way of Knowing." *Mind* 61: 497–512.

Martin, C.B. 1959. *Religious Belief*. Ithaca, NY: Cornell University Press.

Matheson, Jonathan D. 2014. "Disagreement: Idealized and Everyday." In Jonathan Matheson and Rico Vitz (eds.), *The Ethics of Belief*, 315–329. Oxford: Oxford University Press.

Matheson, Jonathan D. 2015. *The Epistemic Significance of Disagreement*. London: Palgrave MacMillan.

Matheson, Jonathan D. 2021. "The Common Consent Argument." In Colin Ruloff and Peter Horban (ed.), *Contemporary Arguments in Natural Theology*, 293–309. London: Bloomsbury Academic.

McGinnis, Jon. 2015. "The Hiddenness of 'Divine Hiddenness': Divine Love in Medieval Islamic Lands." In Adam Green and Eleonore Stump (eds.), *Hidden Divinity and Religious Belief*, 157–174. Cambridge: Cambridge University Press.

McNabb, Tyler Dalton. 2019. *Religious Epistemology*. Cambridge Elements in Philosophy of Religion. Cambridge: Cambridge University Press.

Meister, Chad (ed.). 2011. *The Oxford Handbook of Religious Diversity*. Oxford: Oxford University Press.

Mill, John Stuart. 1975 [1859]. *On Liberty*. New York: W.W. Norton.

Pettigrew, Richard. 2018. *Accuracy and the Laws of Credence*. Oxford: Oxford University Press.

Pittard, John. 2015a. "Religious Disagreement." *Internet Encyclopedia of Philosophy*, ISSN 2161–0002, http://www.iep.utm.edu/rel–disa/

Pittard, John. 2015b. "Resolute Conciliationism." *Philosophical Quarterly* 65: 442–463.

Pittard, John. 2020. *Disagreement, Deference, and Religious Commitment.* Oxford: Oxford University Press.

Plantinga, Alvin. 1995. "Pluralism: A Defense of Religious Exclusivism." In Thomas D. Senor (ed.), The *Rationality of Belief and the Plurality of Faith*, 191–215. Ithaca, NY: Cornell University Press.

Plantinga, Alvin. 2000. *Warranted Christian Belief.* New York: Oxford University Press.

Quinn, Philip L. 2002. "Epistemology in Philosophy of Religion." In Paul K. Moser (ed.), *The Oxford Handbook of Epistemology*, 513–538. Oxford: Oxford University Press.

Quinn, Philip L. 2006. *Essays in the Philosophy of Religion.* Oxford: Oxford University Press.

Rahner, Karl. 1976. *Theological Investigations*, volume 14. London: Darton, Longman, and Todd.

Rea, Michael C. 2018. *The Hiddenness of God.* Oxford: Oxford University Press.

Rice, Rebekah L.H., Daniel McKaughn, and Daniel Howard-Snyder. 2017. "Special (Double) Issue: Approaches to Faith." *International Journal for Philosophy of Religion* 81: 1–6.

Rosen, Gideon. 2001. "Nominalism, Naturalism, and Epistemic Relativism." *Philosophical Perspectives* 15: 69–91.

Rowland, Richard. 2017. "The Epistemology of Moral Disagreement." *Philosophy Compass* 12: 1–16.

Schellenberg, J.L. 1993. *Divine Hiddenness and Human Reason.* Ithaca, NY: Cornell University Press.

Schellenberg, J.L. 2015. *The Hiddenness Argument.* Oxford: Oxford University Press.

Schoenfield, Miriam. 2014. "Permission to Believe: Why Permissivism is True and What It Tells Us About Irrelevant Influences on Belief." *Noûs* 48: 193–218.

Schoenfield, Miriam. 2018. "Permissivism and the Value of Rationality: A Challenge to the Uniqueness Thesis." *Philosophy and Phenomenological Research* 99: 286–297.

Sosa, Ernest. 1999. "How to Defeat Opposition to Moore." *Philosophical Perspectives* 13: 142–153.

Srinivasan, Amia. 2015. "The Archimedean Urge." *Philosophical Perspectives* 29: 325–362.

Srinivasan, Amia. 2019. "Genealogy, Epistemology, and Worldmaking." *Proceedings of the Aristotelian Society* 119: 127–156.

Swinburne, Richard. 2004. *The Existence of God*. Oxford: Oxford University Press, 2nd edition.

Thurow, Joshua C. 2012. "Does Religious Disagreement Actually Aid the Case for Theism?" In Jake Chandler and Victoria S. Harrison (eds.), *Probability in the Philosophy of Religion*, 209–224. Oxford: Oxford University Press.

Titelbaum, Michael G. 2015. "Rationality's Fixed Point (or: In Defense of Right Reason)." *Oxford Studies in Epistemology* 5: 253–294.

van Inwagen, Peter. 1994. "Quam Dilecta." In Thomas V. Morris (ed.), *God and the Philosophers*, 31–60. Oxford: Oxford University Press.

van Inwagen, Peter. 1996. "It is Wrong, Everywhere, Always, and for Anyone, to Believe Anything upon Insufficient Evidence." In Jeff Jordan and Daniel Howard-Snyder (eds.), *Faith, Freedom, and Rationality: Essays in the Philosophy of Religion*, 137–153. Lanham: Rowman & Littlefield.

van Inwagen, Peter. 2010. "We're Right. They're Wrong." In Richard Feldman and Ted A. Warfield (eds.), *Disagreement*, 10–28. Oxford: Oxford University Press.

Vavova, Katia. 2014. "Moral Disagreement and Moral Skepticism." *Philosophical Perspectives* 28: 302–333.

Vavova, Katia. 2018. "Irrelevant Influences." *Philosophy and Phenomenological Research* 96: 134–152.

Watt, William Montgomery. 1994. *The Faith and Practice of Al-Ghazālī*. Oxford: One World.

Weatherson, Brian. 2013. "Disagreements, Philosophical and Otherwise." In David Christensen and Jennifer Lackey (eds.), *The Epistemology of Disagreement: New Essays*, 54–73. Oxford: Oxford University Press.

Weisberg, Jonathan. 2012. "The Bootstrapping Problem." *Philosophy Compass* 7: 597–610.

Weisberg, Jonathan. 2019. *Odds and Ends: Introducing Probability and Decision with a Visual Emphasis*. An Open Access Publication. https://jonathanweisberg.org/vip/

White, Roger. 2005. "Epistemic Permissiveness." *Philosophical Perspectives* 19: 445–459.

White, Roger. 2010. "You Just Believe That Because . . ." *Philosophical Perspectives* 24: 573–615.

White, Roger. 2018. "Reasoning with Plenitude." In Matthew A. Benton, John Hawthorne, and Dani Rabinowitz (eds.), *Knowledge, Belief, and God: New Insights in Religious Epistemology*, 169–179. Oxford: Oxford University Press.

Williamson, Timothy. 2000. *Knowledge and its Limits*. Oxford: Oxford University Press.

Wolterstorff, Nicholas. 2010. *Practices of Belief: Selected Essays*, volume 2. Cambridge: Cambridge University Press.

Zagzebski, Linda Trinkaus. 2012. *Epistemic Authority: A Theory of Trust, Authority, and Autonomy in Belief*. Oxford: Oxford University Press.

2

Disagreement, Testimony, and Religious Understanding

Laura Frances Callahan

1. Introduction

Say you, like many people, have beliefs about religious matters. Maybe you are an Abrahamic theist. Maybe you are an atheist. How should the fact that millions of people disagree with you affect those beliefs?

Plausibly, religious disagreement should cause us to worry that our religious beliefs may not be accurate or may not be rationally formed. Many have argued that such worries should lead us to suspend judgment. For, it is assumed, rationality and/or accuracy are the important desiderata when it comes to religious belief. Where these are in doubt, suspension is required. Matters become more complicated, however, if we think there are *other* important desiderata for religious belief.

In this paper I will suggest that *understanding* is an important desideratum when it comes to many propositions about the (anti) religious character of the universe. Religious epistemologists have typically focused instead on the epistemic desiderata of knowledge, warrant, justification, and rationality.[1] But I'll suggest that understanding—i.e., grasping a system in a holistic and flexible way that involves abilities to put information to use in theoretical and practical reasoning—is important when it comes to religious beliefs.[2] In particular, to have fully appropriate religious beliefs requires understanding (to some degree) the religious character of the universe in such a holistic way. This stems from what we want our religious beliefs to *do*, in orienting us

---

[1] An exception is Scott (2018), who argues for the importance of religious understanding, also emphasizing (as I will) the connection between understanding and action.

[2] There are interesting relationships between understanding and (certain kinds of) knowledge, as well as understanding and rationality. Thus, disagreement literature focusing on knowledge and rationality is already potentially *relevant* to understanding. (E.g., if disagreement undermines rationality and understanding requires rationality, then disagreement undermines understanding.) It is focusing explicitly on understanding that is relatively novel.

Laura Frances Callahan, *Disagreement, Testimony, and Religious Understanding* In: *Religious Disagreement and Pluralism.* Edited by: Matthew A. Benton and Jonathan L. Kvanvig, Oxford University Press. © Laura Frances Callahan 2021. DOI: 10.1093/oso/9780198849865.003.0002

purposefully and rightly toward the universe, including in our behavior, affect, and self-conceptions. This first main claim of the paper sits squarely in religious epistemology.

My second main claim, however, is not particular to the religious case and has implications for epistemology more broadly. I'll argue that suspending judgment about propositions that are deeply embedded in our grasping a broader subject matter, simply because one encounters disagreement, significantly damages understanding. In a nutshell, this is because when we have understanding we appreciate a body of information as interconnected. If we abandon one, deeply embedded belief in the face of disagreement, we must either also give up a broad swath of other beliefs or else exhibit diminished coherence and diminished abilities to draw connections among the beliefs we do have. Both outcomes damage understanding, so suspending judgment on deeply embedded propositions in the face of disagreement stands in tension with understanding and the possibility of understanding.[3]

In making this argument about a tension between understanding and suspending judgment in response to disagreement, *inter alia* I will draw attention to a neglected question. Many if not all of our beliefs support others of our beliefs, and many of our beliefs are themselves supported by other beliefs. Say you and I are "epistemic peers" (or near enough), we discover that we disagree about whether *p*, and we proceed to suspend judgment about whether *p*, as many philosophers recommend. Now, what *further* adjustments (if any) should we make to our body of beliefs? In particular, what adjustments may be required of the beliefs that we previously took to support or be supported by $(\sim)p$?

Taken together, my claim about the value of religious understanding and my claim about the tension between understanding and suspending in response to disagreement suggest that people have a reason not to simply suspend judgment on core religious beliefs upon encountering religious disagreement. This reason stems from the value of understanding in the religious domain. But I wish to be clear up front: a reason not to *simply suspend judgment* does not amount to a reason to blithely *ignore* disagreement. Indeed, disagreement presumably often gives us reasons to re-think our opinions or engage in further inquiry *because* of the value of understanding.

---

[3] I won't be able to give an account here of what it takes for a proposition to be "deeply embedded" in one's understanding. I am inspired by a Quinean picture on which certain beliefs are more central or deeply entrenched in our "webs." See, e.g., Quine and Ullian (1970); Quine (1951: 39–40). See also Murphy (1990) for extended treatment of systems of religious beliefs (theologies) as akin to scientific theories or research programs.

One further clarification: it is natural to categorize, "There is a God," as a religious proposition, but it is not natural so to characterize, "There is no God." We tend to think of the religious domain as including positive claims about transcendent persons, forces, or other entities, whereas claims about the *non*transcendent character of the universe are not considered religious. It seems to me, however, that my arguments for the value of religious understanding carry over, in part, to the value of understanding the *non*religious character of the universe. So although I will talk about "religious understanding" and only sometimes note this as "(anti)religious understanding", I hope that much of what I say about that understanding will apply also to "anti-religious" understanding. (Indeed, some of what I say would seem to apply to moral, socio-political, and philosophical understanding as well, although I lack space to address other domains directly here.)

I will begin with an extended case, which I hope will quickly illustrate the sort of tension I have in mind. In section 3, I sketch a more or less standard epistemological account of understanding. Section 4 is concerned with religious epistemology and briefly supporting the claim that understanding is an important desideratum in the religious domain, such that fully appropriate religious belief requires it. The remainder of the paper will explore tension between understanding and suspending judgment in the face of disagreement. I'll present a case for such a tension (section 5), deal with an important objection (section 6), and then briefly consider a connection between my claims about disagreement and plausible theses about testimony (section 7).

2. A Warm-Up Case

Ada turned up at my office hours during the third week of the fall semester, in some distress. She explained that during her first week at university she'd attended my intro to epistemology class and thought seriously about the epistemic significance of disagreement for the first time. (We'd read Feldman's "Reasonable Religious Disagreements," and Christensen's "Epistemology of Disagreement: The Good News"—unfortunately a freak snowstorm resulted in a class cancellation that required us to skip Kelly (2005)'s "The Epistemic Significance of Disagreement." Simultaneously, she'd been meeting lots of new people, in her dorm and through campus organizations. Having come from a sheltered, highly religious home and community (Christian), she'd been surprised to encounter many seemingly smart, well-informed individuals who were atheists. Some of these individuals had already begun to become her friends. And conversations so far had not dispelled the appearance of real disagreement, nor of her new friends' thoughtfulness and intelligence. When Ada explained that she believed in God's existence in part on the testimony of the Church over time, and on the basis of moral arguments, and on the basis of the cosmological argument, and by abduction on the strange historical story of Jesus Christ..., her new friends seemed unmoved. They simply made other arguments—referencing sociological explanations for religious belief, the problem of evil, and the sufficiency of metaphysical naturalism to explain our universe. These arguments were not *new* to Ada, she explained. She'd thought about them all before and decided they weren't ultimately persuasive. But her new friends—who, again, seemed to be pretty smart and thoughtful people and shared some of her convictions on other matters—came down differently.

Ada realized that this was exactly the sort of situation in which many philosophers would have her suspend judgment and abandon her belief in God's existence. And so she did—or tried to. She declared aloud and repeated to herself silently for days that she did not know whether there was any God and whether Christianity was true. She meditated on the fact of her new friends' disagreement and the persuasiveness of conciliationist arguments in the philosophy of disagreement. And she found—or at least, she reported to me—that she succeeded in suspending judgment on the question whether God exists.

But this, Ada found, left her at sea. For one thing, when she thought about arguments for and against God's existence, it *still* seemed to her as though the arguments for Christianity were better than the arguments against it. Was this because she had other dubious beliefs and assumptions? And which ones were dubious? Should she give up her beliefs about, for example, the historical story of the spread of Christianity, or the objectivist character of morality, or the unsatisfactory explanatory power of metaphysical naturalism? Should she stop trusting the family and community members she had once taken as authorities on religious matters, including ceasing to trust them about other matters? Which other matters?

Other problems did not directly concern reasons or arguments for/against Christianity but what she had taken to be the implications of Christianity for her life. Some of these problems had to do with her habits and emotions. Ada found herself still *wanting* to offer up prayers in distress, still *feeling* gratitude toward God, etc. But now she was unsure about whether these motivations and emotions were fully consistent with her new suspension of judgment about Christianity. They certainly didn't flow from her religious belief as they did before. Other problems were more strictly cognitive. Should Ada's beliefs about, for example, the existence of the soul, the "sinfulness" of humans, the impermissibility of abortion, or the moral status of greed now also change? After all, many of her beliefs about human nature and morality had been connected to and even (partly) inferred from her system of religious beliefs.[4] But now that she was suspending judgment on the metaphysical cornerstone of her previous Christian outlook, it was not at all clear which of these beliefs also had to go, or at least to change. And if she simply held on to the rest of her outlook, she asked me, wouldn't that be sort of disingenuous and unstable?

She explained that she had read and re-read the papers from class. It still seemed to her eminently plausible that disagreement indicates inaccuracy/ irrationality and therefore mandates suspension. But she was puzzled and frustrated as to why there seemed to be no further guidance as to what she should do with the *rest* of her connected web of beliefs, motivations, and emotions, now that she had suspended judgment on the integral question of God's existence. I did not know what to say, except that her frustration was clearly reasonable.

3. Understanding in Epistemology

I'll refer back to Ada sporadically throughout this paper. In this section, I will briefly sketch an epistemological account of understanding.

There's been much recent interest in a kind of understanding that takes as its object subject matters, theories, and/or explanations.[5] Clearly, we also use "understanding" in other ways, as when we talk of understanding the meaning of a sentence, or when we say, e.g., "I understand that Sally is coming to the party," using "understand that" as a sort of hedge-y "believe that." But I'm interested in understanding of the sort we have when we understand, e.g., the human cardiovascular system, Portuguese exploration of the fifteenth and sixteenth centuries, the NY subway system,[6] some explanation of the working

---

[4] More or less skillfully, to be sure. Perhaps Ada took certain things to be implied by her faith that were, instead, more heavily influenced by her political preferences and milieu. Or perhaps Ada tool some things to be supported specifically by Christian faith that were really either made reasonable by monotheistic faith in general or supported directly by religion-neutral metaphysical or ethical commitments. Still, in *Ada's* mind, and to some degree in fact, her religious beliefs used to be very tightly intertwined with many other beliefs about human nature and morality.

[5] Recent influential work includes, e.g., Hills (2009, 2015), Pritchard (2010), Grimm (2011, 2016), Riggs (2003), Elgin (2006, 2009), and Kvanvig (2003).

[6] Grimm (2011) uses this example.

of a lightbulb, or a friend's feelings after the death of a loved one. Such understanding seems necessarily to involve having a whole body of beliefs, seeing the connections between them, and being able to respond appropriately to a range of questions and circumstances in light of those connections. Understanding involves depth of appreciation as well as abilities to draw connections.

Such understanding is often characterized in contrast with knowledge. Knowledge—at least, propositional knowledge—can be atomistic. I can typically know that *p*, regardless of whether I know other propositions that are closely related to p.[7] Knowledge involves true belief. It also (at least paradigmatically) involves justification—having formed one's belief in some reliable, or virtuous, or evidence-respecting, or blameless, or defensible way.

Understanding, on the other hand, seems to involve a structure or system of beliefs, as we've already noted. Moreover, in contrast with knowledge, it does not seem obviously, essentially to involve either truth or particular methods of acquisition. It's plausible to think some of the beliefs that constitute one's understanding of a subject matter can be false, or only approximately true.[8] And, although this will be less relevant for my purposes, there is some reason to think we can acquire understanding in more purely lucky or fortuitous ways.[9] What's essential to understanding seems to be, rather, grasping structures within explanations or subject matters and being able to employ those structures in reasoning or action.

Philosophical accounts of understanding purport to be sensitive to the use of "understanding" in ordinary life and in science. But they are also concerned with identifying a mental state that can fill certain normative roles and solve certain epistemological puzzles. One such puzzle:[10] despite the normative significance of knowledge in epistemology, there seem to be cases in which "merely" knowing something strikes us as a less-than-ideal—and even less-than-ok, not-fully-appropriate—way of relating to the relevant information. Consider, e.g., someone who believes that eating conventionally raised meat is wrong but has no idea why. She was told this by a reliable moral guide, and she simply deferred to their opinion. Even stipulating that her belief is true, and even stipulating that it counts as knowledge, on the basis of having been

---

[7] Those who see the objects of beliefs as sets of possible worlds may disagree with the letter of this claim, although even they typically want to vindicate the possibility that agents can (in some sense) believe a proposition without believing all its logical consequences, e.g., via fragmentation. See Stalnaker (1987), Elga and Rayo (forthcoming).

[8] See especially Elgin (2009).   [9] See especially Pritchard (2010).

[10] Another puzzle is the so-called value problem for knowledge. See especially Kvanvig (2003).

formed via a reliable testimonial exchange, it seems we still have reason to criticize her epistemic position. She knows, but she doesn't have a desirable or fully appropriate grasp of the matter.

This is a case of what is sometimes called "moral testimony," about which there has been much recent discussion.[11] Cases like this prompt a search for some state other than knowledge, which can capture a separate and (at least in some respects) higher epistemic desideratum, which might be lacking in cases where mere knowledge strikes us as problematic or unsatisfactory. Accounts of understanding often attempt to cast understanding as the state we might still want when we find knowledge epistemically unsatisfactory.[12,13]

In the context of reflecting on these cases of moral testimony, I have elsewhere proposed an account of understanding that is largely in line with contemporary epistemological orthodoxy but that differs in one important respect. I argue that we should see understanding as incorporating affective and motivational engagement with propositions and reasons, as well as cognitive engagement. Here I will note just one independent reason for incorporating affective and motivational components in an account of understanding (independent, that is, of the usefulness of doing so in explaining moral testimony): we would not attribute understanding of certain issues—systemic racism, a close family member's suicide, etc.—to individuals who appreciated these things only "coldly," or who only cognitively grasped relevant explanations and rational support relationships. Intuitively, the kind of depth of appreciation that understanding involves can include emotional sensitivity.[14] Of course, in many cases having appropriate emotional sensitivity comes more or less for free. I can be appropriately emotionally sensitive to the workings of a lightbulb pretty easily. *Appropriate* emotional sensitivity might involve a disposition to be impressed or pleased by the intricate electrical system when it functions, or to be puzzled or frustrated when it doesn't. But it would be strange indeed to be disposed to feel ashamed, pitiful, compassionate, guilty, or grateful when the lightbulb did/didn't function (absent a particular story in which it played a special role, of course). It is when it comes to understanding,

---

[11] See Callahan (2020) for an overview; see also, e.g., Jones (1999), Callahan (2018), McGrath (2011), Hills (2009), Sliwa (2012), Enoch (2014), and Howell (2014) for arguments for particular positions in the debate.

[12] There needn't be just *one* state that would be satisfactory when (propositional) knowledge would not be. Wisdom or knowledge-how may be other good candidates, at least when it comes to propositions about the right way to *do* something.

[13] One sees a very similar motivation at work in discussions of understanding that stem from work on the value problem for knowledge. See especially Pritchard (2010), Kvanvig (2003).

[14] Notice that the *virtue* of understanding—or being an understanding person—centrally involves emotional capacities. See Grimm (2016) for discussion.

e.g., each other, morality, or beauty, that the emotional or affective requirements are really substantial.

With this quick sketch of understanding in general in hand, I wish to turn to
the question of the value or importance of understanding, when it comes to
our (anti)religious views.

4. Religious Understanding

As I noted in the introduction, understanding has been somewhat neglected by
contemporary analytic religious epistemologists, who have tended to focus
instead on the topics of putative religious knowledge and warranted or rational
religious belief. However, there are several reasons for trying to remedy this
neglect.[15]

For one thing, understanding is arguably less strictly factive than knowledge. This makes room for the possibility of religious understanding even if
there are often or always significant errors in our appreciation of the divine. Of
course, the leniency here is not unlimited. It is not possible, e.g., to understand
the loving will of the Flying Spaghetti Monster. (One might object that it's
possible to understand the *theology* of the Flying Spaghetti Monster; similarly,
it's possible to understand Christian theology regardless of whether
Christianity is true. But I take it that understanding the (anti)religious character of the universe, through a particular religious tradition or not, is at least a
pseudo-factive affair.) However, at least some (anti)religious propositions *are*
true.[16] We should therefore suspect multiple, differing bodies of (anti)religious
propositions are "true enough" to admit of understanding, at least if we accept
that understanding is not strictly factive.

In support, notice first that a few mistaken beliefs "on the periphery" of
one's cluster of related beliefs seem compatible with understanding.
Borrowing an example from Elgin (2007: 36), "We would be inclined to say
that an historian understood the Athenian victory even if he harbored a

---

[15] I use the term "Religious understanding" in this chapter variously. I mean to talk about having
understanding of the religious character of the universe, or religious truth. Other philosophers,
including Cottingham (2018), advocate using the phrase "religious understanding" adverbially, such
that religious understanding amounts to understanding *the world*, religiously. So, on this alternative
conception, one would have religious understanding by understanding other things—e.g., gravitational
forces, contemporary politics—in a religious mode or way. I do not dispute the fruitfulness of the
adverbial use, but my purposes require a parallel with epistemological work on understanding
according to which it is primarily individuated by objects rather than modes.

[16] At the very least, some negative claims are true.

few relatively minor false beliefs about the matter." Similar examples of propositional understanding are easily constructed. One can understand the risky effects of acid rain while having some false beliefs about, e.g., the full and specific causal mechanisms for various at-risk species.

More to the present purpose, we might think that even a body of beliefs that was primarily or largely false could nonetheless somehow point us toward the truth and thereby count as understanding. Again, from Elgin (2007: 37):

> A second grader's understanding of human evolution might include as a central strand the proposition that human beings descended from apes. A more sophisticated understanding has it that human beings and the other great apes descended from a common hominid ancestor (who was not, strictly speaking, an ape). The child's opinion displays some grasp of evolution. It is clearly cognitively better than the belief that humans did not evolve. But it is not strictly true.

The question to ask, then, is not whether agents' religious beliefs are frequently (strictly) true but whether they constitute a system of beliefs that is true enough or that points us toward truth. It's plausible that significant numbers of (anti)religious people are significantly on to something, in the way their beliefs bear on morality, selfhood, relationship, the universe and causation, the (in)significance of death, the insightfulness of religious figures, etc. And on plausible construals of understanding, this kind of directedness at truth is sufficient for the possibility of understanding.[17]

An additional reason for thinking about religious understanding is that understanding has a tighter connection with right affect and right practice than does knowledge. And right affect and right practice are themselves extremely important on many religious outlooks.

(Anti)religious propositions (e.g., God loves me, this life is one of many in a cycle of reincarnation, Jesus rose from the dead, there are no transcendent beings or forces...) are not merely opinions or bits of trivia to be collected. They call out for acceptance with what we might think of as Kierkegaard's "subjectivity"—a kind of deeply personal, emotional involvement with truths

---

[17] A different objection to the possibility of religious understanding: perhaps "revealed" religious traditions are too *transcendent* for understanding. We certainly could never work out for ourselves the triune nature of God (even assuming that to be true), in the way that we might be able to work out a mathematical theorem, a scientific explanation, or even a moral judgment. But understanding does not strictly require this kind of independence or pure rational insight. Only some degree of appreciating rational support relations is required. And for many matters, having appropriate affective and motivational responses may be ultimately the most important aspects of understanding.

that is ongoing and calls for *de se* re-conceptualization of oneself as living in a certain kind of (anti)religious world.[18,19] This seems to require the broad affective and motivational dispositions that understanding comprises.

Moreover, it's clear that many religious believers should, by the standards of their own religion, *behave* in various ways. Having appropriate affective and motivational responses to doctrine is extremely helpful, if not essential, in such behavior. So is appreciating a system of religious doctrine (at least implicitly) systemically, in a way that involves an ability to see and draw connections. Recall that matters we understand, unlike propositions we merely know or believe, cannot be informationally isolated or inert. Consider that believing some religious propositions—such as, that God loves me, or that he loves mercy—while failing to believe other propositions from the same tradition— such as, that God also loves everyone, or that he also hates injustice, etc.— would be lamentable, from the perspective of that religious tradition. Indeed, even believing broad clusters of religious propositions might be lamentable, if one did not see them as an integrated whole, or if one could not draw connections among them.

After all, the situations in which we find ourselves that have moral and religious import are myriad and complex. A short, simple, or poorly appreciated list of maxims cannot generally suffice to identify the courses of action a religious tradition would have us take. Rather, a highly partial or unconnected grasp of important religious propositions may result in dreadfully disjointed and inconsistent acts of faith or piety. One might tithe but totally lack generosity toward individuals one encounters. One might pray regularly for one's family but remain unmoved by causes of social justice. Indeed, it may be simply impossible for the beliefs undergirding any kind of faithful way of life appropriately so called to be too paltry or piecemeal. While there seem to be many subject matters—e.g., tax law, ornithology, tree-pruning—in which a non-expert may be quite appropriately content to know only the snippets of

---

[18] "What does that mean, objective faith? It means a sum of axioms. But suppose Christianity were nothing of the kind; suppose, on the contrary, that it were inwardness..." (Kierkegaard 2009: 181).

[19] One might think that this is far more plausible for certain religious views than for what I'm calling anti-religious views. But at least some with anti-religious views are adamant that these too should touch us inwardly. Dawkins, e.g., frequently suggests that atheism should shape the way we fundamentally conceive of ourselves and the universe. He claimed in a 2008 debate:

I regard it as ... a privilege to be a scientist and therefore to be in a position to understand *something of the mystery of existence, why we exist.* I think that religious explanations although they may have been satisfying for many centuries, are now superseded and outdated. I think moreover ... the understanding we can get from science of *all those deep questions that religion once aspired to explain are now better, more grandly, in a more beautiful and elegant fashion explained by science.* (Emphasis mine)

information she needs in particular practical decision contexts, religion is not like this and seems to require more.

To have religious understanding, then, is to grasp and be able to use a system of interrelated (anti)religious propositions in affectively/motivationally charged ways. This seems highly important and valuable—at least, given that one's (anti)religious beliefs are "true enough." For this rich grasping of a system of beliefs promotes integrity and consistency in one's patterns of behavior and may also—depending on the content of one's beliefs and whether there really are divine beings—make possible a loving relationship with the divine.[20]

Think back to Ada. Prior to starting college, Ada appreciated Christian doctrine as a system. She could see and draw connections between her various metaphysical and ethical beliefs. She was disposed to act and feel in ways integrated with her beliefs about God and Jesus. And she saw both rational support for her religious beliefs and rational implications of those religious beliefs in her *other* beliefs—e.g., about morality, miracles, and reliable testifiers. If—and I want to highlight that this is a *very* big "if"—Ada's Christian beliefs were true enough, then it seems she had understanding. And this understanding, if she had it, was incredibly valuable, both "religiously," or with respect to the aim of relating appropriately to the (anti)religious character of the universe, and epistemically. Ada had not only some beliefs that, we are assuming, were fairly accurate—she had a deep appreciation of their connections and facility employing them in reasoning.

In the next section, I shall argue that suspending judgment simply in response to disagreement diminishes such understanding.

5. Suspending in Response to Disagreement Diminishes Understanding

For simplicity, let's set up a toy case in which a subject S has understanding of some system Y. We needn't stipulate that Y is a (anti)religious system of doctrine; the argument in this section is intended to be quite general. Since

---

[20] There are fascinating questions about how personal relationship with the divine would in turn relate to knowledge or understanding of the divine. It may be that dependency relations go both ways here: some understanding is necessary for relationship, which in turn is necessary for deeper/broader understanding or (inter)personal knowledge, which makes possible a closer relationship. Or, more radically, interpersonal knowledge and understanding may be identical in the divine case. On interpersonal and personal knowledge in religious contexts, see, e.g., Benton (2018) and Keller (2018).

S understands Y, she must have a host of beliefs relevant to Y, which she appreciates as deeply intertwined. (Perhaps some of these are general principles, and others are particular applications, for example.)

Now, let's take a belief that we might think of as "key" to S's understanding—a belief on which many of her other beliefs about Y are based. Let's call this S's belief that p. S's belief that p partly constitutes her understanding Y. S's further beliefs in "x", "y", and "z", which are propositions supported by "p," similarly partly constitute her understanding. The same is true of S's beliefs in "q", "r", *and* "s", which are propositions that support "p." S appreciates these support relationships, and she has some requisite level of cognitive, emotional, and practical facility with Y-related reasoning.

What happens when S stops believing that p, when she suspends judgment in response to disagreement? In particular, what should happen to S's beliefs, "q", "r", "s", "x", "y", and "z"? Clearly, much depends on the cause of S's suspending judgment about whether p. Did S acquire new first-order evidence casting doubt not only on "p" but on some of "x", "y", "z", "q", "r", or "s", or the connections between these claims and "p"? I am assuming that cases in which we suspend *purely* or *simply* in response to disagreement are not like these.[21] Indeed, this is precisely what's so interesting about disagreement cases. Cases in which we suspend purely in response to disagreement are cases in which we simply suspend judgment on whether p, *without* acquiring any new material for first-order reasoning about p.[22] It should still seem to S as though "q", "r", and "s" *would* support "p", were they true. And it should still seem to S as though "p" *would* support "x", "y", and "z", were it true. So, when S suspends judgment about whether p purely in response to disagreement, there are two possibilities:

(1)   S suspends about whether p, although she continues to believe that q, r, s, x, y, z, and it still seems to her these rationally support/are supported by "p".

(2)   S suspends about whether p, and she no longer believes (at least some of) "q", "r", "s", "x", "y", "z".

In either case, I claim S's valuable understanding of Y is diminished.

---

[21] A similar stipulation is often made in the literature on moral testimony: only cases of "pure" moral deference seem to strike us as fishy. See, e.g., McGrath (2011).

[22] Other, non-disagreement cases that fit this mold (such as cases of pure deference) seem similarly problematic.

This seems not to have been sufficiently considered, in the literature on disagreement. Sure, everyone admits that suspending judgment in the face of disagreement might involve losing what had been a true or rational belief, or even an item of knowledge.[23] But perhaps we must accept this as the cost of doing business as a rational agent in a social context including diverse, intelligent opinions.[24] I am highlighting a further cost, by asking a neglected question: now that one has suspended judgment on whether p, what exactly is one supposed to do with all one's other beliefs that had hitherto seemed rationally connected to "p"? It seems to me that both options are quite costly when "p" is a proposition deeply embedded in one's understanding of a subject.

Consider case (1). Here, the appreciative and ability elements of understanding are threatened, since S exhibits a new failure of coherence resulting in a diminished *ability* to explain and reason about p-related matters. After all, S now refrains from drawing the conclusion that seems most plausible to her on the basis of "q", "r", and "s". And although she still believes "x", "y", and "z", she cannot support these as well as she used to be able to, when she could cite "p" telling in their favor. Call this the "diminished coherence" threat to understanding.

In case (2), since S ceases to *believe* some of q, r, s, x, y, and z, she may now simply lack enough beliefs about Y-related matters to count as understanding Y. Call this the "skeptical" threat to understanding. Now, one might think this skeptical threat is not very threatening, if we are able to identify just one or two beliefs, other than p, on which we can suspend judgment while retaining coherence and reasoning abilities among our remaining beliefs. After all, we already knew that suspending judgment involved giving up one (possibly true!) belief. Giving up a few more might not seem so bad. But certainly, in cases like Ada's—where "p" ("The Christian God exists") is connected in subtle ways with myriad other of her beliefs—avoiding a diminishment of coherence will require quite a broad skepticism indeed. Hence my focus on beliefs that are "deeply embedded" in our understanding—and hence the footnote referencing Quinean notions of certain beliefs being central in our webs (fn 3).[25]

---

[23] See especially Hawthorne and Srinivasan (2013). They argue that while it may be tempting to claim that we ought only to suspend judgment in response to disagreement when (dis)belief would not constitute knowledge, this claim founders on the non-transparency of knowledge.

[24] Philosophers who endorse a view on which disagreement frequently mandates suspension of judgment include Christensen (2007), Elga (2007), and Feldman (2007).

[25] Broad skepticism may often give way to alternate sets of beliefs and ways of understanding some phenomenon. Perhaps Ada could lose her Christian-influenced beliefs about morality, only to quickly

At least where p is a proposition deeply embedded in one's view of other matters in this way, I contend that no matter what S does with her other beliefs, she suffers broad losses in understanding Y when she suspends on whether p purely in response to disagreement. She may embrace a broad skepticism (the skeptical threat). Or she may continue to host clashing attitudes (the diminished coherence threat). It seems to me neither of these options is very attractive. Of course, if "p" is false, then suspending judgment as to whether p is in an important respect epistemically better than believing "p". And disagreement can sometimes provide us with a powerful reason to think that a belief may be false. But the effects of such suspending, on one's other beliefs and one's understanding more generally, have been oddly neglected in the literature. Is maintaining one false or dubious belief epistemically worse than broad skepticism or incoherence, along with the reduction in understanding they involve? The answer, I submit, is not clear. And it is especially unclear when it comes to domains in which we have reason to think understanding is especially or distinctively valuable and propositions that are central in those domains (such as, that God does(n't) exist). In the next section, I'll deal with an important objection.

6. Proving Too Much: The Preface Paradox

One might worry that I've tried to make a very ordinary and unavoidable phenomenon look frightening. We might characterize the state that S will find herself in, if she takes either option 1 or option 2 above, as a state in which she doesn't take herself to know that the *conjunction* of q, r, s, x, y, z, is true. She may still believe those propositions (as in option 1, the diminished coherence threat) but be unwilling to reason and draw conclusions on the basis of all of them together.

But this description of the diminished coherence threat makes clear a certain resemblance to the "preface paradox." There are in fact *lots* of cases in which we're prepared to assert or believe individual propositions but unwilling to assert or believe their conjunction. Indeed, it seems we routinely and knowingly hold even *inconsistent* sets of beliefs—not just refusing to believe that large conjunctions of our beliefs are true but even confidently

acquire, e.g., secular humanist-influenced beliefs. But at the moment of encountering disagreement no promises of regained beliefs can be made. According to the kind of conciliationist I (and Ada) have in mind, suspension of belief is what is required.

believing that these conjunctions are false. ("I'm quite sure that there's a mistake somewhere in this book.") Perhaps, then, the "diminished coherence" threat should not be worrisome because of its apparent partners in innocence.

Let's think about how this might apply to Ada's case. Perhaps, instead of giving up huge swaths of her beliefs about morality or the history of the church or the trustworthiness of various sources, Ada should just adopt the further belief that there may well be mistakes somewhere in her first-order reasoning. She could simply continue believing each of the individual things she believed before, just as we can continue believing each of the individual claims we make in a book even after we admit in the preface that there may be some mistakes. And any diminishment of coherence, in her not being willing to make the same kinds of inferences to "p" as she was previously, is only of a quite common sort that is often necessary for limited and fallible creatures like ourselves.

I want to resist this minimizing characterization of option (1). For one thing, in describing Ada's case it was natural to think of her genuinely worried and confused about what to do with her remaining beliefs—about the trustworthiness of her home community on other matters, about the "sinfulness" of humankind, etc. This is not nearly so comfortable a state as that of the reflective author prefacing her book.

Second, we should maintain that incoherence, especially where it restricts a person's reasoning abilities and especially when it is known to occur within non-global subsets of a person's set of beliefs, is always an epistemic *flaw*, always a *pro tanto* epistemic bad. Sure—the author in the preface paradox may be perfectly rational, and she may have exactly the beliefs that she should have given her cognitive limitations. However, precisely what the paradox brings out is that her beliefs are nonetheless flawed; they are guaranteed to contain at least one false member.[26] Moreover, they are flawed in that they are not as *useful* as they could be, for reasoning purposes. These beliefs have been somehow disqualified from serving in (at least some particular kinds of) inferences. As Foley says in the course of *defending* the rationality of being knowingly inconsistent in certain cases:

---

[26] Foley forcefully defends the rationality of sometimes being knowingly inconsistent, but he fully recognizes that the rationality of such a state is driven by our limitations:
[N]o matter how the world turns out, you will do less well intellectually than what is ideal. If your beliefs are mutually inconsistent, then not all of them can be true. But to say that an option is sure to be less than ideal is not yet to say that it is sure to be irrational (1992: 116).

This is not to say that the discovery of inconsistency is ever epistemically irrelevant. It isn't. Inconsistency is always an indication of inaccuracy, and because of this, it would be a mistake to base further inquiry on a set of propositions that you know to be inconsistent. It would be a mistake, in effect, to make all of these propositions part of your evidence, since this would risk spreading the error to yet other propositions...So, a convincing *reductio* shows that it is irrational for you to believe the conjunction of its premises, and it puts you on alert about each of the individual premises as well.   (1992: 119)

There are clearly cases—like that of the preface paradox—in which a body of incoherent beliefs or beliefs whose usefulness in reasoning is limited is nonetheless on balance the best body of beliefs for an agent to have. However, it seems to me this does not obviously or necessarily describe the case where we imagine S's (or Ada's) resultant body of beliefs, after giving up on her ability to reason to/from "p", despite still believing each of "q", "r", "s", "x", "y", and "z".

After all, one important difference between S's case and the preface paradox is that S starts with a more coherent set of beliefs and is prompted to change, in adopting a less coherent set. S starts the case positively believing that $p, q, r, s, x, y,$ and z. She then transitions to a state, we are imagining, in which she believes that $q, r, s, x, y, z,$ and "At least some of q, r, s, x, y, z may well be false." (Or perhaps, rather than believing this last proposition, she simply suspends judgment on the conjunction "q and r and s and x and y and z".) This represents a significant loss, with respect to S's coherence and hence her understanding and reasoning abilities.[27] In contrast, the preface paradox does not typically involve an author who starts by believing the conjunction of the propositions of their book and then subsequently admits that at least some are false. There is no change involved in the case, other than perhaps the author's disbelief in the conjunction being brought to their explicit attention in the course of writing the preface.

S's case and Ada's case, then, involve trade-offs in which suspension would represent a significant loss in at least one respect. S started with a set of beliefs that was highly interconnected, coherent, and useful-in-reasoning. She ends, we are imagining, with a state that is less so. Perhaps this loss is compensated for by other gains. But the loss is real. Compare: if there really was an author who believed not just each individual claim in her book but also their

---

[27] It may or may not represent a loss, with respect to other epistemic values. Perhaps S can continue to be *rational*, for example. See especially Foley (1992).

conjunction, and if this belief in the conjunction was important in reasoning about the topic, then I think we should admit that giving up belief in the conjunction and adding in a "preface" type belief about likely errors would represent a kind of loss. Perhaps evidence of fallibility could make the new set of beliefs far superior in expected accuracy. Perhaps this would outweigh the loss of coherence. But it would not negate that loss.

7. Disagreement and Testimony

I've argued for a tension between suspending judgment purely in response to disagreement and understanding. I've furthermore suggested that understanding is highly and particularly valuable in the religious domain.

One might notice a certain structural similarity to other arguments that I and others have made, in thinking about moral testimony. In Callahan (2018), I argue that taking moral claims wholly on testimony is (often) in tension with moral understanding, and I furthermore argue that understanding is highly and particularly valuable in the moral domain (at least, when we take understanding to involve the affect and motivations as well as the intellect).

There's a theme here. In domains where understanding is particularly valuable, we seem to have reason not to simply mold our views according to the opinions of others, without reflection. Such molding—whether in the form of deference to testimony or suspension of judgment in response to disagreement—stands in a general tension with understanding.[28]

It is puzzling to me that these two activities I've lumped together as "simply molding" one's views after the opinions of others—deferring to testimony and suspending judgment in response to disagreement—are not often jointly theorized. On the face of it, it looks as though there should be some connection between cases in which it's appropriate for me to take your word about something, and cases in which learning of your disagreement about something makes it appropriate for me to suspend judgment. After all, the appropriateness

---

[28] This is so despite the fact that in *certain* circumstances deference or suspension can in fact serve to further understanding. Deferring to moral testimony can sometimes serve as a scaffolding for broader moral education, and perhaps suspending judgment in response to disagreement sometimes ultimately leads to greater religious understanding as well. But I think common psychological tendencies and common circumstances of adult life prevent these possibilities from being the norm. Generally, if we settle a matter by deferring to someone else, we move on with our lives. Generally, if we suspend judgment in the face of pervasive disagreement, we also move on with our lives, having accepted that pervasive disagreement on the topic prevents our judging on the question at hand.

of both depends on your being in an epistemic position that I should take into account vis-à-vis the matter at hand. Here I just want to suggest one plausible connection, to explain an alternative way one might argue for a reason not to suspend judgment in one's religious opinions on the basis of disagreement.

Literature on disagreement has tended to focus on cases like the following:

Me: (Staring at a restaurant bill, doing some mental math) Looks like we each owe...$18 plus tip.

You: (Also staring at the same restaurant bill) Hmm, I got $22 plus tip.

This is a classic case in which, after we share our opinions about what we owe, you and I should each suspend judgment toward the proposition, "We each owe $18 plus tip," purely on the basis of learning what each other thinks about this.[29] (Notice that there is no complication arising from the value of understanding here—"we each owe $18 plus tip" is not deeply embedded in our understanding of some broader system.) Now consider a different, even more common sort of case:

Me: (Staring at a restaurant bill, doing some mental math) Looks like we each owe...$18 plus tip.

You: (Eating the last fry) Sounds good—say, what time does the lecture start?

In this version of the case, you should again adopt a new attitude toward the proposition, "We each owe $18 plus tip," purely on the basis of learning that I believe this proposition. You should, it seems, come to believe it, deferring to my testimony. The two cases differ in that the first is a case of mutual change on the basis of disagreement, whereas the second is a case of one-sided change on the basis of testimony. Though the connection between such cases is under-theorized, I propose that whenever it's appropriate to suspend judgment in a particular case of disagreement, it would also have been appropriate to deferentially believe in a "counterpart," testimonial case.

The testimonial counterpart cases I have in mind can be constructed as follows. Consider a case of disagreement in which two subjects—S1 and S2—start with certain total bodies of evidence prior to learning of their disagreement—E1 and E2:

---

[29] See Christensen (2007: 193) for the now-classic restaurant case.

Generic disagreement: S1 believes p on the basis of E1, whereas S2 believes ~p on the basis of E2. S1 and S2 communicate their beliefs to each other.

Now suppose that instead of both parties having already had positions on the proposition at hand (*p*) before they began discussing it, one of the parties instead had no position as to whether *p*, perhaps because she had not considered the matter. And instead of both parties sharing their beliefs with each other, suppose that just the opinionated party communicates their belief as to whether *p* to the uncommitted party:

Generic testimonial counterpart (for S1):   S1 has E1, although she has not formed any assessment of whether *p* or the likelihood of *p* (perhaps because she has not considered *p*). S2 believes ~p on the basis of E2. S2 communicates their belief to S1.

I claim that whenever, in a case of the form described in Generic disagreement, S1 would appropriately suspend judgment purely in response to the discovered disagreement with S2, it is also the case that S1 would appropriately believe purely in response to S2's testimony, in the testimonial counterpart case. Stating this officially:

DISAGREEMENT-TESTIMONY ENTAILMENT (DTE):   If it is fully appropriate to suspend judgment in response to a particular case of disagreement, then it would also have been fully appropriate to defer to testimony in a testimonial counterpart case (constructed as described above).

DTE is subjunctive conditional, with an actual world antecedent. And, I claim, it is highly plausible.[30] Notice, first, that appropriate deference to testimony seems more common than cases of appropriate suspension in response to disagreement. We take each other's word all the time ("The lecture starts at 3:00," "Hi, I'm Juan,"), whereas cases of abandoning our opinions in the face of

---

[30] Unlike its converse. DTE-converse would claim that if it would be fully appropriate to defer to testimony in a relevant counterpart case, then it is fully appropriate to suspend judgment. But consider the case in which I happen to have just looked at the latest, updated train schedule. I saw that the train, which used to leave at 1:45, now leaves at 2:00. You, not knowing any of this, casually tell me the train leaves at 1:45. Although it may have been fully appropriate for me to defer to your testimony had I *not* seen the new schedule, I am not now under pressure to suspend judgment.

disagreement—though common—are not as pervasive.[31] Perhaps this is because the epistemic qualifications needed to make me *change* my mind about something should be more impressive than the qualifications needed merely to inform me about some matter on which I hold no opinion. If I'm to suspend judgment in response to your disagreement, I must not see myself as far better positioned (through either ability or evidence exposure) to have assessed the matter at hand. On the other hand, I can receive testimony from you even if I think myself vastly superior in this regard. I can ask you for the time because I don't feel like digging out my extraordinarily accurate pocket watch.

At any rate, my interest here is primarily in how this connection makes possible an alternative argument for the conclusion I've argued above. The first stage of this alternative argument would establish that there's *some, pro tanto,* reason not merely to defer to religious testimony. (Recall that deference to testimony is a kind of acceptance of another person's testimony, wholly on their word, without significant reflection on the part of a hearer.)

1.   It is often—at least in some respect—inappropriate to simply defer to moral testimony, for the reason that (a) understanding is distinctively important in the moral domain, and (b) deferring to testimony is generally in tension with understanding. (Understanding explanation of moral testimony)

2.   Understanding is also distinctively important in the religious domain. (Value of religious understanding—see section 4)

3.   It is often—at least in some respect—inappropriate to simply defer to religious testimony, for the reason that (a) understanding is distinctively important in the religious domain, and (b) deferring to testimony is generally in tension with understanding. (From 1, 2)

The next stage of the argument would employ DTE to connect 3 to a claim about disagreement:

4.   Whenever it's fully appropriate to suspend judgment in response to a particular case of disagreement, it would also have been fully appropriate to defer to testimony in a testimonial counterpart case (constructed as described above). (DTE)

---

[31] Further support for the comparative point: nonreductionists have argued that reductionism is implausible because we simply cannot know very much at all—and in particular can't assess the reliability of testimony—without first relying on testimony. See, e.g., Coady (1992).

5. It is often—at least in some respect—inappropriate to suspend judgment in response to religious disagreement. (From 3, 4)

There are some obvious vagaries and ambiguities here. In particular, the "often" and "in some respect/fully" qualifiers are annoying but necessary.[32] The reason for talking about moral/religious testimony being inappropriate *in some respect* is that discouraging understanding is clearly at most a *pro tanto* reason not to defer to religious testimony. Such considerations may be outweighed, such that all-things-considered religious testimony would be in some sense appropriate though still regrettable and not "fully" appropriate. The reason for the "often" qualifiers is that testimony merely *tends* to discourage understanding. There are admittedly some cases—indeed, arguably all or most cases involving children fall into this category—in which testimony serves as a scaffolding or incentive for further exploration, rather than a hindrance to it.

I offer this argument in the twin spirits of (i) perhaps convincing someone who was not convinced by my argument that suspending judgment in response to disagreement directly damages understanding, and (ii) calling attention to some interesting, underexplored questions about the relationship between testimony and disagreement, which focusing on the value of understanding makes salient. Taking understanding seriously in the religious domain may mean not only admitting a new reason to be stalwart in the face of disagreement but also admitting a new reason to be wary of simple deference to religious testimony.

8. Conclusion

To any who were hoping for a concrete recommendation in Ada's case, I apologize. I have none. So much depends on the particulars, which even a multiple-paragraph sketch of her case cannot provide. However, one thing I will claim is that—if Ada's system of Christian religious beliefs really constituted understanding, prior to her encountering disagreement[33]—she has a

---

[32] Though one might worry that the two separate uses of "often" results in invalidity, it seems to me the vagueness here is innocuous. Line 5 says that—granting premise 3—we should think this "often" generalization extends to those possible cases of religious testimony that we would construct as counterparts to cases of religious disagreement. I do not see a good reason to doubt this.

[33] It is an interesting question how this conditional claim about Ada's reasons relates to the question what Ada should do, when she is *uncertain* whether her beliefs constitute understanding. Plausibly the mere risk of such a loss of understanding is sufficient to generate a reason of some strength not to suspend judgment.

considerable reason not to directly suspend judgment upon encountering disagreeing interlocutors. This is so even if the disagreement is an indication of potential inaccuracy or irrationality. The loss of other beliefs, coherence, and/or reasoning abilities that would ensue should be reckoned a great cost, with respect to both epistemic and religious ends.[34,35]

References

Benton, Matthew A. 2018. "God and Interpersonal Knowledge." *Res Philosophica* 95: 421–447.

Callahan, Laura Frances. 2018. "Moral Testimony: A Re-Conceived Understanding Explanation." *The Philosophical Quarterly* 68: 437–459.

Callahan, Laura Frances. 2020. "Moral Testimony." In Miranda Fricker et al., eds. *The Routledge Handbook of Social Epistemology*, 123–134. London: Routledge.

Christensen, David. 2007. "Epistemology of Disagreement: The Good News." *Philosophical Review* 116: 187–217.

Coady, C.A.J. 1992. Testimony: A Philosophical Study. Oxford: Clarendon Press.

Cottingham, John. 2018. "Transcending Science: Humane Models of Religious Understanding." In Fiona Ellis, ed. *New Models of Religious Understanding*, 23–41. Oxford: Oxford University Press.

Dawkins, Richard. 2008. *The God Delusion Debate (Transcript)*, <http://www.protorah.com/wp-content/uploads/2015/01/The-God-Delusion-Debate-Full-Transcript.pdf>

Elga, Adam. 2007. "Reflection and Disagreement." *Noûs* 48: 478–502.

Elga, Adam and Agustín Rayo. Forthcoming. "Fragmentation and Information Access." In Cristina Borgoni, Dirk Kindermann, and Andrea Onofri, eds. *The Fragmented Mind*. Oxford: Oxford University Press.

Elgin, Catherine Z. 2006. "From Knowledge to Understanding." In Stephen Hetherington, ed. *Epistemology Futures*, 149–716. Oxford: Clarendon Press.

Elgin, Catherine Z. 2007. "Emotion and Understanding." In Georg Brun, Ulvi Dogouglu, and Dominque Kunzle, eds. *Epistemology and Emotions*, 33–50. London: Ashgate.

---

[34] One question this raises is whether such losses or potential losses are ones the Ada herself can take into account as she considers whether Christianity is true. After all, if belief is "transparent," in the sense that Shah and Velleman (2005) claim, then "[T]he only way to answer the question *whether to believe that p* is to answer the question *whether p* (499)." This question must wait for another paper.

[35] Many thanks to the editors of the volume for helpful comments, as well as audience members at the Society of Christian Philosophers group session of the 2019 Eastern APA.

Elgin, Catherine Z. 2009. "Is Understanding Factive?" In Adrian Haddock, Alan Millar, and Duncan Pritchard, eds. *Epistemic Value*, 322–330. Oxford: Oxford University Press.

Enoch, David. 2014. "A Defense of Moral Deference." *The Journal of Philosophy* 111: 1–30.

Feldman, Richard. 2007. "Reasonable Religious Disagreements." In Louise Antony, ed. *Philosophers Without Gods: Meditations on Atheism and the Secular Life*, 194–214. Oxford: Oxford University Press.

Foley, Richard. 1992. Working Without a Net: A Study of Egocentric Epistemology. New York: Oxford University Press.

Friedman, Jane. 2017. "Why Suspend Judging?" *Noûs* 51: 302–326.

Grimm, Stephen. 2011. "Understanding." In Sven Bernecker and Duncan Pritchard, eds. *The Routledge Companion to Epistemology*. New York: Routledge.

Grimm, Stephen. 2016. "How Understanding People Differs From Understanding the Natural World." *Philosophical Issues (Noûs supplement)* 26: 209–225.

Hawthorne, John and Amia Srinivasan. 2013. "Disagreement Without Transparency: Some Bleak Thoughts." In David Christensen and Jennifer Lackey, eds. *The Epistemology of Disagreement: New Essays*, 9–30. Oxford: Oxford University Press.

Hills, Alison. 2015. "Understanding Why." *Noûs* 50: 661–688.

Hills, Alison. 2009. "Moral Testimony and Moral Epistemology." *Ethics* 120: 94–127.

Howell, Robert J. 2014. "Google Morals, Virtue, and the Asymmetry of Deference." *Noûs* 48: 389–415.

Jones, Karen. 1999. "Second-hand Moral Knowledge." *The Journal of Philosophy* 96: 55–78.

Keller, Juliano Lorraine. 2018. "Divine Ineffability and Franciscan Knowledge." *Res Philosophica* 95: 347–370.

Kelly, Thomas. 2005. "The Epistemic Significance of Disagreement." In Tamar Szabó Gendler and John Hawthorne, eds. *Oxford Studies in Epistemology, Volume 1*, 167–196. Oxford: Oxford University Press.

Kierkegaard, Søren. 2009. *Concluding Unscientific Postscript*. Alastair Hannay, ed. Cambridge: Cambridge University Press.

Kvanvig, Jonathan L. 2003. *The Value of Knowledge and the Pursuit of Understanding*. Cambridge: Cambridge University Press.

McGrath, Sarah. 2011. "Skepticism about Moral Expertise as a Puzzle for Moral Realism." *Journal of Philosophy* 108: 111–137.

Murphy, Nancey. 1990. *Theology in the Age of Scientific Reasoning.* Ithaca, NY: Cornell University Press.

Pritchard, Duncan. 2010. "Knowledge and Understanding." In Duncan Pritchard, Alan Millar, and Adrian Haddock, eds. *The Nature and Value of Knowledge: Three Investigations,* 1–88. Oxford: Oxford University Press.

Quine, Willard V.O. 1951. "Two Dogmas of Empiricism." *The Philosophical Review* 60: 20–43.

Quine, Willard V.O. and J.S. Ullian. 1970. *The Web of Belief.* New York: Random House.

Riggs, Wayne. 2003. "Understanding 'Virtue' and the Virtue of Understanding." In Michael DePaul and Linda Zagzebski, eds. *Intellectual Virtue: Perspectives from Ethics and Epistemology,* 203–227. Oxford: Oxford University Press.

Scott, Kyle. 2018. "Religious Knowledge versus Religious Understanding." In Fiona Ellis, ed. *New Models of Religious Understanding,* 134–150. Oxford: Oxford University Press.

Shah, Nishi and David Velleman. 2005. "Doxastic Deliberation." *The Philosophical Review* 114: 497–534.

Sliwa, Paulina. 2012. "In Defense of Moral Testimony." *Philosophical Studies* 158: 175–195.

Stalnaker, Robert. 1987. *Inquiry.* Cambridge, Mass.: MIT Press.

3

How Confident Should the Religious Believer Be in the Face of Religious Pluralism?

Sanford C. Goldberg

Arguments from religious diversity or disagreement purport to support skepticism regarding justified (or rational) religious belief. In this paper I explore the prospects for resisting these sorts of argument. Those who would resist can (i) argue that the principles that convict the faithful of irrationality overreach, and would establish a more widespread skepticism about rational belief, (ii) downgrade their disagreeing interlocutor(s), (iii) appeal to epistemic permissivism, or (iv) argue that the believer is no worse off, epistemically speaking, than the atheist or agnostic non-believer. After presenting what I regard as the best version of the argument from diversity or disagreement, I argue that any believer who hopes for truth will not get much solace from any of these responses.[1]

1.

Religious diversity is pervasive: there are the theists, the atheists, and the agnostics. Among the theists there are the various religions; and within the major religions, there are the various sects, groups, or denominations.[2] Insofar as we represent this diversity as involving distinctive beliefs, pervasive diversity amounts to pervasive disagreement among those with these beliefs.

[1] I would like to thank the participants of the 2016 Bellingham summer seminar on The Virtue of Faith, led by Dan Howard-Snyder (and supported by the Templeton Foundation), who heard and commented on an earlier version of this paper. Thanks also to Matt Benton, Mike Bergmann, and Jon Kvanvig, who provided excellent comments on earlier versions of the paper. (None of them are responsible for any of the errors here.)
[2] As King (2008: 847–648) notes, intra-religious disagreement may be more significant, epistemically speaking, than inter-religious disagreement.

Sanford C. Goldberg, *How Confident Should the Religious Believer Be in the Face of Religious Pluralism?* In: *Religious Disagreement and Pluralism*. Edited by: Matthew A. Benton and Jonathan L. Kvanvig, Oxford University Press.

It has long been recognized that such pervasive diversity and disagreement poses a threat to the rationality of the relevant beliefs in this domain. Many authors have appealed to such diversity and disagreement to argue for *skepticism regarding the rationality or justification of religious belief*; many non-skeptics have felt the need to address such concerns. Such diversity- or disagreement-based arguments for skepticism have been developed in various different ways; and corresponding to each there have been defenders of religious belief who have aimed to address the worries. In this paper my aim is to suggest what I regard as the core concern raised by the diversity- or disagreement-based argument for skepticism, and to argue that none of the recent attempts to rebut these arguments succeeds in meeting the concern as it is presented here. This is not to say that those arguments do not succeed at all; it is merely to make clear that if they succeed in doing what they set out to be doing, this is only because what they set out to do is not as ambitious as one might have hoped. In any case, they fail to secure the possibility of reasonable or justified religious belief in any sense of "reasonable" or "justified" which is tightly connected to knowledge.

2.

In my opinion, the strongest version of a diversity- or disagreement-based argument for skepticism about the rationality of religious belief aims to highlight the grounds we have for the following proposition:

BAD PROSPECTS   The prospects that one oneself has reached the truth in matters of systematically contested religious belief are not good.

By "religious belief" here I will understand any belief whose content is that of an affirmative positive claim concerning matters pertaining to a supernatural and/or spiritual realm, including claims appealing to entities or features of that realm to justify certain (religious) practices.[3] The appeal to the fact of diversity, construed as amounting to a pervasive sort of disagreement regarding matters religious, is meant to highlight that each of us has good reason to endorse BAD PROSPECTS. As I will be presenting the argument from religious diversity/disagreement, it is not committed to the claim that BAD PROSPECTS is *true*

---

[3] This does not include beliefs that express a commitment to atheism; I will discuss these at some length below.

(though I for one think it is). The claim to which this argument is committed, rather, is that the fact of disagreement gives each of us *a good reason* to think that BAD PROSPECTS is true. It is in terms of this contention that the argument from religious diversity/disagreement draws its main conclusion:

DEFEATING DOUBT   One has good grounds for doubting whether one has arrived at the truth in matters of systematically contested religious belief.

The result is that even if one's route *was in fact reliable*—the prospects that one attained truth are very good (the billions of others who disagree being themselves mistaken)—even so, whatever reliability-generated justification would otherwise have been conferred on one's belief is *defeated*. The fact of pervasive disagreement is, in short, an undercutting defeater.[4]

I regard this as the strongest version of the argument from religious diversity/disagreement. Several features of this version of the argument are worth highlighting at the outset.

First, this version of the argument is highly concessive to the defender of the rationality of religious belief. For it can grant at least two important claims that are often used in defense of the rationality of religious belief, and yet still succeed in reaching its conclusion. Thus, it can grant the defender both of the following claims:

BASIC   Religious belief is basic belief, that is, belief whose status as justified or not depends not on the goodness of the reasons on which it is based but on the reliability of the process or method through which it is formed.

RELIABLE METHOD   One's route to religious belief is in fact a reliable one.

That the argument above can grant BASIC is important,[5] since in the past two or three decades many of the most highly influential defenses of the rationality of religious belief appeal to externalist epistemology (either Reliabilism or Proper Functionalism): their strategy is to appeal to one or another externalist epistemology, together with the claim that religious belief is basic belief (and that the relevant route is reliable when properly functioning), to reach the

---

[4] I will speak of the proposition, [p], as a *defeater* for a subject S's belief that r when the presence of [p], among the set of contents S believes, renders S's belief that r *unjustified*. I will speak of a defeater [p] for S's belief that r as a *rebutting* defeater when [p] constitutes evidence that the proposition that r is false. And I will speak of [p] as an *undermining* defeater when [p] constitutes evidence that S acquired or sustained the belief that r in an unreliable fashion.

[5] Compare King (2008: 846).

conclusion that religious belief is justified belief. The argument above is easily adapted to targeting such views, since in effect the argument above advances the hypothesis that the fact of pervasive diversity and disagreement establishes DEFEATING DOUBT even in the face of whatever justification one's belief might otherwise have enjoyed through having been formed in a reliable fashion. And this is also why the foregoing argument can grant RELIABLE METHOD. The point is that even if one's method was reliable, DEFEATING DOUBT still holds: one has good reasons to doubt whether one got things right.

Second, and relatedly, the argument above need not make any strong assumptions about the reasons we need to have in order to be entitled to rely on our basic belief-forming processes. In particular the argument above need not assume either of the following two doctrines:

JJ   If S is justified in believing that p, then S is justified in believing that S is justified in believing that p.

REASONS   For all belief-forming processes BFP, if S's reliance on BFP is to yield justified belief, then S must have (undefeated) reasons to regard BFP as reliable.

That the argument from religious disagreement/diversity (as I am presenting it) has no need to assume either JJ or REASONS is important. If the argument *were* to assume either JJ or REASONS, then (1) those defenders of the rationality of religious belief whose defense appealed to epistemic externalism could dismiss the argument as question-begging, and (2) a case could be made for thinking that the argument above overreaches, generating skeptical conclusions far beyond those pertaining to religious belief alone.[6]

As I present it, the argument from religious diversity/disagreement need not assume either JJ or REASONS. What it does need to assume is something that the vast majority of epistemic externalists themselves embrace, namely, that

DEFEAT$_{DOX}$ For all basic belief-forming processes BFP, S's belief that p formed through BFP is justified only if S has no adequate (undefeated) reasons to regard this belief as unreliably formed.[7]

---

[6] In effect, the first generation of externalist defenders of justified religious belief responded to the then-prevalent objections in both of these ways. See e.g., Alston (1988, 1991) and Plantinga (2000).

[7] See Feldman (2003), who is responding to Plantinga (1995). The defeater-like principle Feldman settles on is not DEFEAT$_{DOX}$, but it is similar (and is deployed in a similar dialectical spirit).

I assume that any externalist view which hopes to yield a plausible account of justification will need to have some way to accommodate the phenomenon of defeat.[8] And I submit that DEFEAT$_{DOX}$ amounts to a plausible condition on doxastic defeat. To ensure its plausibility, I stipulate that a reason is adequate in the relevant sense *only if* that reason itself is in epistemically good order—either it is well-supported (if inferred from other reasons), or it is the output of a properly functioning reliable process (if basic).[9]

It is important to be clear how it is DEFEAT$_{DOX}$, rather than either JJ or REASONS, that drives the argument from religious diversity/disagreement. On my reconstruction, the argument aims to establish that the fact of religious diversity/disagreement constitutes a defeater for the justification or rationality of any religious belief that is systematically contested. If we are to reach this conclusion, it suffices (on the assumption of DEFEAT$_{DOX}$) to show the following: the fact of religious disagreement/diversity constitutes an adequate, undefeated reason to regard the relevant religious belief as unreliably formed. In other words, it suffices to show that we have good reason to think that BAD PROSPECTS holds (with the further result that DEFEATING DOUBT holds). Such an argument needs no claim implying that one is never justified in believing anything through a process unless one can certify the reliability of the process. Rather, the relevant claim is that one is never justified in believing anything through a process *one has adequate (undefeated) reasons to regard as not sufficiently likely to attain truth* (whatever the justificatory status of one's belief would be if one *didn't* have those reasons).[10]

Might one worry that the argument's reliance on DEFEAT$_{DOX}$ would force us to identify a relevant reference class in which to advance the claim of poor prospects for truth?[11] If so, one might object to this argument as critics of reliabilism have used the "generality problem" to object to reliabilism as a theory of justification.[12] But this worry can be met: the relevant reference class

---

[8] For the need to acknowledge defeaters within a broadly externalist view of justification, see e.g., Bergmann (2005, 2006). (Bergmann himself is an externalist defender of the rationality of religious belief, suggesting that even those interested in defending this hypothesis will do well to accept DEFEAT$_{DOX}$.) Not everyone agrees; see Larsonen-Aarnio (2010, 2014), Williamson (2014), and Baker-Hytch and Benton (2015).

[9] This stipulation is concessive. In effect, my disagreement-based argument against rational religious belief aims to show that pervasive disagreement constitutes a defeater, and this stipulation places (epistemic) restrictions on what can count as a defeater.

[10] In fact, although I won't argue for it here, my own view, in Goldberg (2017, 2018), is that we can add to DEFEAT$_{DOX}$ the following condition on what I, following Lackey (1999), call "normative" defeat. However, it would take me too far afield to defend this, so here I will work with DEFEAT$_{DOX}$ only.

[11] I thank Jon Kvanvig for indicating the need to address this.

[12] See e.g., Conee and Feldman (1998).

is the class of religious beliefs regarding which there is systematic disagreement. One advantage of this characterization of the reference class is that there is no need to commit oneself to any particular claim about the nature of the process-type involved in the formation of religious belief. If religious beliefs are the result of a distinctive type (or distinctive types) of cognitive process, then this argument shows that (we have reasons to believe that) this type is/ these types are unreliable. If religious beliefs are *not* the result of a distinctive type of cognitive process—they are instead the result of processes used throughout our cognitive lives, not just in connection with religious belief— then the argument shows that (we have reasons to believe that) this type is/ these types are unreliable *when producing religious beliefs*. As an analogy, consider vision as a belief-forming process-type: it is a highly reliable type, but we have reason to believe that it is unreliable *when utilized for objects in one's peripheral vision, or at a great distance etc*. The result is that subjects have an undercutting defeater for beliefs formed through vision *in those contexts*.

Beyond avoiding JJ and REASONS, a third virtue of the argument from religious diversity/disagreement (as presented above) is this. If the argument is successful, it should generalize to cover any sort of account on which religious belief is rational belief—whether it embraces externalist epistemology or not. For the point is that the fact of pervasive diversity/disagreement is a certain kind of evidence—higher-order evidence—which, whatever one's epistemological orientation, is such that it renders one's religious beliefs unjustified.[13]

Fourth, and finally, the argument above can assimilate considerations pertaining to "irrelevant causal influences" on belief (a topic of recent discussion). My own sense is that arguments from "irrelevant causal influences" are successful only to the degree that they give us reason to regard the relevant belief as having been formed in an unreliable way.[14] So whether or not arguments from irrelevant causal influences can be reduced to arguments from disagreement (for which, see White 2010), it will be my contention that irrelevant causal influences are epistemically significant insofar as they provide reasons to endorse BAD PROSPECTS.

As I am construing it here, then, the argument from religious disagreement/ diversity has two key contentions. The first is that the fact of religious diversity/disagreement gives us good reason to endorse BAD PROSPECTS, that is, good reason to endorse the low likelihood that a contested religious

---

[13] The idea that skeptical arguments from disagreement might be better put as arguments from higher-order evidence is developed in King (2016).
[14] Compare Vavova (2018).

belief of ours is true. The second is that this reason itself constitutes a defeater for the relevant religious belief (= DEFEATING DOUBTS). Insofar as the fact of religious diversity/disagreement gives us good reason to endorse BAD PROSPECTS, and that having good reason to endorse BAD PROSPECTS constitutes DEFEATING DOUBT, we reach the following conclusion: the fact of prevalent diversity/disagreement constitutes a defeater for any of one's contested religious beliefs. In essence, this, together with DEFEAT$_{DOX}$, warrants a conditional claim: if one *has* this reason (essentially, if one is *aware of* the prevalence of diversity/disagreement), then none of one's contested religious beliefs are justified. And this conditional claim is the skeptical conclusion.

I have defended the argument's two key contentions—that we have good reason to endorse BAD PROSPECTS, and that this establishes DEFEATING DOUBT—elsewhere,[15] so here I will be brief. (The real action of the paper will be in responding to the various attempts to rebut these brief arguments.[16])

Take the claim that we have good reason to endorse BAD PROSPECTS. In this connection I note several features of the prevalent diversity in religious belief: it includes some *peer disagreement*; it has persisted despite the efforts of various groups at conversion (forced and otherwise), proselytization, conversation, and argumentation aimed at getting others around to one's own religious views, and despite the fact that so many people (many of whom are at least as well-off, epistemically, as one oneself on the matter at hand) are extremely motivated to get it right (given the rewards they anticipate if they do, or the punishments they anticipate if they don't); and there would appear to be no reasonable method or methods by which to decide these matters.[17] So on any given matter on which one's own belief is in the decided minority, where there are smart and otherwise knowledgeable people on the other side(s), where the disagreement has been persistent, and where one can't explain away all of the opposition, the chance that one is right are not particularly good. To be sure, one can continue to insist that one is right, despite all of this, and one might even think that one's evidence, including one's private evidence, warrants it. But one ought to be tempered by the facts that others with whom one disagrees can and will do the same in their turn,

[15] See e.g., Goldberg (2009, 2012, 2013a, 2013b).
[16] Goldberg (2013b) presents this sort of argument for a negative conclusion about the rationality of religious beliefs in the face of disagreement. Interesting responses have been published since, and my goal here is to show why the responses don't undermine the force of the argument. (With thanks to Jon Kvanvig for indicating the need to make this clear.)
[17] This latter point has been contested; I will return to it below, p. 72.

and (assuming there is a fact of the matter) the two sides can't both be right. So unless one has reasons to think that one's total evidence, including one's private evidence, is more likely to lead one to get it right than the total evidence, including private evidence, of one's disagreeing interlocutors are likely to lead them to get it right, to just that extent one has a reason to regard any of one's contested religious beliefs as no more likely to be true than are any of those with whom one is disagreeing. And since there are many such people who figure into many distinct religious subgroups (not to mentions the agnostics and atheists), we have good reason to endorse BAD PROSPECTS.

Of course, if we have good reason to endorse BAD PROSPECTS, the case for DEFEATING DOUBT is straightforward. Assume that one has a good reason to regard any of one's contested religious beliefs as unlikely to be true. Then it would seem that one has a defeater for any of one's contested religious beliefs whenever one is aware of the pervasive disagreement itself. Note that this does not assume that one has a good reason to regard one's belief-forming process or method as unreliable in general; perhaps it is such a reason, perhaps it isn't.[18] But at the very least, it's a reason for thinking that even if one's process or method *is* reliable in general (say, because it is standardly employed in other, *non-religious* domains in which it produces mainly true beliefs when it produces any beliefs at all), even so, it would be epistemically dangerous to rely on this belief-forming process or method in the domain of religion itself.[19] Simply put, in that domain the likelihood that any of the beliefs it produces is true is low. In this sense, our reason to endorse BAD PROSPECTS would be a reason to think that *within the domain of religion*, one's way(s) of forming beliefs are unreliable. Here I highlight the analogy I introduced above: vision is a highly reliable way of forming beliefs, but when one is trying to reach judgments about things far away, in one's peripheral vision, under bad lighting, vision is not reliable. One who relied on vision in such circumstances would not arrive at justified belief—and this, despite the fact that vision is a generally reliable way to arrive at true belief. So, too, on the (concessive) assumption that the belief-forming process(es) one uses to arrive at religious belief are generally reliable: even so, given the epistemic dangerousness of the context of religion itself, as attested to by the systematic controversies within that domain, one who relied on these processes in such circumstances would have good grounds for doubt that one has arrived at the truth in this way—and

---

[18] See above, p. 70; and see Goldberg (2009) for a more extended discussion.

[19] I underscore that this analysis does not rely on any particular view as to which process-types are involved in the formation of religious belief. See above, p. 70.

this, despite what is being (concessively) assumed to be the fact that the process(es) in question is/are a generally reliable way to arrive at true belief.

Or so it is, according to what I regard as the strongest skeptical argument from religious diversity or disagreement.

3.

Recently, there have been several attempts to rebut or defang this argument, in an effort to preserve the rationality of religious belief. I will address each of these in turn.

One response to the skeptical argument from religious disagreement/diversity proceeds by using the standard framework in discussions of the epistemology of disagreement. The set-up is one in which two "epistemic peers" find themselves disagreeing on some topic. (Two people are peers with respect to a topic when each is roughly equally likely to get it right on the matter at hand.) In this framework, one way to respond to the skeptical argument from religious disagreement is to explain away the disagreement by arguing that the religious believer's disagreeing interlocutor is not actually her peer, but rather is intellectually worse off when it comes to addressing the matter at hand than the religious believer herself is. Of course, if this approach is to succeed in defanging the skeptical thrust of the argument from *pervasive* diversity and disagreement, it must be generalized: it will have to be argued that religious diversity and disagreement, though enduring and pervasive, can nevertheless *always* be explained away as the result of the other sides' lack of relevant evidence, or lack of competence, or... Indeed, it is for this reason that my own presentation of the argument from religious disagreement does not rely on the standard framework of "peer" disagreement, since in my view the significance of considerations of peerhood are somewhat compromised when the disagreement is systematic.[20] However, we might still wonder whether such an approach affords a way for the defender of rational religious belief to respond to the argument from religious disagreement. This sort of response received a boost from some of Plantinga's reflections from the 1990s (see e.g., Plantinga 1995), but it has recently been defended with vigor by Michael

---

[20] See Goldberg (2013a) for a defense of this claim.

Bergmann (2015). In this section I argue that there are many reasons to think that this is unsuccessful as a reply.[21]

Bergmann's core claim is that "in certain actual circumstances that aren't uncommon for educated westerners" the religious believer can preserve the rationality of her religious belief by "rationally demoting" those would-be peers on the other side of the debate. To argue for this, Bergmann begins by noting that there are several ways in which one's acquiring evidence of a peer disagreement might rationalize one's "demoting" the other side so that they are no longer regarded as a peer on the matter at hand. He distinguishes three kinds of relevant evidence in a case of peer disagreement regarding p: *p-evidence*, which is evidence for the disputed claim; *Rp-evidence*, which is evidence that one's own belief that p "is formed in a reliable and non-misleading way"; and *R~p-evidence*, which is evidence that one's would-be peer's belief that ~p is "formed in a reliable and non-misleading way" (Bergmann 2015: 30). Bergmann's claim is that "when your p-evidence and Rp-evidence are strong and your R~p-evidence is weak…, it is rational to demote an assumed peer." (30) In line with this, Bergmann's core allegation is that "in certain actual circumstances that aren't uncommon for educated westerners," this will often be the case for religious believers in would-be peer disagreement with others over religious matters.

He warms us up to this possibility by giving an example modeled on an earlier example given by Plantinga (2000: 40). Here is Bergmann's version:

STOLEN FRISIAN FLAG CASE: The police haul you in, accusing you of stealing my Frisian flag again. The evidence against you is strong. There are reliable witnesses claiming to have seen you at my house at the time the crime occurred. You are known to have a motive to do me harm. In addition, this sort of theft is in keeping with your past behavior. And the flag was found on your property, close to the place you had hidden it when you stole it before. The jury, upon hearing the evidence, is convinced and believes that you are

---

[21] Two points from my colleague Jennifer Lackey (2018) are worth having in mind throughout discussions of peerhood and religious disagreement. First, the issue in play cannot be simply whether the religious believer does *in fact* downgrade those would-be peers on the other side; the question is whether she is *entitled* to do so. Second, there is some question as to the relevant conception of peerhood that is relevant. Lackey herself identifies four (the first three of which she regards as improper for the purpose at hand). According to Lackey, peerhood might involve *rough evidential and cognitive equivalence on the topic at hand* (EP₁), *rough equivalence in intellectual virtue* (EP₂), *rough equivalence in the likelihood to be mistaken conditional on disagreeing about the matter* (EP₃), or *rough equivalence in justification in their respective beliefs regarding the question at hand* (EP₄). Interestingly, for the purposes here I think the matter is not crucial, since I think that on any of them the religious believer will have the sort of defeater mentioned in DEFEATING DOUBT. See also Lackey (2014).

guilty. But you have a clear memory of being on a solitary hike near Mount Baker at the time, although you have no witnesses who can confirm this. You report this clear memory to the jury, but they aren't impressed, especially because you also have a history of telling feeble lies in the past to cover up your crimes. (Bergmann 2015: 34)

Clearly, this is a case in which, from the jury's (third-person) point of view, it is reasonable to assign a very low probability to the hypothesis that you are innocent—and yet, despite this, the probability *you* should assign to your innocence is extremely high (perhaps up to practical certainty). In the first instance, the probative force of this case is that of an existence proof: it is a positive instance of a case in which (i) some subject S has extremely strong and direct (albeit first-personal) confirmation of hypothesis H, (ii) despite this there is ample objective evidence for ~H, so (iii) the probability another person rationally should assign to H is very low, and yet (iv) it remains rational for S to assign a very high probability to H (perhaps up to practical certainty).

Of course, Bergmann hopes to do more than show that there are cases in which (i)–(iv) hold; he wants to argue that some cases of religious belief— those that obtain "in certain actual circumstances that aren't uncommon for educated westerners"—*are* such a case. And this requires more than that STOLEN FRISIAN FLAG constitutes a positive instance of (i)–(iv); it requires that STOLEN be a good analogy for the cases of religious belief in question. The claim would be this: even though it is true that from another person's (third-person) point of view, it is reasonable to assign a very low probability to the hypothesis that your religious beliefs are true, despite this, the probability *you* should assign to the truth of your religious beliefs is very high, i.e., you remain rational in so doing. The key question, of course, concerns whether this is a good analogy.

Bergmann thinks it is. This is because he thinks that the religious believer's *p-evidence* is very strong. This he construes as *the seeming that God exists*, which (he contends) can be triggered by any number of things: feelings of guilt or of being forgiven, or of gratitude or desperate fear; admiration for the grandeur and majesty of nature, as well as its minute intricacy; response to the testimony of others; an appreciation for apparent design in nature; or of a feeling of being moved by Scripture. On Bergmann's reconstruction, that theists have "strong theistic seemings" (2015: 37) provides one explanation of their persistent theistic beliefs; and presumably this, together with (what he regards as) the fact we have no reason to deny these seemings, can be used as the basis of theism. In Bergmann's own words,

One explanation of this persistent theistic belief is that these theists have strong theistic seemings—strong in the sense that they continue to result in a strong inclination towards theistic belief even in the face of much opposition, opposition which these theists deem to be ultimately unconvincing.

(Bergmann 2015: 37)

Bergmann also thinks that the believer's *Rp-evidence* in connection with a belief in God's existence can be strong too, albeit "not easy to recognize" (38). He writes,

Just as we have noninferential knowledge about our immediate physical environment by means of sense perception and about our past by means of memory, so also we have a faculty of common sense by means of which we have noninferential knowledge of first principles.   (Bergmann 2015: 38)

This comes by way of the "felt veridicality" of the first principles we endorse: we endorse them because of this felt veridicality, and our awareness of this felt veridicality is an awareness of evidence for the reliability of the faculty that produces belief in the principles themselves (Bergmann 2015: 41). While he does not regard this as particularly strong evidence, he argues that it protects theistic belief from certain objections to the reliability of the processes (41). Taken together, Bergmann thinks, these pieces of can evidence *outweigh* the *R~p-evidence* the believer has. Here Bergmann writes that in his own case the R~p-evidence *he* has is "not very strong" (47). He writes that the arguments for atheism are not particularly compelling, and often there is a way to explain away the atheist's "capacity or tendency to have appropriate theistic seemings" without forming theistic belief (48). If this is so, then the theist can demote the atheist from the status of peer, and explain away the disagreement as the result of an epistemic asymmetry—thereby preserving the rationality of belief in the face of diversity/disagreement.

Bergmann's position does not withstand scrutiny.

Let's start with the case in STOLEN FRISIAN FLAG. I grant that this is a case in which (i)–(iv) hold. But it is important to see why it is imminently plausible to think that (i)—the claim that S has extremely strong (first-personal) confirming evidence for the hypothesis in question—holds. The answer is straightforward: it is not contentious that perception, memory, and simple reasoning are, and are regarded as, reliable sources (or preservers) of information. For this reason, in contexts of epistemic assessment, these processes have the status of "innocent until proven guilty": a subject is presumptively entitled to rely on them in belief-fixation except when she has reasons for suspicion. What underwrites (i) are experiences and memories that derive from sources of this type—that is, sources on which one is presumptively entitled to rely. What is more, to one who has had such experiences and memories, the more "objective" (third-personal) sources of evidence here need not, and in this case should not, bear against one's rational confidence in the information one acquired through those sources. This is because one's warranted confidence in the experiences and memories is extremely high— something that reflects in part the status of perception and memory as sources or preservers of information—and *nothing in the objective (third-personal) evidence calls into question the reliability of these processes on this occasion.*[22] For consider again the facts that constitute the objective evidence against you:

> There are reliable witnesses claiming to have seen you at my house at the time the crime occurred. You are known to have a motive to do me harm. In addition, this sort of theft is in keeping with your past behavior. And the flag was found on your property, close to the place you had hidden it when you stole it before.

None of these facts calls into question the reliability of your memories. Rather, if the objective (third-personal) evidence calls *anything* into question, what it calls into question is the sincerity or trustworthiness of your *statements about* your memories, not your memories themselves. This is precisely why we have an asymmetry in the rational reaction between the first-person and the third-person case: it remains rational for you to assign extremely high credence to the hypothesis that you are innocent, since your opinion on the matter is fixed by reasoning from your own (first-personal) experiences and memories, and does not depend on your statement on the matter; whereas others depend on your statement on the matter, which, from their perspective, is called into question by their substantial third-personal evidence.

I submit that the foregoing analysis makes plain why STOLEN FRISIAN FLAG is not a good analogy for religious belief. In the case of religious belief, it is simply not true that one's (first-personal) experience as of God's existence (what Bergmann construes as a *seeming as of God's existence*) is produced by sources that ought to be ascribed the status of "innocent until proven guilty."

---

[22] There are occasions when the third-personal evidence *would* or *should* prompt one to question one's own memory; perhaps one learns that one has been under the influence of a memory- or perception-affecting drug, for example. But I assume that this is not such a case.

After all, sources that have this status are presumed to be reliable, whereas it is precisely (one's right to presume) the reliability of one's source for religious belief that is at issue in the epistemology of religious disagreement.[23] Given the fact of pervasive religious diversity and disagreement, it is unreasonable in the extreme to regard the method(s) or process(es) as producing truth in the domain of religious propositions. The two cases are not analogous.

If an analogy with the case of religious belief is wanted, I would propose the following (in place of STOLEN FRISIAN FLAG). S has what she regards as a highly reliable route to judgments in some domain. It turns out that many people who also regard themselves as having a reliable route to judgments in that same domain systematically disagree with the judgments she forms. And among the opinions that her interlocutors have is the opinion that there *is* no reliable faculty of the sort S thinks she has. To be sure, there are yet others who share S's views; and among these people there is the belief that it is the *others* who are mistaken about the status of the alleged faculty in question. In short, the situation is a mess. In such a context, is it obvious that S is entitled to have the sort of confidence in her judgments (and in the reliability of her route to those judgments) as the subject in STOLEN FRISIAN FLAG is entitled to have? It strikes me that the answer is a resounding no. The subject in STOLEN FRISIAN FLAG is entitled to confidence insofar as she is relying on what everyone should agree is a reliable route to truth; the only question that third parties can be taken to be raising concern whether she is being sincere (something that she is in a position to discern first-personally). Not so in the present (analogous) case: what third parties mean to doubt includes precisely whether the route S has to belief-formation is in fact a reliable one. This would appear to be a crucial difference between the cases. Indeed, this is a difference between STOLEN FRISIAN FLAG and the religious case, since in effect the religious case is the same in structure as the analogy just described. Given this, it would appear that no appeal to STOLEN FRISIAN FLAG can help the religious believer avoid the conclusion drawn above: the fact of pervasive religious diversity and disagreement constitutes a good reason to doubt the reliability of one's contested religious beliefs.

Since I suspect that the temptation to deny the point will be great here, I want to reiterate that our conclusion is reached in a way that does not depend on either JJ or REASONS—that is, it does not require that one have reasons to regard any process as reliable prior to being entitled to rely on it. On the contrary, as the skeptical argument presented above makes clear, we can grant

---

[23] See e.g., Goldberg (2015).

that there are process-types whose reliability one is entitled to take for granted. Indeed, the argument above *depends* on this assumption, since in effect it asserts an asymmetry between ordinary perception and memory, which are in play in STOLEN (and whose reliability can be taken for granted), and whatever it is that is producing theistic seemings, on the other. Precisely what makes a process-type one whose reliability can be taken for granted is a complicated affair; I have had my say elsewhere.[24] But it should be clear that if a process is to be a candidate for such a presumption, it should be reliable when working properly in normal conditions, and it should be such that those who employ it are good at discerning when it is working properly and when conditions are normal (and they reliably refrain from employing it when these conditions are not met). The defender of religious belief will be hard-pressed to defend the idea that the processes that produce religious belief meet this condition. For if so, the fact of pervasive religious diversity and disagreement would be impossible to explain.[25] So the argument from pervasive religious diversity and disagreement does not depend on any internalist requirement such as JJ; nor does it depend on REASONS or on the repudiation of basic belief-forming processes on which we are presumptively entitled to rely (without first having confirmed their reliability).

I have been arguing, against Bergmann, that the analogy between religious belief and the belief in the STOLEN FRISIAN FLAG case breaks down on the very point at issue—namely, whether the processes that lead to religious belief have the status of "innocent until proven guilty." On the contrary, insofar as we assume that there are cognitive processes distinctive to religious belief,[26] the argument from disagreement calls precisely this into question. If this is correct, then there is no presumptive entitlement to rely on the process(es) in question, in which case the subject who would rely on them needs reasons to regard them as reliable (in the case at hand). But of course the very fact of pervasive disagreement gives us a reason to doubt the relevant reliability in the domain in question.

A second point against Bergmann's position is this: he appears to needlessly restrict relevant considerations that bear on the matter presently before us. In this respect I have two complaints.

First, in construing the rationality of religious belief in broadly evidentialist terms, he is bracketing the possibility of appealing to theoretical virtues such as

---

[24] See Goldberg (2014, 2015, and 2018).

[25] Admittedly, this requires argumentation, the likes of which I tried to provide in Goldberg (2009).

[26] It is to be borne in mind that this is a concessive assumption: Bergmann cannot use the STOLEN FRISIAN FLAG case as he does if this assumption is denied.

simplicity and parsimony. This is unfortunate: one consideration that has appealed to many agnostics and atheists over the years is the idea that, all else equal, it would be better (in terms of our attempts at a true picture of the world) to do without the substantial hypothesis of a divinity. Insofar as two competing hypotheses are otherwise equally good, it is preferable that we endorse the more parsimonious one. Agnosticism and atheism are often advanced on just these grounds, as (unlike their theistic counterparts) neither postulates God's existence. To be sure, Bergmann will disagree that the agnostic or atheistic hypotheses are as good as their theistic counterparts; but my point here is that if only evidence counts, we will not be able to ascribe the sort of significance to arguments from simplicity or parsimony that we ought to ascribe to them. So even Bergmann must allow that if the atheist is right that she can account for everything that the theist accounts for, then there is a basis for preferring atheism to theism. This need not make Bergmann too upset, since presumably he believes that the atheist cannot do so; but at the very least it acknowledges that the atheist has more at her disposal than a flatfooted evidentialist can recognize.

But I have a second complaint about Bergmann's needlessly restricting the considerations that bear on the question at hand. When he considers the $R{\sim}p$-evidence, he considers only arguments for atheism and finds them wanting. But since one of the arguments itself is the argument from pervasive diversity and disagreement, it is improper merely to note in passing that he finds these arguments unpersuasive. At the very least, there would appear to be a strong prima facie case for the unreliability of the processes or methods, at least as these produce belief in the religious domain. Short of that, it would appear wrong to think that the $R{\sim}p$-evidence is weak; on the contrary, the evidence would appear to be rather substantial.

I conclude, then, that Bergmann's case for "rational demotion" is weak.

4.

More recently, interest in "irrelevant causal influences" on belief has led several recent authors to re-assess the argument from religious disagreement.[27] One strategy for resisting the skeptical pull of the argument from irrelevant causal influences, offered by Miriam Schoenfield, has been to appeal to (and defend) a

---

[27] Not everyone agrees that the problem for religious belief raised by irrelevant causal etiology is a version of—or raises the same issues as—the problem raised by disagreement. See White (2010).

doctrine known as *permissivism*. For our purposes here, permissivism is the denial of a familiar and well-known doctrine in the epistemology literature:

UNIQUENESS   For any body of evidence E, and proposition p, relative to S's possession of E there is only one doxastic attitude it would be rational for S to take towards p. (Schoenfield 2014: 195)

Schoenfield also thinks that establishing permissivism (= the denial of UNIQUENESS) can help secure the rationality of religious belief, and it is interesting to see whether her argument on this score can succeed in defanging the argument from religious diversity/disagreement as I have presented it above.

Schoenfield holds that there is both an intuitive case and a theoretical case to be made for permissivism. The intuitive case is simply that there would appear to be cases of rational disagreements between peers, and this is inexplicable if UNIQUENESS is true. She explains:

> ... it seems implausible to appeal to subtle differences in evidence to explain all cases of seemingly rational disagreement. [In addition,] ... attempting to make too much of these subtle differences comes at a significant theoretical cost: it makes it difficult to explain how we can frequently do a good job at figuring out who is best placed to answer particular questions.
> (Schoenfield 2014: 194)

Schoenfield's theoretical case for permissivism is that many—and arguably all—plausible theories of epistemic justification presuppose permissivism (Schoenfield 2014: 197). Of the two, it is the latter sort of argument will be of greater interest to me here. The question I want to ask is this: is it the case that any plausible theory of epistemic justification will (not only presuppose permissivism, but also) vindicate religious belief's status as justified in the face of "causally irrelevant etiology" and the problems raised by diversity and disagreement? To address this, I will grant (for the sake of argument) that said theories do presuppose permissivism, and will focus only on how this is supposed to vindicate the rationality and justifiedness of religious belief.

According to Schoenfield's brand of permissivism, there are (as she puts it) "multiple evidence 'dials' corresponding to different permissible ways of weighing the evidence (different epistemic standards)." (Schoenfield 2014: 200) She allows that it can happen that "all of the permissible standards warrant the same attitude," but she insists that it can also happen (at other times) that "the different standards warrant different attitudes." (200) Insofar as religious believers have different standards from one another and from non-believers, then, it can happen that, even so, for some (or perhaps many or even all) religious believers, their standards warrant their attitudes.

Several things about this sort of argument concern me.

For one thing, its conclusion would appear to be only a possibility claim: even if it is successful, Schoenfield's argument would show only that *it is possible* for one to have religious beliefs that are justified, despite one's awareness of the facts of irrelevant causal etiology and religious diversity and disagreement. This conclusion stops short of vindicating the particular beliefs one has, still less does it vindicate the rationality of religious beliefs generally. It seems to me that work would need to be done to show that, given what Schoenfield has argued, this or that particular belief is in fact warranted by one's standards.

But perhaps this worry is not such a great one. After all, Schoenfield's argument has been crafted so as to respect those epistemic standards that have persisted, so perhaps for any religious tradition that has endured, there are standards that sanction its followers' beliefs as justified. Indeed, this sort of picture underlies her characterization of why she thinks irrelevant etiology concerns do not undermine the rationality of religious belief. I quote her at length:

> In the case we are imagining, ... the community [in which you were raised] not only caused you to believe in God, but instilled in you rational standards of reasoning that warrant belief in God (this is why you find the arguments for theism plausible). If you had grown up in a different community, you would have been instilled with a different set of rational standards which would have warranted atheism. Since the case is permissive, you were guaranteed to end up with a rational belief no matter what. So, if worries about the rationality of one's beliefs are what explain why sometimes we should decrease confidence in [irrelevant influence] cases, we will never have to be worried by irrelevant influences in permissive cases.
>
> (Schoenfield 2014: 206)

Her thought appears to be that religious communities are such that the standards of rationality that evolve in those communities sanction their religious beliefs as rational.

Even if we grant this, a more serious worry looms. Suppose that Schoenfield has a perfectly general argument that could be applied to religious beliefs from any robust religious community, showing that with respect to at least many (if not most or all) of those beliefs, they are justified (by the standards of rationality employed by the believers in question). My worry then would be: what sort of thing is being designated by this use of "justified"? In particular, is it a sort of property that necessarily corresponds to a high probability that one's belief is true? I think the answer is negative.[28]

Interestingly, for her part, Schoenfield is not only aware of this sort of worry, but develops and defends it herself. This is because she is interested in defending the principle of Rational Independence as against the principle of Truth Independence, both of which I reproduce here verbatim:

RATIONAL INDEPENDENCE: Suppose that independently of your reasoning about p, you reasonably think the following: "were I to reason to the conclusion that p in my present circumstances, there is a significant chance my belief would not be rational!" Then, if you find yourself believing p on the basis of your reasoning, you should significantly reduce confidence in that belief.

TRUTH INDEPENDENCE: Suppose that independently of your reasoning about p, you reasonably think the following: "were I to reason to the conclusion that p in my present circumstances, there is a significant chance my belief would not be true!" Then, if you find yourself believing p on the basis of your reasoning, you should significantly reduce confidence in that belief. (Schoenfield 2014: 204)

Schoenfield's line of reasoning is this: TRUTH INDEPENDENCE implies the falsity of permissivism (which allows for rational belief in the face of even systematic disagreement so long as different legitimate epistemic standards sanction both sides); so if (as Schoenfield argues) permissivism is true, TRUTH INDEPENDENCE is false; and in that case TRUTH INDEPENDENCE cannot be used to argue for a rational requirement to surrender one's belief in the face of irrelevant causal etiology. Such a requirement could only be established by appeal to RATIONAL INDEPENDENCE. And, while Schoenfield accepts RATIONAL INDEPENDENCE, permissivism ensures that if standards are permissive and one's own standards are among the legitimate ones, one's belief formed in conformity with those standards is not irrational merely because one acknowledges irrelevant causal etiology.

---

[28] Here an argument in the same spirit can be found in Vavova (2018).

Clearly, this argument stands or falls with the cogency of Schoenfield's argument for permissivism; those who are unmoved by that argument will be unmoved more generally by this sort of defense of the rationality of religious belief. But I am not interested in providing a direct response to Schoenfield's case for permissivism. Rather, I want to focus instead on the sort of solace the religious believer can take from Schoenfield's argument *even if it is sound.* I submit that the answer is: not much. Simply put, even if Schoenfield is granted her conclusion, so that religious believers remain rational in their religious belief after acknowledging irrelevant causal etiology, this sense of "rational" should not give them any confidence regarding the *truth* of their belief.

Indeed, on this score, I think I can do no better than endorsing Schoenfield's own argument on this score. She writes,

> If TRUTH INDEPENDENCE is [true], then you should decrease confidence in [cases in which you recognize the irrelevant causal etiology of your religious beliefs]. Why? Because independently of your reasoning about religious matters, you should think that there is a significant likelihood that you would form a false belief as a result of your community's influence. (... [Y]ou can see this by imagining that you are judging the likelihood of forming a true belief about God's existence before you joined the community and reasoned about the question. In this state you know that you will come to believe in God on the basis of your community's influence, but you are agnostic about God's existence. Thus, you will think that there is a significant chance that the belief you will form will be false. This is the perspective you have to occupy when you set aside your reasoning about religious matters).
>
> (Schoenfield 2014: 206)

I do not think I can improve on this argument. Schoenfield's position is that, while this is so, TRUTH INDEPENDENCE is false, for overshooting the mark, as it recommends a decrease in confidence in many cases in which it is deeply unintuitive that we should decrease confidence—namely, the cases that motivate permissivism. Insofar as I want to question her position without directly calling permissivism into question, the key issue is this: on the assumptions that there exist multiple rational standards (i) each one of which can be rationally defended by its proponents (and so each one of which is rational by its own lights), yet (ii) which offer different verdicts in cases involving widespread disagreement, what significance should be attributed to the claim that a subject's belief can be vindicated as rational *by the lights of such a model*?

Here Schoenfield thinks that one who recognizes being in such a situation (involving multiple rational standards satisfying (i) and (ii)) should not be moved to reduce confidence in one's own belief, since after all, by one's own lights one remains rational in one's belief. I submit that insofar as Schoenfield is right about this, it only goes to show how little significance there is to being rational in this sense. For—and on this point Schoenfeld is explicit in her agreement with me!—the recognition that one oneself is in such a situation should prompt one to recognize that objectively speaking "there is a significant likelihood that [one] would form a false belief as a result of [one's] community's influence." So insofar as one cares about truth, one should not believe as one does: one has what has all the trappings of a defeater.[29] (Here I note that this is no mere allegation of the fallible nature of our belief-forming processes; the point is that there is a *significant* likelihood of falsity.) If it remains true that your belief is nevertheless rational (i.e., in conformity with your own community's epistemic standards), you might well think: *so much the worse for the significance of being rational in this sense.*

Of course, insofar as one wants to insist on the significance of being rational, one cannot ultimately grant Schoenfield's conclusion that religious believers remain rational in their religious belief even after acknowledging irrelevant causal etiology. Thus, the foregoing is best seen as a *reductio*: granting that conclusion for the sake of argument, we can show that it leads to the absurdity of holding that a belief remains rational despite one's having excellent (objective) reason to regard it as unlikely that the belief in question is true. No doubt, the religious believer might think to take solace in the thought that she has these (objective) reasons only when she brackets her current reasoning about God; once she resumes thinking as a theist, she resumes having reasons in support of her theism (and reasons that defeat the alleged defeater). But my claim is that once she recognizes the causally irrelevant etiology of her beliefs (and more importantly its effects on the likely truth of her beliefs), this should be little solace.

It is worth making the same point in terms of the argument from religious diversity and disagreement, as I have framed it above. Schoenfield concedes that (bracketing the reasoning in support of the contested religious belief in question) one's awareness of the irrelevant causal etiology of one's belief yields a reason to accept BAD PROSPECTS. Presumably she also grants that, continuing to bracket that reasoning, BAD PROSPECTS supports DEFEATING DOUBTS. But Schoenfield insists that *this is not the perspective from which to*

---

[29] See Vavova (2018) for an argument in a very similar vein.

assess the rationality of religious belief. It seems to me that this insistence comes too late in the dialectic to be of any help. To see this, note that the truth of DEFEATING DOUBTS would call the rationality of religious belief into question. To avoid this result, Schoenfield must insist again that this is not the perspective from which to assess the religious believer's belief. But it is hard for me to see how this sort of reply is anything other than a retreat to a notion of rationality that, because it is compatible with one's acknowledgment of low objective chances of truth of one's belief, is not epistemically robust. I conclude that the cost of success of Schoenfield's argument is too high: it succeeds at showing that contested religious belief is rational, but at the cost of diluting the notion of rationality to something that should provide little comfort to anyone interested in truth. This is seen in the fact that Schoenfield's conclusion is compatible with BAD PROSPECTS (read as making a statement about the objective likelihood of truth).

5.

A third response to be considered in connection with the argument from religious diversity and disagreement maintains that the believer is no worse off than the non-believer (whether atheist or agnostic). Here is how Mike Bergmann presents the case:

> the atheist has exactly parallel problems [to the ones faced by the theist who rationally demotes the atheist]. If she is going to hold on to her atheism and demote the theist, then she too will have to do what seems offensive and arrogant, concluding that people who are ethical and bright are mistaken on an important topic, when there is no apparent way to resolve the difficulty through rational discussion. Likewise, the atheist's demotion cries out for explanation: why is it that she, the atheist, is able to have better evidence and to respond to it correctly when the theist fails in this regard? Here too, the stories that might naturally come to mind (according to which there are no theists who are intelligent, good, mature, and wise) seem rather implausible. Without a plausible story, it might be tempting to think that the atheist shouldn't demote the theist.
>
> A similar problem afflicts the principled agnostic—the one who says that, in light of the fact that rational discussion doesn't enable us to settle the issue of whether theism is true, we should withhold judgment, believing neither

theism nor atheism. In effect, this sort of agnostic is saying that theists and atheists should each demote themselves (as well as each other) on the topic of theism. This agnostic demotes them both, as well as herself, on that topic. But notice that the principle agnostic demotes theists and atheists on the topic of when it is rational to demote, but doesn't demote herself on that topic. Thus, she too will be faced with problems similar to those faced by the atheist and the theist. The agnostic will have to do what seems offensive and arrogant, concluding that people who are intelligent and virtuous are mistaken on the important topic of whether their beliefs with respect to theism are rational. This alleged problem the agnostic notices on the part of intelligent atheists and theists cries out for explanation. But it will be difficult for the principled agnostic to produce a plausible explanation of this alleged problem. Here too, it's tempting to think that if the agnostic doesn't have a plausible explanation available, she shouldn't be demoting them in this way.

(Bergmann 2015: 50–51)[30]

I am unmoved by this argument. An analogy will help to explain why. Suppose that there is a group of people who come to find that they disagree rather systematically about some topic, and that this disagreement persists despite efforts of each side to convince the other sides. Among their disagreements are the proper methods to use in arriving at belief in this domain. Both sides appeal to methods that the other side doesn't employ and regards as illegitimate; and neither side can establish the truth of its views (or the reliability of its distinctive methods) by appeal to the methods that both sides have in common.[31] Now along comes another group of people who, surveying all of this, infer that there are no reliably formed beliefs in this domain; so where the various disputing parties believe various things in this domain (in the face of the disagreement of others), this new group of people refrains from believing anything on these topics, on the grounds that the disagreement itself is some reason to conclude that no one has arrived at reliable belief. These are the agnostics. I submit that such a group is not itself a party to the dispute in the same way that the competing parties are: its cognitive state is one of *not* believing things, where the state of agnosticism is justified by appeal to their evidence for thinking that there are no reliable beliefs to be had on these topics.

---

[30] Compare Plantinga (1995).
[31] In speaking of the methods that both sides have in common, I have in mind such methods as perception, memory, reasoning, etc.

Surely that view is not itself subject to defeaters of the sort facing the other disputants.

In fact, I can imagine how there might be others—call these the "atheists"— who go further. They reason as follows. Various people have been highly motivated to arrive at reliable belief on these matters; they have had plenty of time to do so; among them are otherwise highly epistemically competent individuals; and nevertheless even among such otherwise highly epistemically competent individuals who have had the time and desire to find truth, disagreement is systematic. From this the members of this group draw an inference to the best explanation: the reason why we find such disagreement despite every effort among the otherwise highly competent is that *there is no (first-order, affirmative) truth on the relevant topic.* So while the agnostics refrain from belief, the atheists come to believe the negations of the various (first-order, affirmative) propositions believed by proponents of one or another view.

I submit that there are cases of the sort described above where such an abductive inference yields a belief which, far from a party to the very dispute itself, is justified. Consider, for example, belief in the non-existence of such things as ghosts, goblins, witches, djinnis, and so forth. It is easy to imagine how a consensus on these matters could have been reached by reflection on the prior disagreement, among people who believed in such creatures, concerning the various properties and characteristics exemplified in this domain.[32] That is, reflecting on the various disagreements (among those who believe in, e.g., witches) regarding what witches were like or who they were, at a certain point in the history of this disagreement one might reasonably conclude that none of the disputants knew what they were talking about; and further still, on the assumptions that the disputants were sincerely trying to arrive at truth and that they had ample time to do so, the further conclusion would be that the domain in question is one in which there are no interesting (affirmative) truths about witches. And this would appear to be an analogue regarding witches of what atheism is regarding religion. But if that's so, then positions analogous to atheism, formed as an inference from widespread disagreement, need not automatically be party to the very disagreement they use as their evidential basis.

---

[32] This is easy to imagine even if in point of fact the consensus (or near-consensus) was not reached on these matters in this way.

6.

In this paper I have presented what I regard as the best version of the argument from religious diversity/disagreement, whose conclusion is that on matters of contested religious doctrine there is no rational belief (at least among those who are aware of this diversity/disagreement); and I have argued that none of the recent attempts to resist this argument succeed. More generally, the lesson seems to be this: insofar as religious believers care about truth, the recognition of religious diversity/disagreement gives them a compelling reason to question whether they have attained truth.

References

Alston, William P. 1988. "Religious Diversity and Perceptual Knowledge of God." *Faith and Philosophy* 5: 433–448.

Alston, William P. 1991. *Perceiving God: The Epistemology of Religious Experience.* Ithaca, NY: Cornell University Press.

Baker-Hytch, Max and Matthew A. Benton. 2015. "Defeatism Defeated." *Philosophical Perspectives* 29: 40–66.

Bergmann, Michael. 2005. "Defeaters and Higher-Level Requirements." *Philosophical Quarterly* 55: 419–436.

Bergmann, Michael. 2006. *Justification without Awareness.* New York: Oxford University Press.

Bergmann, Michael. 2015. "Religious Disagreement and Rational Demotion." *Oxford Studies in Philosophy of Religion* 6: 21–57.

Conee, Earl and Richard Feldman. 1998. "The Generality Problem for Reliabilism." *Philosophical Studies* 89: 1–29.

Feldman, Richard. 2003. "Plantinga on Exclusivism." *Faith and Philosophy* 20: 85–90.

Goldberg, Sanford C. 2009. "Reliabilism in Philosophy." *Philosophical Studies* 124: 105–117.

Goldberg, Sanford C. 2012. "Defending Philosophy in the Face of Systematic Disagreement." In Diego Machuca, ed., *Disagreement and Skepticism*, 277–294. New York: Routledge.

Goldberg, Sanford C. 2013a. "Disagreement, Defeaters, and Assertion." In David Christensen and Jennifer Lackey, eds., *The Epistemology of Disagreement: New Essays*, 167–189. Oxford: Oxford University Press.

Goldberg, Sanford C. 2013b. "Does Externalist Epistemology Rationalize Religious Commitment?" In Timothy O'Connor and Laura Frances Callahan, eds., *Religious Faith and Intellectual Virtue*, 279–298. Oxford: Oxford University Press.

Goldberg, Sanford C. 2014. "Interpersonal Epistemic Entitlements." *Philosophical Issues* 24: 159–183.

Goldberg, Sanford C. 2015. "Epistemic Entitlement and Luck." *Philosophy and Phenomenological Research* 91: 273–302.

Goldberg, Sanford C. 2017. "Should Have Known." *Synthese* 194: 2863–2894.

Goldberg, Sanford C. 2018. *To the Best of Our Knowledge: Social Expectations and Epistemic Normativity*. Oxford: Oxford University Press.

King, Nathan L. 2008. "Religious Diversity and its Challenges to Religious Belief." *Philosophy Compass* 3/4: 830–853.

King, Nathan L. 2016. "Religious Skepticism and Higher-Order Evidence." *Oxford Studies in Philosophy of Religion* 7: 126–156.

Lackey, Jennifer. 1999. "Testimonial Knowledge and Transmission." *The Philosophical Quarterly* 49: 471–490.

Lackey, Jennifer. 2014. "Taking Religious Disagreement Seriously." In Laura Frances Callahan and Timothy O'Connor, eds., *Religious Faith and Intellectual Virtue*, 299–316. Oxford: Oxford University Press.

Lackey, Jennifer. 2018. "Experts and Peer Disagreement." In Matthew A. Benton, John Hawthorne, and Dani Rabinowitz, eds., *Knowledge, Belief, and God: New Insights in Religious Epistemology*, 228–245. Oxford: Oxford University Press.

Lasonen-Aarnio, Maria. 2010. "Unreasonable Knowledge." *Philosophical Perspectives* 24: 1–21.

Lasonen-Aarnio, Maria. 2014. "Higher-order Evidence and the Limits of Defeat." *Philosophy and Phenomenological Research* 88: 314–345.

Plantinga, Alvin. 1995. "Pluralism: A Defense of Religious Exclusivism." In Thomas D. Senor, ed., *The Rationality of Belief and the Plurality of Faith*, 191–215. Ithaca, NY: Cornell University Press.

Plantinga, Alvin. 2000. *Warranted Christian Belief*. New York: Oxford University Press.

Schoenfield, Miriam. 2014. "Permission to Believe: Why Permissivism is True and What it Tells Us About Irrelevant Influences on Belief." *Noûs* 48: 193–218.

Vavova, Katia. 2018. "Irrelevant Influences." *Philosophy and Phenomenological Research* 96: 134–152.

White, Roger. 2010. "You Just Believe That Because...." *Philosophical Perspectives* 24: 573–615.

Williamson, Timothy. 2014. "Very Improbable Knowing." *Erkenntnis* 79: 971–999.

4

Religious Disagreement Is Not Unique

Margaret Greta Turnbull

1. Introduction

Religious disagreement seems, to many, to be a unique form of disagreement.[1] Numerous epistemologists have tried to understand what it means to rationally respond to specifically religious disagreement.[2] In fact, some philosophers have argued that the distinguishing features of religious disagreement allow those who hold religious beliefs to hold on to their religious beliefs even in the face of disagreement. Even those who maintain that we must adjust our beliefs in response to learning of disagreement have argued that religious disagreement is an exception to this policy (for example, Bogardus 2013).

In this paper, I will argue that religious disagreement is not unique. There is no special problem of religious disagreement because the features which have been claimed to distinguish religious disagreement from other sorts of disagreement, on closer inspection, closely resemble features of numerous other sorts of disagreement. Further, I'll argue that recognizing that religious disagreement is not unique makes religious disagreement less, rather than more, concerning for the religious believer who would like to rationally hold on to her religious beliefs.

---

[1] This view is often held implicitly in the literature rather than explicitly. But see Matheson: "it might be thought that religious disagreement is special—that religious disagreement is importantly unlike other disagreements in science, politics, and philosophy more generally, and that such a difference renders religious beliefs immune from the defeating effects of discovered disagreement" (Matheson 2019, p. 8). Note that in this paper, I do not mean to implicate the oft-discussed Uniqueness Thesis about rationality (Feldman 2007) in using the term "unique." I use the term "doxastic attitude" to refer to the coarse-grained attitudes of belief, disbelief, and suspension of judgment as well as degreed attitudes, including credences or degreed beliefs. Thanks to Charity Anderson for discussions of these issues and to Matt Benton and Jon Kvanvig for helpful comments on this paper.

[2] Perhaps some of the authors I discuss do not hold the view that religious disagreement is unique. Regardless, in this paper I will provide them reasons to refrain from adopting this view and will offer an argument in later sections that given the non-distinctiveness of religious disagreement, religious disagreement is less concerning for religious believers than we otherwise might have thought it to be. See Benton (2019) and Frances (2015) for surveys of the epistemology of religious disagreement.

Margaret Greta Turnbull, *Religious Disagreement Is Not Unique* In: *Religious Disagreement and Pluralism.*
Edited by: Matthew A. Benton and Jonathan L. Kvanvig, Oxford University Press. © Margaret Greta Turnbull 2021.
DOI: 10.1093/oso/9780198849865.003.0004

To ward off some immediate objections, I'll begin by clarifying the aims of my argument. I will not argue that the *content* of religious belief, the evidence we take to support it, the standards by which we evaluate it, and the ways agents come to hold it, are not, in certain ways, distinctive. I know of no other form of widely held belief on which some portion of our relevant evidence is taken to come from communication with the divine as it does in religious experience. Rather, I will argue that the *form* of religious disagreement is not unique. As I will argue, the structure of religious disagreements, despite the in many ways distinctive content of religious belief, is more like than unlike many other sorts of disagreement.

I will also avoid making claims about disagreement among epistemic peers. Stefan Reining (2016), Jennifer Lackey (2014), and others have shown that the question of who counts as an epistemic peer in religious disagreements is a tricky one. The features of religious belief make it difficult to determine, for example, who shares my evidence in religious contexts on David Christensen's (2007) account of peerhood or who is as equally likely as I am to be mistaken about religious questions on Adam Elga's (2007) understanding of peerhood. I think we face similar problems in determining the presence of peerhood in just about every other context of disagreement, as Nathan King (2012) and Lackey (2010) have recognized.

But I will avoid use of the technical term "epistemic peer" in order to sidestep extant confusion about what that term might mean in religious contexts. I am interested in disagreements in which, upon learning that the disagreement exists, it is rational for us to carefully consider whether our religious beliefs might be mistaken and whether adjustment in our religious beliefs might be called for.[3] I think focusing on these disagreements will allow us to approximate the target disagreements of interest to participants in the peer disagreement literature while setting aside determinations of whether agents engaged in religious disagreement are, in fact, epistemic peers, under the technical definition.

I will examine disagreements of this type about a specific religious proposition, t: *God exists*. In section 2, I will canvas two major ways that religious disagreement has been taken to be distinctive: religious evidence and evaluative standards for religious belief. I argue in section 3 that these features do not distinguish religious disagreement from other forms of disagreement. In section 4, I show that the loss of religious disagreement's distinctiveness

---

[3] However, I take these arguments to equally support the claim that other sorts of religious disagreement, such as disagreements between experts and novices, are not unique or distinctive.

need not worry the theist who would wish to rationally hold on to her religious beliefs in the face of religious disagreement. I conclude in section 5.

2. In What Ways Could Religious Disagreement Be Unique?

Canvassing the literature on religious disagreement shows us that authors have taken two prominent features to make religious disagreement different from other forms of disagreement. First, I'll discuss how epistemologists have understood the evidence relevant to religious disagreement to be distinctive. Then, I'll consider discussions of the apparently peculiar standards by which we evaluate religious believers as credible and the role of these standards in religious disagreement.

Several philosophers have indicated that religious experience and its use in the justification of religious belief can make religious disagreement distinctive. These authors agree that in religious disagreement, unlike other forms of disagreement, believers of t sometimes have access to a form of evidence, religious experience, to which non-believers of t do not and cannot have certain kinds of access. William Alston (1991, Ch. 7) and Alvin Plantinga (2000, pp. 443–457, especially p. 454) suggest that since religious believers have access to religious experience, this additional evidence can allow believers of t to rationally hold on to t in the face of challenges from religious pluralism. Reining (2016, p. 408) argues that religious believers sometimes undergo perceptually unique religious experiences which involve "none of the standard senses." This evidence can allow believers of t to justifiably hold on to belief in t when they meet those who have not had such religious experiences and believe ~t.[4] Similarly, Kirk Lougheed (2018, 184–190) uses Philip Wiebe's (2015) articulation of religious experience as a form of intuitive knowing to argue that believers of t have access to evidence which defies communication. This evidence then justifies them in holding on to belief in t in the face of disagreement with those who do not have access to these incommunicable

---

[4] See also Kraft (2007, pp. 427–428) and Bergmann (2017, pp. 36–41) for related arguments. Dormandy (2018) addresses the problem of weighting religious experience and similar sorts of evidence as compared to more readily communicable, public forms of evidence, in pursuit of resolving religious disagreement. Discussion of religious experience shares a common thread with discussions of religious disagreement and transformative experience in religious contexts. See De Cruz (2018, especially p. 270).

religious experiences.[5] Tomás Bogardus notes that in cases of religious disagreement involving "believers who base their beliefs at least in part on private religious experiences they've had," his preferred Equal Weight view does not require individuals to adjust their beliefs in response to learning of the disagreement since this view only requires individuals who have access to the same evidence to adjust their beliefs (2013a, p. 15). These authors seem to share a common view that in order to truly share one's evidence with a partner in disagreement, one must be able to articulate and communicate most, if not all, of the content of one's evidence from experience.[6] Further, since religious experience is a distinctive form of experience which resists this type of communication and articulation to those who have not had the experience, the common thread through these arguments holds it can be rational for those who have had religious experiences to go on holding on to their religious beliefs in the face of disagreement with non-believers.

Others have argued that the standards by which we epistemically evaluate religious believers make religious disagreement distinctive. As Frederick Choo notes rightly, "there is disagreement on what the relevant credibility-conferring features are when it comes to assessing religious propositions" (Forthcoming, p. 5). Members of different religious traditions as well as members of the same religious tradition often find it difficult to determine which qualities make reasoners reliable in religious contexts. Since determining how one should respond to disagreement involves assessing the reliability or credibility of the reasoner with which one is in disagreement, the peculiar evaluative standards in religious contexts are sometimes seen as making religious disagreement distinctive.

John Pittard (2014) offers an extensive argument for this distinctiveness of epistemic evaluative standards in religious contexts. I'll leave the rather intricate details of Pittard's argument to his own work, but briefly, his argument runs as follows. First, religious traditions often reject "standard theories of

---

[5] Van Inwagen (2010, pp. 26–27) flirts with a similar view. Lougheed (2018) also discusses the possibility that self-trust in the theist's own beliefs, the immediacy of the theist's beliefs, and the theist's ability to introspect on her own experiences may allow the believer of t to remain rationally steadfast (2018, S2.1, S2.2, and S2.3 respectively). But Lougheed is right to point out that these routes to steadfastness are by no means unique to religious disagreement. Likewise, DePoe (2018, p. 260) and Bogardus (2013, p. 15) argue that the religious believer may be in a position to "just see the truth of their religious views". However, both Bogardus and DePoe offer as their examples of this phenomenon non-religious contexts where individuals can directly see that their beliefs are true. Clearly then, this route to steadfastness is not understood as being a unique feature of religious disagreement.

[6] In what follows, I'll use the term "incommunicable," in the sense these authors seem to intend it, to indicate bodies of evidence, the majority of whose content cannot be articulated and communicated to those who have not had the religious experience.

epistemic credentials" on which believers are viewed as generally reliable if they possess "analytic sophistication, thorough acquaintance with the publicly available evidence, certification by prestigious institutions...raw intelligence, freedom from corrupting bias, etc." (2014, p. 87). In the place of these standard theories of epistemic credentials, religious traditions substitute "non-standard theories of epistemic credentials" on which standard qualities do not contribute greatly to the reliability of religious reasoners and are replaced by distinctive qualities such as "love of one's fellow human beings, love and desire for God, humility, detachment from material possessions" etc. (2014, pp. 88–89). Further, Pittard argues that these non-standard theories of epistemic credentials are "self-favoring" (2014, p. 90). On self-favoring theories of epistemic credentials, according to Pittard, those who are not members of one's religious tradition are not viewed as being as epistemically reliable as those within it (2014, p. 90).[7]

Similar to arguments making use of religious experience, Pittard argues that these distinctive features of evaluative standards in religious contexts allow religious believers to resist arguments that they must give up confident religious belief in the face of religious disagreement. Pittard notes that on Christensen's (2007) popular account of conciliatory responses to disagreement, "conciliatory pressure generated by a disagreement correlates with the strength of the independent reasons for trusting my disputant" (2014, p. 84). But religious believers who hold these distinctive non-standard theories of epistemic credentials lack reason to trust their disputants since these non-standard theories of epistemic credentials are self-favoring. So the conciliatory pressure generated by a disagreement with those outside of their religious disagreement will be negligible, concludes Pittard (2014, p. 96).

We've seen that these two features, religious experience and evaluative standards, can be understood as making religious disagreement a particularly unique kind of disagreement, one in which its often rational for religious believers to hold on to religious belief in the face of disagreement.

---

[7] Pittard does not once use the term "peer" in his paper, though he develops Christensen's (2007) conciliationism which is explicitly aimed at peer disagreement. However, the target of his argument is clearly consistent with the target of the present work since though participants in these disagreements will eventually downgrade each other as reliable reasoners with respect to the subject of the disagreement, it is still possible and even likely that it is rational for them to carefully consider the reasoning behind their beliefs and to ask whether adjustment might be called for. This reflection will, in Pittard's understanding I take it, result in the downgrading of each other as reasoners.

3. Religious Disagreement Is Not Unique

But religious disagreement is not unique. The features of religious belief which I've just discussed do not justify the claim that religious disagreement is distinctive.

First, consider the claim that religious experience constitutes an at least partially incommunicable, private form of evidence, one which allows us to hold on to religious belief in the face of disagreement with those who have not had such experiences. To think that this feature of religious disagreement makes religious disagreement unique, we would need to think that other disagreements outside religious contexts do not have this feature. In other words, we'd need to think that non-religious disagreements seldom (if ever) involve one party possessing evidence whose content is mostly incommunicable and to which their partner in disagreement cannot gain access to.

Of course, it's obvious that many non-religious disagreements involve one party having access to evidence which the other party does not. Perhaps one party is an expert on the topic under disagreement and the other member is a novice who cannot access technical evidence. However, much of the literature on religious disagreement concerns disagreement between individuals who, other than the religious experience which forms a disparity between them, are roughly each other's epistemic equals (see especially, Reining 2016). To effectively argue that this type of religious disagreement is not distinctive, we need to find similar non-religious disagreements in which the individuals involved do not resemble an expert and a novice but instead are on a more equal epistemic playing field and yet fail to share relevant evidence.

Even given this narrower focus, it's easy to determine that in many non-religious contexts, one partner in disagreement often possesses evidence which is not possessed by the other partner in disagreement. Further, the content of this unpossessed evidence resists communication to the other partner even when the partners in disagreement are similarly well-informed. Alvin Goldman (2010) notes that most of the time, sharing of evidence occurs at a different time than belief acquisition. As Goldman puts it, "one often forgets even past observations that play a lively causal role in belief acquisition. These now-forgotten observations are relevant to the current justificational status of a belief that has been preserved over time, but they are not available for 'sharing' when asked for one's evidence" (2010, pp. 211–212).[8] And even if a

---

[8] Conee and Feldman (2004, p. 232) and their followers hold the view that evidence consists only in those states which are occurrent or present to the awareness of the believer. But this view of evidence has been dismissed as implausible by numerous epistemologists, including McCain (2014, pp. 45–49).

particular disagreement does not, in fact, involve evidence which one has forgotten, the threat that one may have forgotten relevant evidence remains. Given the fallibility of our memory and our awareness of such fallibility, we can never be sure that we have, in fact, remembered all the evidence on which our belief rests. And so many of our disagreements, whether religious or not, easily involve evidence which is not possessed by one partner in disagreement and which resists communication to the partner who does not have it.[9] Reflecting on the fact that disagreement in any context often involves evidence which one has forgotten forces us to recognize that the incommunicable evidence feature of religious disagreement does not make religious disagreement distinctive. I'll now consider several objections to this argument.

First, perhaps we quite regularly forget pieces of evidence on which we base our beliefs, but surely we do not regularly forget *crucial* pieces of evidence. My response to this worry is twofold. First, there certainly are some disagreements in which we are unable to remember and therefore are unable to share crucial pieces of evidence relevant to our beliefs. In these cases, we have incommunicable evidence involved in non-religious disagreement and so we again find that religious disagreement is not unique.

Second, the evidence on which we base our beliefs is often quite fragmented. It is seldom just one piece of evidence which leads us to adopt a justified belief. Instead, there is often a host of pieces of evidence (and background beliefs) which result in our adopting a particular belief. My belief in the thesis of scientific realism, for example, is based on numerous pieces of evidence, as Goldman recognizes, including the rejection of numerous counterexamples I've considered, the weight I give to the opinion of other philosophers who agree and disagree with the view, the ways my intuitions bolster the premises in support of the view, and even my perception of my intellectual acuity at the time I originally considered the arguments for and against it (Goldman 2010, p. 211). While forgetting just one small fragment of evidence may not always spell trouble for achieving some sort of evidential parity between members of a disagreement, forgetting even a few of these fragments may directly impact the belief's justificatory status. Forgetting why I've rejected just one particular counterexample for example, to adapt an example from Goldman, could easily alter my attitude toward scientific realism from belief to disbelief

[9] Nathan King (2012, pp. 253–258) offers further arguments to this effect. Goldman (2010, pp. 210–212) provides further arguments for the incommunicability of evidence in religious and non-religious contexts alike which do not rely on the fallibility of memory which I do not have space to consider here.

(2010, p. 211).[10] The fragmentation of evidence means that much of our evidence is crucial, however small it may appear to be. So the threat that our memory makes pieces of evidence, even small fragments of evidence, incommunicable, gives us reason to think that important, incommunicable evidence is a feature of quite a decent amount of our disagreements.

But perhaps religious disagreement is still distinctive, says the objector, even given Goldman's worries about memory and evidence sharing. In scientific contexts, the objector points out, we take great pains to share our evidence, such that it is virtually impossible that we have forgotten any of the evidence relevant to our belief in scientific hypotheses and theories. So we can communicate our evidence in the contexts of scientific disagreements. And religious disagreement is distinctive because in religious disagreements, we cannot communicate the portions of our evidence which come from religious experience.[11] But this line of objection fails to show us that religious disagreement is distinctive. Instead, it seems to provide an argument that scientific disagreement is distinctive.[12]

The problems for evidence sharing articulated by Goldman apply to our disagreements regardless of subject matter. Evidence which cannot be shared can feature in disagreements about the weather, morality, religion, and past events alike because the fallibility of memory can strike in the context of any subject matter. If the objector is correct that these memory-related problems do not occur in scientific contexts, then this will be the exception to our worries about evidence sharing, not the rule. Perhaps scientific disagreement is distinctive. I am not concerned with such an argument here. However, Goldman's argument that our capacity to remember and communicate relevant evidence is faulty shows us that problems of evidence access and communication are not unique to religious disagreement.

Consider another objection. Perhaps religious disagreement is distinctive not because of the form of the evidence provided by religious experience, but because of this incommunicable evidence's content.[13] Members of the New Atheism coalition, for example, seem to understand religious experience to be

---

[10] My suspicion is that forgetting a fragment of evidence will result in alterations to our doxastic attitude even more often when we consider degreed doxastic attitudes like credences.

[11] Lougheed (2018, p. 187) discusses a similar objection.

[12] I'll note in passing that I'm unconvinced that the premises of this argument are true. See Turnbull (2019, Ch. 2) for an argument that evidence sharing in scientific contexts is not as straightforward as is often assumed.

[13] Relatedly, it might be that religious disagreement is distinctive not just because of the form of religious evidence, but because of the type of claim involved in t. Perhaps religious disagreement is distinctive because it involves affirming the existence of a divine being, on which the entire religious belief structure depends, on the basis of this evidence which only believers of t seem to have good access

akin to wish-fulfilling projections that have more in common with untrustworthy hallucinations than perceptual experiences which have been publicly
proven to be generally reliable. Perhaps religious disagreement is distinctive
because it involves an exceptionally untrustworthy source of evidence.

However, this objection misses the mark given the type of disagreement I've
identified as of interest to this paper and to authors in the literature on
religious disagreement. If you hold that religious disagreement is distinctive
because religious experience is such an untrustworthy source of evidence, it
won't be rational for you to consider carefully whether your beliefs are
mistaken and whether adjustment in your doxastic attitude toward t might
be called for when you, the non-believer of t, find yourself in disagreement
with a religious believer about t. You view religious experience as so wildly
unreliable that those who trust it are not the kind of people whose beliefs you
take seriously in the first place. So if you hold that religious disagreement is
distinctive because religious experience is exceptionally untrustworthy, you
won't find any of the discussions in which I'm intervening to be plausible in
the first place.

But even if religious disagreement is not distinctive in this way, it might be
that non-standard, self-favoring evaluative standards make religious disagreement distinctive, as Pittard suggests. Again, to defeat the claim that religious
disagreement is unique, I'll argue that in non-religious contexts, we can readily
find non-standard, self-favoring evaluative standards at play. In these contexts,
as in religious contexts, individuals reject common credentials of epistemic
reliability (such as terminal degrees, raw intelligence, and the other qualities
Pittard lists) and embrace non-standard sets of evaluative standards which are
self-favoring, which are "unlikely to give an adherent of the religious belief
system of which the [standards are] a part a reason for thinking that those who
dispute the belief system are as epistemically qualified as those who accept it"
(Pittard 2014, pp. 87, 90).[14] While individuals in these non-religious contexts

---

to. But this objection also fails to distinguish religious disagreement from other sorts of disagreement.
Moral disagreement often includes disagreement about the existence of certain mind-independent
moral norms. So moral disagreement can involve disagreement about weighty ontological claims. And
it is often somehow apparent to some parties in disagreement that these independent, static moral
norms exist (for example, absolutists about morality) and not at all apparent to other parties in moral
disagreement that such moral norms exist (for example, certain relativists about morality). The
evidence for the existence of these moral norms also often seems to be based in the sorts of moral
intuitions which cannot readily be articulated and transferred to other members of disagreement.
Thanks to Matt Benton for encouraging me to consider this version of the objection.

[14] Pittard also argues that these evaluative standards involve "opaque" epistemic credentials.
According to Pittard, "a credential C proposed by religious belief system B is opaque just to the extent
that there is no reliable way to tell whether someone possesses C if one does not know whether this
person accepts the claims of B" (2014, p. 90).

will not use non-standard, self-favoring evaluative standards of the same content as standards in religious contexts, these non-religious standards will share the same structural features of being non-standard and self-favoring as those invoked in religious disagreement.

We can find non-standard, self-favoring evaluative standards being used in moral and political contexts.[15] First, consider moral disagreement and the evaluative standards being invoked to assess the reliability of reasoners in moral contexts. I propose that the evaluative standards in these contexts are non-standard. While the set of evaluative standards in moral contexts might include standard credentials, I think we rely more heavily on non-standard credentials, including awareness of the personal needs and desires of other agents, integrity, compassion, and a sense for the balance between justice and mercy in assessing moral reasoners.[16] In addition, these credentials are often self-favoring.[17]

For illustration, take Alex Rosenberg's (2015) discussion of disputes over the morality of honor killing in Eastern cultures. Persons who hold that honor killing is morally impermissible are often appalled that some cultures permit the practice. Similarly, those who hold that honor killing is morally permissible can readily view those outside their moral belief system as thoroughly failing to appreciate the social importance of honor. Those who are of the belief systems which hold that honor killing is morally impermissible will be unlikely to count as reliable moral reasoners those who are of belief systems on which honor killing is morally permissible.[18] So we can see how in moral disagreement, evaluative standards which are non-standard and self-favoring are at least sometimes invoked.

Similarly, in political contexts, we can find non-standard, self-favoring evaluative standards at play. We frequently use non-standard credentials, such as a person's willingness to accept social responsibility, their ability to evaluate fairness, and to be sensitive to the rights of others in evaluating them as a political reasoner. Members of opposing political parties notoriously often

---

[15] Thanks to Harrison Lee for helpful discussion about this issue.

[16] See Schwitzgebel and Rust (2014) for confirmation of the view that the most relevant standard credentials do not guarantee moral character. This realization should encourage us that non-standard credentials are needed to assess the trustworthiness of moral reasoners.

[17] Elga (2007, pp. 492–494) is in agreement with me.

[18] The evaluative standards at play here also seem to involve opacity, in Pittard's terms. For example, those who hold the belief system on which honor killing is impermissible will likely only be able to confidently judge as compassionate those who share their belief system.

refuse to recognize each other as reliable political reasoners.[19] In the US, Republicans frequently decry their opponents' alleged insensitivity to matters of national security and lack of respect for the rights of private citizens in their decision-making and Democrats often regard their opponents across the aisle as being consistently insensitive to the needs of the poor and vulnerable.

A worry emerges. Both of the areas of disagreement in which I've just argued that non-standard, self-favoring evaluative standards are invoked are areas of particularly contentious disagreement, involving the clash of whole belief systems and not merely the clash of a few propositions. Perhaps non-standard, self-favoring evaluative standards only help to make a new class of distinctive disagreements, one which includes religious disagreement among other sorts of broad, fundamental disagreement.

But even if my argument only results in the new classification the objector suggests, I've still accomplished the aim of the present argument. We've successfully moved from the claim that religious disagreement is a unique form of disagreement on its own to the claim that it resembles other forms of disagreement, though it does not resemble every other form of disagreement. And I think this result squares with some of our pre-theoretic intuitions about the terrain of disagreements. In some ways, we expect to find disagreement in politics, ethics, religion, and perhaps philosophy to be fundamental and intractable in a way that disagreements about a simple proof in formal logic are not. Reflecting on the structure of moral and political disagreements shows us that since non-standard, self-favoring evaluative standards are invoked, religious disagreement resembles these forms of disagreement.

We can conclude that religious disagreement is not wholesale unique. The features which were used to argue that religious disagreement was unique do distinguish religious disagreement from *some* other forms of disagreement but they fail to justify the view that religious disagreement is unlike every other form of disagreement.

4. Consequences for the Epistemology of Disagreement

In this section, I will articulate what follows from the recognition that religious disagreement is not unique. In general, I think the consequence of accepting

---

[19] For related empirical research which suggests that members of opposing parties understand the issues of central importance to contemporary governance more and more divergently, see Pew Research Center (2019). For empirical support of the related claim that we broadly discount as reliable reasoners those whose political views differ from our own, see Marks et al. (2019).

this view is that religious disagreement is much less worrisome to those who might wish to hold on to their belief or non-belief in t after encountering the kind of disagreement I've been concerned with here. Anecdotally, I think many individuals tend to be quite comfortable holding on to their moral and political beliefs in spite of the fact that other well-informed individuals may disagree with them about moral or political issues. Religious disagreement is sometimes met with more concern, perhaps because some theists are themselves concerned by the incommunicability of some of the evidence on which they base their beliefs. Recognizing that religious disagreement is not unique helps to calm some of these worries.

But what of the arguments which hold that the allegedly distinct features of religious disagreement allow individuals to rationally maintain their beliefs in the face of religious disagreement? First, I'll consider the impacts of the view I've been defending for those who hold non-conciliatory views of disagreement, on which it is sometimes rational to hold on to your original beliefs after learning of disagreement. Then, I'll consider how my conclusion affects the arguments proposed by those who hold conciliatory views of disagreement, on which learning of disagreement requires me to adjust my original doxastic attitudes about the matter under disagreement.

Proponents of non-conciliatory views of disagreement need not be threatened by the view that religious disagreement is not unique. Proponents of non-conciliatory views of disagreement already hold that it can sometimes be rational to hold on to our original doxastic attitudes in the aftermath of disagreement and some of them have argued that incommunicable evidence in religious contexts can serve this role of making it rational to hold on to your original doxastic attitude toward t. Goldman and I have argued that we often find ourselves in disagreements in which we cannot communicate the content of our evidence in contexts outside of religious contexts. So in the aftermath of this argument, non-conciliationists who hold that incommunicable evidence can make it rational to hold on to your original doxastic attitude in the face of disagreement will find the set of disagreements in which their preferred non-conciliatory response to disagreement applies to be widened to include cases in which we rely on our memory to assist us in evidence sharing.

Further, I think my argument can increase the dialectical advantage of non-conciliationists who believe t. Since non-theists can readily sign on to the idea that the failure of our faculties of memory may make some evidence incommunicable, the incommunicability of evidence from religious experience should seem less suspect to non-theists assessing the rationality of theists who hold on to their belief in t in the aftermath of disagreement. As

I foreshadowed earlier, this added advantage for non-conciliatory theists will only arise in discussions with non-theists who, unlike those of the New Atheist sort, do not, in a question-begging fashion, dismiss private religious experience based on their content. Nevertheless, recognizing that religious disagreement is not unique does not hinder the non-conciliatory position in the context of religious disagreement. Rather, this recognition increases the plausibility of holding on to belief in t in the face of religious disagreement.[20]

Proponents of conciliatory views of disagreement find themselves in a bit more trouble given my conclusion that religious disagreement is not unique. This is because proponents of conciliatory views of disagreement like Pittard and Bogardus used the distinctive features of religious disagreement to argue that religious disagreement, in certain circumstances, could be an exception to the rule that we must adjust our doxastic attitudes on learning of disagreement. My sense is that some conciliationists want to have rational, confident religious beliefs in the aftermath of disagreement with non-theists. Unfortunately, I think my argument spells trouble for this sort of conciliationist.

First, if conciliationists accept my argument that incommunicable evidence arises in numerous disagreements outside of religious contexts, they will find themselves using their preferred conciliatory response to disagreement much less often than they might wish. Recall Bogardus's admission that in cases of disagreement where an individual relies on "private religious experiences," his preferred conciliatory view does not tell us whether conciliation is required, "for all the [Equal Weight] view says, it's reasonable to maintain one's religious beliefs in such cases of disagreement" (2013, p. 15). But if one's beliefs are based on incommunicable evidence in cases of disagreement across the board, when our memory fails to offer up the evidence we originally based our beliefs on, then the Equal Weight view and conciliatory views like it are perfectly compatible with steadfastly holding on to our original beliefs after disagreement.

Proponents of conciliatory views who wish to hold on to theistic belief in the face of religious disagreement are left with a problem. They must either come up with an argument that private, incommunicable evidence in religious contexts ought to be treated differently than other sorts of private,

---

[20] Proponents of non-conciliatory views of disagreement, including Lackey (2010), are usually primarily concerned with the justificatory status of the original doxastic attitude towards the proposition under disagreement. Consequently, they are only indirectly concerned with the standards by which we evaluate our partners in disagreement. I have omitted discussion of the consequences of the non-distinctiveness of evaluative standards in religious contexts on non-conciliatory views of disagreement.

incommunicable evidence or they must accept that in many, many disagreements which involve the use of our memory to reproduce the evidence on which we base our beliefs, their preferred conciliatory view is perfectly compatible with holding on to our original doxastic attitudes rather than conciliating in response to disagreement.

Second, if conciliationists accept my argument that non-standard, self-favoring evaluative standards arise in non-religious disagreements, they will find themselves with a similar problem. Pittard has argued that non-standard, self-favoring evaluative standards can result in those who hold conciliatory views of disagreement rationally resisting the typical conciliatory advice to adjust one's belief in response to disagreement. I've argued that similar sorts of standards are at play in moral and political disagreements. So proponents of conciliatory views of disagreement seem, on Pittard's argument, to be committed to the idea that conciliating is not required in religious, moral, or political contexts. Now Adam Elga (2007, pp. 492–494) has already recognized that conciliatory views may not be committed to conciliationism in the contexts of these fundamental sorts of disagreement, so perhaps this consequence is not so concerning to some proponents of conciliatory views. However, perhaps there are other proponents of conciliatory views who want conciliationism to call them to conciliate in moral and political contexts, but not in religious contexts. If so, as I've argued, they will be forced to adopt a different argumentative tack, arguing that religious disagreement is the exception to the rule of conciliating on some other basis than non-standard, self-favoring evaluative standards.

5. Conclusion

I have argued that religious disagreement is not unique. The features which have previously been understood as making it distinctive, religious experience and non-standard, self-favoring evaluative standards, have analog features in various non-religious disagreements. Anecdotally, I've suggested that recognizing that religious disagreement is not in its own, unique class of disagreements will allow those who hold religious beliefs to find religious disagreement less threatening.

For non-conciliationists in favor of the incommunicable evidence justification for remaining steadfast in their doxastic attitudes, my argument also widens the scope of disagreements in which they may remain rationally steadfast and gives them an additional dialectical advantage in discussions of religious disagreements with those who do not share their religious beliefs. So discovering that religious disagreement is not unique makes religious disagreement less worrisome to non-conciliationists.

But the results are perhaps not quite so happy for all proponents of conciliatory views of disagreement. In the aftermath of my arguments, religious disagreement will, indeed, be less worrisome for conciliationists who are comfortable with the fact that their own conciliatory view will allow them to hold on to their original beliefs in a wide range of cases in addition to religious disagreements, including disagreements in which we rely on our memory to communicate the evidence on which we originally based our beliefs, as well as moral and political disagreements. For proponents of conciliatory views who are not happy with this consequence, new arguments will need to be advanced to argue that religious evidence and evaluative standards do not resemble the non-religious evidence and evaluative standards which I've argued that they do. Absent production of these arguments, we can conclude that religious disagreement is not unique and that this fact makes it less, rather than more, worrisome for those who would wish to rationally hold on to their beliefs in the face of religious disagreement.

References

Alston, William P. 1991. *Perceiving God: The Epistemology of Religious Experience.* Ithaca, NY: Cornell University Press.

Benton, Matthew A. 2019. "Religious Diversity and Disagreement." In Miranda Fricker, Peter Graham, David Henderson, and Nikolaj J.L.L. Pedersen (eds.), *The Routledge Handbook of Social Epistemology*, 185–195. London: Routledge.

Bergmann, Michael. 2017. "Religious Disagreement and Epistemic Intuitions." *Royal Institute of Philosophy Supplements* 81: 19–43.

Bogardus, Tomas. 2013. "Disagreeing with the (Religious) Skeptic." *International Journal for Philosophy of Religion* 74: 5–17.

Choo, Frederick. Forthcoming. "The Epistemic Significance of Religious Disagreements: Cases of Unconfirmed Superiority Disagreements." *Topoi* 1–9. Published early view, 2018. https://doi.org/10.1007/s11245-018-9599-4

Christensen, David. 2007. "Epistemology of Disagreement: The Good News." *The Philosophical Review* 116: 187–217.

Conee, Earl and Richard Feldman. 2004. *Evidentialism: Essays in Epistemology.* New York: Oxford University Press.

De Cruz, Helen. 2018. "Religious Conversion, Transformative Experience, and Disagreement." *Philosophia Christi* 20: 265–276.

DePoe, John. 2018. "Hold on Loosely, But Don't Let Go." *Philosophia Christi* 20: 253–264.

Dormandy, Katherine. 2018. "Resolving Religious Disagreements: Evidence and Bias." *Faith and Philosophy* 35: 56–83.

Elga, Adam. 2007. "Reflection and Disagreement." *Noûs* 48: 478–502.

Feldman, Richard. 2007. "Reasonable Religious Disagreements." In Louise Antony (ed.), *Philosophers without Gods*, 194–214. Oxford: Oxford University Press.

Frances, Bryan. 2015. "Religious Disagreement." In Graham Oppy (ed.), *Routledge Handbook of Contemporary Philosophy of Religion*, 180–191. New York: Routledge.

Goldman, Alvin. 2010. "Epistemic Relativism and Reasonable Disagreement." In Richard Feldman and Ted Warfield (eds.), *Disagreement*, 187–213. Oxford: Oxford University Press.

King, Nathan L. 2012. "Disagreement: What's the Problem? Or, a Good Peer is Hard to Find." *Philosophy and Phenomenological Research* 85: 249–272.

Kraft, James. 2007. "Religious Disagreement, Externalism, and the Epistemology of Disagreement: Listening to Our Grandmothers." *Religious Studies* 43: 417–432.

Lackey, Jennifer. 2010. "A Justificationist View of Disagreement's Epistemic Significance." In Adrian Haddock, Alan Millar, and Duncan Pritchard (eds.), *Social Epistemology*, 298–325. Oxford: Oxford University Press.

Lackey, Jennifer. 2014. "Taking Religious Disagreement Seriously." In Laura Frances Callahan and Timothy O'Connor (eds.), *Religious Faith and Intellectual Virtue*, 299–316. Oxford: Oxford University Press.

Lougheed, Kirk. 2018. "Is Religious Experience a Solution to the Problem of Religious Disagreement?" *Logos and Episteme* 4: 173–197.

Marks, Joseph, Eloise Copland, Eleanor Loh, Cass R. Sunstein, and Tali Sharot. 2019. "Epistemic Spillovers: Learning Other's Political Views Reduces the Ability to Assess and Use their Expertise in Nonpolitical Domains." *Cognition* 188: 74–84.

Matheson, Jonathan. 2019. "Disagreement Skepticism and the Rationality of Religious Belief." In Kevin McCain and Ted Poston (eds.), *The Mystery of Skepticism: New Explorations*, 83–104. Boston: Brill.

McCain, Kevin. 2014. *Evidentialism and Epistemic Justification*. New York: Routledge.

Pew Research Center. 2019. *Public's 2019 Priorities: Economy, Health Care, Education and Security All Near Top of List.*

Pittard, John. 2014. "Conciliationism and Religious Disagreement." In Michael Bergmann and Patrick Kain (eds.), *Challenges to Moral and Religious Belief: Disagreement and Evolution*, 80–100. Oxford: Oxford University Press.

Plantinga, Alvin. 2000. *Warranted Christian Belief.* New York: Oxford University Press.

Reining, Stefan. 2016. "Peerhood in Deep Religious Disagreements." *Religious Studies* 52: 403–419.

Rosenberg, Alex. 2015. "Can Moral Disputes Be Resolved?" *The New York Times.* July 13, 2015. Retrieved from: https://opinionator.blogs.nytimes.com/2015/07/13/can-moral-disputes-be-resolved/

Schwitzgebel, Eric and Joshua Rust. 2014. "The Moral Behavior of Ethics Professors: Relationships Among Self-Reported Behavior, Expressed Normative Attitude, and Directly Observed Behavior." *Philosophical Psychology* 27: 293–327.

Turnbull, Margaret Greta. 2019. *Uncovering the Roots of Disagreement.* Ph.D. Dissertation. Boston College, Chestnut Hill, MA.

van Inwagen, Peter. 2010. "We're Right. They're Wrong." In Richard Feldman and Ted A. Warfield (eds.), *Disagreement*, 10–28. Oxford: Oxford University Press.

Wiebe, Phillip H. 2015. *Intuitive Knowing as Spiritual Experience.* New York: Palgrave Macmillan.

5

Is There Something Special About Religious Disagreement?

Richard Feldman

The invitation to contribute to a book about religious disagreement prompted me to wonder about the topic: Is there something distinctive about religious disagreement that makes it a suitable topic for examination? On other topics, say, mileage standards for automobiles, if there were discussions of disagreement related to it, they would very likely be substantive discussions of the environmental and economic impact of various options, not philosophical discussions about the disagreement itself. There is, presumably, nothing special to say about disagreements on that topic. When confronted with a disagreement about it, one just evaluates all the relevant information as best one can and comes to a conclusion. No doubt one's preferences and priorities will play some role in one's thinking, but the topic does not raise distinctive philosophical issues about disagreement. Religion may seem to be different, at least to the extent that devoting specific attention to religious disagreement does seem warranted. Nevertheless, I come to the topic with the view that it's just another topic, to be addressed like others, even if it is one of utmost importance to so many people. My conclusion will be the same, though there are some complicating factors.

There are, of course, differing views about the epistemology of disagreement generally, with some people leaning toward more conciliatory approaches according to which learning of the existence of disagreeing peers generally affects what it is reasonable believe whereas others are less inclined toward conciliation. I take a generally conciliatory attitude toward disagreement. I will not attempt to defend that perspective here but instead will discuss its implications for religious disagreement. I also want to emphasize that my topic is not the rationality of religious belief, but rather whether disagreement about religion somehow affects the rationality of belief in a way that differs from the way disagreement affects the rationality of belief about other topics. That is, is there something distinctive about religious disagreement along these lines?

Richard Feldman, *Is There Something Special About Religious Disagreement?* In: *Religious Disagreement and Pluralism*. Edited by: Matthew A. Benton and Jonathan L. Kvanvig, Oxford University Press. © Richard Feldman 2021.
DOI: 10.1093/oso/9780198849865.003.0005

I'll begin, in section 1, by characterizing this general view of disagreement. In sections 2 and 3 I will try to clarify the topic. In section 4 I will consider and reject the possibility that there are distinctive epistemic principles governing religious disagreements. And in the remaining section I'll discuss evidence and religious disagreement. This is where some complications arise.

1. Some Starting Points

In this section, I'll describe a few points that set the stage for what follows. While they are not beyond controversy, I will not argue for them here.

i) As already noted, I take a broadly conciliatory view toward disagreement.[1] That is, I think that, generally, when you learn that a well-informed peer disagrees with you about some topic by denying something you believe to be true, you thereby gain some evidence against the proposition you believe. This evidence typically weakens your justification for your belief and the epistemically appropriate response is to adjust accordingly.

ii) As I see it, the evidence one obtains in cases of disagreement may be what I and many others have described as "higher-order evidence"— roughly, evidence about evidence—or as more ordinary first-order evidence.[2] The clearest case of the former is the evidence one obtains from testimony that one's original evidence does not support what one thinks it does. That is, one thinks that some evidence supports or implies some conclusion and one's peer denies this. The clearest case of first-order evidence is direct evidence concerning the proposition in question, as when one's peer informs you that the fingerprints at the crime scene are not those of the suspect you believe to be guilty. The bare fact that a peer denies the proposition you believe is akin to testimonial evidence against the proposition you believe. It doesn't fit neatly into either of these categories, although I see it as more like higher-order evidence. My reason for this is that I think that learning of the peer's belief provides evidence that the peer has some evidence, though you don't know what it is, for believing as he or she does. Thus, it is evidence about the existence of evidence, and thus in the

[1] See Feldman 2009.   [2] For recent discussions of higher-order evidence, see Whiting 2020.

higher-order evidence category. In any case, it is evidence to be taken into account.

iii) There are cases in which encountering a disagreement requires no adjustment, as when you know that your peer is impaired or that you are far better situated with respect to determining the truth about the contested proposition. In such cases, the new evidence obtained from the interaction with your peer is undermined by your other evidence. Some might say, instead, that these considerations undermine the other person's status as your peer and thus deprive the peer's assertions of the evidentiary weight they'd otherwise have. Either way, such cases are exceptions to the general point that disagreement provides evidence that requires modification of one's view.

iv) I think that the conciliatory response to disagreement applies to a vast range of topics. Whether we are disagreeing about American history or athletic accomplishments or climate change, disagreement typically makes an epistemic difference. I take this view seriously, in the sense that the fact that I have disagreeing peers on many topics that I care deeply about does give me pause. It makes me worry that there may be something I'm not aware of or something I'm misunderstanding. In large part, the topic in this paper is whether this general approach to disagreement applies to propositions about religious matters just as it applies to these other areas of inquiry.

v) Any actual disagreement is embedded in a larger context that can affect the extent of its impact. If I already know that there is widespread disagreement about a topic, then encountering one more person who disagrees with me may not have much of an effect. It's just another person on that side of the issue and my background information already supported the idea that there were many such people. Of course, additional facts about the individual in question might make a difference. For example, if I learn of a disagreement with someone with whom I almost always agree, the fact that this person differs with me on this issue might have added impact. Where agreement is anticipated, disagreement can have a greater impact. Where disagreement is anticipated, it will have little impact.

My goal in this paper, then, is to examine my perspective on religious disagreement—that it is like disagreement in other domains—to see if it withstands scrutiny. My conclusion will be a qualified "yes." The qualification results partly from some questions, which will emerge along the way, about exactly what is at issue and partly from some issues concerning religious experience.

2. Clarifying the Topic

One reason that it is often difficult to answer questions about whether things are alike or different is that things are generally alike in some respects and different in other respects. That issue arises in this case. It will therefore be useful to clarify the topic, as I hope to do with the following points.

i) There are philosophically uninteresting ways in which religious disagreement does differ from disagreement about all other matters. The most obvious is its subject matter: religious disagreement is about religious matters while other disagreements are not. This, of course, is wholly trivial. Analogously, disagreements about baseball are distinctive because they are about baseball and disagreements about other topics are not. Differences in subject matter clearly are not differences of interest here. The question, then, must be whether there is some philosophically significant way in which religious disagreements differ from other disagreements. I don't have any well-developed account of what counts as a philosophically significant difference, but I hope that the idea will be clear enough as the discussion proceeds.

ii) Disagreements differ from one another in a whole host of ways. One can respond to a disagreement with amusement, annoyance, feelings of threat or fear, or any number of other attitudes. Whether there are interesting general patterns to these kinds of responses is an empirical matter that could well be studied.[3] It's possible that such studies would reveal something distinctive about how people do in fact respond to religious disagreement. There's no doubt that a great many people lean toward tolerance, but there surely are others who think that religious belief is simply irrational.[4] While this is a topic of interest, it is not my topic.

iii) Similarly, religious belief is particularly important to many people, and perhaps this is a good reason to treat it with deference and respect. But this is distinct from the question of the evidential significance of disagreement and is not my topic here.

iv) There are potential disagreements about religion that are clearly similar in all philosophically significant ways to common disagreements about other topics. For example, one can find numerous

---

[3] See De Cruz 2017 for a discussion of philosophers' attitudes toward disagreement.
[4] For an examination of why some think religious belief is simply irrational, see Frances 2016.

discussions about a decline in attendance at weekly religious services. There are reports of religious leaders lamenting the decline. But the reality of the decline is in fact disputed.[5] This is a straightforward empirical issue that happens to be about religion. Disagreement about it is comparable to potential disagreement about whether attendance at baseball games has declined in recent years. There are, of course, ways in which the claims in each case can be made more precise: Does "attendance" at a religious service require actually paying attention, or could sitting in the lobby looking at one's phone count? Similarly, does "attendance" at a baseball game require paying attention to the game, or does sitting in a stadium restaurant talking with friends count? However, the key point is that there's nothing special, in any way relevant to the present discussion, about this sort of disagreement about religion. The same is true of many other potential disagreements about religious matters, including some concerning more sensitive issues. For example, disagreements about the interpretation of religious texts or the historical facts about the origins of religious practices can be like interpretive or historical disagreements in other domains. They need not present distinctive philosophical issues. But the existence of these routine disagreements about religion does not settle my intended question. That question, then, must not be whether all disagreements about religion differ in some philosophically significant way from all disagreements about other topics.

v) Perhaps, then, the question about the distinctiveness of religious disagreement is best understood as a question about the distinctiveness of disagreement about a particular class of religious propositions. A plausible idea is that it concerns those disagreements that constitute the more fundamental aspects of religious views, especially those about the existence or nature of god. I'll call these "core religious beliefs" and will not attempt to specify more carefully just what is included. It is clear that there is in fact disagreement about such matters. Atheists differ from others about the existence of god. Theists differ on the nature of god.[6] Thus, plausibly, the central question is whether disagreements about core religious propositions

---

[5] Presser and Chaves 2007.

[6] One account of similarities and differences among religions may be found here: https://www.religioustolerance.org/relcomp.htm.

differ in some philosophically significant way from disagreements about other topics.

vi) The topic needs still further refinement, since there can be disagreements about core religious propositions that clearly do not raise distinctive philosophically interesting questions. People might disagree about what the core religious beliefs of some individual or group are. But such a disagreement is a psychological or sociological disagreement similar to others in those domains. The focus here must be disagreements in which the contested proposition is itself a core religious proposition. Our topic, then, is whether such disagreements are in some philosophically interesting way distinctive. So understood, a disagreement about what the core religious beliefs of the majority of people in some particular community are is not itself the relevant kind of disagreement about a core religious proposition.

vii) For the purposes of this discussion, it is essential that the disagreement in question is a genuine disagreement about the truth value of a proposition, not a difference in commitment to a way of living one's life. A person who chooses to live as a faithful practitioner of a particular religion will differ in notable ways from a person who chooses to live as an atheist or as a faithful observer of a significantly different religion. While there almost surely will be propositions about which they disagree, the difference in behavioral commitments is not a disagreement of the sort under discussion here. The focus is differences in beliefs about the truth of core religious propositions.[7]

viii) Further, for some, religious attitudes are a matter of faith rather than evidence-based belief. The issues associated with the epistemic impact of disagreement simply may not be relevant in that case. They are not the topic of this discussion.

ix) The question about the distinctiveness of religious disagreement can be formulated as a question about the uniqueness of core religious disagreement. However, if such disagreements are relevantly like a number of disagreements in a small number of other domains, they still may deserve being described as distinctive. In what follows, I will take the question to be about this broader, and admittedly less precise, issue rather than about the uniqueness of core religious disagreement.

---

[7] Section 3.8 of De Cruz 2017 examines the extent to which philosophers see religious differences as more "preference-like" than "fact-like."

x) For a great many people, religious disagreement falls into the category described earlier of cases in which learning that a particular peer disagrees is not likely to have any significant epistemic impact because, in realistic contemporary settings, the existence of disagreement among informed peers about such matters is a well-known background condition. While there are real or possible cases of people living in isolated homogeneous communities and in ignorance of religious differences, the issue under discussion here concerns people who already know that there are peers who do not share their beliefs about religious matters. While it may come as a surprise to learn that a particular person differs from you on religious matters, such a discovery merely situates that person in an already familiar group. Typically, there is no reason to think that this will have any notable impact on the epistemic status of the propositions in question.

xi) Of course, the known existing disagreement is itself a fact that may have evidential import. This suggests that the question about disagreement of significance here is not "What is it reasonable to believe upon learning of a disagreement?" Instead, it is "What is the impact of disagreement on reasonable or justified belief?" where the existence of this disagreement might be already known but, possibly, not appropriately reflected in one's beliefs. And the question about religious disagreement is whether there is something distinctive about religious disagreement in this regard. In what follows, it will sometimes be convenient to write about "learning of a disagreement," but my real focus will be on the epistemic impact of disagreement. While imagining the evidential impact of religious disagreement by considering someone who has previously been ignorant of such disagreement might be a useful approach, that will not be the focus here.

3. How Could It Be That Core Religious Disagreement Is Distinctive?

At a few points in the discussion that follows I will use what I believe to be a typical example to investigate the possibility that core religious disagreement is in some way epistemically distinctive. The example is my own atheism, my belief that there is no god.[8] One of the points from section 2 is clearly

---

[8] This picks up a theme from my earlier paper, Feldman 2007.

SOMETHING SPECIAL ABOUT RELIGIOUS DISAGREEMENT? 115

applicable here: I've long known that there is widespread disagreement on this matter, just as I know this about many other issues. The question, then, is not whether encountering a theist among my colleagues somehow differentially affects my religious belief but rather whether my knowledge of the existence of widespread disagreement on the matter has a differential impact on the epistemic status of my belief.

In thinking about this, it is important to keep clear about two different questions. One question is about the effect this background knowledge has on the degree of justification I have for my belief. This is a question about the epistemic significance of disagreement. In evidentialist terms, my atheistic belief is justified to the extent that it is supported by my overall evidence. We can separate my evidence into two categories: (i) my evidence that so many other intelligent and thoughtful people believe differently than I do and (ii) all my other evidence. This first question is whether the combination of (i) and (ii) supports my belief less well than (ii) alone does. The general conciliatory outlook I have suggests that the answer to this question is "yes."[9]

The second question concerns whether the answer to this kind of question in the case of religious belief is for some reason different than the answer in the case of other beliefs. Thus, I have beliefs about social policy, economic policy, scientific issues such as climate change, and so on. In each case, my evidence can be segregated in the way just described and we can ask whether the total body of evidence supports my belief less well than my evidence excluding the information about disagreement would support it. The conciliationist says that, in general, the answer is "yes." But the central question here is whether this general answer does not apply, or does not apply in the same way, to my religious belief.

If core religious disagreement is distinctive, then, it could be because, unlike other domains, no conciliation is called for or because a greater or lesser degree of conciliation is called for. And it could be that the situation is unusually asymmetrical in that a greater degree of conciliation is called for by one side of the disagreement than the other, e.g., if the existence of theists has a greater evidential impact on atheists than the existence of atheists has on theists.

There are at least two notably different ways in which it might turn out that core religious disagreement is distinctive. First, it could be that there are

---

[9] This formulation overlooks a complicating factor: it could be that the combination of (i) is evidence against my belief, but the combination of (i) and (ii) does not support my belief less well than (ii) alone because (ii) contains defeaters of the evidence provided by (i).

epistemic principles governing disagreement generally that do not apply in the case of religious disagreement. That is, the principles might have a religious exemption. Second, it could be that, although the same general principles apply, there are differences in core religious propositions or our belief in them or our evidence for them which have the result that the same principles yield importantly different outcomes. I'll discuss the first of these two possibilities in section 4 and the second in section 5. It is the second one that makes it difficult to give a simple response to the question of the distinctiveness of religious disagreement.

4. Special Principles

As just explained, one way in which core religious disagreements might differ from other disagreements is that there are general principles about epistemically proper responses to disagreement that do not apply in the case of core religious disagreement. An advocate of conciliation would endorse some principle according to which disagreement with a peer generally requires that one's beliefs should be tempered in light of the disagreement. For reasons that will become clear shortly, I will not attempt to formulate any such principle more precisely. The religious exemption idea would hold some version of a principle according to which the epistemically appropriate response to learning of a disagreement with a peer is to modify one's belief in the direction of one's peer's *except in the case of disagreement about core religious propositions.*

I have two reasons, neither close to conclusive, for thinking that nothing remotely like this is right. First, I don't see a reason to think that there is a something about religious disagreement itself that could possibly warrant special treatment. In saying this, I am not simply dismissing the possibility that there is something distinctive about core religious disagreement. Rather, the thought is that if there is something distinctive about it, this is due to the distinctive status of core religious propositions or our beliefs regarding them. The exception to the general rule, if there is one, is derivative from some larger category into which these propositions or beliefs fall. For example, one might think that religious disagreement works differently than most disagreement because core religious beliefs fall into some larger category of beliefs whose epistemic situation is distinctive. Any such basis for the religious exemption will fall more neatly into the second kind of response, discussed in the next section, according to which the standard principles apply, but as a result of facts about the cases they yield interestingly different results in the case of core religious disagreement.

My second reason for doubting that there is a religious exemption to general epistemic principles specifically about disagreement is that I doubt that there are any general principles specifically about disagreement, hence I doubt that there are principles for which there can be a religious exemption. (I acknowledge that the lack of a general principle does not imply that there is no principle applicable to particular classes of cases.) Questions about the epistemology of disagreement can be framed as questions about what one is justified in believing when confronted by a disagreeing peer (or about what is the appropriate way, from an epistemological perspective, to take into account the fact of disagreement). In my view, the questions raised by disagreement are questions about the significance of the evidence brought forth in cases of disagreement. There are not special principles about what's justified in cases of disagreement, differing from the principles applicable in other cases. For an evidentialist, what's justified is what's supported by one's evidence.[10] That remains true when one is confronted by a disagreeing peer and when one is taking into account dissenting views. There is, in this sense, nothing special about disagreement. Further, there is nothing all that special about peer disagreement. The fact that non-peers disagree is, equally, information to be taken into account in forming one's beliefs.

I want to acknowledge that I haven't argued, and thus have not shown, that there are no principles specifically about disagreement. Nor have I argued that there aren't any principles about religious disagreement. To be clear, my view is not that there is no principle applicable in the case of disagreement. It's just that there is no *special* principle specifically about disagreement. Rather, the general principle is to believe in accordance with one's evidence, and that applies to cases of disagreement generally and, as I will discuss below, to core religious belief as well.

5. Evidence and Core Religious Disagreements

I turn now to the evidence associated with core religious disagreements. The question here is whether there is something distinctive about the evidence we

---

[10] For a defense, see my book co-authored with Earl Conee: *Evidentialism: Essays in Epistemology*, Oxford: Clarendon Press, 2004.

have in core religious disagreements that makes the impact of disagreement distinctive.

To the extent that core religious belief is based on evidence, it is likely that the evidence in any particular case falls into one or more of three categories: testimony—one can come to one's core religious beliefs on the basis of what one is told by family members, friends, religious leaders (and texts), and others; arguments—people's religious beliefs can be influenced by the many well-known (or not so well-known) arguments about the existence or nature of god; religious experience—people have experiences which, they think, provide insight into core religious propositions.[11]

Testimony (including texts) and arguments on the topic, I think, do not make religious disagreement distinctive. That is, if one encounters a peer who disagrees about core religious propositions, and the source of that disagreement derives from differing testimony or differing analyses of arguments, the epistemologically appropriate response to that disagreement is just like the appropriate response to an analogous disagreement about any other topic. I can see no reason to think that the mere fact that the subject matter is religion introduces reason to treat the testimony or the arguments in some special way. In particular, I see no reason to think that, simply because the topic is religion, disagreement arising from a difference in testimony or a difference in analysis of arguments can be dismissed as evidentially insignificant or treated in any distinctive way. In the case of testimony, the issues to consider include the sincerity and reliability of the source. In the case of arguments, the issues include the merits of the premises and the strength of their connection to the conclusion. This is true regardless of the topic. That, I admit, is not much of an argument, but I find it hard to find any reason at all to support the contrary view.

I want to be clear that I'm not here taking a stand on what the proper response to disagreement is. It may be that conciliation is called for in some cases but not others. It may be that when one finds some argument particularly compelling, that impression of it makes it reasonable to maintain one's view even if others report not finding the argument compelling. Whatever the truth of the matter, it applies equally to religious and non-religious disagreements.

This leaves experiential evidence as a potential source for the distinctiveness of religious disagreement. This kind of evidence raises what strikes me as the

---

[11] Some might add memory to the list. I don't object to that, but what's remembered would presumably be things that fall into the categories listed.

most challenging questions related to religious disagreement.[12] Religious experiences can be unusually private, powerful, and hard to communicate. People differ notably in whether they have them or, if they do, what they are like and what they make of them.[13] Some think that only people with certain powers or training are able to have such experiences. Of course, some people have no such experiences at all or, if they do, they do not take them to have the significance religious believers take them to have. Let's imagine, then, a religious disagreement in which the religious believer's belief is based on religious experience and the non-believer's belief is based on the absence of such experience (along with whatever other considerations may bear on the belief).

It will be useful in what follows to have for comparison a simple example of a disagreement arising out of differing experiential evidence in a perceptual rather than a religious matter. Here's one: Imagine two people sitting in their home when one says that she heard someone knock on the front door. The other says that he heard no such thing. They disagree, at least at first, about whether there was a knock on the door.

There are number of factors we might look at in the knock on the door example to see our way through the disagreement. These include:

i) Track Records: In the knock on the door case, one or both of the people might know that one person suffers from hearing loss, frequently fails to hear things, and could easily miss a knock; they might know that one of them suffers from auditory hallucinations and could readily seem to experience a knock that didn't actually occur; they might know that the person who didn't hear it is frequently distracted and misses things in the environment. In short, there can be knowledge of track records bearing on reliability.

ii) Accuracy of Interpretation: This is similar to the track record point, but slightly different. In the knock on the door case, the circumstances might be such that it is easy to mistake a different sound, such as clanging pipes or a car door being closed, for a knock on the door. A person with poor hearing or someone who tends to be distracted or deep in thought might frequently make such mistakes. Again, information about the circumstances might help in thinking through the matter.

[12] For an excellent discussion of these issues, see Pittard 2015.
[13] Frances provides a useful classification, identifying potential religious experiences as meditative, "mind-blowing," calm, and "overall," where the last includes the strong sense that the world in general results from intentional design. See Frances 2016, 19.

iii) Honesty: In any actual case of disagreement, each party to the disagreement has to make an assessment of the honesty of the other person who reports a different experience and belief. There is generally at least some chance, even if minimal, that the other person is joking or lying or otherwise misreporting the experience and belief.

iv) Plausibility: If we have information about the plausibility of there being a knock on the door, that too can affect what final judgment is most reasonable. If, for example, the home is located in a place to which no one else has access, there might be almost no chance that someone knocked on the door, and this has a bearing on what conclusion is justified.

Somehow, when information about these points is available as background evidence, or can be acquired, you can weigh it and come to a conclusion. It may be that in some cases one's own perceptual experience is so clear and vivid, and so devoid of any indications of error, that it is most reasonable to dismiss the other person as mistaken for one reason or another. This attitude can apply to either side of the disagreement. While it might be clearest in the case of the person who did experience something, in this case, the knock on the door, it might also apply to the person who didn't hear it. That person might think: "I was paying close attention. I have good hearing. If there were a knock on the door, I definitely would have heard it. So, something is going wrong with the other person." This may well be reasonable, and it would be bolstered by some specific information about the other person supporting this response. It's worth noting, however, that the conciliatory response may well be reasonable in some cases. That is, it might be most reasonable to conclude that "Something has gone wrong with one of us, but I have no idea which one. I'll suspend judgment on the matter." The details of the situation may determine what is best. There's no simple formula determining how all these factors add up, but there is also nothing particularly mysterious about it.

The religious experience example may seem different. For one thing, we don't have much that's useful regarding track records.[14] For another, the point about accuracy of interpretation seems particularly contentious. In the knock on the door case, there is a kind of mutual understanding of at least the nature of the experience and the evidential significance of experiences of that kind.

---

[14] There can be cases of theists who regularly claim to experience other sorts of things that other people think are not present. And non-theists who miss things that plainly are present. Perhaps they have relevant track records. But I set these kinds of cases aside.

This can be missing in the religious experience case. The person who didn't hear the knock on the door (presumably) knows what's it like to hear a knock on the door, and the person who did hear it knows what it's like not to hear that sound. But the religious experience case differs, at least for many of us. As a non-believer who has not had such experiences, or not experienced shared events (such as, say, first seeing a newborn child) in the same way as those who attach religious significance to it, I must admit that I don't really grasp what it's supposed to be like. This point, perhaps, is not symmetrical, in that the believer presumably does understand the absence of religious experience in specific cases.

This last point brings to the fore two crucial questions about religious experience for the present discussion: one concerns the evidential significance of religious experience for the person who has the experience; the second concerns the evidential significance of reported religious experiences for those who receive such reports. The second question only gets its footing if the first question gets some sort of affirmative answer. That is, if religious experience provides no evidence in support of religious belief for the person who has it, then, presumably, a person who is told of another's religious experience does not thereby gain evidence for those beliefs. Applied to my own case, if religious experience does not provide the person who has the experience with evidence supporting religious belief, then it's hard to see why someone reporting such an experience to me would provide me with evidence that undermines my atheism.[15]

Where does this leave us? I have no simple answer, but I do have a few comments:

i) In some cases, a disagreement is simply dismissible, as for example, an encounter with someone who contends that the earth is flat and that all the photos from space are fakes, I'll simply dismiss this, and I'll do so with full justification. Similarly, if I feel tired but, for some reason, you tell me that I'm not tired, I'd say that I'm in a far better position to judge the matter and will reasonably maintain my belief.[16] In these cases, I think, there are decisive defeaters for the evidence derived from the disagreement. Those who think

[15] There is a generalization of this point that is not correct. A person might have an experience that does not contribute to the justification of a particular proposition for that person but the report of that experience to another person, with different background evidence, might contribute to its justification. For example, telling you doctor how you feel might contribute to the doctor's justification for some conclusion while not doing so for you.

[16] There may be exceptions. For example, if you are a doctor who has just completed an examination and you say that I'm confusing being tired with being depressed, it may behoove me to modify my view.

that religious experience provides no evidence whatsoever for religious belief may see the disagreement this way.[17] But I do not. There may also be those who think that non-believers are simply refusing to acknowledge plain reality. Thus, interestingly, there may be people on both sides of the issue who agree that it is a disagreement in which the other side is easily dismissed. But that's not my view. As I see it, people with widely differing beliefs on core religious propositions can be thoughtful and intelligent individuals who are trying to get things right. It would be a mistake to simply dismiss them or their views.

ii) From a very high level of abstraction, core religious disagreement looks quite similar to the perceptual disagreement and other disagreements stemming from experiential differences. The epistemically justified response to the disagreement takes into account the information obtained about the other person's experience, weighs it against one's own experience, and comes to a conclusion. Information about track records, accuracy of interpretation, and so on contribute to the verdict. The details matter and different cases will have different outcomes.

iii) Looking a little more closely, however, reveals puzzling differences, in that it can be difficult, especially for the person not having religious experience, to fully appreciate and assess the reported religious experience. This does not change the general principle, as just described in point (i), but it does muddy its application to the case. There is, then, a way in which core religious disagreement differs from these other cases.

iv) One of the points that emerges from the examination of these examples is that they are cases in which there are ineliminable evidential differences between the people who disagree. In the knock on the door case, they've had their different experiences and that cannot be changed. At best, they can learn what they can understand about the experiences of the other. The cases are not, then, like those in the philosophical literature in which people are supposed to have the same evidence.

v) These ineliminable differences in the evidential situations *may* provide a basis for each side of the disagreements to maintain their initial beliefs. These differences could be significant enough to justify different conclusions, despite the similarity in other aspects of the bodies of evidence. In the knock on the door case, it could be that each person, given all their evidence, is reasonable in thinking that because their own experience was so clear and vivid and they lack background evidence pointing one way or the other, the most plausible explanation is that the other person is somehow mistaken or dishonest. In that

---

[17] See, for example, Hitchens 2007.

case, each person (assuming their own honesty) would be justified in retaining their belief. Perhaps the same is true in the religious experience case: each person has a sufficiently strong experiential basis for maintaining belief. I will note that this is not because I think that there is some sort of preferred status for one's own experience simply because it is one's own. Rather, the idea is that, as I imagine the case, the clarity and vivacity of the experience might provide an evidential basis for one's conclusion. This strikes me as a defensible view about the matter. I will acknowledge that I do not have any compelling argument to favor this view over a more conciliatory approach.

vi) It might be helpful to think about the situation from the perspective of a neutral observer of the case. Imagine an observer of the knock on the door case who has no independent information about the matter and hears only what the two parties to the disagreement report. Track records and the like do not help resolve the matter. This observer might plausibly draw the conclusion just described—they are both reasonable in maintaining their beliefs—but also would have no basis (assuming no independent evidence), to favor one side over the other. The situation can be framed in terms of correlations: the observer knows that hearing a knock-like sound is correlated with there being a knock on the door, and not hearing it is correlated with there not being one. Absent additional information, the two points balance each other out. Suspension of judgment about what actually happened would seem to be the proper attitude for such an observer.

vii) This highlights the significance of the absence of useful track record information to bring to bear on the religious disagreement issue. If a neutral observer knew that religious experiences were correlated with being in the presence of a supernatural being, then the actual truth of the matter is settled. Similarly, if the person who lacks religious experience has that background knowledge, that person should defer to the believer. It would be comparable to a person wearing sound-blocking headphones deferring to a person without them about what the latter person hears in their surroundings. In other words, in the case of religious disagreement, it isn't that there are competing track records to consider, but rather an absence of any known records that can be helpful here.

viii) In commenting on the knock on the door example earlier, I identified the "plausibility" of there being a knock on the door as a factor to be considered in thinking through the disagreement. A main consideration here is what one's background information indicates about the likelihood of there being a knock on the door at that time and place. Crucially, at any given time, there may or may not be someone at the door; it's a contingent matter and changes over time. If a knock is likely, as when you are expecting someone to arrive, then this might provide some reason to assign credibility to the person who claimed to hear a knock. If it is unlikely, then greater credibility might go to the person who didn't hear it. The reasonable thing to think at any time is determined by the combination of experiential and other background evidence one has at that time.

Religious belief differs in that the truth value of core religious propositions does not change over time (at least as they are commonly understood). This alters the role that the background considerations of plausibility might play. While it might be true that religious experiences are more likely to occur in some situations than in others, the truth value of the core religious proposition is not sometimes true and sometimes false. If I know that someone had a religious experience at some previous time, and this experience is evidentially significant, then it has a lasting impact and affects the rationality of subsequent beliefs. This is notably different from the knock on the door example, in which the truth value of the target proposition is variable.

ix) The arguments for and against the truth of core religious propositions might be counted as part of the background plausibility considerations. Of course, if that evidence points clearly one way or the other, then it is less clear that religious experiences play any crucial evidential role. This would leave religious disagreement as disagreement much like other disagreements where the considerations at issue largely derive from the assessment of competing arguments. That is, religious disagreement would not be distinctive.

x) If religious experiences do have an evidential role, perhaps, then, it is best to see the issue as being whether the truth of the religious propositions best explains the experiences. If so, religious disagreement can be seen as similar to other disagreements stemming from differences over what best explains some phenomena. There can be competing views about this, just as there can be competing views about many other matters, including cosmology and issues at the limits of science.[18] My goal here is not to resolve the question of how to resolve disagreements of this sort, though I will acknowledge that my inclination toward a conciliatory approach does have its appeal in many of these cases. Suspending judgment is an option. In any case, this puts religious disagreement in a category with other familiar disagreements. If correct, it supports my initial inclination to say that religious disagreement is not entirely distinctive.

[18] See Smeenk and Ellis 2017.

6. Conclusion

I've claimed that religious disagreement is not unlike other disagreements in that, to the extent that religious belief is based on evidence, the rational response to religious disagreement is to take on board whatever new evidence it presents. If religious experience is a source of evidence for religious belief, then the fact that religious experience is private and perhaps incommunicable in a way that other experiences are not introduces an element that distinguishes those religious disagreements deriving from such experience from other familiar disagreements. Possibly these irremediably different bodies of evidence may affect what's justified for different people in a way that diminishes the pull toward conciliation. However, it may be best to see core religious disagreement as similar to other theoretical disagreements in which the best way to interpret the data, in this case, religious experience, is in dispute. In that case, the answer to the question with which I started is that religious disagreement is not distinctive, but rather is much like other disagreements in which issues of best explanations come to the fore.

I'll conclude with a brief comment on the fact that religious experience is of such significance to so many people. When a person finds an issue, or a belief about an issue, particularly significant, it may be more difficult to acknowledge the evidential import of a differing view. But this is a psychological fact about reactions, not a fact about the evidential significance of the disagreement. The related epistemological idea might be that given the significance of religious belief (or disbelief) it is wise to give people latitude: if it's so important, it is acceptable for them to believe as they wish. In my view, these kinds of considerations might provide good reason to treat those who disagree with respect and consideration. It is useful to be careful about your choice of arguments to engage in. But these considerations are not about the epistemic significance of the evidence. And, further, the claim that it is epistemically permissible to believe as one wishes in these cases is at odds with another conclusion one might draw from the that fact beliefs are particularly important to people, namely that more, rather than less, is needed for rational belief or knowledge as the importance of a proposition goes up.[19]

---

[19] For a brief discussion of this, see Ichikawa and Steup 2018.

References

Conee, Earl and Richard Feldman. 2004. *Evidentialism: Essays in Epistemology*. Oxford: Clarendon Press.

De Cruz, Helen. 2017. "Religious Disagreement: An Empirical Study among Academic Philosophers." *Episteme* 14: 71–87.

Feldman, Richard. 2009. "Evidentialism, Higher-Order Evidence, and Disagreement." *Episteme* 6: 294–312.

Feldman, Richard. 2007. "Reasonable Religious Disagreements." In Louise Antony (ed.), *Philosophers without Gods*, 194–214. Oxford: Oxford University Press.

Frances, Bryan. 2016. "The Irrationality of Religious Belief." *Think* 15: 15–33.

Hitchens, Christopher. 2007. *God Is Not Great: How Religion Poisons Everything*. New York: Twelve/Hachette Book Group.

Ichikawa, Jonathan Jenkins and Matthias Steup. 2018. "The Analysis of Knowledge." *The Stanford Encyclopedia of Philosophy* (Summer 2018 Edition), Edward N. Zalta (ed.), https://plato.stanford.edu/archives/sum2018/entries/knowledge-analysis/

Pittard, John. 2015. "Religious Disagreement." *Internet Encyclopedia of Philosophy* ISSN 2161–0002, http://www.iep.utm.edu/rel–disa/

Presser, Stanley and Mark Chaves. 2007. "Is Religious Service Attendance Declining?" *Journal for the Scientific Study of Religion* 46: 417–423.

Smeenk, Christopher and George Ellis. 2017. "Philosophy of Cosmology." *The Stanford Encyclopedia of Philosophy* (Winter 2017 Edition), Edward N. Zalta (ed.), https://plato.stanford.edu/archives/win2017/entries/cosmology

Whiting, Daniel. 2020. "Higher-Order Evidence." *Analysis* 80: 789–807.

6

Transformative Experience and the Problem of Religious Disagreement

Joshua Blanchard and L.A. Paul

1. Introduction

Peer disagreement presents religious believers, agnostics, and skeptics alike with an epistemological problem: How can confidence in any religious claims (including their negations) be epistemically justified? There seem to be rational, well-informed adherents among a variety of mutually incompatible religious and non-religious perspectives, and so the problem of disagreement arises acutely in the religious domain. In this paper, we show that the transformative nature of religious experience and identity poses more than just this traditional epistemic problem of conflicting religious beliefs. In encountering one another, believers, agnostics, and skeptics confront not just different beliefs, but different *ways of being a person*.

To transition between religious belief and skepticism is not just to adopt a different set of beliefs, but to transform into a different version of oneself. We argue that the transformative nature of religious identity intensifies the problem of pluralism by adding a new dimension to religious disagreement, for there are principled reasons to think we can lack epistemic and affective access to our potential religious, agnostic, or skeptical selves. Yet, access to these selves seems to be required for the purposes of decision-making that is to be both rational and authentic. Finally, we reflect on the relationship between the transformative problem of religious disagreement and what it shows about the epistemic status of religious conversion and deconversion, in which one disagrees with one's own (transformed) self.

In §2, we briefly characterize the problem of religious disagreement in its general form, which we view as a species of the more general problem of peer disagreement. In §3, we introduce the phenomenon of distinctly transformative experience, with an eye toward discussing the special case of religious experience. In §4, we describe at length how the transformative nature of

Joshua Blanchard and L.A. Paul, *Transformative Experience and the Problem of Religious Disagreement* In: *Religious Disagreement and Pluralism*. Edited by: Matthew A. Benton and Jonathan L. Kvanvig, Oxford University Press.
© Joshua Blanchard and L.A. Paul 2021. DOI: 10.1093/oso/9780198849865.003.0006

religious experience seriously exacerbates and complicates the problem of religious disagreement. In §5, we pose a newer problem of religious disagreement that arises especially in cases of religious conversion or deconversion: disagreement with one's own potential (or past) self. Finally, in §6 we offer concluding remarks.

2. The Problem of Religious Disagreement

The problem of religious disagreement is a species of the more general problem of peer disagreement. The problem of peer disagreement, in its basic form, is the problem someone faces when she believes that p and knowingly encounters someone who believes that $\sim p$ from a context of approximately equivalent reasoning ability, evidence, and position to know whether p.

The problem of disagreement is especially acute for religious believers. There is a dizzying variety of mutually inconsistent religious beliefs in the world, much of it undergirded by centuries, sometimes millennia, of deep thought alongside profound individual and collective experiences. The fact of religious pluralism means that, for virtually any religious belief that p, anyone who believes that p will face the problem of peer disagreement.

Concomitant with the fact of pluralism, intrareligious epistemology has a tendency to exacerbate the problem of disagreement even further for religious believers. For example, unlike publicly available and easily repeatable experiences that might ground scientific or other ordinary belief, the religious experiences that partly undergird religious belief can be radically private in nature, recalcitrant to repetition and even, in some cases, to linguistic expression. Moreover, the major religious traditions themselves are partly constituted by epistemological frameworks that sometimes require parochial sources of knowledge, e.g., particular scriptures, traditions, teachers, or even *sui generis* cognitive faculties. This exacerbates the problem because when two religious believers disagree, their disagreement may be epistemically incommensurate within any single epistemological framework. Contrast this with two people who disagree about where the closest coffee shop is located, or who come up with different answers to a mathematical problem: especially if they are epistemic peers, they are likely to agree about the basic epistemological framework for figuring such matters out. Not so for religious belief.

Like its parent problem, the problem of religious disagreement is plausibly theorized as a problem of higher-order evidence, that is, evidence about the link between one's beliefs and the first-order evidence or other *desiderata* of epistemic standing that undergird it. The fact that *S* disagrees with an epistemic peer, *S**, provides *S* with higher-order evidence *about the link between S's belief that* p *and the evidence or S's epistemic standing*, not necessarily evidence about *p* itself. Through disagreement, *S* acquires defeasible evidence that there is something faulty in *S*'s evidence, reasoning, epistemic character, position, or some other aspect of *S*'s epistemic situation.

We do not reject any of this standard characterization of the problem of religious disagreement, as far as it goes. We argue that reflecting on the nature of transformative experience shows that religious disagreement is not *only* a matter of disagreement about particular religious propositions, or *only* a matter of disagreement with others. After introducing the concept of transformative experience, we address those issues in turn.

3. Transformative Experience

The standard, intuitive model of rational decision-making assesses the rationality of decisions with reference to an agent's assessment of the probabilities and subjective values of the outcomes of her various options, typically in light of the assessments and preferences that she has at the point of decision. This model works well for lots of decisions that we make. Suppose you're going to the movies and deciding whether to see the historical drama or the space opera. You've seen and liked plenty in both genres, and you already know that you're more in the mood for sci-fi. But you check online and see that the drama has considerably better reviews. The decision involves a potential gamble, but it's not a mystery *how* you go about making it—you're well enough informed about the probabilities and values to rationally make and act on a judgment.

But it turns out that many other decisions that we make, including everyday decisions, involve deciding whether to have what Paul (2014) calls a *transformative experience*. Suppose you're applying for graduate school and deciding whether to pursue philosophy or theology. You've studied and enjoyed both subjects, and you've recently been on a philosophy kick. Like picking movie genres, this decision also involves a gamble, but it's of a structurally different sort. You're *not* necessarily well enough informed about the probabilities and values to rationally make and act on a judgment, at least not in the standard way. The decision point involves a gamble, but not just a gamble on whether you'll enjoy yourself. You're gambling *on the very self that you'll become.* Pursuing philosophy may transform you in a way that pursuing theology wouldn't—and *vice versa.* You have a rough idea of what it will be like, what and who *you* will be like, coming out of the movie theater, but this is not so for the divergent paths of graduate study in philosophy or theology.

Transformative experiences are those experiences that change the agent in certain deep ways—especially, experiences the very having of which modify an agent's future beliefs and valuations in a manner inaccessible to her current cognitive makeup. The nature of transformative experience seems to *preclude* authentic rational decision-making—at least, on the standard model. This is partly because, in order to assess the subjective values of the experiential outcomes of one's options for oneself, one must in a sense project oneself into the future experiences and determine what their value is. That is to say, one must be able to have a certain kind of empathy with one's (potential) future self. But if the candidate experiences will themselves transform one's evaluative stance (Paul calls these *personally transformative experiences*), one loses the ability to make these valuations—at least in any direct way. Vis-à-vis rational decision-making, you don't know what a transformative experience is like until it's too late. The same goes for beliefs and other epistemic attitudes. Epistemically transformative experiences teach you something new, something that you could not know or see except through having the experience. So, if you want to gain this new information, and you aren't willing to rely solely on the testimony of others, you have to, in a sense, take a leap in the dark.

Because our discussion focuses on the largely *sui generis* phenomenon of religious experiences, it is worth re-emphasizing that our lives are chock-full of transformative decision-making. Everything from deciding whether to have children, to planning for end of life care, to embarking on gender transition, to thinking about illness or choosing medical treatments, involves making choices that may result in personal and epistemic transformation. Transformative experience is, then, quite ordinary.[1]

4. Having Religious Beliefs and Being a Religious Person

There is a thin, purely doxastic aspect of being religious that poses the problem of religious disagreement but does not necessarily implicate the additional

---

[1] On having children, see Paul (2015). On end-of-life care and issues having to do with dying, see Thompson (2020). On gender transition, see McKinnon (2015). On illness, see Carel, Kidd, and Pettigrew (2016). On medical research, see Paul and Healy (2018).

problems of transformative experience. For example, someone might transition from bare atheism to bare theism in such a way that has little to no implication for their other beliefs, practices, evaluative assessments, and so on.[2] Ordinary religious belief, however, is not like this. Religion is not an exclusively epistemic phenomenon, but in its major forms implicates the whole of a person's life. To be a religious person is not just to have some stereotypically religious beliefs, but to adopt a *way of being in (and seeing) the world.*

In the context of considering religion in the real world, asking the question "What should I believe?" is really part of asking the question, "Who shall I become?" Becoming religious or irreligious is becoming a different kind of person, a person with a radically different set of lived experiences, values, and beliefs. The distinctive nature of religious transformation means that peer disagreement is not just a matter of conflicting belief, but of conflicting ways of being a person. The standard examples in the literature on peer disagreement, including examples having to do with mere religious beliefs, are not adequate to capture the full force and scope of this conflict.[3]

To appreciate the complexity of religious disagreement in the context of possible transformative experience, it's useful to consider an example of a confrontation between a skeptic and a religious believer. Although what follows is certainly not the only kind of confrontation there might be between believer and skeptic, we think it is sufficiently representative to serve our discussion.[4]

First, consider the believer. The believer exults in the rich satisfaction of his faith, in the communal life, traditions, and revelations which attend the experience of opening his mind to God. His belief in God, we can assume, is not arrived at by mere rational deliberation. Rather, his faith is a matter of a total and all-encompassing re-orientation of his life.[5] For the believer, Pascal's description of God's relationship to believers strongly resonates:

[H]e is a God who fills the soul and heart of those whom he possesses; he is a God who makes them inwardly aware of their wretchedness and his infinite

---

[2] Antony Flew (2007)'s transition from atheism to mere deism is a possible example. See also Oppenheimer (2007).

[3] For a different and important perspective on a puzzle raised by transformative experience for religious disagreement, see De Cruz (2018). De Cruz argues that the transformative nature of conversion makes it difficult to tell whether someone you regard as a peer should still be so regarded by you after they (de)convert. Her central question is whether and how transformative conversion changes the evidential value of what would otherwise be peer disagreement.

[4] For an extended discussion of the material in this section, see Paul (forthcoming).

[5] For an extended discussion from the Christian perspective that we find highly congenial, see Abraham (2006).

mercy; who unites himself to the depths of their soul; who fills their soul with humility, joy, confidence, love; who makes them incapable of any other end but himself.   (Pascal 2005: S690, 227–228)

Moreover, the believer finds within himself no ability to conceive of relationship with God as anything but good. In the words of Marilyn Adams, "intimate relation to [divine goodness] is...incommensurately good for created persons."[6]

Now consider the skeptic. The skeptic has no such experience of God and desires no such relationship. He sees no compelling physical evidence for the existence of God, and reasons that, if there were a God, there'd be some sort of compelling evidence of his existence.[7] Moreover, the godless perspective on life does not depress him. In fact, the skeptic finds that his lack of belief in God (and, in particular, an afterlife) imbues the world with a distinctive value, a kind of preciousness that it would not otherwise have. As rationally sensitive people, both the believer and the skeptic feel the need to confront their disagreement head-on; they recognize that it won't do simply to retreat into their respective first-order beliefs. The skeptic concludes that belief in God probably amounts to indulging in a psychological need for comfort. He doesn't begrudge the believer for having such a need, but he has no desire to engage in what he takes to be an exercise in self-deception. From his perspective, he is the clearer thinker: in the cold hard light of day, he reasons to the most likely conclusion.

The believer, when confronted with the reasoning of the skeptic, argues that the skeptic has jumped the epistemic gun: in order to be properly receptive to the evidence, one must first be open to detecting it. To borrow the terminology of Paul Moser, the skeptic must be properly "attuned" to the kind of "purposively available evidence" that God would provide, that is to say, evidence available only to those with the kind of attitudes and character that are conducive to the sort of relationship with created persons that God would want.[8] To properly assess the case for and against belief, the skeptic should not only open his mind to the metaphysical possibility of divine creation, but he must additionally develop an openness to the possibility of total, unmitigated submission to the will of another—God. While this all surely involves rational inquiry, it also involves religious practice and radical transformation of

---

[6] Adams (1999, 26 and 82–83).
[7] J.L. Schellenberg has developed this intuitive thought in a variety of creative ways. For an up-to-date treatment, see Schellenberg (2015).
[8] Moser (2008).

character. Only under these conditions can he expect to detect evidence that would be relevant to his assessment, should there be any.

But the skeptic may reasonably refuse. Why? It may seem that refusal to be open to the perspective of the other side, refusal to fully participate in the activities the believer finds significant, smacks of intolerance and irrationality. If the skeptic is truly interested in unbiased assessment of both sides of the question, how can he refuse to engage in this way? In our example confrontation, isn't it the skeptic who is really engaging in an act of self-deception, a case study of closed-mindedness?

Not necessarily. Both the pleas of the believer and the resistance of the skeptic suggest that their dispute has additional structure beyond mere epistemic disagreement.

Notice that the religious experience of conversion is just the sort of transformative experience that can radically revise both one's epistemic perspective and personal commitments. In his classic study of religious experience, William James describes cases of instantaneous conversion as events in which "often amid tremendous emotional excitement or perturbation of the senses, a complete division is established in the twinkling of an eye between the old life and the new."[9] Deciding to potentially undergo such an experience is to make a decision of tremendous personal consequence.[10] As James writes,

> It makes a great difference to a man whether one set of his ideas, or another, be the centre of his energy; and it makes a great difference, as regards any set of ideas which he may possess, whether they become central or remain peripheral in him. To say that a man is "converted" means, in these terms, that religious ideas, previously peripheral in his consciousness, now take a central place, and that religious aims form the habitual centre of his energy.[11]

So, if having a religious experience is transformative, then issues concerning alien perspectives and preferences arise. In this context, we can understand the skeptic's resistance as involving aversion to becoming a certain kind of possible self. Right now, of course, he is sure he is right—he does not believe God exists, and he does not think he *should* (in the epistemic sense) believe that God exists.

---

[9] James (2004, Lecture 10, p. 162).
[10] See De Cruz (2018)'s important qualification that transformative conversions need not be instantaneous, but can be (and, as empirical research suggests, usually are) gradual (267–8).
[11] James (2004, Lecture 9, p. 147).

But there is more than that. He fears that, if he truly imagined or engaged with the perspective of the believer—perhaps going so far as to experimentally engage in religious practice and open his mind up to total submission to God—it might change not just his beliefs, but his character and values in a way that, from his current perspective, he cannot sanction. He is not quite afraid, in the first instance, that he'll simply gain new evidence that, given his current preferences and perspective, will change his assessment of the situation; on the contrary, he's happy to read some natural theology here and there. Rather, he is afraid that having a religious experience will corrupt his intellectual capacities and wider cognitive life somehow. That is, he is afraid that having a religious experience will transform him both epistemically and personally. It will transform him in a way that will make him psychologically alien to his current self—and only *then* will he (that is, his alien self) find what seems to be evidence for God. Of course, *that* potential self won't have any problem with this, but that's precisely part of what is so disturbing by the skeptic's present lights.

Now, what sort of experience is involved here from the point of view of the believer? The believer takes it to be the spiritual experience of recognizing the divine, mediated by a distinctive cognitive faculty, perhaps what John Calvin famously defended as the *sensus divinitatis*. The *sensus divinitatis*, or the faculty that tends to produce belief in God in the right circumstances, involves one's capacity to know God. It has a cognitive, quasi-perceptual component, and when exercised, endows one with a grasp or understanding of God's divine majesty.

Alvin Plantinga, following both Calvin and Jonathan Edwards, describes sensing the divine as analogous to experiencing the world in other sensory ways, such as tasting honey or seeing red for the first time. But religious experience, unlike these examples, is not merely epistemic. Like Pascal, Moser, and James, Plantinga understands such experiences as involving a reorientation of the whole person. He writes, "Conversion . . . is fundamentally a turning of the will, a healing of the disorder of affection that afflicts us. It is a turning away from love of self, from thinking of oneself as the chief being of the universe, to love of God."[12]

On this account, the exercise of the *sensus divinitatis* involves experiencing the moral and authoritative qualities of God in a way that necessitates change in the subject of the experience. Once you have the experience, you very naturally and easily are moved to faith. You naturally reflect and develop a

[12] Plantinga (2000, 311).

belief in God *via* this very reflection—it's not hypnosis or like being drugged. On a picture where manifesting one's capacity to engage with the divine leads one noninferentially and naturally to believe in and wholly submit to God, we can interpret the resistance of the skeptic as a resistance to any future that involves the real possibility of becoming someone who is not currently a *candidate self* for him.[13]

So, it's not mere fear of epistemic change that keeps the skeptic from taking belief seriously as an option. Rather, it's fear of losing one's connection to one's past selves, and of becoming a future self who is alien to one's current self.

These reflections give us a better model for what is going on in the disagreement between the skeptic and the believer. The skeptic isn't merely stubbornly defending the *status quo*, and he isn't merely resisting a change in perspective. Instead, the skeptic is confronted with the argument that to truly and fairly assess the value of believing in God, he should open his mind and allow himself to potentially transform into a radically alien self.

Mere descriptions of this experience fall short, of course, just as mere descriptions—for the uninitiated—of what it is like to see red or what it is like to taste honey, fall short. The skeptic must have the experience itself in order to understand and fully grasp the divine.

This poses a familiar problem, cast in a new light. The trouble is that, *if* the skeptic is deliberating over whether to allow himself to have the experience, he cannot cognitively model how he will respond to the experience before he has it. He simply has to have the experience to know what it is like and how he will respond. In the case of religious disagreement over theistic faith, the issue of whether or not to become a religious person is inextricably linked to the issue of whether or not to believe in God. Suppose the skeptic wants to do every-thing he can to find out whether God exists, but *also* wants to preserve an authentic, recognizable self in the course of doing so. He may be incapable of doing both of these things.

This means that the skeptic must decide whether to allow himself to have the experience of sensing the divine without knowing, in the most salient respect, what to expect, and potentially without being able to determine whether his subsequent experiences are veridical.

That is to say, if he opens his mind so that he can experience God, he risks losing (his current self's) control of his values, preferences, and beliefs, and

---

[13] By "candidate self," we mean something different from what William James calls a *live option*. Even a self that is a live option may nevertheless not be a "candidate self" for you, in the event that the self's beliefs and values would be fundamentally alien to those you currently hold.

becoming someone who is psychologically alien to him now—whether or not God really exists. In particular, he risks becoming someone who thinks very differently about the fundamental nature of the world and who evaluates experience very differently from how he does now, and he finds such a perspective and having such a value structure to be cognitively alien to who he presently is.

So, the skeptic risks losing permanent control of his beliefs and preferences in a way that entails he would be alienated from the future self that would result from the change. And this is why the skeptic refuses to entertain the perspective of the believer or to explore the possibility of awakening the *sensus divinitatis* in himself.

The worry, of course, isn't just one for the skeptic. We've spent our time developing the case for the skeptic, but the same goes, *mutatis mutandis*, for the believer, especially one who is deeply and authentically repulsed by the forlorn existence of the skeptic. From the believer's point of view, it may be that only "the fool says in his heart, 'There is no God.'"[14] From his current standpoint, he may think that non-belief is the result of "sin and its cognitive consequences," a *malfunction* of the *sensus divinitatis* due to various moral failings, especially a kind of arrogance that resists submission to God.[15]

With this, we can see how confronting religious disagreement in a rational manner implicates the problems of exploring religious transformative experience and the problematic metaphysics of the self. In the case of religious disagreement, one cannot escape problems of endogenous belief change and self-deception. This discussion of religious disagreement also brings out deep ways in which empathy for our other selves connects to ideas about how we understand, control, and form ourselves, and to central issues involving living in a religiously pluralistic society.

5. Transformative Self-Disagreement

Religious pluralism raises the problem of disagreement in a straightforward and particularly acute way, and we have shown how problems of transformative experience complicate how one responds to it. But by reflecting on the nature of transformative experience and its relationship to religious belief and personhood, we can see that religious conversion raises an additional,

---

[14] Psalm 14:1.   [15] See Plantinga (2000, chapter 7).

distinct problem of disagreement, namely, *disagreement with one's former or possible selves.*[16]

To see the problem clearly, we need to carefully distinguish between two kinds of conversion. Imagine someone raised in a secular environment who has never encountered the arguments of natural theology. Such a person may encounter these arguments, convert, and rightly judge that their conversion involved an advancement of knowledge (at the very least, knowledge of more reasons in favor of theistic belief). So described, this is not the kind of conversion that raises a problem of *peer* disagreement with oneself, because the pre- and post-conversion selves are decidedly not epistemic peers, even by their own lights. The *transformative conversion* at issue in this paper is of a different kind. The convert may not have learned new, objective information, but instead come to see the world—that is, the same old facts—in a new light. In such a case, the convert may not find it possible to imaginatively inhabit her own old perspective, and the potential convert may not find it possible to imaginatively inhabit her possible new perspective. Compare: after deciding to see the sci-fi movie, you can easily access what it was like before you saw it. And you could imagine either liking or hating the movie ahead of time. But after, say, having a child, it's remarkably difficult to imaginatively re-inhabit what your world was like before, and you can't (accurately) imaginatively inhabit the new world with your child before you have them.

Intuitively—but, we think, mistakenly—religious (de-)conversion even of this second, transformative kind is thought to be either an advancement or a regression. Often this depends on whether one is taking an internal or external point of view. For example, a convert to a religious or irreligious perspective may claim that their newfound identity reflects an advancement of their knowledge of the world or an improvement in their character. Likewise, a detractor (say, someone dismayed that their family member has become religious) may think the opposite, that the convert has in fact become more ignorant or confused about the world.[17]

---

[16] Helen De Cruz (2018) introduces and addresses the problem of how a convert should see her former self vis-à-vis epistemic peerhood (268–270). De Cruz sees this problem as one about *irrelevant influences*: the convert has reason to worry that her new beliefs are the result of causes that are not sensitive to the truth. De Cruz marshals sociological and other evidence to argue that it is not obvious that post-conversion beliefs have a comparative advantage here. "The factors underlying conversion cases do not seem to be more epistemically vicious or benign than factors underlying original religious belief formation (for example, parental religious affiliation)" (170).

[17] For an extended discussion of how one ought to react to the conversion of a peer, see De Cruz (2018, 271–275).

This is all regarding how conversion looks from the inside versus the outside, where the subject of the conversion is understood to be necessarily "on the inside." The standard assumption is that, from the inside, conversion necessarily looks like an advancement. But if we assume that a religious convert has undergone a *transformative conversion*, then the convert in fact may face a problem *even from within her own perspective*, because in the deepest metaphysical sense she is *not* "on the inside" with respect to *both* her former and newly converted selves.[18] Given the epistemically and personally transformative nature of such a conversion, the convert may not be in a position to evaluate the conversion from an epistemically or personally neutral perspective.

If the convert is aware of the problems of transformative experience, then she can know what her situation is—*vis-à-vis* transformation—and hence she can know that she is not in a position to know that she has advanced rather than regressed. Because she is not in a position to neutrally distinguish between her former and current epistemic positions, her relationship to her former self is structurally identical to the relationship of epistemic peer disagreement. To be sure, all that stands between her post- and pre-conversion self may be the conversion experience or process itself, but this is precisely the divide across which she cannot evaluate her epistemic and personal transformation.

This means that religious believers and skeptics who arrive at their positions through (de)conversion are permanently faced with a problem of peer disagreement even beyond the usual problem of disagreement posed by pluralism. We call this the problem of *transformative self-disagreement*.

How should the convert respond to this problem? We think that the best responses will follow whatever are the best responses to peer disagreement generally. For example, if you're a dogmatist who thinks that it is reasonable to stand one's ground in the face of peer disagreement, then you should think this in the case of transformative self-disagreement as well. According to this view, it is rationally permissible to fully endorse one's post-conversion beliefs, even though one does not have independent reason to think that one is in a better

---

[18] De Cruz (2018) argues that, even in cases of transformative conversion, the convert has one additional piece of evidence, namely the knowledge "that her religious beliefs can be changed" (270). Our response to this is twofold. First, this doesn't address the *forward-looking* aspect of the problem that we present, the problem of disagreeing with one's *potential* or *future* self. But more to the point, we don't see why a person cannot, pre-conversion, know that her beliefs can change. After all, it's precisely a change in beliefs (and way of being a person) that a would-be convert is justifiably worried about on our account. Our story about the believer and the skeptic in the previous section plausibly presupposes that both individuals know that they *can* change.

position to know than before. If you're a conciliationist who think that it is reasonable to "split the difference" or otherwise lower your credence in your own beliefs in the face of peer disagreement, then you should think this in the case of transformative self-disagreement as well. According to this view, it is rationally obligatory to lower one's credence in light of the fact that one has no independent reason to think that one is in a better position to know than before.

Our understanding of the problem of religious disagreement with oneself, especially as it relates to the conciliationist response to that problem, is connected to a problem developed by Daniel Garber for the epistemology implicit in Pascal's famous wager argument. According to Garber, "wagering" for God (by engaging in religious practice as if God exists) is a kind of inquiry that may reveal God's existence to the wagerer *only if God exists*, but may nevertheless produce belief in God *even if God does not exist*. One incurs a certain epistemic risk by engaging in religious practice, according to Garber. One the one hand, if Pascal is right, there is a kind of synchronic guarantee: Wagering that God exists makes it very likely that one will eventually come to (synchronically, internally) rationally believe that God exists, whether or not God exists. This is because, by one's *post-wagering* lights, it will be rational to believe in God. But one also takes a diachronic risk: The process by which one comes to eventually (synchronically, internally) rationally believe that God exists is (diachronically, externally) rational only if, in fact, God exists. But you can't evaluate whether or not God exists other than by your current lights, which wagering itself transforms. Hence, if God does *not* exist, it seems that wagering will land one in an epistemically bad position; not only will one have a false belief, but one will be diachronically irrational. But worst of all, the fact that one is diachronically irrational will be *rationally inaccessible* to one after wagering, because it will be indistinguishable from one's position in the event that God does exist.

Garber's own novel question is how we should believe and act *after* wagering, given that we are aware of both our synchronic and diachronic positions. With respect to belief, Garber thinks that the post-wagering believer should continue to believe, though she should continually review her evidence in light of the live possibility that she is "in the grips of a cognitive illusion."[19] With respect to action, Garber thinks that—in light of the diachronic risk undertaken—the believer should be extremely cautious in her employment of post-conversion assumptions, at least when the stakes are high. Understood

---

[19] Garber (2009, 53).

as a way of responding to transformative self-disagreement, we think that this response is consonant with conciliationist positions in the literature on peer disagreement. The transformed believer (or skeptic) does not merely face the possibility of illusion. She faces that possibility, but she faces it partly because she faces disagreement with her own former self, who she has no grounds for assessing as anything other than an epistemic peer.

6. Conclusion

Although the problem of religious disagreement is a species of the general problem of peer disagreement, it brings with it special problems involving transformative experience. We have highlighted two such special problems. The first problem is that religious disagreement does not consist in a mere conflict of beliefs, it consists in a conflict between different ways of being a person. This fact alone makes it intelligible and rational that one might resist full engagement with one's peers who disagree on religious matters. The second problem is that religious disagreement does not only exist between oneself and one's peers—it exists in a strong form across one's own selves. This suggests that the problem is even more serious than has been recognized, for unlike one's external peers, one cannot escape the specter of one's former, pre-transformed self.

References

Abraham, William J. 2006. *Crossing the Threshold of Divine Revelation*. Grand Rapids: Eerdmans.

Adams, Marilyn McCord. 1999. *Horrendous Evils and the Goodness of God*. Ithaca, NY: Cornell University Press.

Carel, Havi, Ian Kidd, and Richard Pettigrew. 2016. "Illness as Transformative Experience." *Lancet* 388: 1152–1153.

De Cruz, Helen. 2018. "Religious Conversion, Transformative Experience, and Disagreement." *Philosophia Christi* 20: 265–275.

Flew, Anthony. 2007. *There is a God*. New York: Harper Collins.

Garber, Daniel. 2009. *What Happens After Pascal's Wager: Living Faith and Rational Belief*. Milwaukee: Marquette University Press.

James, William. 2004 (1902). *The Varieties of Religious Experience*. New York: Touchstone.

McKinnon, Rachel. 2015. "Trans*formative Experiences." *Res Philosophica* 92: 419–440.

Moser, Paul K. 2008. *The Elusive God: Reorienting Religious Epistemology.* Cambridge: Cambridge University Press.

Oppenheimer, Mark. 2007. "The Turning of an Atheist." In *The New York Times Magazine*, https://www.nytimes.com/2007/11/04/magazine/04Flew-t.html

Pascal, Blaise. 2005. *Pensées.* Roger Ariew (trans.). Indianapolis: Hackett.

Paul, L.A. 2015. "What You Can't Expect When You're Expecting." *Res Philosophica* 92: 1–23.

Paul, L.A. 2014. *Transformative Experience.* Oxford: Oxford University Press.

Paul, L.A. and Kieran Healy. 2018. "Transformative Treatments," *Noûs* 52: 320–335.

Paul, L.A. Forthcoming 2022. "The Paradox of Empathy." *Episteme.*

Plantinga, Alvin. 2000. *Warranted Christian Belief.* Oxford: Oxford University Press.

Schellenberg, J.L. 2015. *The Hiddenness Argument: Philosophy's New Challenge to Belief in God.* Oxford: Oxford University Press.

Thompson, Evan. 2020. "Death: The Ultimate Transformative Experience." In Enoch Lambert and John Schwenkler (eds.), *Becoming Someone New: Essays on Transformative Experience, Choice, and Change*, 269–288. Oxford: Oxford University Press.

7

The Apologist's Dilemma

Nathan L. King

Suppose one of you wants to build a tower. Won't you first sit down and estimate the cost to see if you have enough money to complete it? For if you lay the foundation and are not able to finish it, everyone who sees it will ridicule you, saying, 'This person began to build and wasn't able to finish.'

(Luke 14: 28–30 NIV)

Consider the religious apologist. Such a person seeks to provide a rational defense of her religious beliefs. She tries to show that these beliefs are true, and that they are reasonable to hold. As she does this, she comes into contact with people who disagree with her views, and who reject her arguments. In these enlightened times, she must approach this situation with a keen awareness of religious diversity and disagreement—and thus with epistemic humility. But in an intellectual setting that calls for humility, the apologist faces a dilemma about the rational force she takes her arguments to have.

The problem arises in the following way. In the typical case, the apologist will take her arguments to rationally justify her own beliefs. She will think that these arguments suffice to render these beliefs rational, perhaps even in the face of disagreement. Here is a related question:

> Should the apologist think that those who disagree with her—even after hearing her arguments—are rational in denying her beliefs, or in suspending judgment about them?

In this paper, I will suggest that both affirmative and negative answers to these questions come with potential costs—thus, the dilemma. After explaining this dilemma, I will count the costs of taking either path. The first path, what I'll call *the way of the sledgehammer*, subjects the apologist to the charge of arrogance, and suggests a commitment to the implausible claim that she has "knockdown arguments" for her views. The second path—what I'll call *the*

Nathan L. King, *The Apologist's Dilemma* In: *Religious Disagreement and Pluralism*. Edited by: Matthew A. Benton and Jonathan L. Kvanvig, Oxford University Press. © Nathan L. King 2021. DOI: 10.1093/oso/9780198849865.003.0007

permissive path—threatens to make the apologist's enterprise incoherent, and to undermine the very beliefs for which she argues. It also threatens to worsen the problem of divine hiddenness and, for some apologists, the problem of Hell. I will explore various ways in which the costs of traveling each path may be reduced. My main aim, however, is to show that the apologist cannot sensibly isolate her views about religious disagreement and apologetic strategy from her views about other issues in epistemology and the philosophy of religion.

1. The Dilemma Stated

The dilemma addressed in this paper is closely related to recent work on the epistemology of disagreement. Such work has largely focused on questions like these:

- Can it be rational for someone to retain her beliefs in the face of disagreement with someone who is as at least roughly as reliable and well informed as she is?
- When she acknowledges this qualified dissenter as such, can she rationally retain her own beliefs?

The answers to these questions remain under dispute, despite scores of papers published on the epistemology disagreement over the past fifteen years.[1] For present purposes, we'll embrace affirmative answers, at least for the sake of argument. We'll do this in order to address the question posed in our introduction. For our question occurs downstream of affirmative answers to the questions about disagreement posed just above. Granted that it's rational to retain one's own belief in the face of disagreement, is it also rational to think that an informed dissenter's incompatible attitude is rational?[2] More

---

[1] For important early contributions to this literature see Kelly 2005, Christensen 2007, and Feldman 2006 and 2007. See also the essays in Feldman and Warfield 2010, Machuca 2013, and Christensen and Lackey 2013. For an introduction to the epistemology of religious disagreement, see King and Kelly 2017. Note that I do not here assume that religious disagreements are commonly *peer* disagreements— disagreements between *equally* reliable persons who share the *same* body of evidence. I strongly suspect that they are not, because I suspect that genuine peerhood, and acknowledged peerhood, are quite rare (see King 2012 and 2016).

[2] Richard Feldman raised this question early in the epistemology of disagreement literature. See Feldman 2007. This question has not yet received the same degree of attention as questions about the rational status of retaining one's own beliefs in the face of disagreement.

specifically, is this rational *for the religious apologist, after* she has shared her apologetic arguments with her dissenter?

We'll focus on the latter, more specific version of the question, for two reasons. First, the theme of this volume is not just disagreement in general, but religious disagreement, in particular. Second, as we will see, by virtue of her religious commitments, the religious apologist faces theoretical costs that do not accrue to thinkers engaged in disagreements about other topics.

One last stipulation. In what follows, we will understand the *religious apologist* to be a proponent of a theistic religion. Such an apologist affirms the existence of a God who is omnipotent, omniscient, wholly good, and the Creator of the world. Apologists for (for instance) Christianity, Islam, and Judaism count as religious apologists in this sense. Buddhists and other non-theists do not count as religious apologists in this sense, even if they are devoutly religious and argue rigorously for their views. (Exclusion of this sort demands explanation. The reason for our restriction is that the costs of embracing the idea that one's dissenter is rational in this dissent are different for the theistic apologist than they are for the non-theistic apologist. The theist faces problems that non-theists, including religious non-theists, need not face.)

So then, can the religious apologist sensibly think that those who do not believe in God, despite being aware of her arguments, are rational in their non-belief? We can get a rough and ready grasp of the problem by imagining the following dialogue:

APOLOGIST: [Gives several arguments for her views].... So that's my case for my belief in God. I think it shows that my beliefs are both true and rational.

DISSENTER: OK, but what do you think about the beliefs of people—like me—who have heard your arguments and don't find ourselves moved by them to convert to your view? Are we rational in our non-belief or not?

APOLOGIST: Interesting question. Why does my answer matter? I've already shown that my beliefs are true and rational. What else is there for me to do?

DISSENTER: Well, on the one hand, if you say "no"—if you say your dissenters are irrational in their non-belief once they've heard your arguments—then you seem arrogant and overbearing. You must think that you have knock-down arguments for your views, arguments so good that anyone who rejects them must be a fool. On the other hand, if you say "yes"—if you say that non-believers can be rational in their unbelief even *after* hearing your arguments—then why do *you* hold your views on the basis of those arguments? After all, by your own admission, it can be rational not to do so. And if you think *that*, what, in your view, could be the point in giving the arguments? Worse, if you say "yes," you're admitting that rational non-belief occurs—and that admission raises the problem of divine hiddenness. A wholly good and all-powerful God wouldn't allow non-culpable, much less *reasonable* non-belief. So, if you give the "permissive" answer to my question, you should end up an atheist. And even if you don't, you might end up believing in a God who is a real jerk—a God who punishes people for not believing in him when, by your own admission, they might be *rational* in not believing.

APOLOGIST: Um....

Hereafter, we will assume that the apologist's dissenter has heard and understood the apologist's arguments. We can state the dilemma more precisely like this:

1. Either the religious apologist thinks that her dissenter is rational in that dissent, or she thinks her dissenter is not rational in that dissent.

2. If the religious apologist thinks her dissenter is not rational in that dissent, then she expresses arrogance, and reveals her commitment to the implausible belief that she has knockdown arguments for her views.

3. If the religious apologist thinks that her dissenter is rational in that dissent, then she is hard-pressed to explain why her own religious beliefs are rational; in addition, she undermines the apologetic enterprise, she makes the problem of divine hiddenness worse, and she may reveal her commitment to unpalatable eschatological views.

Thus,

4. The religious apologist either expresses arrogance and reveals her commitment to the implausible belief that she has knockdown arguments for her views *or* she is hard-pressed to explain why her own views are rational, she undermines the apologetic enterprise, she makes the problem of divine hiddenness worse, and she may reveal her commitment to unpalatable eschatological views.

In short, if she doesn't admit that her dissenter can be rational, the apologist ceases to be humble. But if she admits that her dissenter can be rational, she ceases to be a real apologist for *her* position. Her commitment seems wishy-washy, and may even be self-defeating. Either way, the dilemma suggests that the prospects for humble apologetics are not good.

The dilemma is validly formulated. If its premises are true, then the religious apologist has bills to pay, whatever she thinks about the rational status of her dissenter's attitude. Of course, someone might want to split the horns of the dilemma. That is, one might note that the religious apologist could suspend judgment about the rational status of her dissenter's attitude, thereby denying (1). We will address to this possibility in section 4. There, we'll see that this position, too, comes with costs.

For now, let's consider the other two possibilities: thinking that the dissenter is irrational, and thinking that he is rational. That is, let's consider what can be said on behalf of (2) and (3). We'll consider objections to these premises and their supporting arguments in section 5.

2. Potential Costs of the "Sledgehammer" Response

Start with (2). In taking this path, the religious apologist thinks that, once her arguments have been heard and understood, anyone who dissents from her religious views (anyone who denies them or suspends judgment about them) is irrational. In this connection, Michael Murray describes a kind of apologetics that aims to

> show the unbeliever that they are rationally compelled to believe in the central features of the Christian view and that the failure to do leaves them *irrational* in this respect.... This is what we might call "sledgehammer apologetics." The sledgehammer apologist thinks that apologetic arguments deliver the intellectual equivalent of knockout punches by making it impossible for unbelievers to rationally continue in their unbelief.[3]

The sledgehammer apologist, in short, thinks that the arguments for her views are not only good, but that they are *so good* that they can be rejected only at the cost of irrationality.

Similarly, Kelly James Clark describes Aquinas's project in natural theology as follows:

> Aquinas self-consciously tried to use premises that all rational beings are obliged to accept, taking logical steps that are obvious, thereby *demonstrating*

---

[3] Murray 1999, 10–11. Murray does not himself endorse this variety of apologetics.

or *proving* the existence of God to nearly any sane person. His proofs would demonstrate that the unbeliever is rationally obliged to believe in God.[4]

Given Clark's description, Aquinas qualifies as a sledgehammer apologist. Arguably, so do many other thinkers, including Anselm, Descartes, and Leibniz.[5]

2.1 Knockdown Arguments: An Implausible Commitment?

Why might someone find sledgehammer apologetics too costly? One reason is that sledgehammer apologetics apparently require the apologist to think she has "knockdown" arguments for her views—arguments that, once heard and understood, render dissent irrational. Sledgehammer apologetics and knockdown arguments walk hand-in-hand—or maybe fist-to-fist. But many philosophers have given up on the idea of "knockdown" arguments. For instance, in assessing his own work, David Lewis remarks,

> The reader in search of knockdown arguments in favor of my theories will go away disappointed. Whether or not it would be nice to knock disagreeing philosophers down by sheer force of argument, it cannot be done. Philosophical theories are never refuted conclusively.[6]

Likewise, Peter van Inwagen:

> There are...no knockdown arguments in philosophy. There are no philosophical arguments that all qualified philosophers regard as compelling.[7]

Knockdown arguments, if there are any, offer conclusive[8] evidence for their conclusions—and every qualified philosopher discerns that the arguments do this. More precisely, knockdown arguments are such that every qualified

---

[4] Clark 1990, 4.

[5] Each of these thinkers argues for God's existence by appeal to premises that are supposed to be self-evident, or obvious to all rational persons. And each seeks to lead the hearer toward the theistic conclusion by way of valid inference from these self-evident premises. By virtue of seeking to prove God's existence in this way, these thinkers qualify as sledgehammer apologists. For discussion of their theistic arguments see Chignell and Pereboom 2015.

[6] Lewis 1983, x.   [7] Van Inwagen 2009, 105.

[8] Some authors speak in terms of "conclusive" evidence or reasons, while others speak of "decisive" reasons. I treat these terms as synonyms, for the purposes of this paper.

person who hears and understands them, and has no reason to doubt that she understands them, *should* believe their conclusions on the basis of their premises, which are themselves supported by very strong reasons. Not to do so would be irrational.[9] But, Lewis and van Inwagen suggest, there are no such arguments. And if there aren't, then there can be no sledgehammer apologetic arguments, or at least no philosophical ones.

Suppose this is right. While it might make us wary of sledgehammer apologetics, it would not explain *why* there are no knockdown arguments. One possible explanation—and a second reason to be wary of sledgehammer apologetics—concerns the underdetermination of theory by data. Michael Murray explains the relevance of underdetermination in the present context:

> [N]ew evidence which seems to count against a theory is instead *incorpo-rated into* the theory .... any given data set admits a large variety of explana-tions, and...no amount of data can decisively select for one theory or explanation over all of the competitors.... One lesson to be learned from this is just that there is no sledgehammer apologetics. There are no argu-ments for the truth of Christianity that force the atheist or non-Christian to their intellectual knees. The unbeliever can always backtrack and give up some other belief instead.[10]

Similarly, Kelly James Clark affirms,

> Of course, the argument from design does not *demonstrate* the existence of God. A whole host of hypotheses are equally compatible with the evidence, and the evidence does not rationally force one to accept one hypothesis over another. This is not to say that God did not create the world; it implies only that the propositional evidence for God's creating the world does not speak with one voice. The propositional evidence is ambiguous with respect to the competing hypotheses and should not be expected to persuade all rational creatures.[11]

---

[9] I owe this notion of a knockdown argument, as well as the quotations from Lewis and van Inwagen, to Nathan Ballantyne. See Ballantyne 2014; also Keller 2015. In the quotations from Lewis and van Inwagen, one can discern both descriptive and normative elements, corresponding to whether qualified hearers *would* or *should* be convinced by a given argument. The normative sense is the relevant one, for present purposes. Note also that those who take themselves to have knockdown arguments are not merely claiming that one should accept their conclusions on the basis of their premises *if* they accept those premises. (This would make any valid argument a knockdown argument, which is too strong.) They are saying that one should accept the premises as well, because these are supported by very strong reasons. Aquinas is a good example here.

[10] Murray 1999, 12–13.   [11] Clark 1990, 34.

And elsewhere:

> The thinking theist must recognize that a number of competing hypotheses are consistent with the evidence.[12]

There are two distinct points here. The first point is that that at most, the apologist's argument will reveal that the non-believer must give up *some* belief—that the apologist's premises are inconsistent with some claim the non-believer currently holds. However, this does not by itself show that the non-believer would be irrational if she did not come to believe in God. Granted she must give up something, it does not follow that atheism, or agnosticism, or some other attitude inconsistent with the apologist's conclusion, is the thing to jettison. The second point is that the evidential data, on which the apologist and the non-believer are agreed, is consistent with more than one hypothesis. So, one might think, it does not uniquely favor the apologist's conclusion. There are really two kinds of underdetermination here—what theorists call *holist* underdetermination and *contrastive* underdetermination, respectively.[13] Taken together, one might think, these two underdetermination arguments provide a powerful one-two punch against knockdown arguments—and thereby, against sledgehammer apologetics.

Here is a third challenge, one that highlights just how ambitious the sledgehammer approach can appear. Consider this claim, which the sledgehammer apologist endorses:

a. If the non-believer rejects my religious beliefs even after having heard my arguments for them, then he is irrational in so doing.

Notice that this claim is perfectly general. As stated, it applies to *anyone* who rejects the sledgehammer apologist's argument, irrespective of the non-believer's *reasons* for rejecting these arguments, and irrespective of the non-believer's other relevant evidence. Thus, by endorsing (a), the sledgehammer apologist must apparently endorse the following:

b. Irrespective of the content, quality, or extent of the non-believer's evidence prior to encountering my apologetic arguments, the non-believer is irrational if he persists in non-belief after having heard my arguments.

---

[12] Clark 1990, 45.

[13] I owe this distinction to Kyle Stanford. See Stanford 2017. For a detailed discussion of underdetermination and the related topic of holistic rationality, see Kvanvig 2014, chapters 4 and 5.

(b) is a strong claim. Many will find it implausibly strong. For it implies that, for all possible non-believers and their corresponding evidence bases, adding the apologist's arguments to those evidence bases renders non-belief irrational. To put it colloquially, it amounts to the apologist saying, "I don't care what your evidence is. Mine is better. It's decisive. And once you've heard it, you're irrational to disagree." This claim is supposed to hold whether the apologist is a neophyte or a seasoned expert, and whether the non-believer is a neophyte or a seasoned expert. It is supposed to hold if the non-believer happens to have no evidence against theism or theistic arguments (so far, so good). But it is also supposed to hold if the non-believer is a philosophical expert who knows more about the relevant evidence than the apologist knows.[14] Importantly, it is supposed to hold even if the non-believer has experienced a life of terrible tragedy and suffering—say, as a survivor of the Holocaust or the Gulag—and thereby has what many will regard as *experiential* evidence against theism.[15] It's also supposed to hold even if the non-believer rationally thinks (prior to hearing apologetic arguments) that no such arguments can be successful. In short, the sledgehammer apologist thinks, her evidence overrides[16] all. However, unless the apologist is familiar with *all* of the non-believer's evidence prior to presenting her arguments, this seems like an implausible stance to take. Thus, one might think, it is unwise for the religious apologist to grasp the first horn of our dilemma.

2.2 A Failure of Humility?

An overarching concern is about sledgehammer apologetics is that the approach involves claiming more for one's argument than it actually shows. It involves, for instance, claiming not only that one's premises are good evidence for one's conclusions, but that they *prove* one's conclusions, or render alternative conclusions irrational. Moreover, it apparently involves accepting such claims in a way that floats free of any counterevidence or objection the non-believer may have—no matter how strong, and even if the apologist has not heard them.

At least initially, such a position can seem arrogant, or at best to express a failure of intellectual humility. Such humility, on the account of the trait most

---

[14] On the perils of reasoning about evidence one does not possess, see Ballantyne 2019, chapter 7.
[15] For discussion of such experiential evidence against theism, see Benton, Hawthorne, and Isaacs 2016.
[16] Given the current political climate, I cannot bring myself to write "trumps" here.

salient here, amounts to being aware of, and responding appropriately to, one's intellectual limitations. As Dennis Whitcomb, Heather Battaly, Jason Baehr, and Daniel Howard-Snyder put it, "[Intellectual Humility] consists in proper attentiveness to, and owning of, one's intellectual limitations."[17] This trait stands as Aristotelian mean between the vices of servility and arrogance. Arrogance can concern either the attentiveness condition or the owning condition (or both). One might express arrogance by being oblivious to one's intellectual limitations—say, by simply failing to register them. Or, one might express arrogance by responding inappropriately once one becomes aware of a limitation—as when one ignores the limitation, or denies having it, or doesn't care about it, or does nothing about it, or becomes angry when someone points it out.[18] The latter reactions are failures to *own* limitations, even if one is appropriately attentive to them.

If this account of humility is on the right track—indeed, if limitations-owning is even necessary for humility—then sledgehammer apologists can easily fail to express humility.[19] For, in order rationally to make the comparative judgment implied in (b) above, one needs reason to think that one's apologetic arguments can beat all comers. This requires, at a minimum, having rational beliefs about the types and instances of counterevidence one's dissenters might have, and a rational trust in one's ability to judge that such counterevidence isn't good enough to override the evidence provided by one's own apologetic arguments. These conditions are not easily met. Meeting them requires a firm and thorough grasp of a broad array of evidence, along with good access to the potential contents and workings of a potential dissenter's mind. Perhaps some expert apologists meet these conditions. I don't dismiss that possibility, and we'll consider it in more detail below. It is nevertheless easy to see how, for many apologists, even attempting—much less claiming—to meet the conditions is beyond their intellectual limitations. For many theists, sledgehammer apologetics can't be humble apologetics.

---

[17] Whitcomb, Battaly, Baehr, and Howard-Snyder 2017, 520.

[18] See Whitcomb, Battaly, Baehr, and Howard-Snyder 2017 for detailed explorations of these dimensions.

[19] Some Christians might object to the account of humility assumed in this section. Limitations-owning is not even necessary for humility, they might think. For, from a Christian perspective, Christ is the central exemplar of humility—and yet Christ does not have intrinsic limitations to own. Rather, at the Incarnation, Christ takes on limitations that are extrinsic to his nature. Thus, the limitations-owning account is too strong. For development of this objection, see Kvanvig 2018, section 9.4. For present purposes, it should help to note that, irrespective of what ends up being the true account of *humility*, the failure to own one's epistemic limitations is clearly a failure of intellectual virtue *of some sort* (perhaps a failure of modesty?). This is enough to ground an important concern about sledgehammer apologetics. Those who reject the limitations-owning account of humility are encouraged to recast the worry accordingly.

3. Potential Costs of the "Permissive" Response

Is the other path of the dilemma less costly to travel? By way of reminder, that option involves the apologist saying that at least some non-believers can encounter, seriously consider, and reject her arguments without thereby falling into irrationality. On the face of it, it is an attractive option. It allows the apologist to say that her dissenters are rational in their dissent—something that sounds enlightened and charitable. The option also allows the apologist to avoid claiming that her arguments are knockdown arguments, and to avoid perilous comparative judgments about the probative force of evidence she may not even possess.

However, there appear to be costs for traveling the permissive path.

3.1 Up-Front Costs

Two kinds of costs are salient. The first kind concern the potential instability of the position that says, "given the evidence we share, my belief and your non-belief belief are both rational." The apologist incurs these costs just by taking the permissive path. Call these "up-front costs." The second kind concern ways in which the permissive path exacerbates theological problems the apologist already has—e.g., the problem of divine hiddenness or the problem of Hell. Such problems are not directly in view just by virtue of the apologist's taking the permissive path. They come into view only when we consider the permissive path in connection with some other theological problem. Call them "hidden costs." Let us explore these costs in turn.

3.1.1 Permissivism and Belief

In a well-known paper, Richard Feldman argues that taking what we've called "the permissive path" is incoherent. To show this, he imagines a detective trying to determine which of two defendants, Lefty or Righty, is guilty of a crime. (It is given that one, and only one, defendant is guilty.) There is strong evidence that Lefty is guilty, but also strong evidence that Righty is guilty. Given this, one might think that the total relevant evidence licenses *both* the belief that Lefty is guilty and the belief that Righty is guilty, so that one can rationally hold either belief, given this evidence. Thus, if there were two detectives assigned to the case, it could turn out that one could reasonably hold that Lefty is guilty, the other could reasonably hold that Righty is guilty, and that each could agree that the other detective is reasonable in holding the contrary attitude. Feldman argues that this assessment of the case is mistaken:

> It is clear that the detectives should suspend judgment in this sort of case.... The evidence for Lefty is evidence against Righty. Believing a particular suspect to be guilty on the basis of this combined evidence is simply not reasonable. Furthermore, it is hard to make clear sense of the thought that the other belief is reasonable. Suppose one of the detectives believes that Lefty is guilty. She can then infer that Righty is not guilty. But if she can draw this inference, she cannot also reasonably think that it is reasonable to conclude that Righty is guilty. This combination of beliefs simply does not make sense.[20]

Feldman thinks that these considerations lend support to the Uniqueness Thesis, which he construes as the claim that "a body of evidence justifies at most one proposition out of a competing set of propositions (e.g., one theory out of a bunch of exclusive alternatives) and that it justifies at most one attitude [belief, disbelief, or suspending judgment] toward any particular proposition."[21] To deny the Uniqueness Thesis is to embrace *Epistemic Permissivism*, from which our "permissive path" derives its name.

The debate over Uniqueness and Permissivism occupies a literature of its own.[22] That debate concerns whether a given body of evidence can in fact justify or make rational more than one competing attitude toward some proposition. Note, though, that what's at issue here—and what Feldman considers in the second half of the passage just quoted—is a question that occurs one level up. Namely:

> When one believes that P on the basis of evidence E, can it be rational to *acknowledge* or *believe* that E also makes it rational for someone else to believe not-P on the basis of E?

On Feldman's assessment, to think that it can, one would apparently have to deny that evidence for P is evidence against ~P. But this line is hard to hold. To see why, we might expand a bit upon Feldman's reasoning. By the rule of

---

[20] Feldman 2007, 204–205.
[21] Feldman 2007, 205. I have included the bracketed words for clarification.
[22] For a helpful introduction see Kopec and Titelbaum 2016. For important primary works, see White 2005 and 2013, Kelly 2013, Ballantyne and Coffman 2011, and Matheson 2011.

double-negation, P is equivalent to ~~P. Thus, one might think, if evidence E supports P, then it supports ~~P. Hence, because ~~P is directly contradictory to ~P, to whatever extent E supports P, it serves as evidence against ~P. Or, to put the point in terms of probability, it is an axiom of the probability calculus that

$$Pr(\sim P) = 1 - Pr(P).$$

The debate between P and not-P is a zero-sum game, and the evidence can't back both sides. If you believe P but think your evidence makes ~P probable, you are in effect denying that it makes P probable. Alternatively, to whatever extent you think the evidence makes ~P probable, you are committed to thinking that it makes the belief that P that much less probable—that much less rational to believe, given your evidence.[23]

Return to our main thread. We are considering the religious apologist who thinks that, while her arguments render her own belief rational, they also make (or at least *leave*) it rational to deny her beliefs. If the reasoning just rehearsed is sound, this position is incoherent. In acknowledging her dissenter's disbelief as rational even given her apologetic arguments, the apologist appears thereby to admit that her own beliefs aren't rational, given those arguments. (Or alternatively, to whatever extent she affirms that her dissenter's beliefs are rational, given her apologetic arguments, she undermines the extent to which those arguments make rational her own beliefs.) But if she admits that her arguments can make (or leave) rational *both* belief and disbelief in her religious views, awkward questions arise. (Here I rehearse an argument inspired by Roger White.[24]) Why does the apologist hold the views she does, rather than those of her dissenter, *given* that she acknowledges both beliefs as rational on the evidence she has shared? And, on the assumption that rationality is a guide to truth, why should she think her beliefs are true? For by her own lights, if she takes rationality as a guide to truth, she's just as likely to get the truth by holding the negation of her beliefs as by holding the beliefs themselves. As White asks, why should she then bother forming her beliefs on the basis of the evidence, rather than by, say, popping a belief-inducing pill?

---

[23] The argument rehearsed in this paragraph is inspired by, and bears obvious similarities to, arguments developed in White 2005 and 2013.

[24] White 2005, 447ff.

3.1.2 Permissivism and the Apologetic Enterprise

Consider next not the permissive apologist's attitudes toward her first-order religious beliefs (e.g., about the existence of God, or the truth of her particular religion); rather, consider the apologist's attitude toward her task as an apologist. By virtue of taking herself to be an apologist, she takes herself to offer evidence and arguments for her religious beliefs. As a *permissive* apologist, she takes the view that, even after she has shared her arguments with the non-believer, the latter can still be rational in that non-belief. But if that's right, what could be the point of sharing those arguments in the first place? For then it seems that, by the apologist's own lights, the non-believer will be as likely to get the truth by denying the conclusions of the apologist's arguments as by embracing them.

3.2 A Hidden Cost: Unpalatable Eschatology

If the Feldman–White sort of arguments just canvassed are correct, then the cost of grasping the "we're both rational" horn of the dilemma is a certain kind of epistemic incoherence. This is an "up-front" cost of grasping that horn. Let us now explore some "hidden" costs. I say they are "hidden" because they aren't directly in view when we are considering the permissive strategy. Rather, they come into view when we consider the combination of Permissivism and some other factor.

To begin to grasp the first hidden cost, note that many religious apologists engage in their enterprise because they believe that the eternal destiny of their audience depends upon it. Apologetics is for them a tool for *evangelism*—for sharing the good news about God—good news that allows people to avoid the horrors of eternal damnation. To get a sense of the urgency involved here, consider these lines from a popular Christian meme:

Evangelism is hard. Watching people you love go to Hell is harder.

Similarly, nineteenth-century preacher Charles Spurgeon pleads,

If sinners will be damned, at least let them leap to Hell over our bodies. And if they will perish, let them perish with our arms about their knees, imploring them to stay. If Hell must be filled, at least let it be filled in the teeth of our exertions, and let not one go there unwarned and unprayed for.[25]

---

[25] Spurgeon 1861, v. 7, p. 15.

Some thinkers draw close connections between the hope of drawing others into saving faith (on the one hand) and their apologetic efforts (on the other). Consider these remarks from actor turned Christian apologist Kirk Cameron. Christians should do apologetics, he says,

> Not just to score points, but to save sinners. And it's easy to get this out of perspective, because apologetics can be so powerful. Apologetics appeals to truth and argumentation, and it's hard, and it's unforgiving, and it's like a granite rock that can be wielded around, and people can get clobbered with it, and it can do lots of damage, if it's used carelessly. We know that without Christ people are going to Hell. We want to save them. We want them to come to Christ. And that brings honor and glory to Jesus, who sacrificed Himself for them.[26]

Any theist who aligns with Spurgeon and Cameron faces an important ethical-eschatological problem. For she thinks that God condemns some people to Hell, or some other such punishment, in part because these individuals have incorrect beliefs about God—say, they believe there is no such person. (Alternatively, on this line of thinking, if people don't receive negative eternal judgment *because* of incorrect beliefs, correct beliefs are still an important—perhaps essential—means or constituent of their receiving salvation.)

This problem is well known and is hard enough to resolve—if it can be resolved—in its own right.[27] But now suppose that the religious apologist *also* holds that those who reject her apologetic arguments can be rational in so doing. Such an apologist is then committed to the claim that those who reject her apologetic arguments are destined for divinely administered punishment *despite* the fact that their non-belief is rational. They must be willing to recite the following speech: "My dissenter rejects my religious beliefs, which are essential to his salvation. Even though he's rational in his non-belief and is thus making good use of the cognitive faculties God has given him, God is planning to go ahead and send him to Hell, anyway." It is hard to see how God, so described, could be anything other than diabolically evil. (If there is such a way, I am constitutionally incapable of seeing it.) At any rate, it seems clear that for the apologist who already faces the problems that arise for a traditional view of Hell, taking the permissive path will make for even more treacherous travels.

---

[26] Cameron 2019.   [27] See, e.g., Kvanvig 1993 and Walls 1992.

3.3 Another Hidden Cost: Divine Hiddenness

Many theists subscribe to the claim that God wishes to know and be known by human beings, and to enter into a loving relationship with them. However, it is widely acknowledged that God—if such a being exists—is sometimes *hidden*. That is, at least for some people, at some times, God's existence is not apparent. Perhaps in part because of God's hiddenness, some people do not form the belief that God exists.

But here the question arises: can such non-belief be rational? An affirmative answer gives rise to atheistic arguments from divine hiddenness. J.L. Schellenberg has developed the version most salient for our purposes:

1. If there is a God, he is perfectly loving.
2. If a perfectly loving God exists, reasonable nonbelief does not occur.
3. Reasonable non-belief occurs.

Thus,

4. No perfectly loving God exists. (from 2, 3)
5. There is no God. (from 1, 4)[28]

This argument is importantly connected to the dilemma that concerns us in this paper.[29] For suppose the religious apologist takes the permissive path of our dilemma—the path on which the non-believer can rationally resist her apologetic arguments. In that case, she has in effect granted premise (3) of the argument from hiddenness. The theist is committed to (1) by virtue of being a theist, and steps (4) and (5) follow from previous steps. Thus, if she takes the permissive path, the apologist will be forced to deny or undermine Schellenberg's second premise.

---

[28] This is the official version developed in Schellenberg 2006, 83. In more recent work (Schellenberg 2015), he prefers to speak in terms of *non-resistant* non-belief instead of *reasonable* non-belief. I use the earlier—"reasonable non-belief" formulation here, because it is directly relevant to the permissive path of our dilemma. For the permissive apologist has granted that non-belief can be *reasonable* or *rational*. Plausibly, however, granting that non-belief can be reasonable also commits the permissive apologist to the corresponding claim that non-belief can be non-resistant—that is, formed in a way that does not involve resistance to a relationship with God, if God exists. It is at least very natural to think that a non-believer who is reasonable in her non-belief is thereby not *resisting* belief. If this is right, then by taking the permissive branch of our dilemma, the apologist reduces the resources by which she can resist both the 2006 and the 2015 versions of Schellenberg's argument.

[29] For further work that connects the topic of religious disagreement to that of divine hiddenness, see Matheson 2018.

Can she do so successfully? There is a large and complex literature devoted to assessing that question—that is, to the assessment of (2) and various revisions of it. We won't enter that discussion here.[30] For now, note the close connection between the views one takes on Permissivism and the positions one takes on hiddenness. The apologist who takes the permissive view can't deny step (3).

Indeed, such an apologist appears committed to something even stronger than (3). As it stands, (3) is consistent with any number of ways reasonable non-belief might occur. One might never have heard of God, might never be exposed to evidence—propositional or not—for God's existence. Or one might be raised in a social setting in which one's best epistemic resources—including experts in one's community—point toward non-belief.[31] The permissive apologist doesn't just grant these possibilities. She *also* grants:

3*: Reasonable non-belief occurs *even* among people who have been exposed to my best apologetic arguments.

If this is right, two consequences follow. First, as already noted, embracing (3*) commits the apologist to (3), and this narrows the range of her available responses to Schellenberg's argument. Second, embracing (3*) commits the apologist to the failure of the very apologetic means God designed to extract people from non-belief-inducing circumstances. On that way of thinking, God would remain hidden to non-believers, in the sense that non-belief is rational for them, even *after* the apologetic evidence for God's existence was made known. It might seem a very strange God who would set the world up in this way. Taking the permissive route, then, threatens to make the problem of divine hiddenness worse for the theist than it would be otherwise.

4. A Third Path?

There are prospective costs for traveling both the way of the sledgehammer and the permissive path. In light of this, the apologist might consider seeking a third way.

---

[30] For discussion of several possibilities (though related to *non-resistant* non-belief, rather than of *rational* non-belief) see Howard-Snyder and Green 2016, section 3. For fuller discussion of theistic responses to divine hiddenness, see Howard-Snyder and Moser 2002, Green and Stump 2015, and Rea 2018.

[31] For a careful treatment of social epistemology in defense of faultless non-belief, see Greco 2015.

The only option I can see here is to suspend judgment about whether, having heard one's apologetic arguments, one's dissenter can remain rational in his non-belief. Such a position is possible—when faced with a "yes" or "no" question, one can sometimes say, "I don't know." And in some cases, this is what one should say. Is the apologist's dilemma such a case?

One benefit of going agnostic about the epistemic status of her dissenter's belief is that the apologist off-loads an important cost of traveling the first path—namely, the belief that she has knockdown arguments for her views. For as we saw above, an apparent cost of taking the sledgehammer way is that, in order to do so, the apologist must embrace the notion that her arguments are knockdown arguments. Suspending judgment about the rationality of her dissenter's beliefs leaves it open for the apologist to disavow this commitment, which—as far as our dilemma is concerned—should also forestall the charge of arrogance. So, there seems to be a benefit to going the agnostic, path-splitting route.

What about costs?

First, consider an extension of the Feldman–White argument discussed above. There, the thought was that if the apologist positively believes that her dissenter's belief is rational, given evidence, E, she must, on pain of incoherence, think that E does not make rational her own belief. Now suppose that, instead of *believing* that her dissenter's belief is rational, given the evidence, the apologist instead suspends judgment about this. She then holds the following combination of attitudes:

- My belief that P is rational, given evidence, E.
- I suspend judgment about whether my dissenter's belief that ~P is rational, given E.

Is this combination of views coherent? One might think not. For again, it seems that evidence for P is evidence against ~P, and vice versa. So, if our apologist thinks her belief is rational given her evidence, she should be able to deduce that the contradictory belief is not rational, given that same evidence. That is, she should think that her dissenter's belief is not rational, given the same evidence, instead of suspending judgment about this proposition. To suspend judgment here would be a failure to respond properly to her evidence concerning the higher-level claim about whether her dissenter's belief is rational. Worse yet, by suspending judgment about the rational status of her dissenter's belief, the apologist seems to threaten the status of her own first-order belief about P. For it seems that if she suspends judgment about whether

E makes ~P rational to believe, she should also suspend judgment about whether E makes P itself rational to believe.[32]

Given the reasoning just rehearsed, there is an additional cost of seeking a third path. Namely, doing so can make it difficult for the apologist to make sense of her enterprise. By virtue of being an apologist, she thinks that an important part of her calling is to provide evidence for her religious beliefs, thereby helping those currently outside her faith to enter into it. A third-path-seeking apologist suspends judgment about the following claim:

> If I share my apologetic arguments with the non-believer, this will make it *irrational* for her *not* to adopt my beliefs and, insofar as belief is concerned, to adopt my faith.

Provided the reasoning in the above paragraph is sound, if the apologist suspends judgment about this claim, she should also suspend judgment about:

> If I share my apologetic arguments with the non-believer, this will make it rational for her to adopt my beliefs and, insofar as belief is concerned, to adopt my faith.

But if she suspends judgment about *this* claim, it becomes unclear what she could take to be the point of sharing her arguments with the non-believer. For the very point of sharing those arguments is to enable the non-believer *rationally* to adopt the apologist's faith. Suspending judgment about the claim just above seems to leave the apologist in the position of thinking her efforts may very well be pointless. She'll be saying to herself, "I'm giving these arguments in order to bring the other to rational belief in my faith. But for all I know, he'll be rational even if he rejects my view after hearing these arguments." As far as the coherence of apologetic activity is concerned, the costs of splitting our dilemma seem similar to those of taking the permissive path.

Next, consider eschatological costs. (These costs will accrue only to certain theistic apologists.) Recall the difficulty of taking the permissive path while embracing the idea that God visits eternal punishment on non-believers. The idea, again, is that the permissive apologist embraces both of the following propositions:

---

[32] For a similar point, see Feldman 2006, 234. Though I am inclined to endorse this argument, I do not claim it is decisive. Those who believe in epistemic *akrasia* or epistemic level-splitting will be inclined to reject it. I cannot address their arguments here. For relevant discussion, see Roush 2017.

- Non-belief is rational, even for those who have heard my apologetic arguments; and
- God punishes non-believers eternally in Hell.

Given the argument developed in section 3, this combination of views makes God out to be a moral monster, who permanently punishes those who *literally* don't know better than to refrain from belief in God. Someone who holds the conjunction of these claims should, I think, conclude that God is evil. Now consider someone who believes the second claim, but suspends judgment about the first. Such a person believes that God punishes non-believers, but confesses ignorance about whether the non-belief that issues in that punishment is rational. Though perhaps not as bad as *believing* that God punishes rational non-belief, such a stance seems problematic. If thinking that God punishes rational non-belief commits the apologist to the claim that God is evil, then suspending judgment about this claim should at least prompt doubts about God's goodness.

5. Cost-Cutting Measures

The arguments sketched in section 4 are not decisive. They may be resisted in various ways, some of which we'll explore below. The point for now is that arguably, the apologist who splits the horns of our dilemma faces costs that mirror those of taking the permissive path. Some philosophical dilemmas may be dismissed simply by splitting their horns. Not so the Apologist's Dilemma. Here, carving out a third path requires substantive philosophical work, work that parallels that needed to reduce the costs of traveling one of the other paths. Deciding which path to take is no simple matter; it requires careful accounting. In light of this, it will be worthwhile to consider how to reduce trail fees for the other two paths.

5.1 A Cheaper Sledgehammer?

In section 2, we considered two prospective charges that the apologist incurs by taking the way of the sledgehammer: the charge of arrogance, and the implausible belief that she has knockdown arguments for her religious doctrines. Let's take these charges in turn.

5.1.1 Reducing the Arrogance Charge

Above, we explored the idea that the apologist expresses arrogance, or at best a failure of humility, if she thinks it would be irrational for the non-believer to remain steadfast in the face of apologetic arguments. There, the idea was that in thinking that her apologetic arguments will *always* render non-belief irrational for those who hear them, the apologist must think she has knock-down arguments for her beliefs. Recall that there is a plausible connection between the belief that one has knockdown arguments, on the one hand, and a failure of humility, on the other. For in thinking that her arguments will always render non-belief irrational, the apologist is apparently committed to:

> b.   Irrespective of the content, quality, or extent of the non-believer's evidence prior to encountering my apologetic arguments, the non-believer is irrational if he persists in non-belief after having heard my arguments.

But to embrace (b), the apologist seems to presuppose a vast amount of knowledge about the content, quality, and extent of *any possible* dissenter's evidence base. It is easy to see how the apologist who thinks this might be failing to acknowledge her cognitive limitations, and thus given the notion of humility as limitations-owning, is failing to express humility.

As far as humility goes, two separate charges might appear on the apologist's bill. The first is that by embracing (b), she shows that she lacks intellectual humility as a character trait. She shows that she is not a humble *person*. The second charge is that the apologist fails to express humility in the intellectual act of embracing (b); embracing this claim is not an intellectually virtuous *act*.

The apologist need not pay the first (character-based) charge just on account of thinking that (b) is true. That is, just thinking that one has knockdown arguments for one's views, even if this is not rational, does not mean that one fails to be a humble person. Singular actions are not normally regarded as sufficient evidence that a person has or lacks a given character trait. This is in part because people can act uncharacteristically. Someone who is usually honest might lie in rare or extreme circumstances. Someone with a stable habit of lying might tell the truth when it suits him to do so. Someone who is normally courageous might commit an occasional act of cowardice. A cowardly person might perform an act of bravery. And so on. Likewise, it is possible that, even if embracing (b) is not a characteristically humble intellectual act, an otherwise humble apologist might do so. Alternatively—for those who don't construe beliefs as intellectual acts—even if a characteristically humble person will not normally believe (b), such a person might hold this belief in a way that is out of character, but that need not keep her from having the trait itself.

So much for the first charge. The second is milder. It says only that in embracing (b), the apologist fails to express humility in that very act. It says that humble thinkers won't typically believe that they have knockdown arguments, when they are thinking in a way characteristic of their humility. The apologist could be guilty of this charge while nevertheless remaining a humble person in general.

Even so, failures of humility should be taken seriously. Does the apologist fail to act humbly just by virtue of thinking she has knockdown arguments for her religious views? I doubt it. The correct answer to the question is, "it depends." Depends on what? On the content, quality, and extent of the apologist's evidence concerning her beliefs and their logical and doxastic contraries.[33] To think that *any* apologist who thinks she has knockdown arguments for her beliefs *ipso facto* fails to be humble, is to ignore the possibility that the apologist is rational in thinking her arguments are knockdown-quality. In a way, this is to skirt the same mistake one is attributing to the apologist herself. The apologist's critic claims that by embracing (b), the apologist exceeds her intellectual limitations. She presumes to grasp a vast body of evidence for and against her views, and to be the cognitive superior of dissenters whose judgments about the force of that evidence are incompatible with her own. But the apologist's critic seems to be doing something similar here. Namely, he presumes to have extremely good access to the content, quality, and extent of the apologist's evidence base, and to the apologist's capacities for assessing her evidence. For without a great deal of evidence relevant to these matters, he would not be in position to judge that the apologist is exceeding her limitations in embracing (b). In claiming that any apologist who embraces (b) thereby fails to be humble, the critic runs the risk of exceeding his own intellectual limitations.[34]

Of course, even if embracing (b) doesn't *automatically* bespeak arrogance, it could turn out that many, most, or all of the apologists who actually embrace (b) do fail to express humility. The question whether *a given* apologist exhibits a failure of humility in believing (b) is closely tied to the following questions:

Can it be reasonable for the apologist to think she has knockdown arguments for her views—arguments that, once heard and understood, make it irrational for anyone to persist in non-belief? If so, *how*?

---

[33] E.g., disbelief and suspending judgment.   [34] See Plantinga 1995 for a parallel discussion.

As a means of further exploring the arrogance charge, let us turn to these questions.

5.1.2 More Modest Knockdown Arguments

The apologist we are considering believes that irrespective of the non-believer's evidence prior to encountering her apologetic arguments, this non-believer is irrational if he persists in his non-belief after having heard those arguments. This is just to say that the apologist believes she has knockdown arguments for her views. Can thinking this ever be reasonable?

I'm not sure that it ever actually is. But to see how it *could* be, we can start with a more modest claim the apologist might believe instead:

> There is at least one non-believer such that, given his evidential situation, if I were to share my apologetic arguments with him, it would be irrational for him to persist in non-belief.

Imagine a non-believer who suspends judgment about God's existence, not because he has considered the relevant evidence and judged it inconclusive, but because he isn't even familiar with it. Suppose our apologist knows this, and that she also reasonably thinks her arguments provide powerful evidence for her religious beliefs. Couldn't she sensibly think that if she were to share these arguments, the apologist would thereby render belief in her religious doctrines more rational than disbelief, and more rational than suspending judgment, for her friend? It is hard to see why not. In fact, it is easy to imagine that such a thing actually happens once in a while. But if this is right, then it is at least *sometimes* reasonable for an apologist to think that a dissenter's evidence base is such that, if apologetic arguments were added to it, non-belief would cease to be a rational option. Our question concerns whether and how the apologist could reasonably think that, given the apologetic arguments at her disposal, *every* case—and thus every evidence base—has this feature.

There are at least two ways in which the apologist might wish to reduce the cost of taking such a position. First, she might construe the claim that she has knockdown arguments *cumulatively,* so that it applies not to her arguments taken individually, but rather to the arguments taken together. She need not take, say, some version of the cosmological or design argument to be a knockdown argument in itself. Rather, we can envision her putting forth a large number and range of arguments, dubbing its inclusive disjunction her "argument" for her religious beliefs, and claiming that *that* argument always suffices to make non-belief irrational. Her "argument" might consist in, say,

Plantinga's famous "two dozen (or so) theistic arguments," all suitably developed, or in those arguments conjoined with additional arguments developed by (say) Richard Swinburne or St. Thomas Aquinas or others.[35] Such a move will make the apologist's claim about the epistemic efficacy of her arguments more plausible than it would be, taken to apply to a single argument. When her "argument" is really a cumulative case, her claim to dialectical superiority rests on a much larger proportion of the total relevant evidence than it would if she were relying on a single argument to deliver the "knockout blow."[36]

Here's a second cost-cutting strategy. Recall Clark's description of Aquinas's project in natural theology:

> Aquinas self-consciously tried to use premises that all rational beings are obliged to accept, taking logical steps that are obvious, thereby *demonstrating* or *proving* the existence of God to nearly any sane person. His proofs would demonstrate that the unbeliever is rationally obliged to believe in God.[37]

Notice—there are really two aims here. The first is to prove or demonstrate God's existence, presumably with something approaching certainty. The second is to show that the non-believer is obligated to believe in God. Accomplishing the first task would be sufficient for accomplishing the second. But the tasks are separable. Success in the second task does not require success in the first. In thinking that her arguments always render non-belief irrational, the apologist need not think that these arguments render her religious beliefs *demonstrated* or *certain* or *proven*. She need only think that they make belief more reasonable than disbelief, and more reasonable than suspending judgment.

To see this, recall the definition of *knockdown argument* with which we are working. On that definition, such an argument has this essential feature: every qualified person who hears and understands it, and has no reason to doubt that she understands it, *should* believe its conclusion on the basis of its premises, which are themselves strongly supported. Nothing in this definition suggests that having such an argument renders one's beliefs certain, nor that taking oneself to have such an argument implies taking one's evidence to render one's belief certain. Indeed, in taking oneself to have a knockdown argument, one need only take the argument to render belief more rational than both disbelief and suspending judgment.

[35] See Swinburne 2004, and the essays in Dougherty and Walls 2018.
[36] On the logic of cumulative case arguments, and combined "weak" arguments, see Swinburne 2004 and DePoe and McGrew 2013.
[37] Clark 1990, 4.

Taken together, these cost-cutting strategies reduce the apologist's claim to possess knockdown arguments to this:

c. If any non-believer were exposed to the very wide range of well-developed arguments for my religious beliefs that I am prepared to present, and if he understood these arguments and lacked reason to doubt that he understood them, then these arguments would render it more rational for him to adopt my beliefs than to disbelieve them or suspend judgment with respect to them.

This claim is weaker than some other nearby claims that the apologist need not embrace. It doesn't require dismissing counterevidence for one's views as completely lacking in epistemic efficacy. It doesn't require thinking that some single argument should knock the unbeliever to the canvas. And as we've seen, it doesn't require thinking that even one's cumulative argument demands or licenses certainty about the content of one's conclusions, whether for oneself or for the non-believer. Employing our two strategies in tandem, then, reduces the bill the apologist must pay for thinking that she has knockdown arguments for her views.

Even so, the nuanced and diminished claim, (c), is very strong. The apologist should accept it only with caution, and only after ardent and extended study. It should only be embraced by apologists who have good reason to think that:

- they are thoroughly familiar with the arguments needed to develop and present a cumulative case for their religious beliefs;
- they are thoroughly familiar with the arguments and experiential evidence supporting beliefs contrary to their own;
- they have strong reason to trust in their capacities to make rational judgments about the probative force of large, cumulative bodies of evidence; and
- they have more reason to trust the reliability of their own capacities to make such judgments than they do to trust the capacities of those who are familiar with the same evidence but who come to contrary judgments about its probative force.

Perhaps there are apologists who meet these conditions. I doubt that there are many. (As a religious believer who sometimes argues for his views, I am confident that *I* don't meet them, and indeed could not meet them without the help of several consecutive sabbaticals.) To see why, consider just the first three bullet points, which concern assembling and making rational judgments about the probative force of cumulative bodies of evidence. As is widely recognized, even the evaluation of single arguments can be mentally taxing. Thus, Pascal:

> The metaphysical proofs of God are so far removed from man's reasoning, and so complicated, that they have little force. When they do help some people it is only at the moment when they see the demonstration. An hour later they are afraid of having made a mistake.[38]

And when we consider a *cumulative* apologetic case—the collection of Plantinga's two dozen arguments, say—the difficulty increases dramatically. As Timothy and Lydia McGrew note,

> Cumulative case arguments are indeed particularly difficult to evaluate.... In the nature of the case, such arguments draw on many details and often require, for their full appreciation, more than a passing acquaintance with multiple disciplines. Beyond this, there is the sheer cognitive difficulty of appreciating the evidential impact of multiple pieces of evidence on a single point; we are apt to focus on two or three considerations and discount the rest. Finally, the pieces of evidence must themselves be not only considered in isolation but coordinated, that is, considered in connection with each other."[39]

Moreover, to meet the conditions above, the apologist will not only need to assemble and evaluate a cumulative case *for* her own beliefs, but also to do the same with respect to the arguments and evidence *against* her beliefs. Otherwise, she won't be in position to make the comparative judgment that (c) requires. This is a formidable intellectual task. Apologists who lack good reason to think they can perform it should not embrace (c). To do so would be to fail to attend to and own their intellectual limitations. It would thus be a failure of humility.

5.2 The Permissive Path: Cost-Cutting Measures

If few apologists can afford to travel the way of the sledgehammer, the ones remaining may wish to consider how to reduce the costs of taking the permissive path.

---

[38] Pascal 2008, 63.   [39] McGrew and McGrew 2009, 617.

5.2.1 Eschatological Price Slashing

As we saw above, for some religious apologists, there is an eschatological cost of taking the permissive path. Some religious apologists embrace the idea that God will visit eternal punishment on those who do not believe in God during their earthly existence. And if the apologist also holds—per the permissive horn—that some of these people are *rational* in their non-belief, then it is difficult to see how she can continue to hold that the God she worships is morally good. For in that case, she holds that some people are subject to eternal punishment for their non-belief, despite this non-belief being rational and thus a good use of God-given rational faculties.

Many religious apologists will want to reject the combination of views just described. They will find it unpalatable to think that God could punish people who are rational in their non-belief. Accordingly, they might abandon not their Permissivism, but rather, the idea that God punishes people for non-belief—at least when such non-belief is rational. One way to do this is to embrace universalism—the doctrine that all people are eventually "saved" by God.[40] Another way, one that falls short of universalism, is to embrace the idea of eschatological "second chances."[41] Perhaps, the apologist might think, even the best apologetic arguments fail to render non-belief irrational for individuals during their earthly existence. But for all this, at some point in the afterlife, all individuals will come face to face with God, and *this* encounter will make non-belief irrational. It is only after such an encounter, and presumably after a chance to relent, that non-believers will be punished for their non-belief. A third possibility is that God judges people only according to what they have reason to believe, so that, while irrational non-believers may be punished for their non-belief, rational non-believers are not. All of these possibilities deserve further exploration. The point for now is just this: for apologists concerned about the eschatological costs of the permissive path, there are several ways to lower the price.

5.2.2 Dealing with Divine Hiddenness

Recall this key claim in Schellenberg's atheistic argument from divine hiddenness:

  3. Reasonable nonbelief occurs.

The apologist who takes the permissive path is logically committed to this premise. When conjoined with the claim that a perfectly loving God would not

---

[40] See, e.g., Adams 1993 and Talbott 2014.   [41] See Buckareff and Plug 2005.

permit reasonable non-belief, (3) entails that no perfectly loving God exists. Inasmuch as theists are committed to the claim that if God exists, God is perfectly loving, it then follows that there is no God.

As we have seen, a cost of the permissive path is that it deprives the apologist of a strategy for responding to the hiddenness argument—namely denying (3). When it comes to that argument, the permissive apologist must resist

2. If a perfectly loving God exists, reasonable nonbelief does not occur.

If she cannot do so, her permissive strategy will have led the religious apologist into atheism. From the perspective of a theistic apologist, this would be a maximally poor outcome.

Can the permissive apologist find a sensible way to resist (2)? We cannot answer that question here.[42] In order to answer the question properly, we would need to engage a large and substantive body of literature on the hiddenness problem. But reflection on this fact reveals an important point: the cost of the permissive path cannot ultimately be tallied independently of ongoing debates about divine hiddenness. That is, we cannot ultimately tell how much the permissive path will cost the apologist without first discerning whether or not there is a plausible way to resist (2) that is consistent with the permissive strategy. An important lesson to draw is that it is a mistake to treat the topic of religious disagreement in the abstract, as though it swings free from other topics in the philosophy of religion.

5.3 Making Sense of the Permissive Apologetic Enterprise

In section 3, we saw that taking the permissive path of the Apologist's Dilemma threatens to make the apologetic enterprise incoherent. The point of giving apologetic arguments, one might think, is to give one's interlocutor reasons to convert to one's own position. But the permissive apologist believes that even if she provides the non-believer with such reasons, non-belief may *still* be rational. What, then, could be the point of giving the arguments? For, by the apologist's own lights, they fail to provide compelling reasons for conversion.

---

[42] But see Howard-Snyder and Green 2016, section 3, for discussion of several attempts. See also Howard-Snyder and Moser 2002, Green and Stump 2015, and Rea 2018.

Faced with this question, the apologist should distinguish between different aims of her enterprise. Here are a few:

- To show that non-belief in the doctrines of her religion is irrational;
- To show that her religious beliefs are rational;
- To show that there is enough evidence for her religious doctrines to put them "on the table" for rational discussion;[43]
- To show that non-doxastic attitudes like *hope, acceptance* and certain varieties of *faith* in religious doctrines can be rational.[44]

The permissive apologist judges that her arguments fail in the first aim. She must therefore make sense of the other aims in a way that is independent of that aim. She must find ways to show that the latter aims are valuable—epistemically or religiously—even if the first aim is not tenable.

Some apologists who adopt the first (sledgehammer) aim also accept the legitimacy of more modest permissive aims. Here, for instance, is J.P. Moreland:

Two senses of rationality are relevant to the question [of what it means to say a belief is rational]. A belief P can be rational in the sense that it is a rationally *permissible* belief. A belief P is permissible in case believing P is just as warranted as believing not-P or suspending judgment regarding P in light of the evidence. A belief P can also be rational in the sense that it is a rationally obligatory belief. A belief P is obligatory if believing P has greater warrant than believing not-P or suspending judgment regarding P in light of the evidence. In my view, the evidence in this book contributes to making the belief that the Christian God exists at least permissible and, I would argue, obligatory.[45]

Likewise, William Lane Craig, himself no friend of permissive apologetics, affirms:

Apologetics is...vital in fostering a cultural milieu in which the gospel can be heard as a viable option for thinking people. In most cases, it will not be arguments or evidence that bring a seeker to faith in Christ—that is the half-

---

[43] For discussion of this aim, see Matheson 2019.

[44] On the importance of such states in the religious life, see Audi 2011, Howard-Snyder 2013, and McKaughan 2013.

[45] Moreland 1987, 13. Bracketed words added for clarity.

truth seen by detractors of apologetics—but nonetheless it will be apologetics which, by making the gospel a credible option for seeking people, gives them, as it were, the intellectual permission to believe.[46]

If apologetic arguments suffice to show that the apologist's belief is rationally permissible, this is epistemically significant. For one of the most prominent critiques of religious belief over the past century or so has been that belief in God is *not* rationally permissible. If apologetic arguments are capable of establishing the rational permissibility of belief in God, then, they thereby undermine a very prominent critique of such belief. Accomplishing this—though it falls short of the grand aim espoused by sledgehammer apologists—would thus provide a way for the apologist to make coherent sense of her enterprise.

What about the aim of merely putting her religious beliefs "on the table" for discussion? Can the permissive apologist sensibly regard this as epistemically worthwhile, even if she thinks that her arguments don't make non-belief irrational, and may not even suffice to make belief rational? Let's explore two reasons to think she might.

First, some critics of belief in God make extremely strong claims about the state of the evidence concerning God's existence. Here, for instance, is Sam Harris:

> What I'm advocating...is a kind of conversational intolerance...All we need is a standard of intellectual honesty where people who pretend to be certain about things they're clearly not certain about, receive some conversational pressure. This would all be accomplished if we treated everyone who spoke about God on the floor of the Senate as though they had just spoke [sic] about Poseidon.... Clearly that would be the end of that person's political career. And yet *it's not like someone discovered in the third century that the biblical God exists and Poseidon doesn't. These claims have exactly the same status.*[47]

In like manner, Richard Dawkins opines:

> The universe does not owe you a sense of hope. It could be that the world, the universe, is a totally hopeless place. I don't as a matter of fact think it is, but even if it were, that would not be a good reason for believing in God. You

---

[46] Craig 1999.   [47] Harris 2005. Emphasis added.

cannot say 'I believe in X,' whatever X is—God or anything else—'because that gives me hope.' You have to say 'I believe in X because there is some evidence for X.' In the case of God, there is not a tiny shred of evidence for the existence of any kind of god.[48]

These claims are extremely strong. The apologist who claims merely to provide enough evidence to put God's existence on the table for discussion, makes a comparatively modest claim. That modest claim, however, is strong enough to make logical contact with the evidential claims of thinkers like Harris and Dawkins. And inasmuch as these thinkers are—for better or worse—quite prominent, it is easy to see how the apologist might think it worthwhile to rebut their claims by providing evidence, however modest, for her views.

Here is a second reason the apologist might think it worthwhile to provide evidence for her beliefs, even if, by her own lights, that evidence does not suffice to justify those beliefs. Consider the enterprise of scientific research. When scientists are careful about their work, they make sure not to draw grand conclusions from single studies. Careful researchers shy away from language like "this study *shows* that X and Y are highly correlated" or "our experiment *proves* that P causes Q." Instead, when researchers' individual studies are suggestive, the lesson to draw is that *further inquiry is merited.* A single study can provide some evidence for the hypothesis in question, while also providing evidence that the hypothesis is worthy of further research— perhaps in the form of replication attempts, or in the form of differently designed studies of the same phenomenon. Importantly, to make sense of this enterprise, the researchers need not think that their studies show that the negation of their hypothesis is irrational to believe, given the evidence that they supply. They need not think it is irrational to suspend judgment about their hypothesis. From an epistemic point of view, their study puts their hypothesis on the table for discussion, and justifies further inquiry—that's all, and that's significant. Likewise, the permissive apologist might think, her apologetic arguments don't always suffice to justify intellectual conversion. Perhaps, despite this, they provide rational encouragement for the non-believer to continue his inquiry—to run his own study, as it were. This might involve seeking further dialectical evidence in the form of additional arguments for or against religious beliefs. But crucially, it might also involve seeking direct evidence relevant to the beliefs, in the form of religious

[48] Dawkins 2008.

experience. For if God is real, one might think, among the most important evidence to be had is evidence gathered by seeking God directly by way of prayer, religious services, or a kind of devotional experiment.[49] Of course, there's no telling how such evidence-seeking will go. It is possible that the non-believing seeker will uncover no new evidence during the inquiry. The point for now is just this: if apologetic arguments suffice to put the given religious beliefs on the table for discussion, they encourage the further inquiry. In cases where this occurs, the apologist's arguments will have played an important epistemic role. That is perhaps enough for the apologist to make sense of her enterprise, even if she judges her arguments to fall short of more ambitious aims.

There are still further possibilities. Perhaps, short of making religious *belief* rational, apologetic evidence can justify states like *hope*, (non-doxastic) *affirmation*, or (non-doxastic) *faith*. We cannot explore these possibilities in detail here. But arguably, such states can foster one's commitment to religious practices (e.g., prayer, reading Scripture) in the absence of belief, and in the presence of doubt. Many apologists will take such practices to be conducive to encounters with God—the supreme religious good. It therefore seems that the permissive apologist can appeal to a number of epistemic and religious goods in order to make sense of the apologetic enterprise, even if she thinks her arguments fail to render non-belief irrational. To deny this is to take a truncated view of the relevant epistemic and religious goods.

5.4 Permissivism Without Pill-Popping

Recall the Feldman–White argument discussed above. There, the idea was that by taking the permissive path, the religious apologist undermines the rationality of her own beliefs. If the apologist thinks that those who hear and understand her arguments can remain rational in non-belief, then why should she adopt those beliefs instead of denying them or suspending judgment about them? After all, by her own lights, given the evidence she has shared, all of these attitudes are rational. Moreover, given the view that both her belief and its negation can be rational, why should she think that her belief is *true*? For if she thinks that both her belief and its negation can be rational given the evidence she has shared with her dissenter, it seems arbitrary for her to think that *her* belief is the more likely to be true. Why,

---

[49] See Franks Davis 1986.

then, should she hold her belief on the basis of that evidence, rather than by popping a belief-inducing pill?

This sort of argument targets directly the extreme Permissivism (and the denial of the Uniqueness Thesis) characteristic of permissive apologetics. We won't address it with anything approaching the attention it deserves.[50] Nevertheless, to see how the apologist might respond, note that proponents of Permissivism's rival—the Uniqueness Thesis—grant that different portions of a body of evidence can support different attitudes toward the same proposition. What they deny is that a *total* body of evidence can do so. Thus, White's official formulation of Uniqueness:

> Uniqueness: If an agent whose total evidence is E is fully rational in taking doxastic attitude D to P, then necessarily, any subject with total evidence E who takes a different attitude to P is less than fully rational.[51]

This is crucial in the present context because, first, even if Uniqueness is true, it is far from obvious that it applies to the case of the permissive apologist. For many such individuals, the apologetic arguments they share in the midst of discussion are only part of their total relevant evidence. More to the point, many such individuals *take* their arguments only to comprise only part of their total evidence. The latter might well include religious experience, testimony from experts in the apologist's religious community, and the like. If she takes E to be her total evidence, she will take the evidence consisting in their arguments, call it "E-," to be a proper subset of E. But crucially, in taking E- to support either their religious beliefs or the denial of those beliefs, she need not think that E itself does. Indeed, she might very well think that holding her religious beliefs is the only rational way to respond to E. So, even if the White–Feldman argument is sound, it is not clear that it reduces the permissive apologist to theological pill-popping, because it does not apply to her case.[52]

Now, one might worry that this tack is purely evasive—that it ignores the epistemic anarchy that ensues unless one embraces Uniqueness. But as Thomas Kelly has observed, to deny Permissivism, one need only think that there are *some* permissive cases—cases in which a body of evidence makes rational more than one doxastic attitude.[53] One can deny Uniqueness, Kelly

---

[50] But see White 2005 and 2013, and Kelly 2013.   [51] White 2013, 312.

[52] A further salient possibility: perhaps in *giving* the arguments comprising E-, the apologist does not thereby succeed in ensuring that her dissenter *possesses* E-. For more on this possibility, see Anderson 2018. Thanks to Matt Benton for helpful discussion here.

[53] See Kelly 2013, especially section 1.

notes, even if one thinks that many or most cases are *not* permissive. Now consider E- (the apologist's arguments). In taking the permissive path, our apologist must deny

c. If any non-believer were exposed to the very wide range of well-developed arguments for my religious beliefs that I am prepared to present (E-), and if she understood these arguments and lacked reason to doubt that she understood them, then these arguments would render it more rational for her to adopt my beliefs than to disbelieve them or suspend judgment with respect to them.

To deny (c) is to think that there are *some* non-believers whose evidence (and perhaps their background beliefs) is such that even when E- is added to them, their new total evidence still renders non-belief rational. But crucially, to deny (c) is not to say that all non-believers and their corresponding evidence bases and background beliefs are like this. Indeed, the apologist might deny (c) while also claiming that with for many non-believers and their corresponding evidence bases and background beliefs, the addition of E- would render non-belief irrational. She might even take this stance when it comes to the non-believers with whom she is most familiar. So, a certain way of traveling the permissive path might accord with the spirit of sledgehammer apologetics, albeit without some of the costs that accrue to the latter, and without the costs that attend the most extreme versions of Permissivism. Of course, that this position is *possible* does not entail that it is *viable*. That matter depends crucially on whether the apologist's arguments *would* render (or leave) non-belief rational, once added to the non-believer's evidence. But this can only be determined by taking a close look at the arguments themselves.

6. Conclusion

The main purpose of this paper has been to explore the Apologist's Dilemma—the dilemma that arises when the apologist considers the rational status of her dissenter's belief. Having shared her evidence with her dissenter, should the apologist take her dissenter's beliefs to be rational, or not? I have suggested that both answers come with costs. And while there are ways to cut the costs of traveling both paths, it is not wholly clear which path is the least costly, on the whole. In this respect, our treatment of the Dilemma is analogous to two competing housing contractors who are willing to provide only rough estimates concerning the cost of their labor, but who can't provide a guaranteed and accurate estimate until the work is done. The apologist who wants to discern whether she should travel the way of the sledgehammer or the permissive path is, I think, in a similar situation. And so are we. Determining which path is most cost effective requires careful consideration of several thorny issues in the philosophy of religion and epistemology, including the possibility of knockdown arguments, the problem of divine hiddenness, and the quality of the relevant apologetic arguments themselves. The safest conclusion to draw is that for many apologists, the cost-counting should continue for some time.[54]

References

Adams, Marilyn McCord. 1993. "The Problem of Hell: A Problem of Evil for Christians." In Eleonore Stump (ed.), *Reasoned Faith: Essays in Honor of Norman Kretzmann*, 301–327. Ithaca: Cornell University Press.

Anderson, Charity. 2018. "On Providing Evidence." *Episteme* 15: 245–260.

Audi, Robert. 2011. *Rationality and Religious Commitment.* Oxford: Oxford University Press.

Ballantyne, Nathan. 2014. "Knockdown Arguments." *Erkenntnis* 79 (S3): 525–543.

Ballantyne, Nathan. 2019. *Knowing Our Limits.* New York: Oxford University Press.

Ballantyne, Nathan and E.J. Coffman. 2011. "Uniqueness, Evidence, and Rationality." *Philosophers' Imprint* 11/18: 1–13.

Benton, Matthew A., John Hawthorne, and Yoaav Isaacs. 2016. "Evil and Evidence." In Jonathan Kvanvig (ed.), *Oxford Studies in Philosophy of Religion*, Vol. 7, 1–31. Oxford: Oxford University Press.

Buckareff, Andrei A. and Allen Plug. 2005. "Escaping Hell: Divine Motivation and the Problem of Hell." *Religious Studies* 41 (1): 39–54.

Cameron, Kirk. 2019. "Balancing Apologetics and Evangelism." Blog post at livingwaters.com, April 4, 2019. https://www.livingwaters.com/balancing-apologetics-and-evangelism/

Chignell, Andrew and Derk Pereboom. 2015. "Natural Theology." *The Stanford Encyclopedia of Philosophy.* https://plato.stanford.edu/entries/natural-theology/

---

[54] Thanks to Matt Benton, Nathan Ballantyne, Jon Kvanvig, and Jon Matheson for helpful comments and suggestions.

Christensen, David. 2007. "Epistemology of Disagreement: The Good News." *Philosophical Review* 116 (2): 187–217.

Christensen, David, and Jennifer Lackey (eds.). 2013. *The Epistemology of Disagreement: New Essays*. Oxford: Oxford University Press.

Clark, Kelly James. 1990. *Return to Reason: A Critique of Enlightenment Evidentialism and a Defense of Reason and Belief in God*. Grand Rapids, MI: Eerdmans.

Craig, William Lane. 1999. Review of Michael J. Murray (ed.), *Reason for the Hope Within*. *Philosophia Christi* 1: 129–133.

Dawkins Richard. 2008. Interview on *The Big Questions*. April 7, 2008. Accessed at: https://www.youtube.com/watch?v=of-8Q3HySjE&t=44m08s

DePoe, John and Timothy McGrew. 2013. "Natural Theology and the Uses of Argument." *Philosophia Christi* 15(2): 299–309.

Dougherty, Trent and Jerry L. Walls (eds.). 2018. *Two Dozen (or so) Arguments for God: The Plantinga Project*. New York: Oxford University Press.

Feldman, Richard. 2006. "Epistemological Puzzles about Disagreement." In Stephen Hetherington (ed.), *Epistemology Futures*, 216–36. Oxford: Oxford University Press.

Feldman, Richard. 2007. "Reasonable Religious Disagreements." In Louise Antony (ed.), *Philosophers without Gods*, 194–214. Oxford: Oxford University Press.

Feldman, Richard and Ted A. Warfield (eds.). 2010. *Disagreement*. Oxford: Oxford University Press.

Franks Davis, Caroline. 1986. "The Devotional Experiment." *Religious Studies* 22 (1): 15–28.

Greco, John. 2015. "No Fault Atheism." In Adam Green and Eleonore Stump (eds.), *Hidden Divinity and Religious Belief*, 109–25. Cambridge: Cambridge University Press.

Green, Adam and Eleonore Stump (eds.). 2015. *Hidden Divinity and Religious Belief*. Cambridge: Cambridge University Press.

Harris, Sam. 2005. Lecture on Harris, *The End of Faith*. C-SPAN2, November 15, 2005. Retrieved from: https://www.youtube.com/watch?v=qrScXF98tH0

Howard-Snyder, Daniel. 2013. "Propositional Faith: What it Is and What it Is Not." *American Philosophical Quarterly* 50 (4): 357–372.

Howard-Snyder, Daniel and Adam Green. 2016. "Hiddenness of God," *Stanford Encyclopedia of Philosophy*. Retrieved from: https://plato.stanford.edu/entries/divine-hiddenness/#ArguNonrNonb

Howard-Snyder, Daniel and Paul K. Moser (eds.). 2002. *Divine Hiddenness: New Essays*. New York: Cambridge University Press.

Keller, John. 2015. "On Knockdown Arguments." *Erkenntnis* 80 (6): 1205–1215.

Kelly, Thomas. 2005. "The Epistemic Significance of Disagreement." In Tamar Szabó Gendler and John Hawthorne (eds.), *Oxford Studies in Epistemology*, vol. 1, 167–196. Oxford: Clarendon Press.

Kelly, Thomas. 2013. "Evidence Can Be Permissive." In Matthias Steup, John Turri, and Ernest Sosa (eds.), *Contemporary Debates in Epistemology*, 298–313. Malden, MA: Wiley-Blackwell.

King, Nathan L. 2012. "Disagreement: What's the Problem? or A Good Peer is Hard to Find," *Philosophy and Phenomenological Research* 85 (2): 249–272.

King, Nathan L. 2016. "Religious Skepticism and Higher-Order Evidence." In Jonathan Kvanvig (ed.), *Oxford Studies in Philosophy of Religion*, vol. 7, 126–156. Oxford: Oxford University Press.

King, Nathan L. and Thomas Kelly. 2017. "Disagreement and the Epistemology of Theology." In William Abraham and Frederick D. Aquino (eds.), *The Oxford Handbook of the Epistemology of Theology*, 309–324. Oxford: Oxford University Press.

Kopec, Matthew and Michael G. Titelbaum. 2016. "The Uniqueness Thesis." *Philosophy Compass* 11/4: 189–200.

Kvanvig, Jonathan L. 1993. *The Problem of Hell*. New York: Oxford University Press.

Kvanvig, Jonathan L. 2014. *Rationality and Reflection*. Oxford: Oxford University Press.

Kvanvig, Jonathan L. 2018. *Faith and Humility*. Oxford: Oxford University Press.

Lewis, David. 1983. *Philosophical Papers*, vol. 1. Oxford: Oxford University Press.

Matheson, Jonathan. 2011. "The Case for Rational Uniqueness." *Logos & Episteme: An International Journal of Epistemology* 2 (3): 359–373.

Matheson, Jonathan. 2018. "Religious Disagreement and Divine Hiddenness." *Philosophia Christi* 20: 215–225.

Matheson, Jonathan. 2019. "Disagreement Skepticism and the Rationality of Religious Belief." In Kevin McCain and Ted Poston (eds.), *The Mystery of Skepticism: New Explorations*, 83–104. Boston: Brill.

Machuca, Diego (ed.). 2013. *Disagreement and Skepticism*. New York: Routledge Press.

McGrew, Timothy and Lydia McGrew. 2009. "The Argument from Miracles: A Cumulative Case for the Resurrection of Jesus of Nazareth." In J.P. Moreland and William Lane Craig (eds.), *A Companion to Natural Theology*, 593–662. Malden, MA: Blackwell.

McKaughan, Daniel. 2013. "Authentic Faith and Acknowledged Risk: Dissolving the Problem of Faith and Reason." *Religious Studies* 49 (1): 101–124.

Moreland, J.P. 1987. *Scaling the Secular City: A Defense of Christianity*. Grand Rapids, MI: Baker Books.

Murray, Michael. 1999. "Introduction." In Michael Murray (ed.), *Reason for the Hope Within*, 1–19. Grand Rapids, MI: Eerdmans.

Pascal, Blaise. 2008. *Pensées and Other Writings*. Trans. Anthony Levi. Oxford: Oxford University Press.

Plantinga, Alvin. 1995. "Pluralism: A Defense of Religious Exclusivism." In Thomas D. Senor (ed.), *The Rationality of Belief and the Plurality of Faith*, 191–215. Ithaca: Cornell University Press.

Rea, Michael C. 2018. *The Hiddenness of God*. Oxford: Oxford University Press.

Roush, Sherrilyn. 2017. "Epistemic Self-Doubt." *The Stanford Encyclopedia of Philosophy*. Retrieved from: https://plato.stanford.edu/entries/epistemic-self-doubt/

Schellenberg, John. 2006. *Divine Hiddenness and Human Reason*. Ithaca: Cornell University Press.

Schellenberg, John. 2015. "Divine Hiddenness and Human Philosophy." In Adam Green and Eleonore Stump (eds.), *Hidden Divinity and Religious Belief*, 13–32. Cambridge: Cambridge University Press.

Spurgeon, Charles H. 1861. *Spurgeon's Sermons*, vol. 7. Woodstock, Ontario: Devoted Publishers.

Stanford, Kyle. 2017. "The Underdetermination of Scientific Theory." *The Stanford Encyclopedia of Philosophy* October 12, 2017. URL: https://plato.stanford.edu/entries/scientific-underdetermination/

Swinburne, Richard. 2004. *The Existence of God*. 2nd edn. Oxford: Oxford University Press.

Talbott, Thomas. 2014. *The Inescapable Love of God*. Eugene, OR: Wipf and Stock.

Van Inwagen, Peter. 2009. *Metaphysics*. 3rd edn. Boulder, CO: Westview Press.

Walls, Jerry. 1992. *Hell: The Logic of Damnation*. Notre Dame, IN: University of Notre Dame Press.

Whitcomb, Dennis, Heather Battaly, Jason Baehr, and Daniel Howard-Snyder. 2017. "Intellectual Humility: Owning Our Limitations." *Philosophy and Phenomenological Research* 94: 509–539.

White, Roger. 2005. "Epistemic Permissiveness." *Philosophical Perspectives* 19: 445–459.

White, Roger. 2013. "Evidence Cannot Be Permissive." In Matthias Steup, John Turri, and Ernest Sosa (eds.), *Contemporary Debates in Epistemology*, 312–323. Malden, MA: Wiley-Blackwell.

8

Rationalist Resistance to Disagreement-Motivated Religious Skepticism

John Pittard

1. Introduction

Many epistemologists writing on disagreement have argued that our responses to disagreement should exhibit a certain kind of epistemic impartiality. In particular, these "strong conciliationists" claim that we ought to give equal weight to the views of those who, judged from a dispute-neutral perspective, appear to be our "epistemic peers" with respect to some disputed matter. In this paper, I consider whether there is a plausible epistemic impartiality principle that would require us to give up confident religious (or *irreligious*) belief in favor of religious skepticism. The discussion is carried out within the formal context of Bayesian epistemology, since doing so helps render perspicuous the strong conciliationist's commitments and the challenges facing these commitments. I argue that the strong conciliationist's commitment to epistemic impartiality is untenable, at least in contexts like the religious domain where the primary questions under dispute cannot be cleanly separated from questions about what qualifications are needed to reliably assess those primary questions. I recommend that we reject strong impartiality requirements in favor of a rationalist view which holds that rational insight can sustain justified confidence even when impartial grounds are lacking. In the paper's final section, I defend the "religious acceptability" of this rationalist epistemology.

2. The Key Commitment of the (Bayesian) Strong Conciliationist

In this section and the following two sections, I draw on formal epistemology to clarify what I take to be the key commitment that lies behind a prominent view on the rational significance of disagreement, a view that I will call

John Pittard, *Rationalist Resistance to Disagreement-Motivated Religious Skepticism* In: *Religious Disagreement and Pluralism*. Edited by: Matthew A. Benton and Jonathan L. Kvanvig, Oxford University Press. © John Pittard 2021.
DOI: 10.1093/oso/9780198849865.003.0008

"strong conciliationism." An assumption of my discussion is that the correct disagreement policy, whatever it may be, is generally compatible with Bayesianism, which is the consensus view in formal epistemology. More specifically, I will assume that the correct disagreement policy is applicable to what may be called a "precise and opinionated Bayesian agent." For present purposes, I will define such an agent with reference to a disagreement situation where subjects *S1* and *S2* disagree about *p*, and where *S1* knows some information about *S2* before learning *S2*'s view on *p*. *S1* counts as *a precise and opinionated Bayesian agent* if and only if the following conditions are satisfied:

- At any time *t*, *S1*'s opinions can be faithfully modeled by a single credence function C_t that specifies the values (real numbers between 0 and 1) of her unconditional and conditional degrees of confidence or "credences."

- Just before learning *S2*'s opinion about *p*, *S1* has a credence for *p* and she also has a precise estimate of her own reliability with respect to *p* and of *S2*'s reliability with respect to *p*.[1]

- When *S1* learns *S2*'s opinion about *p*, *S1* updates her credences through a process of *conditionalization*. (More will be said about conditionalization later.)

In assuming that the correct disagreement policy is applicable to a precise and opinionated Bayesian agent, I assume that the correct disagreement policy is at least normally compatible with standard Bayesian conditionalization and that questions about how to respond to disagreement are orthogonal to the question of whether it is always rationally permissible to have a precise credence for some proposition. Most epistemologists writing on disagreement would, I think, be happy to grant these assumptions. While not everyone writing on disagreement carries out their discussion within a Bayesian framework, very few would endorse a policy that is seen to significantly conflict with Bayesian conditionalization. Bayesianism is our best formal account of how to update credences in light of empirical evidence, and policies that diverge from Bayesian prescriptions in a predictable way are subject to formidable objections.[2] And

---

[1] *S1* could arrive at arbitrarily precise reliability estimates on the assumption that she has precise (and knowable) credences for any proposition that posits of her reliability (or of <*S2*'s reliability) that it falls within some determinate range.

[2] An agent committed to following some policy that diverged from conditionalization in a predictable way would be subject to manipulation by a "Dutch Book" strategy, where they are presented with bets that individually look fair but that collectively are guaranteed to result in the subject losing money. For a good overview of the Dutch Book argument for conditionalization, see Hájek 2009. Departure from conditionalization would also lead to violation of an extremely plausible "epistemic reflection" principle of the sort defended in Briggs 2009.

while Bayesians disagree about whether rationality sometimes forbids having a precise credence for some proposition, very few positions on disagreement appear to be committed to any particular resolution of this debate.

Thus, in focusing my discussion on precise and opinionated Bayesian agents, I do not beg the question against major approaches to disagreement. And focusing on precise and opinionated Bayesian agents will help us to characterize the core commitment of strong conciliationism and to identify various alternatives to this commitment. This being said, a small number of philosophers do argue for positions on disagreement that explicitly oppose the rationality of a precise and opinionated Bayesian agent.[3] While I do not think that such positions are correct, I cannot defend that judgment here. For the present, I simply set these positions aside.

Having noted this important background assumption, let's now consider a generic disagreement scenario. In this and all other examples we will consider, it should be assumed that the agents are precise and opinionated Bayesian agents. Suppose I consider some proposition p for the first time, without knowing what other people think about the matter, and after reflection I come to believe that p is true. Let's say that my credence for p is fairly close to 1. (Credence 1 indicates certainty that the proposition in question is true, and credence 0 indicates certainty that it is false.) I then learn that someone named Beatrice has also been thinking about p. Before I learn what Beatrice thinks about p, I am able to acquire a great deal of information about Beatrice that would help me to estimate how reliable she is likely to be in assessing the truth of p. For example, I can learn facts about her intelligence, her level of education, her epistemic track record with respect to similar matters, what information she possesses that might be relevant to an assessment of p, whether there are factors that would obviously bias her thinking, how confident she feels in her judgment about p, how carefully she has thought about the matter, and so on. But what I *cannot* learn about Beatrice at this point is her view about whether p or $\sim p$ is more likely to be true, or any specific details of the reasoning on which she bases her conclusion. The only factors about Beatrice that I can learn are what I will call "p-neutral considerations." P-neutral considerations are considerations whose evidential significance can be appreciated from a stance that is neutral on p and also neutral on

---

[3] For example, see Rosenkranz and Schulz 2015; Elkin and Wheeler 2018. Rosenkranz and Schulz endorse a conciliatory policy as an *alternative* to conditionalization, as they suggest that one should sometimes respond to disagreement not by conditionalizing, but by modifying one's prior conditional probabilities. Elkin and Wheeler suggest that one should respond to peer disagreement by adopting imprecise credences. I will briefly discuss credal imprecision later.

the merits of (potentially controversial) lines of reasoning that might be used to support p or $\sim p$. The point of this scenario is that we are to imagine that I estimate Beatrice's cognitive reliability with respect to p in a way that is not biased by my particular perspective on p or by my perspective on contestable reasoning that bears on p.

Let's suppose that on the basis of p-neutral considerations alone, any reasonable neutral party would estimate Beatrice and myself to be equally reliable. We appear to be equally intelligent, we have equivalent track records with respect to similar questions, we both possess the same information that is relevant to assessing p, we both feel equally confident in our judgment, and so on. Seeing this, I acknowledge that to any reasonable third party, Beatrice and I would appear to be *epistemic peers* (at least when taking into consideration only p-neutral factors).[4]

Let's imagine that on the basis of the p-neutral factors I have learned about Beatrice and her process of evaluating p, I form an estimate of Beatrice's cognitive reliability with respect to p. In other words, I form a view about the probability that Beatrice will believe the truth about p. Call this reliability estimate r_B. Let's also assume that r_B is my best estimate of Beatrice's reliability irrespective of whether p turns out to be true or false. This means that my overall estimate of Beatrice's reliability does not differ from my estimate of her reliability conditional on p or from my estimate of her reliability conditional on $\sim p$. (As I will argue later, strong conciliationism faces problems when we drop this simplifying assumption.)

After learning that Beatrice is like me with respect to p-neutral factors, but *before* learning whether Beatrice believes p or $\sim p$, there's no clear reason to suppose that my initial high credence for p would change. So let's suppose that it remains unchanged. But now, finally, I learn what Beatrice thinks about p, and I learn that she disagrees with my view: my confidence that p is true is matched by Beatrice's confidence that p is false.

How should learning of this disagreement with Beatrice affect my credence for p? Many philosophers have recently argued that in this sort of case I should not think it any more likely that Beatrice is the one in error than that *I* am the one in error, and should therefore adopt a credence for p of approximately 0.5.[5] On their view, since I acknowledge that Beatrice appears to be just as qualified as

---

[4] The term "epistemic peer," introduced in (Gutting 1982), gets defined in many different ways. For our purposes we can say that someone is my epistemic peer with respect to p just in case she has the same quality and quantity of relevant evidence and she is equal to me in her reliability in assessing such evidence.

[5] See, for example, Elga 2007; Christensen 2007; Cohen 2013.

myself on the basis of *p*-neutral considerations—i.e., since she is an apparent epistemic peer—it would be rationally arbitrary for me to trust the cognitive process behind *my* credence for *p* more than I trust the cognitive process behind *her* credence for *p*. Given that we appear to be equally trustworthy, I should give equal weight to each of our initial views.[6]

The view just sketched is quite demanding in that it requires me to exhibit full epistemic impartiality in my response to the disagreement with Beatrice. This commitment to rigorous impartiality is definitive of strong conciliationism. The strong conciliationist holds that I should give equal weight to the views of those who appear (on the basis of *dispute-neutral* considerations) to be my epistemic peer.

Strong conciliationism provides one answer to the question of how I should adjust my credence after learning of the disagreement, but a different sort of answer is provided by standard Bayesian confirmation theory. I say a *different sort* of answer rather than a *competing* answer since the constraint supplied by strong conciliationism and the constraints supported by Bayesianism are mutually consistent, though not mutually entailing. Conciliationism says what the *value* of my final credence should be—0.5—while Bayesianism says what *relation* should hold between my final credence and the credences and views I had just before learning of the disagreement. More specifically, we can appeal to the requirements of Bayesianism in order to identify a function that shows how my credence for *p* just *after* learning of the disagreement should be related to r_B (my reliability estimate for Beatrice) and to my credence for *p* just before learning of the disagreement.

Bayesians use credence functions to represent a subject's doxastic state at any given time. Credence functions specify both the unconditional and conditional credences of a subject. If C is my present credence function, $C(p)$ stands for the value of my unconditional credence for *p* and $C(p|H)$ stands for my conditional credence for *p* on the supposition that hypothesis H is true. Bayesianism provides a theory of how a subject's credences should change in response to new evidence. According to this theory, when I learn evidential

---

[6] Elsewhere, I've argued that the most reasonable version of conciliationism will *not* typically require "splitting the difference" and arriving at a credence halfway between the original credences, despite the fact that conciliationists frequently describe their view as a "split the difference" policy (Pittard 2019a). In particular, if two epistemic peers arrive at opposing views on *p*, and if one of those views was agreed to be antecedently more probable than the other, then we have an impartial reason to give more weight to the disputant who arrived at the view that was antecedently more probable. To avoid complications arising from such cases, we can assume that the disagreements discussed here are ones where the opposing views enjoy equal antecedent probability, or where there is no agreement on which of the opposing views enjoys more antecedent probability (in which case the disputants' judgments of antecedent plausibility are also caught up in the disagreement).

proposition E (and nothing else), I should *conditionalize* on this evidence. This involves setting my new credence for p equal to the *conditional* credence for p given E that I had just before learning E. To apply this to my disagreement with Beatrice, let C_{post} stand for my post-disagreement credence function just after taking into account the evidence supplied by the disagreement, C_{pre} stand for my credence function just *before* learning of the disagreement, and D stand for the evidence that I receive when I learn that Beatrice *disagrees* with me. Conditionalization requires that $C_{post}(p) = C_{pre}(p \mid D)$.

In addition to this diachronic constraint that describes how my credences should shift when I learn new evidence, Bayesianism also supplies synchronic requirements that constrain $C_{pre}(p|D)$. Bayes's theorem says that my credence function should satisfy the following constraint:

$$\text{Bayes's theorem}: \; C_{pre}(p \mid D) = \frac{C_{pre}(D \mid p) \; \times \; C_{pre}(p)}{C_{pre}(D)}$$

Additionally, respecting the law of total probability requires me to satisfy the following constraint:

$$C_{pre}(D) = C_{pre}(D \mid p) \times C_{pre}(p) + C_{pre}(D \mid {\sim}p) \times (1 - C_{pre}(p))$$

Finally, note that r_B, my reliability estimate for Beatrice, determines how probable I should take disagreement to be conditional on $\sim p$ and conditional on p. Specifically, it should be the case that $C_{pre}(D|{\sim}p) = r_B$ and $C_{pre}(D \mid p) = (1 - r_B)$.

Making various substitutions, the Bayesian constraints identified in the previous two paragraphs imply that I should satisfy the following the constraint:

$$C_{post}(p) = \frac{(1 - r_B) \times \; C_{pre}(p)}{(1 - r_B) \times \; C_{pre}(p) + r_B \times (1 - C_{pre}(p))}$$

Even if one is not familiar with the Bayesian principles that lie behind this constraint, it should not be surprising that my confidence for p after learning of the disagreement should be a function of how reliable I estimated Beatrice to be before learning of the disagreement. The above constraint aligns with the intuitive view that the more reliable I estimate Beatrice to be, the more my credence should decrease upon learning of her disagreement.

An interesting result is attained when we combine the strong conciliationist requirement with the Bayesian constraints. Strong conciliationism says what the value of my new credence for p should be: $C_{post}(p)$ should be 0.5, as this is the impartial response that gives equal weight to my apparent peer. Bayesianism does not specify a value for my new credence, but it does say how this new post-disagreement credence should be related to r_B and my pre-disagreement credence for p. These two requirements taken together entail the following constraint on my credence for p *before* learning of the disagreement:[7]

STRONG IMPARTIALITY: It ought to be the case that $C_{pre}(p) = r_B$.

According to STRONG IMPARTIALITY, prior to learning what anyone else thinks about p, my credence for p should be equal to the p-neutral reliability estimate that I have for someone like Beatrice whom I know to be relevantly like me in p-neutral respects.[8] Given the assumption that the correct disagreement policy is applicable to precise and opinionated Bayesian agents, it follows that strong conciliationism is correct only if STRONG IMPARTIALITY is correct.

Here is the upshot of the foregoing discussion. In a context where a Bayesian agent has a precise and opinionated doxastic state both before and after a disagreement, strong conciliationism amounts to a view on what factors may legitimately ground epistemic confidence *prior* to disagreement. This is because Bayesian conditionalization will lead to the impartial *post*-disagreement credences that the strong conciliationist endorses only if *pre*-disagreement credences are set in a suitably impartial way. For this reason, it would be somewhat misleading to characterize strong conciliationism as a policy narrowly concerned with disagreements between apparent epistemic peers. To be sure, a key commitment of strong conciliationism is that in paradigm cases of disagreement between apparent peers (like the one

---

[7] As already explained, Bayesian epistemology requires that $C_{post}(p) = (1 - r_B) \times C_{pre}(p)/[(1 - r_B) \times C_{pre}(p) + r_B \times (1 - C_{pre}(p))]$; and strong conciliationism requires that $C_{post}(p) = 0.5$. Combining these, we get $0.5 = (1 - r_B) \times C_{pre}(p)/[(1 - r_B) \times C_{pre}(p) + r_B \times (1 - C_{pre}(p))]$, which algebraically simplifies to $C_{pre}(p) = r_B$. A derivation of this sort was originally provided by Roger White 2009. White was focused on the relation between subject's pre-disagreement credence and his estimate of his *own* reliability, though in the context of that example it was known that the subject and his disputant were equally reliable. In the present example, it is not known that Beatrice and I are equally reliable. All that is known is that the *impartial* considerations support equal estimates of Beatrice's and my reliability.

[8] Labels given to rules like STRONG IMPARTIALITY include "calibration," "calibration rule," or "calibrationism." For discussion of such requirements, see White 2009; Schoenfeld 2015; 2018; Sliwa and Horowitz 2015; Christensen 2016; Pittard 2019a. Because STRONG IMPARTIALITY focuses on an agent (like Beatrice) who is *relevantly similar* (in p-neutral respects), this constraint is very much like Christensen's "Idealized Thermometer Model" (Christensen 2016, 409).

involving Beatrice and myself), the appropriate response is to give equal weight to each disputant's pre-disagreement credence. But this commitment, together with the commitment to Bayesianism, requires the strong conciliationist to endorse a general impartiality requirement that constrains the values of one's credences whether or not disagreement is ever encountered. Moreover, by appealing to the impartiality constraint on pre-disagreement credences and the requirement of Bayesian conditionalization, the strong conciliationist can arrive at prescriptions for non-peer disagreements where there is an asymmetry in the apparent epistemic credentials of the disputants.

3. Reasons Impartiality and Agent Impartiality

The constraint on pre-disagreement credences that must be endorsed by the strong conciliationist is one that is substantive and highly controversial. To see this, it will be helpful to emphasize how STRONG IMPARTIALITY differs from the more benign claim that prior to the disagreement, my credence for p ought to be equal to my estimate of *my own* reliability on the matter. Letting r_M designate how reliable I estimate *myself* to be in assessing p prior to learning of my disagreement with Beatrice, we can express this more benign claim by saying that it ought to be the case $C_{pre}(p) = r_M$. Since the strong conciliationist will also affirm this latter claim, the strong conciliationist will hold that I ought to satisfy the following constraint: $C_{pre}(p) = r_M = r_B$. The claim that my credence (and estimate of my own reliability) should be equal to r_B is not an innocuous addition to the benign constraint expressed by $C_{pre}(p) = r_M$. STRONG IMPARTIALITY goes beyond this benign constraint in two important respects. First, STRONG IMPARTIALITY requires that my pre-disagreement credences be equal to a reliability estimate that I have or would have for someone who is *not me* (albeit someone who, on the basis of p-neutral considerations, does not appear to be more or less qualified than myself). By tying my initial credence to the reliability estimate I would have for *someone else* who is relevantly similar, STRONG IMPARTIALITY imposes an *agent impartiality* requirement. Second, recall that r_B is a reliability estimate for Beatrice that is based only on p-neutral considerations. In tying my pre-disagreement credence to a p-neutral reliability estimate, STRONG IMPARTIALITY also requires what I call *reasons impartiality*. It will be useful to elaborate on these distinct impartiality requirements that both follow from STRONG IMPARTIALITY. I begin with reasons impartiality.

To clarify the reasons impartiality requirement that follows from STRONG IMPARTIALITY, let's turn to a concrete example.[9] Suppose I am a college student working through a math problem set, and one of the problems requires me to reason through a version of the well-known "Monty Hall Problem." In this problem, a game show contestant's final prize will be determined by which of three closed doors she chooses to open. The winning door, which was randomly determined, accesses a room that holds a car. The other two doors access rooms that contain only a goat. As the contestant knows, the show's host, Monty Hall, always follows the following procedure. After the contestant announces an initial choice (Door 2, say), Monty Hall (who knows which door leads to the car) does not yet allow the contestant to open that door. Instead, Monty Hall opens some door that leads to a goat and that the contestant did *not* initially choose (Door 3, say). Having revealed the goat behind this door, Monty Hall then gives the contestant a choice: she may stick with her initial choice or she may choose to change her choice to the other door that remains closed (in this case, Door 1). (If this procedure leaves Monty Hall with a choice as to which door to open, he chooses at random.) The question is whether switching doors increases the probability that the contestant wins the car. Suppose that this is my first time encountering this problem, and that I am unaware of the history of controversy surrounding the problem.[10] While many highly qualified thinkers initially give the wrong answer to the Monty Hall Problem, let's suppose that I correctly reason as follows: "We can expect that two thirds of the time, the contestant will initially choose a door behind which is a goat. When that happens, the car must be behind the only door that both was *not* the contestant's initial choice and that remains closed after Monty Hall opens a door to reveal a goat. So two thirds of the time, switching to the other door that remains closed will lead to winning the car. Switching leads to a goat only one third of the time, on those occasions when the contestant initially chooses the winning door. Staying put, on the other hand, results in winning the car only when the contestant initially chose the winner, which happens one third of the time. So by switching, the contestant doubles the probability of winning."

Having reached this conclusion, how confident should I be that switching doors is the superior strategy? As already suggested, it is plausible that my credence for this proposition should be equal to my estimate of my reliability in reasoning through the problem. But this requirement does not by itself

---

[9] I also discuss the following "Monty Hall Problem" example in chapter 4 of Pittard 2019b.

[10] See the relevant Wikipedia entry for the interesting details.

place any constraints on the factors that may inform this reliability estimate. In particular, it does not require that my reliability estimate be based only on p-neutral factors. Granted, I *could* estimate my reliability in a p-neutral way. I might, for example, reach a reliability estimate by reasoning as follows: "In past homework assignments when I'm inclined to affirm some particular answer on the basis of reasoning that *seems* clear and conclusive, I've been right 95% of the time. So, my estimate of my reliability in answering this Monty Hall question is 0.95." But suppose instead I reason in this way: "The generic process of 'believing some answer to one of these homework questions when I am highly confident in my reasoning' is only 95% reliable. But that generic process does not determine the reliability of relying on the very specific form of reasoning that led me to my conclusion in the Monty Hall Problem. And that reasoning is cogent, clear, and conclusive. My appreciation of the cogency of that reasoning gives me reason to think that the probability that I am correct on this matter is greater than 95%. My estimate of my reliability in this case is therefore 0.99."

Clearly, this reasoning that lies behind my high reliability estimate does not qualify as being p-neutral. I acknowledge that my confidence cannot be justified on the basis of more generic considerations (like my track record on broadly similar problems) whose significance could be appreciated independently of any particular view on the merits of my reasoning about the Monty Hall Problem. Rather, my high level of confidence is based on the evident cogency of the specific reasoning that led me to my conclusion.

The strong conciliationist must deny that I can rationally base my confidence level directly on the specific reasoning in this way. For suppose I am about to learn Beatrice's answer to the Monty Hall question. I know, let's imagine, that Beatrice's track record on homework assignments is equal to my own and that we are on a par with respect to this and all other accessible p-neutral considerations. But because I think that the p-neutral qualifications that I share with Beatrice only support a reliability estimate of 0.95, I ought to estimate her reliability at 0.95 prior to learning what she thinks about the matter. And if I start with a credence of 0.99 and conditionalize on the fact that someone estimated to be 0.95 reliable disagrees with me, I will not arrive at an "equal weight" credence of 0.5.[11] To get the correct equal weight result, I must start with a pre-disagreement credence of 0.95, which is to say that I must start

---

[11] Starting with a credence for my answer of 0.99 and then conditionalizing on disagreement from a source with 0.95 reliability would result in a final credence of approximately 0.84.

with a credence that comports with a p-neutral reliability estimate and that therefore exhibits reasons impartiality.

STRONG IMPARTIALITY requires not only that we exhibit reasons impartiality in our pre-disagreement stance, but it requires agent impartiality as well. To see how these two forms of impartiality differ, consider a different example. Beatrice and I have been talking for a while when the question arises as to whether we have been talking for more than an hour. After a moment's reflection, I am strongly inclined to judge that we have been talking for more than an hour. This judgment is not based on any explicit line of reasoning, but is a response to its strongly seeming to me that over an hour has elapsed. Suppose that in estimating my reliability in forming this judgment, I reason as follows: "I have such and such p-neutral epistemic credentials, and when someone else with those p-neutral credentials is inclined to a certain view on whether more than an hour has elapsed in a conversation, and when their doxastic inclination is as strong as my present inclination, my best estimate of their reliability is 0.95. But in this situation, it is not merely the case that someone as qualified as me is strongly inclined to judge that more than an hour has elapsed. It is also the case that it seems *to me* that more than an hour has elapsed. And this first-person fact about what seems true *to me* gives me greater reason for confidence than a third-person fact about a relevantly similar seeming of someone whose p-neutral credentials are just like mine. So it is reasonable for me to estimate my reliability as being higher than 0.95. I therefore estimate my reliability at 0.98."

While the above reasoning clearly fails to be impartial, this is not because it appeals to some consideration whose force can be appreciated only by someone who is inclined to agree with me on whether or not an hour has elapsed. Since no part of the reasoning behind my reliability estimate presupposes that my estimate of how much time has passed is correct, I do not exhibit *reasons* partiality. Rather, my reasoning fails to be impartial because it supposes that a first-person fact that p seems true *to me* can have more evidential weight (for me) than the third-person fact that p seems true in a relevantly similar way to someone relevantly like me. Such reasoning exhibits what may be called *agent* partiality, since it supposes that the evidential significance of some doxastic "seeming" may depend on which agent the seeming belongs to (and in particular, whether that agent is *me*) even after we have taken into account all of the non-identifying facts pertaining to the epistemic qualifications of the agent and the qualitative character of the seeming. Importantly, even if Beatrice has some contrary seeming that leads her to disagree with me over whether an hour has elapsed, this need not prevent her from affirming that the reasoning behind my self-favoring reliability estimate is fully rational. Beatrice might think that it is perfectly rational to give additional weight to first-person seemings. Of course, Beatrice could not *adopt* my reasoning, since my reasoning includes first-personal claims that are true if uttered by me but not if uttered by her. But she could recite parallel reasons for estimating her own reliability more highly than she estimates my reliability. And in this case, Beatrice and I might affirm the full rationality of the other's position even as we continue to disagree on how likely it is that an hour has elapsed.

Because strong conciliationists are committed to holding that my initial credence for p should be equal to my reliability estimate for *Beatrice* (and for any other person whose p-neutral qualifications are equal to my own), they are committed to an agent impartiality requirement. This commitment puts them in opposition to epistemologists who hold that the fundamental norms of rationality are "agent-centered" norms that license agent partiality.[12]

Thus far, I've argued that strong conciliationists are committed to STRONG IMPARTIALITY, and that STRONG IMPARTIALITY imposes a reasons impartiality constraint and an agent impartiality constraint on pre-disagreement credences. But on a little reflection, it seems fairly clear that STRONG IMPARTIALITY is not plausible if offered as an absolutely exceptionless requirement.[13] For example, it does not seem that I can have p-neutral reasons for highly estimating my reliability with respect to the proposition that every human being's thoughts, sense impressions, and memories are being manipulated by a malicious and deceptive demon. Someone who was not already inclined to agree with me that this skeptical thesis is implausible would presumably have doubts about the cogency of any reasons I might give for highly estimating my reliability (and the reliability of those relevantly like me) on this matter. Assuming that strong conciliationists allow that we are justified in assigning a low credence to such radical skeptical hypotheses, then presumably they must allow that in this case we can be justified on "partisan" grounds that do not satisfy the requirement of reasons impartiality.

Likewise, if the strong conciliationist allows that she justifiably believes strong conciliationism itself, then it would appear that STRONG IMPARTIALITY does not constrain her initial credence for strong conciliationism. Strong conciliationists have disputants who, judged by p-neutral considerations, appear to be just as qualified to assess strong conciliationism. If strong conciliationists are justified

---

[12] For example, see Huemer 2011; DePaul 2013.
[13] For further defense of the claim that such impartiality requirements cannot be exceptionless, see Pittard 2019a.

in giving their own position more weight even after conditionalizing on facts about the opinions of others, then we can infer that STRONG IMPARTIALITY does not constrain how much confidence they can rationally have for strong conciliationism prior to taking into account others' views on the matter.

Because a reasonable strong conciliationist will likely admit that we are not always required to conform to STRONG IMPARTIALITY, it is more charitable to understand strong conciliationism as holding that STRONG IMPARTIALITY is a highly general constraint that applies to *nearly* all of our beliefs. Those who count as opponents of strong conciliationism will thus be those who affirm that we are often justified in holding a belief with confidence even when such confidence cannot be justified impartially.

It will be useful to have a label for the kind of justification that someone enjoys when they rationally hold a belief with a degree of confidence that is not supportable on purely impartial grounds. Let's say that someone has *partisan justification* for his belief that *p* just in case he is justified in assigning *p* a high credence even though a credence that high does not accord with an impartial estimate of his reliability (where an impartial estimate is one that exhibits both *reasons impartiality* and *agent impartiality*). When someone starts with a partisan estimate of their own reliability and then conditionalizes on disagreement evidence, the resulting credences will not be impartial. Conditionalization will still typically require a diminishment in confidence, perhaps even to a significant degree. But less conciliation will be required than if the subject had started off with credences conforming to STRONG IMPARTIALITY.

If the discussion thus far is on track, then questions about the nature and scope of partisan justification are of central importance to the epistemology of disagreement. Strong conciliationists occupy one extreme end of a spectrum of views on partisan justification. If they are right that we almost never enjoy partisan justification, then it will almost never be reasonable to maintain confidence in the face of disagreement with those who appear (on the basis of *p*-neutral considerations) to be our epistemic peers. But if there are many contexts where partisan justification is available, then it could frequently be rational to maintain significant confidence in the wake of such disagreements.

Do we sometimes enjoy partisan justification? If so, on what grounds? Might it be the case that many religious believers enjoy partisan justification, so that they are not required to weight competing religious (and irreligious) views in an impartial manner? In the next section, I identify three broad accounts of partisan justification that strong conciliationists must oppose.

4. Accounts of Partisan Justification and Their Problems

Let's continue with the example of the previous section where I acknowledge that the impartial reasons I have for trusting my view about p are perfectly symmetrical to the impartial reasons I have for trusting Beatrice's view on the matter (whatever it turns out to be). Again, let us focus on the stage after I have formed my own view about p but before I know Beatrice's opinion. Suppose that, despite this symmetry of the impartial considerations, I estimate of my own reliability on the matter more highly than I estimate Beatrice's reliability. In other words, $r_M > r_B$. Let's also assume that my pre-disagreement credence for p is equal to my estimate of my reliability. This means that $C_{pre}(p) > r_B$, contrary to what STRONG IMPARTIALITY requires.

Given the acknowledged parity of the impartial considerations, it would seem that my self-favoring reliability estimate is justified only if there is some asymmetry in the *non-impartial* considerations, an asymmetry that justifies $r_M > r_B$.[14] One could contest this by endorsing a radically "permissive" conception of rationality according to which $r_M = r_B, r_M > r_B$, and $r_M < r_B$ could all be rationally permissible states for me even though there is no asymmetry in *any* of the factors that are relevant to estimating r_M and r_B. But such a radically permissive view is not especially plausible. Even if there are rationally permissive situations where $r_M = r_B, r_M > r_B$, and $r_M < r_B$ are all rationally permissible states, these would presumably be *nonsymmetric* situations where one sort of rational factor supports $r_M > r_B$, where another sort of rational factor supports $r_M < r_B$, and where no single way of weighing these competing factors is rationally obligatory.[15] But suppose that, for any value v, all the rational factors that might serve to justify me in setting r_M equal to v are perfectly symmetrical to the rational factors that might serve to justify me in setting r_B equal to v. In this case, it does seem that $r_M = r_B$ is the rationally privileged state. At least that is what I will assume going forward. I will henceforth assume that $r_M > r_B$ is justified only if there is some sort of "symmetry breaker" that supports trusting myself more than trusting Beatrice.[16]

---

[14] Recall our assumption that I am a precise and opinionated Bayesian. So we can assume that I have credences pertaining to whether there is some sort of asymmetry, and what that asymmetry may be.

[15] For example, in a piece from Schoenfield defending a permissive view of rationality, she maintains that a rational person could believe atheism on the basis of certain sorts of arguments and considerations (like the argument from evil or "appeals to ontological simplicity") while acknowledging that someone with her same evidence could also rationally believe theism if more weight was given to other sorts of arguments and considerations (Schoenfield 2014, 200–202).

[16] The helpful notion of a "symmetry breaker" is from Lackey 2010.

What sort of factor could reasonably be thought to justify $r_M > r_B$ even when there is acknowledged to be perfect parity in the p-neutral considerations? According to an *agent-centered account* of partisan justification, first-person facts (e.g., facts about what seems true *to me*) might help to justify $r_M > r_B$ even when the third-person facts I am aware of are symmetrical and do not justify $r_M > r_B$.

It is important to distinguish between an agent-centered account of partisan justification, which assigns direct epistemic significance to first-person facts, and a view that takes first-person facts to be significant inasmuch as they shape which third-person facts are accessible. Because you have introspective access to your own cognitive state but not to the cognitive states of others, you will normally have better evidence pertaining to your own cognitive state than to the cognitive states of your disputants.[17] For example, you might know that p seems to you to be obviously correct, while in the case of your disputant you may know only that he or she *reports* (with apparent sincerity) that $\sim p$ seems to him to be obviously correct. This might make it reasonable for you to give somewhat more weight to your own view than to your disputant's view, even if in fact matters seem just as obvious to your disputant as they do to you. This result does not stand in tension with strong conciliationism. In such a case, first-person facts affect what reliability estimates are justified for you by affecting what evidence is available to you. This evidence is still expressible in third-person terms, and your self-favoring reliability estimate can still be impartial in the relevant sense. You give more weight to your perspective not because it is yours, but because you are in a position to know more favorable information about the person who holds that perspective. The agent-centered account, however, assigns epistemic significance to facts that are irreducibly first-personal.

The obvious objection to the agent-centered account of partisan justification is that it is objectionably arbitrary to think that *my* seemings and doxastic inclinations concerning p are more likely to be correct than the similar seemings of someone else whose epistemic qualifications and evidential situation are relevantly just like mine. Granted, the *pragmatic* reasons I have for trusting myself may not be matched by equally strong pragmatic reasons for trusting a relevantly similar person. It may be, for example, that severe doubts about one's own cognitive reliability has a crippling effect that does not similarly follow from doubts about the cognitive reliability of some person

---

[17] For relevant discussion of the epistemic significance of asymmetries in "personal information" in contexts of disagreement, see Lackey 2010; Christensen 2011, 9–10; Pittard 2017, 4399–4404.

who appears to be relevantly similar. Nonetheless, asymmetries in the pragmatic reasons that bear on reliability estimates of oneself and others do not seem to be of *evidential* relevance to these reliability estimates. And it seems irrational to have asymmetric reliability estimates when there is parity in the evidence that bears on these reliability estimates. Even if first-person pragmatic reasons ultimately do play an important role in rationalizing epistemic self-trust, the requirement to give equal credence to propositions evidentially on a par means that our degree of self-trust must be matched by the degree to which we trust others who are similar in every respect that is *evidentially* relevant to estimated reliability.

Setting aside factors that could have significance only from a first-person standpoint, what else could justify my self-favoring reliability estimate? According to an *externalist account* of partisan justification, whether $r_M > r_B$ is justified could depend on factors that are not discernible by me and that are therefore "external" to my cognitive perspective.[18] Suppose, for example, that my belief that more than an hour has passed in my conversation with Beatrice is the product of highly reliable and properly functioning cognitive faculties. And suppose that these faculties, as part of their proper and reliable functioning, also produce the higher-order belief that I am highly reliable in estimating the elapsed time in this and similar situations, and that they produce this belief even when I lack track record data to support this and even when I have good reason to believe that others who appear to be similar to me are *not* very reliable in estimating elapsed time. According to an externalist account of partisan justification, such facts about the reliability of my faculties could directly account for my partisan justification even though these are not factors of which I can be directly aware. On this view, $r_M > r_B$ could be justified for me even though someone else in an internally indistinguishable position but without similarly reliable faculties would *not* be justified in having a self-favoring reliability estimate.

The natural objection to an externalist account of partisan justification is that facts about what is rational for some subject cannot depend on factors of which the subject cannot be aware. According to this objection, rationality is perspectival in that what is rationally justified for someone supervenes on factors that are accessible from her perspective, and factors that are not internally discernible seem not to be accessible in the relevant sense. In

---

[18] Jeroen de Ridder 2014 argues that externalism is the *only* option for those who oppose strong conciliatory verdicts in idealized examples of the sort considered here. In my view, he neglects agent-centered accounts just mentioned and rationalist accounts that I will soon discuss.

support of this "internalist" view, some appeal to the example of "internal twins" whose mental states are internally indistinguishable but who differ with respect to external factors that bear on reliability. While such individuals may differ significantly with respect to knowledge, it seems that they do not differ with respect to their rationality.[19] Of course, this and other arguments for internalism about rational justification have been contested by those epistemologists who endorse an "externalist" account of rational justification. If externalism about justification more generally is correct, then perhaps external factors could help to justify a self-favoring reliability estimate even when there is acknowledged to be perfect internal symmetry.[20]

Suppose we reject externalist accounts of partisan justification, perhaps because we accept internalism about rational justification. Setting aside both agent-centered reasons and external factors, what else could account for the rationality of $r_M > r_B$? The only remaining possibility is that $r_M > r_B$ is justified on account of some factor that has agent-neutral significance and that is internally discernible. Recall that we are assuming that there is perfect parity in the p-neutral considerations and that, *antecedent to information about what a person relevantly like Beatrice (and myself) thinks about p*, the truth or falsity of p has no bearing on estimated reliability of such a person. Thus, if there is an internally discernible factor that helps to justify my self-favoring reliability estimate, this factor must be some fact about my view on p or my reasoning about p, and it must be some factor whose significance cannot be appreciated from a standpoint that is neutral about p. Examples of such factors would include the (alleged) fact that my reasoning about p is cogent or that my view on p has greater intrinsic plausibility than an opposing view on p.

I will now argue that a *non-externalist* and *agent-neutral* account of my justification for $r_M > r_B$ cannot appeal to factors such as the cogency of my reasoning about p or the greater intrinsic plausibility of p unless such factors can be the object of unmediated awareness. Consider again the Monty Hall example above, where I reason correctly on the matter and Beatrice does not. Suppose that when Beatrice shares her reasoning, I initially see no reason for thinking that my reasoning has more or less rational merit than hers. But

---

[19] The literature on the "new evil demon problem" for externalism, which appeals to internal twin cases to raise worries for externalism, traces back to Lehrer and Cohen 1983.

[20] It's worth noting that endorsing externalism about justification more generally does not commit one to externalism about partisan justification specifically. One could affirm that external factors play a role in justifying our trust in the cognitive reliability of those generically like us, while denying that external factors could justify estimating one's own reliability as being higher than those who are generically similar. So in the present example, external factors might help to justify a high value for both r_M and r_B without helping to justify $r_M > r_B$.

I have on my smartphone an advanced app called Reasoning Checker that I regularly rely on to help me distinguish between good reasoning and bad reasoning. Reasoning Checker has been listening in on my conversation with Beatrice, and when I consult the app it says that my reasoning is sound and Beatrice's is not. Beatrice, however, has a competitor app on her phone called Argument Sifter. When she asks Argument Sifter to evaluate the competing arguments, it endorses Beatrice's line of reasoning. Suppose that I am aware of these inconsistent verdicts and have no independent reason for thinking that Reasoning Checker is any more or less reliable than Argument Sifter. Nonetheless, because of Reasoning Checker's verdict, I give more weight to my reasoning than to Beatrice's reasoning and estimate my reliability as being higher than hers.

Suppose Reasoning Checker is in fact the more reliable of the two apps, that it properly evaluated our competing arguments, and that I would have trusted Reasoning Checker whatever its verdict. Given these assumptions, the cogency of my reasoning is a partial cause of my self-favoring reliability estimate. But it seems clear that in this version of the example there is no viable internalist account according to which the cogency of my reasoning serves to justify $r_M > r_B$. Because I cannot directly discern any difference in the rational merits of my reasoning and Beatrice's reasoning, my justification for thinking that my reasoning is cogent depends entirely on my justification in having greater trust in Reasoning Checker than in Argument Sifter (at least in this case). But since I have no internally discernible and agent-neutral reason for trusting Reasoning Checker more than Argument Sifter, my preferential trust in the former could be justified only on agent-centered and/or external grounds (if it could be justified at all).

But now let's change the example so that the role of the apps is filled by unconscious cognitive processing. When Beatrice shares her reasoning, it is still the case that I do not initially discern any difference in the rational merits of my reasoning and her reasoning. But some cognitive module that unconsciously evaluates such arguments correctly determines that my argument is better than Beatrice's, and this result is indicated by a strong feeling of conviction that my reasoning is cogent and Beatrice's is not. This feeling of conviction is "brute" in that it is unaccompanied by any conscious appreciation of the greater rational merits of my reasoning. Meanwhile, the same type of module in Beatrice unconsciously evaluates the arguments and arrives at the incorrect conclusion. This incorrect verdict is indicated to her by a strong feeling of conviction that *her* reasoning is cogent and mine is not. Suppose I know that Beatrice's feeling of conviction is just as strong as my own, but I nonetheless adopt a self-favoring reliability estimate and give more weight to my view.

I suggest that moving the "reasoning checker" into my head does not help the internalist to explain how the cogency of my reasoning could help to justify $r_M > r_B$ in an agent-neutral way. Because I do not *directly* discern that my reasoning is cogent or has greater rational merits than Beatrice's reasoning, my justification for thinking that my reasoning is cogent depends on my justification for putting more trust in my feeling of conviction than in Beatrice's relevantly similar feeling. And since I lack any agent-neutral, internally discernible reason for this preferential trust, my self-favoring reliability estimate could only be justified if external factors or agent-centered considerations play some role.

Recall that we are seeking some symmetry breaker that could serve to justify $r_M > r_B$ even though I know that there is perfect symmetry in the p-neutral considerations and even if external factors and agent-centered considerations cannot contribute to my justification of this self-favoring reliability estimate. The above reasoning suggests that the cogency of my reasoning cannot fulfill this role if I have only mediated awareness of this cogency. Any indicator that mediates this awareness will be relevantly like an indicator that Beatrice enjoys, and preferential trust of my indicator would itself stand in need of justification. It seems, then, that the cogency of my reasoning can supply the right sort of symmetry breaker only if I can have direct and unmediated awareness of this cogency. If that is right, then someone who thinks that I can have partisan justification in my disagreement with Beatrice and who rejects agent-centered and externalist accounts is committed to holding that we sometimes enjoy a rather strong form of rational insight—insight that involves immediate awareness of some factor like the cogency of some bit of reasoning or the greater intrinsic plausibility of some position. I will call such a view a *rationalist account* of partisan justification.

Unlike the agent-centered and externalist accounts of partisan justification, a rationalist account of partisan justification comports well with a common-sense conception of rationality. Intuitively, it is perfectly reasonable for our confidence in some belief to depend directly on the clarity and cogency of our reasons for that belief. It is natural to think that grasping a powerful (and undefeated) argument for p can be sufficient to give one justification to believe p even if one lacks independent reason for highly estimating one's reliability in the relevant domain of inquiry. For example, it is doubtful that our extremely high confidence that $1+1=2$ can be fully justified by our antecedent reasons for thinking that we are reliable with respect to arithmetic (together with the fact that it *seems* to us that 1+1=2). Perhaps we have antecedent reasons for thinking that human beings are reliable in their arithmetical capacities, but the justificatory force of such reasons would seem to be much weaker than the justification that comes from insightfully seeing that 1+1=2. Similar claims apply to the Monty Hall case. I know that it is not all that uncommon to be misled by reasoning that *seems* to me to be sound and conclusive, even though it is not. But in gauging how confident to be about my answer in the Monty Hall case, my grounds for self-trust are not limited to the generic fact that my reasoning strongly seems to me to be sound. I also know the precise character of my reasoning. When I appreciate the cogency of that reasoning, the specifics of that reasoning may provide reason for confidence that cannot be captured in more generic terms.

While a rationalist account of partisan justification might comport well with a commonsense conception of rationality, the account is one that many contemporary epistemologists do not accept. There are two main objections to the account. First, many dismiss the idea of unmediated rational insight as objectionably mysterious (Benacerraf 1973; Field 1989; Boghossian 2001). Unlike perception, rational insight is not a way of knowing contingent empirical facts about our environment. Rather, the objects of rational insight are typically held to be necessary truths. (This does not mean that rational insight has no bearing on propositions that are true or false contingently. The fact that some line of reasoning or body of evidence supports p is arguably a necessary fact, and thus a candidate object of rational insight, even if p itself is contingent.[21]) For example, when I insightfully see that "taller than" is a transitive relation, I see that this *must* be the case, not merely that the transitivity of tallness holds in this world. Since modal facts of this sort are not true in virtue of facts about my empirical environment, it is difficult to see how I could come to be directly aware of such facts.[22]

Second, even if we *do* sometimes enjoy rational insight of the relevant sort, many doubt that such insight could provide autonomous grounds for epistemic self-trust. After all, we sometimes think we have insight into the truth of p when we do not. (A frequently cited example is Frege's mistaken acceptance of a "naïve comprehension axiom" in set theory, which holds, roughly, that corresponding to any property there is a set of all and only those things that have that property.) The fact that we can be misled by merely apparent

---

[21] For an argument that the norms of abductive inference are knowable a priori, see Beebe 2009.

[22] Acknowledging the mystery here, one can ask in reply: Is *mediated* knowledge of such facts any *less* mysterious?

insights suggests that it is not immediately evident to us whether an alleged insight is in fact genuine.[23] Plausibly, if it is not evident to us whether an apparent insight is genuine, then our confidence in response to some insight should be constrained by our antecedent estimate of the probability that some apparent insight that *seems* genuine is *in fact* genuine. If that is right, then the genuineness of rational insight cannot justify confidence greater than what is allowable on purely impartial grounds.

In light of these challenges to rationalist accounts of partisan justification and the aforementioned problems facing other accounts, an understandable reaction would be to side with the strong conciliationist in rejecting these accounts of partisan justification. Assuming that these accounts exhaust the possibilities (as it seems they do), then this would require accepting STRONG IMPARTIALITY.

This conclusion in favor of STRONG IMPARTIALITY at least initially seems to lend strong support to the view that religious skepticism is required of those who are aware of facts pertaining to disagreement. Most of us are aware of a great many people who disagree with us on religious matters and who appear to be just as intelligent, careful, informed on religious matters, and so on. If we should proceed as strong impartiality requires, then it would seem that we should estimate these apparent peers to be just as reliable as ourselves. If that is right, then conditionalizing on facts about disagreement should arguably lead to rather drastic reduction in confidence.

But as I will argue in the next section, there is no straightforward argument from STRONG IMPARTIALITY to religious skepticism.[24] When we turn to religious inquiry, we encounter complicating factors that make STRONG IMPARTIALITY inapplicable. The strong conciliationist's approach to simple disagreements like the one involving the Monty Hall Problem cannot be straightforwardly extended to religious disagreements. And proposals for adapting strong conciliationism to the religious domain are dubious. For this reason, there is pressure to concede that religious inquiry is one context where we do enjoy partisan justification. In this case, we may have reason to embrace one or more of the accounts just canvassed.

---

[23] For a historically informed discussion of this sort of objection to rationalism, see Wolterstorff 1999.

[24] The argument offered here, while new, is similar in spirit to arguments in Pittard 2014; 2019b, 252–280 that question the assumption that religious skepticism is the attitude that best comports with epistemic impartiality.

5. The Failure of Strong Impartiality in the Religious Domain

In the examples discussed so far, I have assumed that, antecedent to information about what I or others think about *p*, the truth or falsity of *p* would have no bearing on my reliability estimates for myself or my potential disputant. In a great many cases, this assumption is entirely reasonable. In the Monty Hall case, for example, whether switching doors is or is not advantageous has no apparent bearing on how likely it is that someone with my qualifications and track record will succeed in reaching the correct conclusion. Similarly, in the case involving the question of the elapsed time in my conversation with Beatrice, there is no apparent reason why my estimate of Beatrice's reliability should depend on whether I think we have been talking for more or less than one hour.

In the religious domain, however, this simplifying assumption often fails to hold. Many religious outlooks are comprehensive worldviews that have implications for a theory of the epistemic credentials that are most important in assessing religious questions.[25] Among those questions that are the subject of significant religious controversy is the question of *what sort of person* is best positioned to attain religious truth.

For example, there is a significant strand of Christian thought that challenges the assumption that those with scholarly credentials in religion or philosophy are especially well-placed to grasp the truth of Christian teaching. The gospel of Matthew records Jesus as praying, "I thank you, Father, Lord of heaven and earth, because you have hidden these things from the wise and the intelligent and have revealed them to infants; yes, Father, for such was your gracious will."[26] In a similar vein, the apostle Paul writes the following to a young Christian church in Corinth:

> Consider your own call, brothers and sisters: not many of you were wise by human standards, not many were powerful, not many were of noble birth. But God chose what is foolish in the world to shame the wise; God chose what is weak in the world to shame the strong; God chose what is low and despised in the world, things that are not, to reduce to nothing things that are, so that no one might boast in the presence of God.[27]

[25] For further discussion of the "non-standard" theories of epistemic credentials supported by religious outlooks, see Pittard 2014.
[26] Matthew 11:25–6 (NRSV).   [27] I Corinthians 1:26–29 (NRSV).

The allegedly privileged position of the "weak" and the "low" is not seen by Paul to be merely a matter of having more information, at least not more information that can be characterized in religiously neutral terms. Rather, those who are not influenced by the spirit of God are unable to properly appreciate and understand the message of God when it is shared with them. As Paul writes, "Those who are unspiritual do not receive the gifts of God's Spirit, for they are foolishness to them, and they are unable to understand them because they are spiritually discerned."[28] Because of such teachings, it seems that there is no religiously neutral, non-question-begging way of deciding how conventional scholarly qualifications bear on reliability in the religious domain.

Consider another example of a religiously motivated theory of epistemic credentials. There is a sophisticated tradition of Buddhist philosophical argumentation for central Buddhist tenets such as the non-existence of an enduring self. Nonetheless, many Buddhists maintain that a rigorous philosophical appraisal of such arguments is not sufficient to appreciate the significance of the conclusions reached by such arguments. Seeing through the illusion of the self and inhabiting a way of understanding the world that is not distorted by self-concern normally requires that one engage in rigorous practices of meditation. Apart from such practices, one is unlikely to achieve more than a shallow and merely theoretical understanding of the non-existence of self (Albahari 2014). Indeed, some argue that attempts to gain a philosophical appreciation of Buddhist doctrine (which language is inadequate to express) can be a detriment to understanding and progress toward enlightenment. Hui-neng, the seventh-century master of the Zen Buddhist tradition, is recorded as saying that the reason some Buddhist disciples "cannot comprehend the buddha-knowledge is because they speculate on it. They may combine their efforts to speculate, but the more they speculate, the farther they are from the truth" (Hui-neng 1990, 114).[29] What is needed is what Hui-neng calls "thoughtlessness," a grasping of the world that overcomes the distortions imposed by human concepts, a wisdom that "sees things intuitively without going through the process of reasoning" (Hui-neng 1990, 116–117). In light of views like this, it is doubtful that we can identify a non-question-begging way of estimating someone's reliability with respect to Buddhism. How much weight we should give to meditative practices versus historical or philosophical

---

[28] I Corinthians 2:14 (NRSV).

[29] This and the following passage are quoted in Blum 2015, 147–148, which provides an interesting and helpful discussion of Hui-neng's "mystical" epistemology of enlightenment.

knowledge, say, is not a matter that can be settled independently of our views on the plausibility of various strands of Buddhist thought.

Because many religious outlooks have significant implications for a theory of religious epistemic credentials, in the religious domain it will often not be possible to form p-neutral reliability estimates as STRONG IMPARTIALITY requires. The following toy example illustrates the problem. Suppose that Kendra is going to consider the merits of religious outlook $R1$, and then after forming her opinion on $R1$ she will learn what Ron thinks. Like many religious perspectives, $R1$ includes a distinctive theory on what epistemic credentials are important in the religious domain. While $R1$ affirms the benefit of many "standard" epistemic credentials (e.g., education, attentiveness, open-mindedness, analytical sophistication, and so on), $R1$ holds that even someone who possesses these standard credentials is unlikely to rightly assess central religious questions if they have not engaged in the particular kind of spiritual practices that, according to $R1$, are typically necessary to free one from deep-seated rational bias. (Such practices might consist of a certain meditative program, involvement in worship of a certain sort, actively serving the needy, studying under a particular kind of guru, etc.) While engagement in these practices is epistemically beneficial according to $R1$, conditional on $R1$ being false, there is reason to think that engagement in the practices might introduce emotional biases that would make one *less* likely to ascertain the truth about $R1$.

Suppose that Kendra and Ron, who are fully aware of $R1$'s distinctive theory of epistemic credentials, both have the same *conditional* reliability estimates for someone who is relevantly like them in $R1$-neutral respects. Table 1 shows their conditional reliability estimates.

It is important to keep in mind that these are reliability estimates about a relevantly similar person antecedent to any information about how the person actually thinks about $R1$. If information about how Kendra actually thinks about $R1$ can inform her estimate of her own reliability (as a rationalist

Table 1 Kendra and Ron's conditional reliability estimates.

	Estimated reliability conditional on $R1$	Estimated reliability conditional on $\sim R1$
Otherwise similar person who has engaged in $R1$ practices	0.9	0.7
Otherwise similar person who has *not* engaged in $R1$ practices	0.3	0.9

account of partisan justification holds), or if first-person facts can inform her estimate of her reliability (as agent-centered accounts hold), then there is no reason to think that Kendra's estimate of her own reliability and her credence for *R1* are constrained by the values in the above table. But according to STRONG IMPARTIALITY, Kendra's credence for *R1* should be governed by her impartial reliability estimate for someone relevantly like her in *p*-neutral respects. And Kendra's unconditional reliability estimate for such a person must also cohere with the *conditional* reliability estimates specified in the table.

While Kendra has not engaged in the practices prescribed by *R1*, she knows that Ron *has* engaged in these practices. So the bottom row is most relevant to a reliability estimate of someone in Kendra's position, while the top row is relevant when estimating Ron's reliability. Finally, suppose that when Kendra reflects on the question of *R1*, she is strongly inclined to judge that *R1* is false.

We may now put to the strong conciliationist the following difficult questions. First, what is the impartial reliability estimate that should determine the value of Kendra's credence for ~*R1*? Second, and perhaps more importantly, how should Kendra's estimate of her own reliability compare to her estimate of Ron's reliability? I suggest that *R1*-neutral answers to these questions are not possible since any reliability estimates that Kendra might adopt would be indicative of a particular view on the probability of *R1*. Let r_K be Kendra's reliability estimate for someone relevantly like herself (i.e., someone who has not engaged in *R1* practices and whose intellectual abilities are relevantly like Kendra's). Given the conditional reliability estimates that Kendra and Ron both endorse, a value for r_K that is close to 0.9 would appear appropriate only from a vantage point that sees ~*R1* as being much more plausible than *R1*. A value for r_K close to 0.3 appears to be appropriate only from a perspective that sees *R1* as being highly plausible. A value for r_K in the neighborhood of 0.6 looks reasonable only if *R1* and ~*R1* are thought to be approximately equal in their plausibility. Because the question of *R1* bears in this way on the reliability estimates that are appropriate for Kendra and Ron, any reliability estimate Kendra adopts would beg the question against some view on the respective plausibility of *R1* and ~*R1*.

One might think that the uniquely impartial approach would be for Kendra to reach her credences for *R1* and ~*R1* by conditionalizing on facts about her opinion and others' views from an initial position that assigns a prior probability of 0.5 to *R1* and a prior probability of 0.5 to ~*R1*. Starting from this "indifferent" state, Kendra would first conditionalize on the fact that she is inclined to believe ~*R1*, leading to updated credence values of 0.44 for *R1* and 0.56 for ~*R1*. If she then learns that Ron believes *R1*, Kendra would conditionalize on this fact leading to updated credence values of 0.7 for *R1* and 0.3 for ~*R1*. Ron's employing this procedure would lead him to the same result, but he would get there by a different path since he learns the evidence in a different order. When Ron starts with "indifferent" priors of 0.5 for *R1* and 0.5 for ~*R1* and then conditionalizes on the fact that he is inclined to believe *R1*, Ron would adopt credences 0.75 for *R1* and 0.25 for ~*R1*. Then, when he learns of Kendra's disagreement and conditionalizes on this fact, his final credences would be 0.7 for *R1* and 0.3 for ~*R1*.

While this approach has the initial appearance of impartiality, this appearance vanishes when we note that ~*R1* may encompass distinct religious outlooks *R2*, *R3*, *R4*, and so on. Suppose, for example, that *R1* is some Buddhist outlook. In estimating one's reliability on religious questions, it does not seem religiously impartial to start from an initial position of 0.5 probability for a Buddhist perspective while dividing the remaining 0.5 credence among all of the other religious and irreligious alternatives.

Even if being indifferent between *R1* and ~*R1* does not yield the right kind of impartiality, perhaps there is a more nuanced "principle of indifference" that does yield a religiously neutral reliability estimate.[30] A plausible principle of indifference would require us to be indifferent between outlooks on a menu of options only when those options exhibit the right kind of parity. But what menu or menus exhibit the appropriate parity? In constructing the right sort of menu, should one start by giving equal credence to atheism and theism, then going on to divide the 0.5 credence for theism among various theistic options and the 0.5 weight for atheism among various atheistic options? Or should one begin by partitioning the possibilities in some other way, perhaps between substance monism and substance pluralism, or between moral realism and anti-realism, or between the view that the self is merely conventional and the view that it is not merely conventional? These are, of course, only a sampling of the ways that someone might go about partitioning the possibilities for purposes of applying an indifference principle and arriving at an allegedly impartial starting position. Which of these ways we choose can have dramatically different results in how much initial credence is assigned to a given religious or irreligious perspective. And it seems unlikely that there is some religiously impartial way of identifying a uniquely correct way of partitioning the possibilities. For this reason, it is doubtful that any sort of indifference

---

[30] The sort of worry raised here for employing an indifference principle are explored in Meacham 2014.

procedure determines a genuinely impartial way to measure and compare the reliability of Kendra and Ron.

The strong conciliationist could respond to this challenge by giving up the assumption that the correct disagreement policy is applicable to a precise and opinionated Bayesian agent. In our example, perhaps Kendra should have neither determinate reliability estimates nor a determinate credence for *R1*. Some Bayesians maintain that precise credences are inappropriate in circumstances where our evidence is in some way impoverished, vague, or "equivocal" (Joyce 2010). It is held that the rational doxastic state in such a situation cannot be modeled by a single credence function, but only by a set of credence functions called the "representor." For an advocate of credal imprecision, the natural view to take on Kendra's case is that some functions in her representor should return a high estimate of her reliability and other functions in her representor should give a low estimate of her reliability. Since the functions in a representor are not weighted in any way, we cannot amalgamate these options to yield a more determinate perspective.

In my view, the incorporation of such divergent outlooks into one's representor would already amount to a rather severe religious skepticism.[31] And a view that requires religious skepticism even prior to knowledge of disagreement strikes me as highly implausible. But I won't press this point or discuss the imprecision approach further, since my assumption in this paper is that strong conciliationism is not committed to the rejection of precise Bayesianism.

I've argued that Kendra has no impartial way of estimating her reliability or of determining her credence for *R1*. Because the question of her reliability with respect to *R1* cannot be settled independently of her view on the truth of *R1*, she has no way of conforming to STRONG IMPARTIALITY. On the assumption that there are some precise pre-disagreement credences for *R1/~R1* that are justified for Kendra, what should the strong conciliationist say about Kendra's case? Perhaps the strong conciliationist could say that an impartiality requirement fixes the maximum and minimum credence that Kendra could legitimately assign to her preferred view, and that within this range (between 0.3 and 0.9, in Kendra's case) any credence assignment is permitted. But this approach concedes that rationality can tolerate credence assignments that are to a significant extent arbitrary (at least from the standpoint of evidential evaluation). This is a damaging concession, since STRONG IMPARTIALITY is to a significant degree motivated by the view that credences that are arbitrary (from an evidential perspective) are rationally objectionable. This opposition

---

[31] For persuasive arguments against extreme credal imprecision, see Rinard 2013.

to arbitrariness lies behind the view that self-favoring reliability estimates require some sort of favorable symmetry breaker and also behind the view that agent-centered facts do not supply the right kind of symmetry breaker. It is therefore doubtful that the strong conciliationist can reasonably affirm that Kendra can arbitrarily choose her credence in this case.

If rationality does not permit Kendra to arbitrarily choose her credence, and if impartial considerations are unable to justify any particular credence, then it must be that the credence that is rational for Kendra is justified at least partly on the basis of some sort of partisan factor, whether that be some agent-centered consideration, an external factor, or rational insight that bears on the question of $R1$'s truth. If some such factor plays a role in determining what credence is justified for Kendra, then we cannot rule out the possibility that Kendra may retain a good deal of confidence even after conditionalizing on the fact of Ron's disagreement. (For example, if Kendra starts with a credence for $\sim R1$ of 0.9 and then conditionalizes on the fact of Ron's disagreement, her updated credence for $\sim R1$ would be 0.75.)

If the strong conciliationist is forced to concede that partisan factors can play a justifying role in the religious domain, this seriously weakens the motivations for strong conciliationism even in contexts where it *is* possible to identify impartial reliability estimates. If one or more partisan factors can play a legitimate epistemic role when impartial reliability estimates are not available, why think that such factors have *no* role to play when impartial reliability estimates *are* available? If rational insight, for example, can ground significant confidence in the absence of an impartial basis for believing oneself to be reliable, couldn't such insight sometimes help to justify confidence that exceeds the level of confidence supportable by impartial grounds alone? The inapplicability of STRONG IMPARTIALITY in the religious domain does not, I grant, show that it is wrong across the board. But the strong conciliationist owes us a principled epistemological theory that explains why impartial considerations should have trumping power even though there is some other independent source of epistemic justification that is efficacious in the religious domain (and in any other domains where impartial considerations are not sufficient to justify any particular doxastic state).

6. Rationalism for the Religious

If we should accept that partisan justification is possible in the religious domain, what account(s) of partisan justification should we accept? My own view is that only the rationalist account of partisan justification is tenable. Giving anything like a full defense of this verdict is not possible here. But in this final section, I briefly defend rationalism against one of the objections sketched earlier and explain why rationalism may be congenial to the religious.

As already noted, one of the main objections to a rationalist account of partisan justification is that even if we could have unmediated insight into the truth or plausibility of p, or into the cogency of reasoning that supports p, we cannot tell when we enjoy such genuine insight. After all, it sometimes seems to us that we have insight into p when we do not. It is therefore claimed that our confidence when we have genuine rational insight supporting p should be equal to our estimated reliability on those occasions when it *seems* to us that we have genuine insight. And in setting our credence in this way, we would fully respect reasons impartiality, since our confidence level would not take for granted the genuineness of our insight.

This objection relies on reasoning which we could state in a more general form as follows: "In situations where you are *not* in state S, it sometimes seems to you that you *are* in state S. In such situations, you cannot tell that you are not in state S. Thus, when you *are* in state S, you cannot tell that you are in state S." As others have noted, this sort of inference looks dubious when we consider dreams. Someone who is dreaming is often strongly inclined to affirm that she is awake. In this sense, at least, it often seems to the dreamer that she is awake. Even if the phenomenal character of dream states differs significantly from the phenomenal character of waking states, dreamers are typically unable to use these differences in order to tell that they are not awake. Does it therefore follow that you cannot presently tell that you are awake?[32] An affirmative answer is difficult to swallow. Here is what we *can* conclude: you cannot discern that you are awake merely by noting that the proposition that you are awake seems true to you. Such a seeming is not a highly reliable indicator. But we arguably are able to discern that we are awake (when we are) because we are directly aware of the coherence and vividness of our present experience, features that we know are not characteristic of our dream experiences (even though while dreaming we may have the *conviction* that our experience is coherent and vivid). Similarly, when we can tell that we have genuine insight into some matter, our awareness of such insight is not achieved merely by noting that the proposition that we have such insight seems true to us. Such a seeming is at best an imperfectly reliable indicator of

---

[32] For more extended discussion that appeals to dreams to argue against impartiality constraints, see White 2010; Pittard 2019a.

insight. Rather, when we can tell that we have genuine insight, we can do so because we are directly aware of the rational merits of some specific belief or way of thinking, merits that are not had by reasoning that is non-insightful.

What shall we say about the other main objection, that rational insight of the sort envisioned is objectionably mysterious? I have little to offer as a direct response to this objection, though some recent work on this problem looks promising.[33] Here, I wish simply to argue that many religious believers are already implicitly or explicitly committed to there being instances of rational insight of a very strong sort, however mysterious such rational insight may be.[34] For such religious believers, the "mysteriousness objection" ought to carry very little weight.

I suggest, first, that skepticism about rational insight cannot easily be squared with classical theism. According to the classical theistic picture, God is a cognitively perfect being. Among the questions that God can answer for Godself with perfect certainty and infallibility are several "religious" questions like the following: "Am I definitely God, or might I be some created being who is being manipulated to think that I am God, that I am governing the created world, and so on?" "While it *seems* to me that I am a necessary being who could not have failed to exist, am I really?"[35] What justifies God in being absolutely certain in God's answers to these questions? Here, a number of views that might be acceptable as accounts of human epistemic justification and human knowledge do not provide an adequate way of characterizing the ideal epistemic position that God occupies with respect to the aforementioned questions. For instance, it is not satisfactory to say that the justification of God's beliefs on these matters stems from the default entitlement of robust epistemic self-trust. Even the deceived non-god has such default entitlement. Surely God's justification in accepting his/her divine identity goes beyond the generic reasonability of accepting (in the absence of any defeaters) whatever doxastic inclinations one happens to have. It would also be problematic if, in order to account for God's justification, one had to appeal to some external factor (like the reliability of the relevant divine cognitive process) that is not internally discernible from God's perspective. For if God cannot be directly aware of the factors that justify God, then this leaves room for divine doubt.

---

[33] See especially Chudnoff 2013; Bengson 2015.

[34] Of course, it may be that there are compelling philosophical reasons to hold that we sometimes enjoy unmediated rational insight, quite apart from one's view on religious matters. My point here is that many religious believers have *additional* reason to endorse a robust form of rationalism, or at least to not be dismissive of it.

[35] For an interesting discussion of the (putative) skeptical worry for God raised by this question, see Pasnau 2017, 121–125.

Plausibly, an account of God's knowledge that accords with our intuitions about cognitive perfection will have to affirm that God's answers to the aforementioned questions are based on rational insights. Such insights must involve unmediated awareness of truths and must possess a kind of luminous clarity that is seen to be incompatible with error. Perhaps God somehow has direct insight into "his" divine identity, or perhaps God has insight into the soundness of an a priori argument that rules out various deceptive possibilities and infers on this basis that "he" must be God. (God, in other words, may be able to make good on this part of Descartes' project in the *Meditations*.) In any case, it is likely that to give a satisfactory account of God's knowledge that skeptical scenarios are false, and also to satisfactorily describe God's knowledge more generally, we will need to posit that God has unmediated awareness of a great many truths (and not merely truths about God's phenomenal states that might be known by means of introspection). Since such awareness does not seem any less mysterious when it belongs to God rather than to us, theists should be relatively unmoved by the mysteriousness objection to rational insight. To be clear, I am *not* suggesting that our rational insight is godlike in its scope or clarity. But once one has posited the perfect manifestation of rational insight in God, one could recognize the possibility of our participating in such insight in some limited way appropriate to finite creatures.

Theism is not the only religious view that provides motivation for a strong version of rationalism. Some Buddhist discussions of the path to enlightenment strongly suggest an epistemology that is rationalist in the relevant sense. Consider the following sampling of passages in which philosopher and Buddhist monk Bhikku Bodhi describes the process of overcoming harmful "cognitive distortions," especially "the delusion of the self" (Bodhi 1994, 114):[36]

Since the final goal to which the path leads, liberation from suffering, depends ultimately on uprooting ignorance, the climax of the path must be the training directly opposed to ignorance. This is the training in wisdom, designed to awaken the faculty of penetrative understanding which sees things "as they are."   (14–15)

The right view of the Four Noble Truths develops in two stages. The first is called the right view that accords with the truths...; the second, the right view that penetrates the truths. To acquire the right view that accords with the truths requires a clear understanding of their meaning and significance in

---

[36] I encountered Bodhi's work in Albahari 2014, where some of these selections are quoted.

our lives. Such an understanding arises first by learning the truths and studying them. Subsequently it is deepened by reflecting upon them in the light of experience until one gains a strong conviction as to their veracity.

But even at this point their truth has not been penetrated, and thus the understanding achieved is still defective, a matter of concept rather than perception. To arrive at the experiential realization of the truths it is necessary to take up the practice of meditation—first to strengthen the capacity for sustained concentration, then to develop insight.   (27–28)

Whereas ignorance obscures the true nature of things, wisdom removes the veils of distortion, enabling us to see phenomena in their fundamental mode of being with the vivacity of direct perception. The training in wisdom centers on the development of insight *(vipassanā-bhavana)*, a deep and comprehensive seeing into the nature of existence which fathoms the truth of our being in the only sphere where it is directly accessible to us, namely, in our own experience.   (113)

The epistemic transformation Bodhi describes here is not merely a revision of one's convictions, whereby what once seemed true (namely, that we have enduring selves) now seems false. In emphasizing that Buddhist insight is the fruit of "direct perception" that is achieved in the sphere of experience that is "directly accessible," the passage suggests that Buddhist enlightenment moves beyond the mediacy of appearances with its potential for error and distortion. Of course, this passage does not explicitly endorse rationalism. But it seems clear that Bodhi thinks that his no-self perspective is rationally superior to the perspective of those who affirm a real self, and that the superiority of this perspective is not to be accounted for in purely external terms. It is not as though the rational advantages are known merely through some reliably produced indicator like a brute feeling of rightness (a feeling that, while perhaps unreliably produced, could also be enjoyed by an opponent of Buddhism). Rather, Bodhi thinks the rational credentials of the no-self view are directly apparent, eliminating any question of whether some putative indicator of epistemic improvement might be misleading and defective. As he says, for someone who has fully traversed the path of insight, "doubt is eliminated because one has grasped the truth proclaimed by the Buddha, seen it for oneself, and so can never again hang back due to uncertainty" (121).

Even if I am right that rationalism comports well with some prominent religious outlooks, rationalism has not fared well in recent work on religious epistemology. "Reformed epistemology" has been the most prominent position in the epistemology of religion over the last few decades, and a central tenet of reformed epistemology is that justified religious belief does not need to be based on an assessment of the internally discernible rational merits of various religious outlooks. William Alston and Alvin Plantinga, the two most prominent figures of reformed epistemology, both maintain that religious confidence can be sustained even while acknowledging that some disputants occupy positions that are no less internally rational than one's own position (Alston 1991, 270–279; Plantinga 2000, 451–457). This runs counter to the exclusively rationalist account of partisan justification that I favor. On this rationalist account, justified confidence in the face of religious disagreement is likely to require that one have rational insight into the merits of one's religious (or irreligious) outlook, insight that justifies one in thinking that one's own position has greater internal rational merits than the positions affirmed by one's disputants.

Why have reformed epistemologists rejected (or at least neglected) a rationalist approach to resisting disagreement-motivated religious skepticism? One reason, I suspect, is that it is thought that a religious epistemology that emphasizes rational insight overintellectualizes religious belief. The view I am commending might seem to imply that justified religious conviction rests on philosophical arguments, and that rational religious belief is possible only for those who can out-argue their opponents on the playing field of natural theology. Relatedly, it might seem that a rationalist epistemology of religious belief would assign very little significance to first-person religious experience. But *first-person* religious experience (and not just the evidence supplied by religious experiences more generally) seems to play a significant role in the formation of people's religious convictions. If we adopt an exclusively rationalist account, must we dismiss the influence of first-person religious experience as an example of irrational agent partiality?

As I argue at length elsewhere (Pittard 2019b, 182–211), emphasizing the importance of rational insight to justified religious belief needn't lead to an overly intellectualist account of religious belief formation. It may be that many of the most important insights for assessing religious questions do not concern the sort of metaphysical principles that feature in the arguments of natural theology. As important or more important than such "philosophical" insights may be axiological, moral, and aesthetic insights that bear on evaluative questions such as whether eternal life could be desirable, whether creaturely freedom and responsibility would be worth pursuing even at the cost of great suffering, whether it is good to valorize the kind of self-sacrificial love depicted in Christian accounts of Jesus' death, whether the God depicted in such and such scriptures would be worthy of worship, and so on. The answer to such evaluative questions has significant bearing on assessment of the truth of religious claims. And if insight into such matters is possible, there is no reason to think it is accessible only or especially to analytically sophisticated philosophers.

Moreover, it is arguable that many of the affectively charged religious experiences that produce and sustain religious belief can profitably be understood as experiences of *insight*. In such experiences, the believer not only acquires some new belief or new level of confidence, but she achieves a more insightful grasp of some evaluative truth that is relevant to religious questions. Consider, for example, the following account of a religious experience from seventeenth-century Christian mystic, Marie of the Incarnation:

> ... there appeared before me all the faults, the imperfections, the impurities which I had committed since being called by the Divine Majesty. What had formerly seemed like nothing to me now seemed horrible in light of the infinite purity of God who demanded exact reparation for all I had experienced. How could one ever express the ways of this divine purity and the demands on souls called to live purely a spiritual life? There is no way to express this or to describe how terrible this divine love can be, penetrating and unrelenting in regard to purity, that irreconcilable enemy of purely human nature.[37]

Marie here describes an experience that led her to a very different evaluation of herself; she went from seeing her faults as "nothing" to seeing them as "horrible." What prompted this changed evaluation seems to be Marie's acquiring a clearer and deeper understanding of God's "infinite purity." In the light of her vision of God's purity, the significance of her sins, and immensity of the gap between her and perfection, is understood more clearly. While she may have previously affirmed that she was a sinner who should repent and who stands in need of God's salvation, she now *grasps* that this is so. At least that is how one sympathetic to Marie's religious outlook might describe this episode. I am not here arguing that she did indeed improve in her self-evaluation. What I do claim, though, is that Marie's description of this "religious experience" is suggestive of deepened insight. It's not merely that some reliable process produced the belief in her that she is deeply sinful.

---

[37] Mahoney 1989, 140–143; as quoted in Katz 2013, 172.

Rather, by juxtaposing her life and a conception of God's holiness, Marie can see this for herself.

In advocating for an account of partisan justification that is exclusively rationalist, I've suggested that justified confidence in the face of religious disagreement is likely to require that one have insight into the greater rational merits of one's outlook on religious matters. It is natural to hear this claim as implying that in a religiously plural context such as our own, personal religious experience will play a marginal role, at most, in contributing to the justification of religious belief. But this implication can be resisted. It may be that many religious experiences are plausibly understood as episodes of insight whereby one more clearly grasps the coherence and cogency of some religious view of the world. And such insight, if genuine, may be required to rationally maintain a degree of confidence on religious matters that cannot be supported on the basis of dispute-neutral considerations.[38]

References

Albahari, Miri. 2014. "Insight Knowledge of No Self in Buddhism: An Epistemic Analysis." *Philosophers' Imprint* 14 (21): 1–30.

Alston, William P. 1991. *Perceiving God: The Epistemology of Religious Experience.* Ithaca, NY: Cornell University Press.

Beebe, James R. 2009. "The Abductivist Reply to Skepticism." *Philosophy and Phenomenological Research* 79: 605–636.

Benacerraf, Paul. 1973. "Mathematical Truth." *The Journal of Philosophy* 70: 661–679.

Bengson, John. 2015. "Grasping the Third Realm." *Oxford Studies in Epistemology* 5: 1–38.

Blum, Jason N. 2015. *Zen and the Unspeakable God: Comparative Interpretations of Mystical Experience.* University Park, Pennsylvania: Pennsylvania State University Press.

Bodhi, Bikkhu. 1994. *The Noble Eightfold Path: The Way to the End of Suffering.* 2nd ed. Kandy, Sri Lanka: Buddhist Publication Society.

Boghossian, Paul. 2001. "Inference and Insight." *Philosophy and Phenomenological Research* 63: 633–640.

---

[38] This chapter benefited from valuable help and feedback from Matthew Benton, Katherine Dormandy, Nathan Dowell, Jonathan Kvanvig, and audience members at a conference hosted by the Center for Religious Studies at Fondazione Bruno Kessler.

Briggs, R. 2009. "Distorted Reflection." *Philosophical Review* 118: 59–85.

Christensen, David. 2007. "Epistemology of Disagreement: The Good News." *Philosophical Review* 116: 187–217.

Christensen, David. 2011. "Disagreement, Question-Begging and Epistemic Self-Criticism." *Philosophers' Imprint* 11: 1–22.

Christensen, David. 2016. "Disagreement, Drugs, Etc.: From Accuracy to Akrasia." *Episteme* 13: 392–422.

Chudnoff, Elijah. 2013. *Intuition*. Oxford: Oxford University Press.

Cohen, Stewart. 2013. "A Defense of the (Almost) Equal Weight View." In David Christensen and Jennifer Lackey (eds.), *The Epistemology of Disagreement: New Essays*, 98–119. Oxford: Oxford University Press.

DePaul, Michael. 2013. "Agent Centeredness, Agent Neutrality, Disagreement, and Truth Conduciveness." In Chris Tucker (ed.), *Seemings and Justification: New Essays and Dogmatism and Phenomenal Conservatism*, 202–221. New York: Oxford University Press.

Elga, Adam. 2007. "Reflection and Disagreement." *Noûs* 41: 478–502.

Elkin, Lee, and Gregory Wheeler. 2018. "Resolving Peer Disagreements Through Imprecise Probabilities." *Noûs* 52: 260–278.

Field, Hartry H. 1989. *Realism, Mathematics, and Modality*. New York: Blackwell.

Gutting, Gary. 1982. *Religious Belief and Religious Skepticism*. Notre Dame, IN: University of Notre Dame Press.

Hájek, Alan. 2009. "Dutch Book Arguments." In Paul Anand, Prasanta K. Pattanaik, and Clemens Puppe (eds.), *The Handbook of Rational and Social Choice*, 173–195. Oxford: Oxford University Press.

Huemer, Michael. 2011. "Epistemological Egoism and Agent-Centered Norms." In Trent Dougherty (ed.), *Evidentialism and Its Discontents*, 17–33. Oxford: Oxford University Press.

Hui-neng. 1990. *The Diamond Sutra and The Sutra of Hui-Neng*. Translated by A. F. Price and Wong Mu-lam. Boston: Shambhala.

Joyce, James M. 2010. "A Defense of Imprecise Credences in Inference and Decision Making." *Philosophical Perspectives* 24: 281–323.

Katz, Steven T. (ed.). 2013. *Comparative Mysticism: An Anthology of Original Sources*. Oxford: Oxford University Press.

Lackey, Jennifer. 2010. "What Should We Do When We Disagree?" *Oxford Studies in Epistemology* 2: 274–293.

Lehrer, Keith, and Stewart Cohen. 1983. "Justification, Truth, and Coherence." *Synthese* 55: 191–207.

Mahoney, Irene (ed.). 1989. *Marie of the Incarnation: Selected Writings*. New York: Paulist Press.

Meacham, Christopher J. G. 2014. "Impermissive Bayesianism." *Erkenntnis* 79: 1185–1217.

Pasnau, Robert. 2017. *After Certainty: A History of Our Epistemic Ideals and Illusions*. Oxford: Oxford University Press.

Pittard, John. 2014. "Conciliationism and Religious Disagreement." In *Challenges to Moral and Religious Belief: Disagreement and Evolution*, edited by Michael Bergmann and Patrick Kain, 80–97. Oxford: Oxford University Press.

Pittard, John. 2017. "Disagreement, Reliability, and Resilience." *Synthese* 194: 4389–4409.

Pittard, John. 2019a. "Fundamental Disagreements and the Limits of Instrumentalism." *Synthese* 196: 5009–5038.

Pittard, John. 2019b. *Disagreement, Deference, and Religious Commitment*. New York: Oxford University Press.

Plantinga, Alvin. 2000. *Warranted Christian Belief*. New York: Oxford University Press.

Ridder, Jeroen de. 2014. "Why Only Externalists Can Be Steadfast." *Erkenntnis* 79: 185–199.

Rinard, Susanna. 2013. "Against Radical Credal Imprecision." *Thought: A Journal of Philosophy* 2: 157–165.

Rosenkranz, Sven, and Moritz Schulz. 2015. "Peer Disagreement: A Call for the Revision of Prior Probabilities." *Dialectica* 69: 551–586.

Schoenfield, Miriam. 2014. "Permission to Believe: Why Permissivism Is True and What It Tells Us About Irrelevant Influences on Belief." *Noûs* 48: 193–218.

Schoenfield, Miriam. 2015. "A Dilemma for Calibrationism." *Philosophy and Phenomenological Research* 91: 425–455.

Schoenfield, Miriam. 2018. "An Accuracy Based Approach to Higher Order Evidence." *Philosophical and Phenomenological Research* 96: 690–715.

Sliwa, Paulina, and Sophie Horowitz. 2015. "Respecting All the Evidence." *Philosophical Studies* 172: 2835–2858.

White, Roger. 2009. "On Treating Oneself and Others as Thermometers." *Episteme* 6: 233–250.

White, Roger. 2010. "You Just Believe That Because…." *Philosophical Perspectives* 24: 573–615.

Wolterstorff, Nicholas. 1999. "Epistemology of Religion." In John Greco and Ernest Sosa (eds.), *Blackwell Guide to Epistemology*, 303–324. New York: Blackwell.

9

How to Be an Inclusivist

Jonathan L. Kvanvig

1. Introduction

There is a standard category scheme for discussing the plurality of religions
and the question of eternal destiny. It begins with a prosaic distinction
between relativists and absolutists about truth, determining which religions
are true, who the adherents of such religions are, and predicting eternal
destiny on that basis. There are thus three central issues involved, and a
standard narrative about priority. The three issues are truth, adherence, and
salvation. The standard narrative has the question of truth coming first,
followed by the issue of adherence, and from these two an explanation of
who is saved and who is not is generated. Both relativists and absolutists thus
endorse an approach I will call the "TAS narrative," where the acronym
reports the order of priority as truth first, adherence next, followed by
salvation.

The standard names for the competing positions within the TAS narrative
are "Exclusivism" and "Pluralism."[1] In Christian contexts, the historical position has been Exclusivist, with Acts 4:12 emblazoned on its banner: "Salvation
can be found in no one else. Throughout the whole world, no other name has
been given among humans through which we must be saved."

The best-known Pluralist is John Hick,[2] who argues for the idea that all
major post-axial religions, ones having their source roughly between 800 and
200 BCE, are windows on the same beyond-our-ken ultimate reality and each
is roughly equal in terms of its capacity to produce saints. Hick endorses a
Kantian distinction about what he terms "The Real," maintaining that these
religions give us pictures of this reality that are structured and constrained by
experience in ways analogous to Kant's idea that what the world is, as
experienced, is one thing and what the world is, in itself, another.

---

[1] See Meeker and Quinn (1999) for discussion of these positions and the issues involved.
[2] See, especially, Hick (1989) and Hick (1999).

Jonathan L. Kvanvig, *How to Be an Inclusivist* In: *Religious Disagreement and Pluralism.*
Edited by: Matthew A. Benton and Jonathan L. Kvanvig, Oxford University Press. © Jonathan L. Kvanvig 2021.
DOI: 10.1093/oso/9780198849865.003.0009

Such an articulation paints a Pluralistic vision, but can hardly be thought of as telling us about the nature of Pluralism as such. A more general attempt can be found in these remarks by Peter Byrne:

> A third answer to the question is given by a pluralist theory of religion. Pluralism borrows from, yet differs from, both naturalism and confessionalism. The pluralist must ascribe cognitive success to a great many of the brands of human religion. (Neither the pluralist nor the confessionalist must attribute success to everything that has counted as a religious tradition in human history.) The pluralist must assert of each of the forms of religion covered by the theory that it provides people with real contact with a sacred, transcendent focus. Pluralism is not committed to asserting that no judgments of superiority of any kind can be made about religions; all that need be asserted is that there is the key cognitive equality mentioned.
>
> The affirmation of this cognitive success and equality does not distinguish pluralism from confessional inclusivism. To a minimal definition of pluralism we must add the element of skepticism or agnosticism with regard to the detailed dogmatic structure of a particular brand of religion. The pluralist must, on reasoned grounds, doubt whether the detailed dogmatics of any particular religion can be known with sufficient certainty to enable such a form of religion to be the means of interpreting the whole that is human religion. There is not the certainty in any particular form of religion to enable its world-view to be the basis for a viable interpretation of religion. In this way pluralism can agree that one brand of religion could conceivably be true while claiming that it is not reasonable for the philosophy of religion to judge of any one particular brand that it is true.   (Byrne 2004, 204)

These remarks contain some hopeful elements. First, the account is metatheoretical without requiring the Kantian elements found in Hick. Second, the account attempts to distinguish Pluralism from both Exclusivism and Inclusivism. But it suffers from a major difficulty: the account is a bit too epistemological to provide a useful metatheory. What is needed is a metaphysical version of the negative point raised by Byrne, the point that expresses reservations about extant religions. We need not only skepticism or agnosticism about the truth of such, but rather something more alethic and metaphysical. For one can be an Exclusivist and a skeptical Christian, claiming that nobody really knows that Christianity is true, even though unbeknownst to us it in fact is, and that salvation requires commitment to the great truths of the Christian faith. That's not Pluralism, even though it expresses reservations of a skeptical and agnostic sort. What is needed, instead of the epistemological focus, is a metaphysical basis for claiming both that there is a transcendent reality with which cognitive contact can be generated through adherence to any of a number of religions and something further about the inadequacies of extant religions. This negative part is that no religion is better, or enough better than its rivals, in terms of such contact so as to sustain a requirement of adherence to that religion as a condition for salvation. We might put this point by saying that for such a version of Pluralism, cognitive contact with a transcendent reality coexists with widespread error about this reality for all major world religions. While this negative point is easily perceived as quite pessimistic about extant religions, the negativity has to be measured. An experience of the Real is not nothing, and central to Pluralism is the embracing of the importance of religious life. So even though pessimism about the adequacy of the central doctrinal tenets of major world religions is part of Pluralism, a second component is the element of cognitive contact with a Reality that is tinged enough with ineffability to require the error theory just noted.

Such an account of Pluralism is clearly metatheoretical, and it can be endorsed even by those who, within a particular context, talk and think like Exclusivists. Such Pluralists could quote the Acts passage with the best of them, acknowledging that the truth for their particular context is some particular religion, while recognizing metatheoretically that there are other contexts and the truth for those contexts is different. One might hold the suspicion that such people suffer doublemindedness, but even if they do, they do not also suffer from any distinctively religious conceptual incoherence. It may be that any version of relativism in any context is incoherent, though I doubt it, but the point is that Pluralism can be given a coherent statement provided that incoherence isn't endemic to relativistic positions of every sort.

The issue here has some affinities with disputes in metaethics, where realists assert a particular point of view, and quasi-realists and attitudinalists sometimes claim to be able to affirm exactly the same claims. In such a case, the realist is trying to assert a metatheoretical perspective that distinguishes the view from the alternatives, but defenders of the alternative view claim to be able to mimic realism by endorsing everything realists was claiming to be distinctive of their position.

The key to avoiding such a metatheoretical impasse is to distinguish first-order positions from meta-positions, regimenting the claims of natural language into appropriate levels in the hierarchy. For example, one's religious practice can be exclusivist in virtue of one's use of Acts 4:12 and a particular exegetical reading of it. But one's philosophical stance on such a practice might be a version of either Exclusivism or Pluralism.

The same can't be said for the opposite combination, where one is a theoretical Pluralist (holding that everyone has multiple correct religions to choose from) but a metatheoretical Exclusivist (maintaining that from a God's-eye point of view, one outside all contexts—or including all other contexts as parts—there is one true religion and adherence to it determines who is saved and who isn't). Our interest here, in any case, is with the metatheoretical perspective. If Pluralists can sound just like Exclusivists at the theoretical level, that is not my concern here. My concern is rather with the division between relativists and absolutists when the TAS narrative is adopted. In this context, the division in question is both exclusive and exhaustive of the metatheoretical options.

Even so, the standard account of the metatheory concerning religious disagreement and the chance of salvation introduces a third category, called "Inclusivism." It is this position that I wish to explore and develop here, and we can begin by considering how a third possibility can arise at all, given what we have just seen about the exclusive and exhaustive distinction just noted. We will begin, then, by considering the views of the primary exponent of Inclusivism, Karl Rahner. I will argue that his view is not, in fact, a metatheoretical position but is rather only a theoretical one. Seeing why this is true will put us in a position to appreciate how alternatives to Pluralism and Exclusivism may arise at the metatheoretical level and will allow us to develop a metatheoretical version of Inclusivism that takes its cues from Rahner but isn't bound by the limitations we find in his thought. We turn then to Rahner's theory of anonymous Christians.

2. Rahner's Anonymous Christian

Rahner characterizes the anonymous Christian as follows:

> We prefer the terminology according to which that man is called an "Anonymous Christian" who on the one hand has *de facto* accepted of his freedom this gracious self-offering on God's part through faith, hope, and love, while on the other he is absolutely not yet a Christian at the social level (through baptism and membership of the Church) or in the sense of having consciously objectified his Christianity to himself in his own mind (by explicit Christian faith resulting from having hearkened to the explicit Christian message) We might therefore put it as follows: the 'anonymous Christian' in our sense of the

term is the pagan after the beginning of the Christian mission, who lives in the state of Christ's grace through faith, hope and love, yet who has no explicit knowledge of the fact that his life is orientated in grace-given salvation to Jesus Christ.   (Rahner 1976, 283)

Here are the central claims in this depiction. First, anonymous Christians have freely accepted God's grace through faith, hope, and love. Even so, they are not adherents of the Christian religion or of any of its sects. In spite of this failure of adherence, such Christians live lives that are focused or oriented "in grace-given salvation to Jesus Christ." We can thus identify three central elements involved in the theory:

I. ACs have *de facto* accepted grace through faith, hope, and love.
II. ACs are not adherents of the Christian religion or any of its sects.
III. The lives of ACs are oriented toward the salvation offered through Jesus Christ.

We will focus on the substance of the theory, but it is also worth noting the argument that drives Rahner to insist on the possibility of anonymous Christians:

. . . the theory [of anonymous Christianity] arose from two facts: first, the possibility of supernatural salvation and of a corresponding faith which must be granted to non-Christians even if they never become Christian; and secondly, that salvation cannot be gained without reference to God and Christ, since it must in its origin, history and fulfilment be a theistic and Christian salvation.

One can only escape this conclusion if one adopts the pessimistic outlook common in the past and disputes the possibility of supernatural salvation for such people, thereby consigning them to hell or limbo, or if one grants salvation merely on the basis of human respectability without reference to God and Christ, or if, finally, one refuses to think about the Christian character in these cases, thus endangering the universality of Christ's redeeming action, which should on the contrary be firmly maintained.

(Rahner 1979, 18)

According to Rahner, there are only three ways to avoid his theory of anonymous Christians, the first two of which are fairly straightforward. First, one might consign vast swaths of humanity to hell or some non-heavenly alternative to hell.[3] Second, one might adopt a soteriological position on which human respectability without reference to Christian doctrine can be sufficient.

To these two Rahner adds a third which is more mysterious. Rahner claims that the universality of Christ's redeeming action must be firmly maintained,[4] and that the third option threatens this point of view. That option involves a refusal to think about something ("the Christian character in these cases . . ."), which is a surprising and at least slightly perplexing remark. For one thing, refusing to think isn't a way of "escaping a conclusion," except in the purely psychological sense of not in fact endorsing it. A better way to parse Rahner's thinking here, however, focuses on the content in question, the claim about the "Christian character" of the particular individuals in question. This third option thus distinguishes between the idea of salvation based on human respectability alone, as in the second option, with salvation based on Christian character. So we need an understanding of Christian character so that it involves something more than human respectability, since I doubt Rahner would have been thinking that Christian character should be recognized in cases not involving respectability.

The final option, then, is better thought of in terms of denying that there is any true Christian character displayed by those who are not adherents of the Christian religion, a position that endangers the universality of Christ's redeeming action, according to Rahner. This option is thus, strictly speaking, not distinct from the other options, since it is compatible with both options. But it adds something by way of explanation: it says eternal destiny is either a matter of gracious atonement or human respectability. So, perhaps what is distinctive about the third option is its skepticism about finding non-Christians who nonetheless go beyond mere human respectability and display Christian character.

So, we can summarize Rahner's basis for the theory of anonymous Christians by noting that there are two ways one might explain away consigning vast swaths of humanity to hell. One way involves a hard-hearted doctrinal stance, and the other involves a hard-headed skeptical resistance concerning the apparent marks of Christian character among those who have not named the name of Christ. Otherwise, one can reject the theory of anonymous Christians only if one divorces salvation from Christian doctrine entirely,

---

[3] If we can agree that the appropriate carving of logical space involves only two possibilities—heaven and hell—we can limit this first option to consigning vast swaths to hell. The argument against there being more than two such possibilities is developed in Kvanvig (1993).

[4] It may be worth noting the hint of anti-Calvinism in this claim, since it would seem to be in tension with the centrality of Limited Atonement to Calvinism.

maintaining that presence in the heavenly community is a function of human respectability alone.

Note the way in which Rahner's theory upsets the metaphysics-first order of explanation. On that order, issues of truth and falsity take priority, followed by the question of adherence, which then issues in some soteriological results. For Rahner, what is explanatorily prior is the question of whether a person has freely accepted grace "through faith, hope, and love." Such a claim makes soteriological issues prior to issues of adherence, since the source of salvation can be present independently of adherence to what is assumed to be the one true religion.

This priority point can then be generalized beyond the particulars of Rahner's own theology. A Hickian pluralist could identify salvation in generic terms as well, and then ground such salvation in generic characterizations that apply to all religions, or all the major post-axial ones, thereby embracing a category of what we might call "anonymous religiosos." If all the interesting religious options were theistic ones, and the source of salvation were something more affective and less cognitive, we might use the label "affective theists" to identify such individuals, even those who are cognitive atheists.

Moreover, there is something quite natural and intuitive in this type of approach. For those of us who reflect both on the impressive character of others and our own moral frailty (to kindly understate), it is easy to view the matter this way: "if salvation eludes them, we have no chance at all." Such thoughts can then prompt a rejection of a metaphysics-driven conception of salvation, in favor of one that begins from attitudinal and characterological starting points.

The general point, however, is that the Rahnerian position reveals a much wider logical space than that which seemed to be in place when the dispute begins with the metaphysics of relativism versus absolutism. Once this point is appreciated, the logical space of alternatives to Exclusivism and Pluralism are much broader than the Inclusivism of Rahner. In order to make the standard category scheme involve categories that are both exhaustive and exclusive, we would have to treat "Inclusivism" as a mere placeholder for anything that isn't a version of Exclusivism or Pluralism. Pretty clearly, however, that term is not being used as a placeholder, nor was it intended to be used that way. Instead, it is a name for a position that Rahner intends to characterize properly, in positive and substantive terms. As such, the standard category scheme is not exhaustive of the logical space in question. Characterizing the space more perspicuously and more adequately is the task of the next section.

3. Generalizing Rahner's Theory of the Anonymous Christian

A first point to note is that if we treat Rahner's ideas as hinting at a proper metatheoretical category scheme, his remarks are insufficiently metatheoretical, tied as they are to the assumption of the truth of Christianity. If we want to articulate a fully metatheoretical position, it will need to be neutral on the question of which religion is true. There should thus be the possibility of anonymous Hindus, anonymous Buddhists, anonymous Muslims, etc., and not just anonymous Christians.

We can make some progress by systematizing our understanding of the religions that we need to include in our characterization. Perhaps something along the lines of John Hick's account will be helpful. Hick focuses on what he terms "post-axial religion," the kind of religions that have their source in the axial age of roughly 800 to 200 BCE,[5] each of which involve the idea of transforming some deeply problematic feature of our present condition into something different and dramatically better. As Hick says,

> Each of the great post-axial streams of religious experience and belief has been shown to exhibit a soteriological structure: a recognition of our human moral weakness and failure or of the pervasive insecurity and liability-to-suffering of all life; the proclamation of a limitlessly better possibility arising from another reality, transcendent to our present selves; and the teaching of a way, whether by "ownpower" spiritual discipline or the "other-power" of divine grace, to its realisation. Thus they are concerned with salvation or liberation . . . and they all affirm a transcendent Reality in virtue of which it is available to us. Thus each in its own way constitutes a gospel, offering good news to erring and suffering human beings.   (Hick 1989, 56)

We thus tentatively begin our metatheoretical task by characterizing the central elements of such religions. All of them offer some hope of salvation, where we treat this notion as a placeholder for the way in which the religion points toward something different and dramatically better that our current condition. In addition, all of them offer a diagnosis of what is troubling or problematic about our current condition. Finally, there is some way each religion posits linking these first two notions, some method or mechanism or characteristic by which humans can move from the problematic to

---

[5] See, especially, Hick (1989), but also Hick (1985, 1999).

something better, some notion of efficacy for escaping the predicament noted. Though some of the terms I will use call up Christian associations, I will use them in a more generic sense, identifying the first element using the language of derangement, dis-ease, and perturbations of the human condition—in short, it is what I will call "the problem of *sin*," limited in semantic content to the etymological heart of that notion involving missing the mark. The hoped-for resolution of the problem of sin is *salvation*, and the path for moving from the problem of sin to the joys of salvation composes the *gospel* according to the religion in question.[6]

From this perspective, it is relatively simple to see how to generalize much of Rahner's theory so as not to presuppose the truth of Christianity. On his theory, recall, anonymous Christians have received "grace" from God through "faith, hope, and love"; they do not adhere to the Christian faith; but their lives are oriented toward the salvation offered through Jesus Christ. Generalizing to include other religions, we can say that Inclusivism involves a recognition that, where R is the religion that is assumed to be the one true religion, there is a problem of sin that R identifies and a promise of salvation from such sin, relative to R, with some account of the gospel for R that does not require adherence to R in order for a given person to achieve salvation from sin.

But here's the rub. First, negative characterizations alone disappoint, and this latter account is negative. Second, Rahner's own account employs distinctively Christian ideas through its appeal to faith, hope, and love as the vehicle for receiving divine grace, so his account provides no help in moving from a negative to a positive characterization. Most important, however, is the restriction that this negative characterization places on the notion of gospel: it insists that we have an account that doesn't require adherence to the religion in question. But that, by itself, appears to be a mistake: why think every religion is so constituted? We thus have work to do in the next section on the notion of gospel itself.

4. The Generic Notion of Gospel

The idea behind the distinction between Pluralism and Exclusivism is a shared assumption about explanatory relationships between the individuation of

---

[6] See also Prothero (2010) for a regimenting scheme that understands major religions in terms of an account of the fundamental problem faced by humanity, the remedy for this problem, and the mechanism by which the remedy is secured.

religions (or sects of religions) and the hopes for salvation that each offers. That assumption is that a proper understanding begins with the issue of which religion is true and then finds the possibility of the fulfillment of the hope in question to adherents of the religion in question. At least, that assumption is made when Pluralism appears in the guise of the relativist, in contrast to the absolutism about truth that characterizes Exclusivism. (Note that relativistic Exclusivism is exactly the same position as relativistic Pluralism, so to maintain the exclusivity of the category structure of our theory, Exclusivism must reject relativism about truth.) The order of explanation thus runs from the question of truth through the question of adherence to the hope of salvation.

Suppose, however, that some pluralist agrees with naturalism, holding that all religions are, in fact, false. To distinguish the view from naturalism, something more positive must be said, and here such a pluralist must, of necessity, say something positive about religion. Perhaps such a pluralist might hold that even though every religion is false, many of them have enough truth in them to make adherence to such a religion effective in securing salvation. Such a perspective minimizes the role of truth in the story, but leaves intact the general order of explanation, which runs from truth to adherence to salvation (TAS).

Yet, if such a pluralism minimizes the role of truth in the story of salvation, it also opens up the possibility that the story of salvation does not arise out of adherence to whatever truth can be found in religion. Or at least, it opens up the possibility that the amount of truth involved in the story of salvation might be small indeed. Moreover, the smaller the role that truth plays in the story, the less sense it makes to let the notion of adherence to a religion play a central explanatory role in the story of salvation. Presumably, if only a small amount of any given religion matters as far as salvation goes, then only adherence to that small amount could be important in an account of the realized hope of salvation. And the slimmer the slice of adherence taken into account, the more one begins to wonder whether larger pieces of the pie are being ignored. That is, perhaps a better understanding of the mechanism by which salvation is realized should not really be focused on the issue of adherence or should not be primarily so focused.

Such a conclusion allows development of a generic inclusivism that can be stated without relying on specifically Christian themes, as does Rahner's. I want to argue that the route to such an account is through the land of the affective and what I will argue is fundamental faith, but in order to make the case for such an account, we need to see why and how an appeal to faith of this sort differs from the faith-based character of some religions, especially the religion of Christianity.

In slogan form, it is the difference between faith in fundamentals and fundamental faith.

Such language is reminiscent of Rahner's idea of non-adherents having accepted God's grace in "faith, hope, and love," thereby running the risk of generating an Inclusivism that is less than fully general. Rahner's focus, however, shows a predilection for a certain type of relationship to God and to some openness on the part of God toward human well-being and flourishing. Such an approach need not involve distinctively Christian elements, but rather is compatible with quite generic theologies and quite generic accounts of the distinctive attitudes and conditions of heart and mind that are central to a relationship to or with God of soteriological significance.

Central to this attempt to generalize is the fundamentality of the attitudinal and characterological elements that do not presuppose the truth of any particular account of the human condition or of the means to remedying it. We can see that both pluralism and exclusivism are metaphysics-first positions, starting from the first two items on the list and deriving an answer to the third in terms of these metaphysical facts. As I'm characterizing inclusivism, it begins from the third element and moves toward the first two items in terms of the nature of the satisfaction of the third element in a given case. There is no really good term for such satisfaction, the kind of satisfaction conditions I'll describe below can be thought of in a quite vague way as conditions generating an ethos of a certain sort.

Such language is enigmatic at best at this point, so a bit of explanation is needed here. The idea is nicely illustrated from a scene in *The Big Lebowski* in which Walter Sobchak is criticizing nihilism by contrasting it with something still deplorable but slightly better: "I mean, say what you want about the tenets of National Socialism, Dude, at least it's an ethos." What I see here is the priority of the ethos over the tenets of National Socialism. The idea is there is first an ethos and then a set of tenets that issue from the ethos. I don't make any claim about what comes first, but I suspect even the etiological priority of the ethos over the tenets, but my primary point is that one can grant the value of the ethos and still find deplorable the doctrine.

In the cases we are considering, the relevant ethos will be a religious one. Moreover, it will involve some notion of faith, in the sense explicated and defended in Kvanvig (2018). It is in this ethos-first sense that I mean to contrast approaches that point to faith in fundamentals, a metaphysics-first approach, with an approach that points to the kind of fundamental faith involved in a religious ethos. The point I will argue for is that such fundamental faith is precisely the right kind of thing to play a role in the story of how a person or community moves from the plagues of the human condition to the state of salvation offered.

I note in passing that this alternative to the metaphysics-first approach taken by Exclusivists and Pluralists raises the possibility of a heretofore unrecognized possibility, that of starting with the second item on the list and deriving accounts of the first and third, in either order. I note this possibility out of an urge to characterize the entire logical space for metatheory here, but will ignore it in what follows, since I have no idea what such an approach would look like.

For inclusivism, however, what might those attitudes and conditions of the heart involve, so as not to involve the presupposition of the truth of a particular religion such as Christianity? Rahner speaks of accepting God's offer of grace through "faith, hope, and love," and while this approach may be adequate, it requires careful treatment in order to avoid the presupposition in question. In particular, there must be some understanding of the attitudes Rahner notes that don't depend on the distinctive tenets of the Christian religion.

5. Faith, Hope, and Love

We may begin by asking whether the appeal to faith, hope, and love is just a vestige of Rahner's Christian sensibilities, or if there is a deeper explanation of how and why an ethotic approach, as advocated here, would appeal to these three elements.[7] The one that seems easiest to defend is the appeal to love, conceived of in Thomistic terms as a willing of the good for a beloved and a desire for union with the beloved. The essential element here is an aversion for the self-absorption that is central to any adequate understanding of how anyone could be lost forever,[8] and thus provides an obvious starting point for an ethotic alternative to the standard metaphysical approach of Exclusivism and Pluralism.

What is needed, then, is an explanation of how and why both faith and hope are required in addition to love, in order for soteriology to be explanatorily

---

[7] There is also a question of whether more than these three are required on a full account of an ethotic approach, but I leave that issue for another time and place.

[8] As I argue in Kvanvig (1993), though this feature is common to all versions of the choice model of hell that I argue for, including Lewis (1940), Swinburne (1983), Stump (1986) and Walls (1992).

prior to the questions of truth and adherence. To get such an account, we first need an explanation of the difference between faith and hope, and as Andrew Chignell has been arguing, the cognitive aspect of attention is central to hope,[9] and this account of hope reveals the central difference that distinguishes hope from faith. To hope for world peace, for example, is to be characterized by certain patterns of attention that are not explicable in terms of cognitive commitments such as belief, acceptance, etc. The standard account maintains that hope involves desiring something that one believes is possible, but such an account doesn't help us see the difference between hope and despair, since both attitudes can be displayed by people who have just the desire/belief complex that defines the standard account. What is missing here is an attentional element. The one who despairs attends to, focuses on the negatives: how unlikely the desired state is, how much disappointment will be experienced if the desire isn't realized, etc. The one with hope attends primarily to the desirability of the state and what the future might look like under a realization of the possibility in question.[10]

I'm suspicious of the desire/belief requirements on hope, but not of the attentional element. My skepticism is primarily about the idea that one has to view the object of hope as possible. There may be reasons for claiming that one can't hope for something that one takes to be impossible,[11] but failure to believe that something is impossible doesn't entail believing that that thing is possible.[12] In addition, I suspect that quite a few hope for things that they don't in fact desire. Perhaps they view the world as better or more beautiful if it involves the presence of certain states or objects, and hope for such presence on the basis of this attitude. Such a hope is compatible with a known lack of wanting or desiring the presence of those states or objects. In particular, reflective people often find themselves lamenting their lack of desire and interest in the right and the good and the beautiful, wondering whether and

---

[9] See, e.g., Chignell (2013, 2014, 2017).

[10] A prototypical example is in *The Shawshank Redemption*, where Andy and Ellis both desire to escape from prison and both realize it's possible. Though there is no indication in the movie that the desires, preferences, beliefs, and levels of confidence are precisely the same for both, such equality is possible. Yet, one despairs and one hopes, a difference explicable by appeal to different attentional foci: one focuses on the dimness of the prospects and despairs and the other focuses on the possibility of success and hopes.

[11] Even this claim needs very careful articulation. The kind of impossibility is going to have to be beyond even the reach of the gods, on pain of making it impossible to hope for a miracle, which is clearly not impossible. But we need not chase precision here.

[12] This point generalizes to other approaches that replace belief that something is possible with some other content, such as that some chance or non-zero probability exists. See, e.g., Benton (2019) and Benton (2021) for a view along these lines.

how they might be responsible for such a condition. For such, however, hope is not impossible.[13]

The important point for present purposes, however, is not the full account of hope but the centrality of the attentional element that separates hope from despair. Faith may involve a pro-attitude of some sort,[14] a feature in common with hope, but the attentional element is not part of the nature of faith.

To the extent, then, that the attentional element is itself something central to the religious ethos being considered, there is reason to side with Rahner in thinking that an ethos-first approach will need to include hope in the story in addition to faith. To anticipate, I'll present an account of faith in the next section that leaves open the possibility of having faith but growing weary and despondent in the task, even approaching despair. Such faith may thus be necessary on an ethotic approach (together with love), but the possibilities of weariness, despondency, and despair call for an admixture that includes hope.

The outline of the ethotic picture thus includes the three Rahnerian elements, but some skepticism is warranted at this, precisely because standard accounts of faith fit better with a metaphysical approach than an ethotic one. If faith is fundamentally cognitive, then it would seem to involve an attitude toward some propositional claims, and we are thus in need of some propositional claims that are not distinctively Christian in order to have an account of salvation that doesn't presuppose the truth of Christianity. So, for example, the object of faith can't be the claim that God was in Christ reconciling the world to himself, even though that is a quite generic claim that every version of Christianity can subscribe to. So, what exactly can faith be, and what are the objects of faith, so that there is any chance of providing an alternative to the more standard metaphysical approach, where one's account of faith requires doctrinal elements from the start, or generic alternatives to specific doctrines, where the generic alternatives still involve metaphysical commitments to characterize the nature of saving faith. To this issue we turn in the next section.

---

[13] I note that such considerations are standard in modern decision theory, where a belief/desire that functions on rational action is replaced with a combination of degrees of belief and preference orderings. The cases I have in mind are those in which one's preferences do not mirror one's desires.

[14] Proponents include Adams (1995), Alston (1996), Audi (2008, 2019) and Howard-Snyder (2013). I note, however, that there are reasons to be suspicious here, of the same sort that led these same theorists to doubt that belief is required for faith. These reasons for suspicion are being developed in unpublished work by Maria Altepeter. Perhaps an account that replaces proattitudes with preferences will be adequate.

6. Faith in Fundamentals and Fundamental Faith

What is clear from the above is that the faith and hope that are central to a Rahnerian subversion of a metaphysical approach have to be more generic than many conservative religious groups can stomach. And the reason why is that the conception of faith central to the faith in the minds of such individuals is cognitive, directed at what John Calvin in the context of Christianity refers to as the "great truths of the Gospel." But for faith to be central to the story of a relationship with God of such a quality as to be capable of eventuating in salvation, it must be something not tied to specific cognitive commitments in this way.

Defenders of cognitive approaches have a ready answer here, however, for they will side with Alvin Plantinga in insisting that whatever else is needed in a proper account of faith, it is built on top of the requisite cognitive elements:

> So believing in God is indeed more than accepting the proposition that God exists. But if it is more than that, it is also at least that. One cannot sensibly believe in God and thank him for the mountains without believing that there is such a person to be thanked and that he is in some way responsible for the mountains. Nor can one trust in God and commit oneself to him without believing that he exists; as the author of Hebrews says, "He who would come to God must believe that he is and that he is a rewarder of those who seek him" (Heb. 11:6).   (Plantinga 1983, 18)

Plantinga agrees that believing in God (and presumably having faith in God) involves more than a cognitive attitude of believing that God exists, but insists that it involves at least this much. Once this claim is accepted, as it is by nearly all conservative Christian groups, we are launched into the project of defining what the fundamentals are for such faith, so as to find the cognitive basis on which to build the kind of faith in God that will be salvifically adequate.[15]

For some, the class of fundamentals will be wide and deep, containing a vast array of great truths of the good news they preach. The more expansive the list, however, the more exclusive the club of the elect, with the extreme being that any cognitive error consigns one to the exile of hell. Less austere accounts acquiesce to human foibles and folly, allowing for a variety of errors and

---

[15] A detailed discussion and rebuttal of Plantinga's claims here, including a corrective concerning the standard translation of the text Plantinga quotes, can be found in Kvanvig (2018, 11–15). Here I bypass the details to focus on the larger issue of the general perspective on the life of faith that such a claim involves.

ignorance concerning the great truths. In any case, if saving faith is built on top of such cognitive requirements, the cognitive requirements will need to be those that constitute adherence to the religion in question, for the point of insisting on faith in the fundamentals is to define adherence to the religion in terms of its essential components.

There is a danger here, however, for it isn't easy to see how this target can be hit. The less austere, the more generic, one's account of the fundamentals, the greater the danger that even non-adherents might be able to qualify for having met the cognitive requirements in question and that the generic formulation isn't one that practitioners actually endorse. What they endorse will likely be, at most, a more specific claim that entails the generic one. In addition, it may be that talk of the fundamentals is explanatorily posterior to a religious life already affirmed, so that there will be no path toward circumscribing the great truths in question apart from such an assumed religious life.

Consider the cost of such an order of explanation in the context of Christianity: there is orthodox Christianity, there is fundamentalist Christianity, there is liberal Christianity, postmodern Christianity, etc. What do all these groups agree on, and what must they agree on to be part of the religion we wish to identify as Christianity? The phrase "In essentials, unity; in non-essentials, liberty; in all things, charity," is charmingly attractive.[16] Moreover, when one notices that the slogan has been adopted by groups as varied as the Moravian Church of North America, the Evangelical Presbyterian Church (US), as well as other groups, one can be forgiven for the suspicion that the charm of the phrase is retained only so long as nobody stands up to say what the essentials are!

Notice also that this clarion call on behalf of Christian Irenicism is ironically a source of further divisiveness. For as soon as the slogan is voiced, one is required to say what the essentials are, and here controversy reigns. If you are attracted to "muscular" Christianity, it is hardly discomfiting to condemn to the flames even the majority of those who swear allegiance to Christ, but for the irenics among us (including myself), it is awkward to say the least to be forced to put down on paper what the well-muscled relish as fuel for the flames.

Things look different when we begin with an account of faith that makes faith central to religious life. On this approach, there is the theological question of what is true and what is false, and there is, we may presume, a core theory or

---

[16] The Latin phrase is often misattributed to Augustine, whose theology would not allow it. Some say the origin is in a tract written by Rupertus Medenius in 1627–1628 during the Thirty Years' War, but the adage seems to have occurred at least five years earlier in the work of Marco Antonio de Diminis. For details, see Nellen (1999).

model that is correct or adequate with respect to the doctrinal issues involved. When the issue of salvation arises, however, the theological question fades into the background, in favor of more pressing questions such as "What must one do or be to be saved?" The Christian answer involves living a life of faith, and if a proper understanding of faith is embraced, this answer may generalize to other religions as well. On the account of faith I have defended in Kvanvig (2018), several things are true about faith. First, faith is fundamentally dispositional, incorporating cognitive, affective, and conative elements. Second, among these elements, if one takes priority over the others, it will be the affective elements, since faith is, to quote the slogan, a disposition to respond in service of an ideal.[17] Central, then, to a life of faith is the notion of an ideal, and whatever we want to say about ideals, it is clear that the attachment to an ideal is fundamentally affective rather than cognitive. Even if cognition is essential to such an attachment, the appreciation of the ideal *as ideal* is not an ordinary, mundane cognitive response to an empirical fact about the world.

An advantage of this account of faith over cognitive ones is that it can be put to metatheoretical use more easily, for the idea of a disposition to respond in service of an ideal is generic enough to present an inclusive conception of religion as faith-based without presupposing the truth of any of these religions. Thus, whereas Rahner's notion of accepting God's grace in faith, hope, and love appeals to a fundamentally Christian understanding of the way in which salvation is to be achieved, an account of salvation in terms of affective faith aimed in service of an ideal can characterize the story of salvation for any religion one wishes.

Once we adopt such a view of faith, there is no longer any reason to identify salvation with cognitive commitment to some list of supposed fundamentals for each religion. This separation of alethic and salvific concerns makes possible an account Inclusivism that distinguishes it from Pluralism and Exclusivism, but without presupposing any distinctive first-order religious perspective.

Central to Inclusivism is a refusal to endorse the pessimistic element of Pluralism. Inclusivists have no need of the central Pluralist commitment to fundamental error for all major world religions. In this respect, Inclusivists agree with Exclusivists, but for a different reason. Inclusivists do not envision the order of explanation as proceeding from truth or reality and adherence to it, in a way that culminates in the hope of salvation. Instead, Inclusivists avoid

---

[17] The account of faith I develop and defend is Deweyan in character, and the slogan in the text is Dewey's. See Dewey (1934).

such a metaphysics-first orientation by endorsing a soteriology-first approach, one that characterizes the hope of salvation in a way that makes a certain kind of life appropriate to and fitting with this soteriology. The life in question is a life of affective faith, understood in terms of a disposition to a response profile in service of the ideal that generates this hope of salvation. The question of doctrinal elements thus comes last, a filling in of the response profile in a way designed to make intellectual sense of this hope and one's allegiance to its source.

Exclusivists may resist here, insisting that the substrate of the disposition in question involves cognitive commitments that are specific enough to line up with the essential truths of the one true religion. Inclusivists have a ready answer, however, for the broadly functional account of faith here would be surprising if the same faith were not multiply realizable, as is typical of functional states. We can grant that the disposition to respond in service of an ideal depends on various combinations of conative, cognitive, and affective elements. But we should expect multiple realizability here as much as with functional states more generally. So Inclusivists have an initial advantage here.

They also have a further advantage. Each metatheory has to explain how the hope of salvation is tied to the story of adherence endorsed, and here Inclusivism tells the beautiful story: the hope of salvation depends on an affective and dispositional attachment to the ideal that is the source of that hope. Metatheories that are metaphysics-first approaches struggle here, trying to explain why attachment to intellectual elements are explanatorily fundamental. It is not hard to wonder why intellectual assent should be given such pride of place and why salvation might reasonably be tied to such.

What remains is to address the issue of how much variability Inclusivism tolerates, even after a given ideal is specified. Some versions of Inclusivism will be more restrictive than others, but the generic version of the view can allow for identification of the relevant ideal in ways that allow for a variety of specific intentional realizations. There is no reason to think, at this level of metatheoretical generality, that an Inclusivist could not hold that a given ideal I can be the object of a disposition for two individuals, one of whom has Jesus of Nazareth in mind and the other of whom has Allah in mind. This possibility is, by now, a rather banal implication of the problem of cognitive significance generating an argument for distinguishing between the object of thought and the content of the thought itself. Under the mode of presentation of Clark Kent, Lois views him as a nerd; under the mode of presentation of Superman, she does not.

More radical possibilities exist as well, complications that I will point to though without endorsing a particular metatheoretical response to them. In light of the distinction between the ideals themselves and the modes in which they can be presented, the individuation conditions for ideals come to be the central focus for any precise version of Inclusivism. On this score, things are complicated by the fact that some of the ideals in question count as what the medievals called "transcendentals": truth, goodness, and beauty, as well as being and the associated notion of unity or oneness. Combine this point with the additional item that there are various names under which one might attach to divinity: "God," "Brahma," "Allah," "Shiva," "Yahweh," "Vishnu," "All-Glorious," "The Great Spirit," etc. And note further the centrality of a concept of transcendence that attaches to deity, one that makes attractive apophaticist strains in theology (even for those who reject apophaticism itself). We are thus somewhere in the neighborhood of Kantian humility with respect to theology.

If we combine this Kantian humility with some way in which our concepts of God and matters theological are nonetheless coherent and not completely inadequate,[18] we have to account for the relation that holds between the theological concepts we use and the metaphysical reality that is being conceived. Now, if we think of the transcendentals as themselves transcendental, then the question is what makes theological concepts attach to God but not to other transcendentals? And, for those people of faith who don't conceive of themselves as particularly religious, but are attached to the Good, the True, and the Beautiful in various ways, what makes their concepts of each attach to these features of reality and not to God?

The issue here is quite simple. If our theological concepts are a way of seeing God through a glass darkly, then non-theological concepts such as goodness, truth, and beauty may also be a way of seeing God through a glass darkly. And if that is so, then lives of faith that are, from a purely cognitive point of view, thoroughly secular, might also be, from a more affective and conative point of view, thoroughly religious.

One final point here is needed, since the more humility is involved in the Inclusivist story, the more Inclusivism comes to resemble certain forms of Pluralism, especially versions such as that of John Hick that make the ineffability of the Real central to rejecting the priority of any extant religion over others. What is important to recall here, however, is the different order of explanation involved. Pluralists join hands with Exclusivists in embracing a

---

[18] For an attempt along these lines, see Bonevac (2012).

metaphysics-first metatheory, and this order of explanation is reversed by Inclusivists. Thus, even in the presence of strong similarities, Inclusivism is a radically different metatheory than Pluralism.

7. Conclusion

Our goal has been to find a way of explaining Inclusivism that is fully general, not assuming the truth of any particular religion in the way Rahner's own approach does. We have found a way to do so, relying on a notion of faith that is affective rather than cognitive, and Deweyan in spirit. As a result, we can formulate a version of Inclusivism that allows the Inclusivist to endorse a theory of religion that is neither hard-hearted nor hard-headed.

References

Adams, Robert Merrihew. 1995. "Moral Faith." *Journal of Philosophy* 92: 75–95.

Alston, William P. 1996. *The Reliability of Sense Perception*. Ithaca, IN: Cornell University Press.

Audi, Robert. 2008. "The Ethics of Belief: Doxastic Self-Control and Intellectual Virtue." *Synthese* 161: 403–418.

Audi, Robert. 2019. "Faith, Belief, and Will: Toward a Volitional Stance Theory of Faith." *Sophia* 58: 409–422.

Benton, Matthew A. 2019. "Epistemological Aspects of Hope." In Claudia Blöser and Titus Stahl (eds.), *The Moral Psychology of Hope*, 135–151. London: Rowman & Littlefield.

Benton, Matthew A. 2021. "Knowledge, Hope, and Fallibilism." *Synthese* 198: 1673–1689.

Bonevac, Daniel. 2012. "Two Theories of Analogical Predication." *Oxford Studies in Philosophy of Religion* 4: 20–43.

Byrne, Peter. 2004. "It Is Not Reasonable to Believe That Only One Religion Is True." In Michael L. Peterson and Raymond J. VanArragon (eds.), *Contemporary Debates in Philosophy of Religion*, 201–210. Malden: Blackwell.

Chignell, Andrew. 2013. "Rational Hope, Moral Order, and the Revolution of the Will." In Eric Watkins (ed.), *The Divine Order, the Human Order, and the Order of Nature: Historical Perspectives*, 199–207. Oxford: Oxford University Press.

Chignell, Andrew. 2014. "Rational Hope, Possibility, and Divine Action." In Gordon E. Michalson, *Religion within the Bounds of Mere Reason: A Critical Guide*, 98–117. Cambridge: Cambridge University Press.

Chignell, Andrew. 2017. "Knowledge, Discipline, System, Hope: The Fate of Metaphysics in the Doctrine of Method." In James O'Shea (ed.), *Kant's Critique of Pure Reason: A Critical Guide*, 259–279. New York: Cambridge University Press.

Dewey, John. 1934. *A Common Faith*. New Haven, CT: Yale University Press.

Hick, John. 1985. *Problems of Religious Pluralism*. New York: St. Martin's Press.

Hick, John. 1989. *An Interpretation of Religion: Human Responses to the Transcendent*. New Haven, CT: Yale University Press.

Hick, John. 1999. "Religious Pluralism and Salvation." In Kevin Meeker and Philip Quinn (eds.), *The Philosophical Challenge of Religious Diversity*, 54–66. New York: Oxford University Press.

Howard-Snyder, Daniel. 2013. "Propositional Faith: What It Is and What It Is Not." *American Philosophical Quarterly* 50: 357–372.

Kvanvig, Jonathan L. 1993. *The Problem of Hell*. New York: Oxford University Press.

Kvanvig, Jonathan L. 2018. *Faith and Humility*. Oxford: Oxford University Press.

Lewis, Clive Staples. 1940. *The Problem of Pain*. London: Geoffrey Bles.

Meeker, Kevin and Philip Quinn (eds.). 1999. *The Philosophical Challenge of Religious Diversity*. New York: Oxford University Press.

Nellen, H. J. M. 1999. "De zinspreuk 'In necessariis unitas, in non necessariis libertas, in utrisque caritas'." *Nederlands archief voor kerkgeschidenis* 79: 99–106.

Plantinga, Alvin. 1983. *Faith and Rationality: Reason and Belief in God*. Notre Dame, IN: University of Notre Dame Press.

Prothero, Stephen. 2010. *God is Not One: The Eight Rival Religions that Run the World—and Why Their Differences Matter*. New York: HarperCollins Publishers.

Rahner, Karl. 1976. *Theological Investigations*. Vol. 14. London: Darton, Longman & Todd.

Rahner, Karl. 1979. *Theological Investigations*. Vol. 16. London: Darton, Longman & Todd.

Stump, Eleonore. 1986. "Dante's Hell, Aquinas's Moral Theory, and the Love of God." *Canadian Journal of Philosophy* 16: 181–196.

Swinburne, Richard. 1983. "A Theodicy of Heaven and Hell." In Alfred J. Freddoso (ed.), *The Existence and Nature of God*, 37–54. Notre Dame, IN: University of Notre Dame Press.

Walls, Jerry. 1992. *Hell: The Logic of Damnation*. Notre Dame, IN: University of Notre Dame Press.

10

The Loyalty of Religious Disagreement

Katherine Dormandy

1. Introduction

Scientific disagreement can bring great insight, especially when the interlocutors are apt to have different perspectives because they have diverse backgrounds and social locations (Longino 1990; Anderson 1995; De Cruz and De Smedt 2013). I have argued that the same applies to *religious* disagreement, that is, disagreement over the nature or existence of ultimate reality and what this means for how we should live (Dormandy 2018a, 2018b, 2020a, 2020b). This includes disagreement with people from other religious traditions, confessions, or denominations; adherents of other religions or none; and people from non-authoritative social locations in one's own religious community.

The sort of disagreement I have in mind is *epistemically oriented*—it aims at achieving epistemic improvements, as opposed to just mutual tolerance. Epistemically oriented religious disagreement is an important source of external criticism, it can reveal bias in our own belief-forming practices, it can offer up new epistemic possibilities, and it can lessen prejudice against other people and their views.

Despite these possible benefits, many religious communities are uncomfortable with religious disagreement. Disagreement is well and good for science, they say. But scientists approach their subject matter neutrally, following their evidence where it leads, whereas religious believers should be *committed*—to their tradition, community, and especially to God, or however they construe the divine. This is especially so in religious traditions that regard God as personal, and religious commitment as relationship, or the quest for relationship, with him.[1] Epistemically oriented religious disagreement, such communities argue, has no place in the life of a committed believer. God has graciously gifted us with revelations about what he is like and how we should

---

[1] I follow the tradition of using "he" of God as an imperfect way, in limited language, to refer to a being who is neither male nor female.

Katherine Dormandy, *The Loyalty of Religious Disagreement* In: *Religious Disagreement and Pluralism.*
Edited by: Matthew A. Benton and Jonathan L. Kvanvig, Oxford University Press. © Katherine Dormandy 2021.
DOI: 10.1093/oso/9780198849865.003.0010

live. When a friend opens up and offers you her truth and emotional connection, it is typically inappropriate to consult third parties, including those who may think poorly of her, for their dissenting opinions. Epistemically oriented disagreement about your friend in this case is disloyal to her; along similar lines, epistemically oriented religious disagreement is disloyal to God.

The reason is that this sort of religious disagreement seems to play fast and loose with God's gracious gift of revealed truths, failing to treat them with the respect and seriousness that they deserve, and even putting them at risk as you entertain alternatives. One particular sort of belief that many religious communities want to protect (certainly not the only one) is beliefs that state or imply that God is in one way or another *good*. Often, a disagreeing interlocutor may view God more negatively than the believer does, at least by the lights of the latter's received beliefs. The disagreeing interlocutor may think, for example, that God is less likely to exist, less perfect, that he is not personal (where the received beliefs construe personhood as a great good), that he *is* personal (where the received beliefs construe personhood as a limitation), and so forth. When a believer engages in epistemically oriented religious disagreement with an interlocutor who construes God more negatively than she does, she seems ready to at least entertain the idea, herself, of downgrading her view of God by the lights of her received beliefs. And this, goes the worry, would be disloyal. Behind this worry stands the idea, called *doxastic partiality*, that believing positively about someone, or at least being strongly disposed to, is an expression of loyalty (Keller 2004; Stroud 2006; Hazlett 2013). So believing negatively, or being open to doing so, is a form of what we may call *doxastic disloyalty*. Relationships with God are no exception; indeed, negative beliefs about God, or an openness to forming them, are a great danger to one's faith in him.

The worry is that engaging in epistemically oriented religious disagreement with someone who construes God more negatively than you is doxastically disloyal. One reason is that this sort of disagreement seems to indicate an uncharitable mindset on the believer's part. After all, it is hard to explain why someone would do this unless she suspected that there might be something to the negative beliefs. Another reason is that, even if you did not believe negatively of God already, epistemically oriented disagreement about him certainly puts you at risk of doing so, and this is enough for doxastic disloyalty. If this is so, then, whatever the epistemic benefits of religious disagreement may be, they come at a price that committed believers should not pay.

But I will argue that epistemically oriented religious disagreement is *not* disloyal. On the contrary, it can be loyal. This is so even if doxastic partiality is true. That is, even if believing negatively about God or being open to doing so is disloyal, you can engage in religious disagreement without doing either. But I then argue that doxastic partiality is false. That is, it is *not* disloyal to form, or be open to forming, negative beliefs about the object of your loyalty— including when this is God. So even when religious disagreement does involve negative beliefs about God or an openness to forming some, engaging in it need not be disloyal. It can even, I argue, be loyal. I advance an alternative account of loyalty, *epistemically oriented* loyalty, that construes loyal doxastic behavior not as seeking to believe *positively* about the other party, but as seeking to believe *truly*. Epistemically oriented loyalty includes abiding by truth-conducive epistemic norms, for the sake of knowing the object of your loyalty as she is.

I'll start with some initial clarifications, including about loyalty (section 2). Then I outline two objections from disloyalty that arise from the doxastic-partiality view. I respond by showing that epistemically oriented religious disagreement does *not* violate doxastic partiality, and can be loyal by its lights (sections 3, 4, and 5). But then I argue that doxastic partiality is false, so that epistemically oriented religious disagreement can be loyal *even when it involves negative beliefs about God or openness to forming them*; this is where I defend epistemically oriented loyalty (section 6). The conclusion draws together various results (section 7).

2. Loyalty, Disloyalty, and Some Preliminaries

2.1 Preliminary Clarifications

I'll begin with some clarifications. *Disagreement* occurs when one person believes a proposition p (or a proposition entailing it), and the other suspends judgment or believes that not-p (or a proposition entailing that not-p); it could also occur when both have the same coarse-grained belief that p but differ in their credences (or subjective probability assignments). The proposition p could pertain to just about anything, including, importantly, higher-order epistemic matters—for example, whether some belief or experience counts as evidence in the domain under discussion, or whether and how much some purported evidence supports a belief. *Engaging in epistemically oriented disagreement* with someone amounts to conversing respectfully and charitably about your respective beliefs, focusing particularly (but not only) on the ways in which they are incompatible. Your aim is not particularly to persuade each other (though you need not be opposed to this happening), but more to see what there might be to learn from each other, if anything, about the domain in question.

Here are some of the epistemic benefits, argued for elsewhere, of epistemically oriented religious disagreement (Dormandy 2018a, 2020a, 2020b). First, it is an important source of external criticism: those dissenting from our perspective are better equipped to notice our unquestioned and undefended assumptions. Second, it can reveal the influence of biases to which individuals and communities are susceptible, such as groupthink or the tendency to weight one's own evidence more just because it is one's own. Third, it can expand our evidential basis, challenging our own views to accommodate the evidence supplied by others' research or theorizing (especially in science), or their understanding and lived experiences (especially in religion). Fourth, it can provide new epistemic possibilities that may previously have escaped our radar, perhaps precipitating a shift of probabilities for the alternatives already open to us. And fifth, it might break down prejudices against people who think differently to us, cultivating cognitive flexibility.

Epistemically oriented disagreement cannot do these things by itself; an attitude of mutual respect must be present and communicated. This is especially so when the topic is religion, which is often emotionally laden and linked with interlocutors' sense of identity. But assuming mutual and communicated respect, epistemically oriented religious disagreement can be a source of great insight. In what follows, *religious disagreement* will mean "epistemically oriented religious disagreement."

A note on God. It is important for present purposes to construe him, if he exists, as a personal being. Some philosophers and theologians complicate or reject this construal. But the idea of a personal God is important. It meshes tightly with the three monotheistic traditions and scriptures, and with the way believers are encouraged to speak and think of God. Moreover, the prospect of loyalty to God, or of God's loyalty to us (for example, of God's keeping his covenant to the descendants of Noah and Abraham), is easiest to make sense of given his personhood. I will thus work here with the assumption that God is personal.[2]

Finally, the prospect of believing negatively about God deserves comment. On many traditional views, God is perfect if he exists at all, so any negative belief about him is incoherent. Other views, in contrast, allow for God to be less than perfect, or even have negative qualities (Potter 2000; Wettstein 2012; Hazony 2012). I want to leave room for such views—not only because many traditions espouse them, but also because, even when the doctrine of a given

---

[2] See Benton 2018b for an account of personal knowledge applied to relationship with God.

tradition construes God as perfect, it can be natural to feel betrayed by God; take Job as an example. This suggests that, for many believers, the prospect of God's existing but being flawed is more of a live possibility than his not existing at all. I will thus suppose that negative beliefs about God are not only coherent, but that taking them seriously does justice to religious tradition and experience.

2.2 Loyalty and Disloyalty

The objector says that the person who engages in religious disagreement conducts herself disloyally toward God. To see what this amounts to, we need an account of *loyal* conduct. Following Keller (2007, chapter 1), we may construe this as involving a certain sort of action performed for a certain sort of motive.

Keller characterizes the action of loyalty as *sticking by* the other person or *taking her side*. This metaphor is an umbrella term that picks out different things in contexts. You might take someone's side by advocating for her, by honoring her through certain rituals, by prioritizing her interests or welfare over those of comparable others, or by identifying with her in the sense of treating her as an extension of yourself (2007, 3–7). I suggest that taking someone's side might also involve casting your lot with her: tying your fate to hers in a way that raises the probability that what happens to her, good or bad, might also happen to you. Keller adds that these sorts of actions, to count as side-taking, must be done with a positive attitude toward the other person, such as respect, reverence, or possibly love (2007, 21).

We may agree with Keller that side-taking can be manifested in these ways. But he agrees that it can also be manifested doxastically, as the inclination to "hold or resist certain beliefs, independently of the evidence" (6). More than this, he holds that *not* showing loyalty in this way is often disloyal. Keller is thus a doxastic partialist. We may accept his general account of side-taking conduct while rejecting this detail, as I will discuss in section 6.

But side-taking conduct, on Keller's view, is not enough to be loyal. In order for your conduct to be loyal, it must also be motivated by an emotional attitude of attachment or association with the other party.[3] This emotional attachment

---

[3] I am characterizing loyal conduct, whereas Keller's aim is an account of *loyalty*. He characterizes this as the emotional attitude of association that disposes you to conduct yourself by taking the other person's side.

or sense of association is directed toward the other party herself, as opposed to some type that she falls under. "When you are loyal to X," says Keller, "what is presented within your motivation, so to speak, is not only X, but X as something to which you are connected in a special way" (2007, 18).

Both the side-taking conduct and the motive are necessary for loyal conduct. You can conduct yourself in a side-taking way without this being loyal, for you may not feel yourself to be particularly associated with the other party. For example, you might notice a stranger being harassed on the street and defend him simply because you are disgusted by the cruelty. And you can feel associated with someone and yet, because you fail to take his side in your conduct, fail to conduct yourself loyally; think of Peter's betrayal of Jesus.

Now that we have an account of loyal conduct, we can give an account of *disloyal* conduct, which is what interests our objector. Keller notes that this is more than simply conduct that is not loyal. We are not disloyal to passersby on the street simply because we do not find ourselves motivated by a sense of association to take their side in random altercations. What more is there to disloyal conduct? Keller argues that disloyalty involves a violation of certain normative expectations that arise in your relationship with the other person. A normative expectation is an expectation *of* someone to do something, as opposed to a predictive expectation, which is a belief *that* he will do it. When a person's normative expectation is legitimate, it corresponds to a norm, or an "ought," that governs the situation at hand, so that failing to conduct oneself in accord with it can legitimately offend the other party. Certain sorts of relationship, such as between friends, family members, or sometimes work colleagues, generate norms to conduct yourself loyally;[4] I will call such a relationship a *relationship of loyalty*.

Loyal and disloyal conduct are thus asymmetrical (Keller 2007). Loyal conduct is possible whether or not you are in a relationship of loyalty, but disloyal conduct is only possible within such a relationship. For example, in the Biblical story, after Ruth's young husband died, Ruth's mother-in-law, Naomi, encouraged Ruth to return to her own people to find a new husband. Ruth was thus discharged from a relationship of loyalty to Naomi, so returning to her people would not have been disloyal. But she chose to stay with Naomi, thereby conducting herself loyally nonetheless.

The norms of loyalty respect the dictum that ought implies can: you are only answerable to them to the extent that abiding by them is within your control (Keller 2007, chapter 10). Suppose for example that a person's conduct in

---

[4] Whether these norms are moral or something else is up for debate.

a relationship of loyalty—say, a marriage—fails to be loyal because his emotional association to his partner has disappeared, so that, lacking this motivation, his conduct does not count as loyal. If this has happened through no fault of his own (say, he had an accident that damaged his brain), his lack of loyalty does not count as disloyal. But if his emotional state results from no more than his unilaterally declining to work at the partnership, his non-loyal conduct can count as disloyal. So—and this will be important for later—to the extent that you have control over conduct that violates norms of loyalty, you are responsible for it and it thus counts as disloyal.

To this account of Keller's, I will add that the norms that arise in a relationship of loyalty are not unconditional. If the object of loyalty does something heinous or violating, such as lying to you or abusing you or others, the norm that you ought to conduct yourself loyally toward her is cancelled. (If *she* still normatively expects loyal conduct from you, she is mistaken.) But this does not mean that there is now an opposing norm requiring you to *cease* conducting yourself loyally; you are merely permitted to cease doing so. You are also permitted to keep conducting yourself loyally, though if the relationship is to be healthy, any loyal conduct you choose to engage in will presumably take different forms than before (see section 6).

In summary, loyal conduct is conduct in which you take someone's side and are motivated to do so by an emotional attitude of association with her. Disloyal conduct is conduct that, in the context of a relationship that generates norms for loyal conduct, does not meet these norms.

3. Doxastic Disloyalty

3.1 Two Types of Doxastic Disloyalty

The objection from disloyalty starts from the two ideas. The first is that religious believers enter into relationships of loyalty with God, and the second is that, in such a relationship, the norms of loyalty mandate that you hold certain received beliefs. These beliefs are seen as gracious gifts from God, and pertain to God himself, his will for human beings, or matters with implications for these, such as which sources are epistemically authoritative. Because holding at least some of these beliefs is normative, says the objector, it is disloyal to stray from them, whether by becoming significantly less confident in them, suspending judgment in them, or disbelieving them entirely.

Why would such changes in your doxastic attitude toward received beliefs be disloyal? There are (at least) two answers, each corresponding to a different form of (supposed) doxastic disloyalty. One form we may call *disloyalty of difference*. The idea is that adhering to certain beliefs themselves is an important way to side with God, so that any divergence is disloyal. This is so even if alternative beliefs portray God more favorably than the received beliefs. For example, someone with the received belief that God is morally changeable might think it disloyal to switch to believing that he is perfect. This might happen, say, if a majority group that has traditionally oppressed her fellow believers construes God as morally perfect. Switching her beliefs would amount to disloyalty to the God who has upheld her community through the ages. Indeed, many religious disagreements arise with people who do not think of God more negatively than you. But I will not discuss such cases here.

What I will discuss is another form of supposed doxastic disloyalty, introduced in sections 1 and 2.2: believing *negatively* about God, or being open to doing so. Whereas disloyalty of difference can arise for received beliefs with just about any content, this form of supposed disloyalty, which we may call *disloyalty of valence*, concerns their content—specifically, whether they ascribe good or bad characteristics to God. The idea, which we saw that Keller endorses, is that a relationship of loyalty generates norms to be strongly disposed to believe *positively* about the other party. I will show later how the objector motivates this idea (section 3.3). Suffice it for now to note that disloyalty of valence consists in believing negatively about the other party (here, God), or lacking the strong disposition to believe positively.

Fairly clear examples of negative beliefs about God are that he is evil or weak, or, in a liberal sense of being "about him," though one that religious communities care very much about, nonexistent. Other examples are less clearly negative, such as the belief that God is very good but not perfect, or the belief that he is perfect but not necessarily so. Whether a belief about God counts as negative, for present purposes, depends on a person's received religious beliefs. For example, if her received beliefs are a form of traditional monotheism on which God is perfect, then for her, the claim that he is good but not perfect is apt to be negative; or if her received beliefs emphasize necessary perfection, then she may regard the attribution of contingent perfection to God as negative. If the received beliefs, in contrast, are a form of open theism, the believer may regard the traditional theist view of God as impassable as negative, on the grounds that it portrays him as uncaring.

A tradition emphasizing God's oneness may think that a Trinitarian view downgrades God. And so forth.[5]

More beliefs might count as disloyal in valence than one might at first think. Consider the belief (or the disposition to believe) that Jesus was born not in Bethlehem, but in Bethany. This might not appear to downgrade Jesus. But if your received belief system regards the belief that Jesus was born in Bethlehem as divine revelation, then rejecting it in favor of the Bethany belief may imply that God is the source of an epistemically flawed tradition, and hence is either not fully truthful or not fully sovereign. There may thus be an overlap between beliefs that are considered disloyal by way of difference, and disloyal by way of valence: the very fact of straying from the received belief system may be taken to imply something negative about the God who is its supposed source.

As important as both forms of disloyalty are in religious contexts, our objector is concerned with disloyalty of valence: the forming of negative beliefs about God, or the openness to doing so. In what follows it is disloyalty of valence that the term "doxastic disloyalty" picks out.

This allows us to specify two features of the kinds of religious disagreement targeted by the objector. First, she is concerned only with disagreements with interlocutors at least some of whose beliefs about God are negative by the lights of one's received belief system. Second, one of the topics on which you engage in disagreement is the truth or falsehood of those negative beliefs.

3.2 Doxastic Partiality

Why would believing negatively about God, or lacking a special disposition to believe positively, be disloyal?

This objection takes its cue from the doxastic-partiality view introduced in section 1. This view[6] says that the norms of loyalty do not just govern our conduct, but also our beliefs or our belief-forming dispositions. The doxastic norms of loyalty can be summarized, with qualifications to be discussed momentarily, as the expectation to *believe positively about the other party,* and *to be strongly disposed to do so.* Supposing, with the doxastic partialist, that these doxastic norms govern relationships of loyalty in general, then *a fortiori*

---

[5] One topic of religious disagreement may be how positive or negative a given portrayal of God is to begin with.

[6] The doxastic-partiality view is held not just for relationships of loyalty, but for friendship, trust, and love, sometimes because these are taken to involve loyalty, and sometimes for independent reasons. I will not distinguish these types of view here.

they govern relationships of loyalty with God. The doxastic partialist says that it is partly constitutive of loyalty to God (or anyone) to believe positively about him, and be strongly inclined to do so. I'll motivate the doxastic-partiality view in section 3.3; for now some clarification.

To be strongly disposed to believe positively about someone is to be disposed to believe positively *even if doing so might skew the accuracy of your overall picture of her.* In other words, believing positively is the default, so that, in the event of a conflict between believing positively and believing accurately, the weights will strongly favor believing positively.[7] Below we will have cause to talk of people who lack the disposition to believe positively (which our objector says is disloyal); I will say that such people are *open to forming negative beliefs.*

The objector understands the doxastic-partiality view as prescriptive—that is, as positing a requirement. This is stronger than the evaluative claim that forming negative beliefs and being open to doing so is simply bad-making (yet perhaps the best option given other considerations).[8] The requirement aspect is important, because believing negatively (or being open to doing so) is said to be *disloyal*—it is something that, in the context of such a relationship, one ought not do. Here is the claim:

The Doxastic–Disloyalty Claim: Being open to forming, let alone actually forming, negative beliefs about someone in a relationship of loyalty is, all else equal, disloyal to that person.

The Doxastic–Disloyalty Claim has an "all else equal" clause. One thing that has to be "equal" is that there must be something that the believer can do to avoid believing negatively or being open to doing so. For we have seen that conduct over which you have no control whatsoever does not count as disloyal, and beliefs and dispositions to believe are often involuntary. So the all-else-equal clause can be read, at least, as "compatibly with doxastic involuntarism."

One might think that beliefs and doxastic dispositions are always involuntary, making the Doxastic–Disloyalty Claim empty. But this is too quick. There are indirect ways of influencing, for example, our intellectual character, what evidence we receive or attend to (Keller 2007, chapter 2), the non-evidential social and psychological forces that we are exposed to, e.g., whom we spend time with, whether we are in a charitable mindset (Keller

---

[7] Strictly speaking one could be disposed to believe positively without ever doing so, but I take it that proponents of the doxastic-partiality view, in its dispositional form (prominently Keller 2007 and Hazlett 2013), take this disposition to be manifested to a great extent.

[8] See Crawford 2019 for discussion.

2007, chapter 2; Stroud 2006), and how we frame apparently negative evidence (e.g., is our friend being unkind or just overenthusiastic?), and so forth. To the extent that such strategies are available, we are responsible for our beliefs and dispositions to believe.

Some argue that compatibility with doxastic voluntarism is *all* that need be equal. This means that virtually nothing apart from an inability to do otherwise excuses you from forming a negative belief or being open to doing so. Not even evidence pointing toward a negative belief excuses you. This means that, if there is a conflict between forming a positive belief and forming an accurate one, for example because of negative evidence, loyalty requires violating epistemic norms and forming the positive one (if you can). That said, doxastic partialists differ over exactly how egregiously you must violate epistemic norms. At one extreme are those who hold that loyalty demands violating them often and egregiously (Kierkegaard 1983; Stroud 2006); at another are those who say that it demands bending them a little (Keller 2007, chapter 2), with others falling somewhere in between (Hazlett 2013). We may call the cluster of views that construes the all-else-equal clause as "compatibly with doxastic involuntarism, and with the expectation that the believer violates epistemic norms" the *strong* version of the Doxastic–Disloyalty Claim.

A weaker version of the Doxastic–Disloyalty Claim does not require the believer to violate epistemic norms. This version, which we may call this the *epistemological* doxastic-partiality view, understands the all-else-equal clause as "compatibly with doxastic involuntarism *and epistemic norms*" (Kawall 2013; Hawley 2014). The believer is expected to believe partially, and be disposed to do so, in a way that respects epistemic norms. The epistemological version might not look like a doxastic-partiality view—after all, it seems to say that, if evidence points toward negative characteristics, loyalty permits you to believe negatively of the other party. But proponents of this version posit, in addition to the Doxastic–Disloyalty Claim so understood, the additional claim that epistemic norms are *permissive*, and so easily yield positive beliefs about the object of our loyalty (Kawall 2013; Hawley 2014; Plantinga 2000b; James 1921). An internalist way of understanding this says for example that, for any given body of evidence and any given proposition that one might believe on its basis, there is typically a range of epistemically acceptable doxastic attitudes, some more positive than others (James 1921; Kelly 2014).[9] The Doxastic–Disloyalty claim, cashed out this way, says that it is disloyal to do anything

[9] A permissive epistemology developed specifically for religious beliefs can be found in Plantinga 2000b.

other than form (or be disposed to form) the most positive belief permitted by epistemic norms.[10]

In whichever form, the objector applies the Doxastic–Disloyalty Claim to relationships of loyalty to God. She supposes, first, that such relationships are possible. Or at least that they are possible for committed religious believers, as long as God exists; whether they are possible for non-believers too may be left open. And she supposes, second, that such relationships come with norms of doxastic partiality. That is, that human beings in relationships of loyalty with God must believe partially about him.[11]

3.3 Arguments for Doxastic Partiality

Why think that the Doxastic–Disloyalty Claim holds, either in general or in relationships of loyalty with God? One category of argument says that doxastic partiality is *intrinsically* loyal, and believing negatively or being open to doing so is intrinsically disloyal. Another category of argument holds that doxastic partiality is *extrinsically* loyal, in the sense of being loyal on account of its consequences, and that believing negatively or being open to doing so is extrinsically disloyal.

Here are three intrinsic arguments for doxastic partiality. First, beliefs are analogous to actions. And partiality in our actions is normative for relationships of loyalty: we treat the objects of our loyalty with a special care not extended to third parties. We should thus treat the objects of our loyalty partially in our beliefs too. This means believing (and being disposed to believe) positively about them (Hazlett 2013).

Second, *commitment* is normative for relationships of loyalty, and this includes commitment to the goodness of the other party's character (Stroud 2006).

Third, the phenomenology of relationships of loyalty is a good guide to their norms, and this favors doxastic partiality: we supposedly feel an impulse to believe well and to be closed (or at least slow) to believe badly of the objects of our loyalty, and when we are the objects of someone else's loyalty, we supposedly want them to do this for us too (Stroud 2006; Keller 2004).

---

[10] Another epistemological version of the Doxastic–Disloyalty Claim says that epistemic norms are lenient on account of being *context-sensitive*. This says that, when we form high-stakes beliefs (e.g., about objects of our loyalty), the evidential standards must be stricter—it must be *harder* to form negative beliefs. Space prohibits discussing this possibility, but see Kawall 2013; Benton 2018a.

[11] Whether the reverse holds on this view—whether a loyal God must believe partially of human beings—I won't discuss.

Here is an extrinsic argument for doxastic partiality. Believing positively about the object of loyalty, and being disposed to do so, will strengthen your relationship with her (Stroud 2006). In contrast, believing negatively, or being open to doing so, will put it at risk because it may weaken your incentive to maintain it; and risking your relationship is disloyal. The above arguments, intrinsic and extrinsic, concern loyalty in general. Their application to relationships of loyalty with God is *a fortiori*.

But the extrinsic argument has special importance in the case of God. For a relationship of loyalty with him amounts to religious *faith*, and faith is standardly considered a great religious good, even a virtue (Kvanvig 2018), so that upholding it is loyal and abandoning it disloyal.[12] The proponent of doxastic partiality may add that negative beliefs about God can threaten one's faith. If the belief is that God does not exist, then, if this belief, as some argue, is necessary for faith (Plantinga 2000b; Mugg 2016), the threat is automatic. If the belief is instead that God is not just or good (or that he does not exist, where this *is* compatible with faith), then it is apt to threaten the person's faith psychologically. Doxastic partiality toward God is thus a way to uphold one's faith in him.

I will address these arguments in section 6.3. First I will assume that the Doxastic–Disloyalty Claim holds (in whichever version), and consider more closely two arguments against religious disagreement that feature it, the Explanation Argument (section 4), and the Argument from Risk (section 5). Both contend that engaging in religious disagreement is disloyal because it involves (or is very likely to involve) forming or being open to forming negative beliefs about God. I argue that *even if* the Doxastic–Disloyalty Claim holds, neither argument succeeds in showing that religious disagreement is disloyal. But I finish (section 6) by arguing that the Doxastic–Disloyalty Claim is false too, so that *even if* religious disagreement involves it, this does not automatically make the believer disloyal—on the contrary, it might even be actively loyal.

4. The Explanation Argument

The first argument starts by asking why a believer would engage in religious disagreement to begin with. The most probable explanation, it says, involves her having negative beliefs about God or being open to forming some. After

[12] But for an argument that it can be loyal to be ready to abandon one's faith, see Dormandy 2018c.

all, unless you at least suspected that the other party were in some way negative or capable of doing something negative, what would interest you in discussing the matter with someone whom you know thinks she is? Negative belief, or openness to it, is very likely to be among the causal factors behind the believer's engaging in disagreement. This argument concludes that a case of religious disagreement, given the Doxastic–Disloyalty Claim, is very likely to be disloyal.

The intuition that negative belief (or openness to it) is likely to be a causal factor in (epistemically oriented) religious disagreement is plausible. One source is the following sort of case.[13] Consider Othello, who engages in open-minded discussion about the character of his life partner, Desdemona, with Iago, whom Othello knows thinks that Desdemona has been unfaithful. This exercise would make little sense, says the objector, unless Othello were at least willing to entertain the idea that Desdemona is not beyond suspicion. Othello's willingness to entertain this idea will very probably feature in the explanation for his engaging in epistemically oriented disagreement with Iago about Desdemona's character. An analogous point holds for disagreement about God with someone who holds beliefs about God that are (by the light of the received belief system) negative. It is very probably motivated by negative beliefs about God, or at least by an openness to forming some.

I will return to this analogy below. Suffice it for now to agree that negative beliefs, or an openness to forming them, can surely explain, in many cases, why someone would engage in epistemically oriented religious disagreement. But lest this possible explanation get too great a portion of our probability distribution, I will present an alternative.

A believer might engage in religious disagreement *without* believing or being open to believing anything negative about God. Take Hildegard, for instance, who is simply fascinated to learn about him from a variety of angles. She might hope to learn, for example, how other religious belief systems and their adherents reflect God's manifold creativity, what they reveal about God's abundant common grace, and how he may be at work in others' lives.

[13] Buchak 2012, 234 uses a similar case to motivate the intuition that faith entails declining to seek evidence. A husband has an envelope containing information about whether his spouse has betrayed him. Seeking new evidence in the form of opening it, she says, indicates a lack of faith. Faith overlaps significantly with loyalty, and one way to seek evidence is to engage in epistemically oriented religious disagreement. Much as Buchak's aims and use of this case differ from the present objector's, I take its use here to be in the spirit of her view. Moreover, analogies between religious faith or loyalty and spousal fidelity are common.

Hildegard might do this fully expecting to learn only more positive things about him. Indeed, her positive image of God might be what motivated her to do this to begin with.

That this alternative explanation also enjoys some probability is supported by a *disanalogy* between the religious case and the Othello case. One prominent way in which people form beliefs about God, more so than about human beings, is by comparing notes with other people who know about him or at least claim to do so. For God, unlike human beings, is not localizable to time and place, and does not predictably manifest himself on demand. (An exception in certain ways, according to Christians, is the briefly incarnated Christ—but even here we only have others' say-so.) So we depend much more, for knowledge of God, on comparing notes with others. Yet human viewpoints are limited and fallible, even those of divinely guided religious communities. It only makes sense, for someone longing to learn about God, indeed to *increase* the number of excellent things she believes about him, to construe the open-minded sharing of perspectives and traditions as an excellent way to do so. So a believer can engage in religious disagreement without any negative beliefs about God or openness to such beliefs—and thus without falling foul of the Doxastic–Disloyalty Claim.

But why, the objector might wonder, would a believer such as Hildegard seek such enlightenment from outside the safety of her religious community and its teachings? One reason is that no group, even one whose beliefs are divinely inspired, is immune to epistemically problematic phenomena such as groupthink, bias, and the influence of ideology (Dormandy 2020b). Another is that religious disagreement is a way to allow God to be who he is. Surely a wonderful or perfect divine creator of the universe can astound in ways that an individual believer, or her temporally and spatially located religious community, could not have imagined. One way to give him this leeway is to see how he might manifest himself in unexpected ways.

So a believer such as Hildegard is not disloyal. But more than this, *she can also be loyal*. First, her religious disagreement, as we saw, may be motivated by an emotional attitude of association with God. Second, her disagreement can be a way of taking God's side. After all, her aim is to know God better as he is, and there is a decent chance, if my arguments elsewhere for its epistemic benefits are on target (Dormandy 2018a, 2020b), that it may help. So engaging in religious disagreement can constitute *loyal* conduct, even supposing that the Doxastic–Disloyalty Claim is true. Moreover, I suggest that it is not particularly less probable that a given disagreement involve a believer like Hildegard than one like Othello.

But the next objection disputes this conclusion. It considers another argument that, even for believers like Hildegard, religious disagreement is disloyal after all.

5. The Argument from Risk

The Explanation Argument looks backward. It notes that a particular believer engages in (epistemically oriented) religious disagreement, and works back to the supposedly most probable cause: a negative belief about God or an openness to forming one. I just argued that an alternative, and not improbable, cause is enthusiasm to know God better, and that disagreement, when so motivated, can be a way of taking God's side and thus be loyal.

But one might think that this conclusion is overhasty. Well-intentioned as a believer such as Hildegard may be, she should know that she is taking a grave risk in exposing herself to the influence of beliefs that she would be disloyal for holding or even considering, supposing the Doxastic–Disloyalty Claim is true. Because of this, engaging in religious disagreement does *not* take God's side. It sides against him: Hildegard is unfortunately conducting herself disloyally. This is the gist of the Argument from Risk. This argument is thus forward-looking: regardless of why a particular believer engages in religious disagreement, the large risk that it runs of doxastic disloyalty typically makes doing it disloyal.

Here is the argument step by step:

Argument from Risk

1.   Engaging in epistemically oriented religious disagreement runs a substantial risk of bringing you to form negative beliefs about God, or of opening you up to doing so (and thus of being disloyal all-else-equal). (**The Risk Claim**)

2.   This risk of (all-else equal) disloyalty is typically substantial enough that even taking it is disloyal. (**The Substantiality Claim**)

3.   **Conclusion:** It is typically disloyal to engage in epistemically oriented religious disagreement. (From 1, 2, and the Doxastic–Disloyalty Claim)

We may grant premise 1, that engaging in religious disagreement runs a substantial risk of bringing you to form, or become open to, negative beliefs about God. (That doing this is also *disloyal* I am accepting for argument's sake, pending section 6.) What premise 2, the Substantiality Claim, adds that this risk is *substantial enough that running it typically constitutes disloyal conduct.* This is the premise that I will dispute.

I'll begin with some clarifications. The "typically" is meant to exclude highly unusual cases not of interest here. But why think that engaging in religious disagreement typically runs such a substantial risk? One reason is evidential. Since your interlocutor believes more negatively about God than you, engaging open-mindedly with her is apt to deliver evidence pointing to a more negative view of God than yours (at least by your lights); this is especially so if she is epistemically and morally admirable. Your exchange may even deliver evidence *mandating* negative beliefs about God, or at least a lowering of confidence in positive ones; the epistemic pressure could also weaken your disposition to believe positively.[14] Note that even permissive evidence can mandate, if all of the doxastic attitudes in the acceptable range are negative. Resisting epistemic pressure can be a psychological challenge: it takes nerve to know what a norm requires and consciously defy it. But second, even if the negative evidence that you risk receiving does not mandate a negative doxastic response, the fact that you have received it could unexpectedly shake your confidence for purely psychological reasons (Plantinga 2000a, 189).

One response to premise 2, the Substantiality Claim, is to deny it by rejecting the "typically": engaging in religious disagreement does *not* typically run such a substantial risk of forming (or becoming open to forming) a negative belief about God that simply doing so is disloyal. Recall the all-else-equal clause. On both versions of the doxastic-partiality view, this clause ensures that you do not count as disloyal if you form a negative belief (or become open to doing so) *involuntarily.* And on the epistemological version of the view, this clause also ensures that you do not count as disloyal if you are obeying epistemic norms. For this reason, one might think that the doxastic-partiality view fails to kick in. Surely a believer who engages in religious disagreement for perfectly loyal reasons, and winds up forming a negative belief or becoming open to doing so, will be exempted from disloyalty by the all-else-equal clause. This is what is typical—not, *pace* Premise 2, a substantial risk of doxastic disloyalty. On this line of reasoning, premise 2 is false.

But this response does not work. Consider first doxastic involuntarism, which excuses the believer on both versions of the doxastic-partiality view. The fact that the believer's response to her negative evidence was involuntary

---

[14] Even if the negative evidence is not strong enough to *mandate*, it might *permit* negative beliefs or a lowering of your confidence in positive ones—so that if you find yourself psychologically distressed by the negative evidence, you may be tempted to accept this permission.

does not exempt her from the charge of disloyalty. After all, engaging in disagreement to begin with was within her voluntary control. Consider an analogy: you are not exempt from responsibility for what you do when you have chosen to get drunk. A similar point applies when we consider obedience to epistemic norms. We may suppose (along with the proponents of the epistemological version of the doxastic-partiality view) that epistemic norms do not mandate engaging in religious disagreement. This means that the believer was not epistemically mandated to engage in religious disagreement to begin with, and is hence not exempted from the charge of disloyalty now that she has done so. So the all-else-equal clause does not falsify premise 2: doxastic partialists still have the result that they take to be true, which is that doxastic risk run by the believer who engages in religious disagreement *is* substantial enough to count as disloyal.

5.1 Declining Religious Disagreement Is Risky Too

I will criticize premise 2, the Substantiality Claim, in a different way. Accepting for argument's sake the idea that risking negative belief is disloyal, and agreeing with premise 2 that one does run a substantial risk of disloyalty by engaging in religious disagreement, I will argue that this does not suffice to make religious disagreement itself disloyal. The reason is that *declining* to engage in religious disagreement runs a comparably substantial risk of disloyalty. Since both alternative actions are risky, I argue, it is not typically disloyal to perform one or the other; we must take matters on a case-by case-basis.

We cannot consider every form of declining religious disagreement. For simplicity I will focus on the form that our objector is most apt to advocate: declining to engage in it on the grounds that doing so is disloyal to God. Assuming that this is motivated by an emotional attitude of association with God, this alternative action appears loyal. In this way it is on a par with engaging in religious disagreement, where this is also motivated by an emotional attitude of association with God. I argued with the case of Hildegard in section 4 that religious disagreement, performed for this motive, can be loyal. But the objector denies this parity. She says that, regardless of how the respective actions appear, the only loyal one of the two, typically, is declining religious disagreement. And the reason arises from the risks that religious disagreement incurs.

But if, as I will argue, declining to engage in religious disagreement because one thinks that it is disloyal *also* runs a substantial risk of disloyalty, then both alternative actions—engaging as well as declining to engage in religious disagreement, even when motivated by an emotional association with God—run a substantial risk of disloyal consequences.

For simplicity I will suppose that the two actions that we are contrasting are the only realistic alternatives. This assumption is not outlandish: a believer motivated by emotional association with God could easily wonder which of the two to perform.

What risks does a person court by declining religious disagreement? Four come to mind. The first two, perhaps surprisingly, involve the believer's forming negative beliefs about God or becoming open to doing so—which is of course disloyal by the objector's lights.

The first risk is that the believer comes to think poorly of God. To see how this might happen, note that there are different ways of thinking of a God who makes declining religious disagreement a criterion of loyalty. He might be like a protective parent wanting to keep his children safe from bad company; a believer content to learn about God within the safe bounds of her religious community might form this picture. But a different sort of believer might rankle under what feels to him like thought-control. Apart from the edict against religious disagreement, this person might not have been tempted to think negatively of God. But given this edict, he may be tempted to think of God as akin to Heinrich Mann's insecure schoolmaster, Professor Unrat. This character insists on rote obedience, feels threatened by lateral thinking and unregulated play, and would prefer a child to keep his uniform clean than to discover new fauna. Thinking of God in this negative way would, by the Doxastic–Disloyalty Claim, be disloyal.

Second, declining religious disagreement on account of its supposed disloyalty might raise the suspicion that your positive beliefs about God would not withstand scrutiny. Why else protect them so delicately from alternative viewpoints? An undergraduate comes to mind who wanted to own his faith for himself by seeing how it could acquit itself in a diverse arena. But he wanted even more to remain loyal to God as he understood loyalty, among other things by avoiding negative beliefs or openness to them. For this reason (and with his parents' encouragement) he attended a small religious college instead of the large secular university that he would have preferred. This stifling of exploration nourished a growing suspicion that the positive beliefs he grew up with might be defective. He became increasingly open to negative beliefs about God and wound up doubting God's existence or power.

So there are at least two ways in which declining to engage in religious disagreement could set in motion a course of events in which the believer forms, or becomes open to forming, negative beliefs about God—and thus, by the Doxastic–Disloyalty Claim, conducting herself disloyally.

The objector might contend that, should these two consequences arise, the negative beliefs (or openness to them) will not often count as disloyal, on the grounds that the all-else-equal claim applies. Often, the believer will be unable to help it (excusing her on the strong version of the doxastic-partiality view), or doing otherwise would violate epistemic norms, since in both scenarios above she has evidence for negative beliefs (excusing her on the epistemological version). If this is so, then declining to engage in religious disagreement does *not* pose a substantial risk of disloyalty.

But this objection does not significantly help the believer who declines religious disagreement. On the question of doxastic voluntarism, the believers in both scenarios could do more to avoid these negative doxastic changes. They might for instance engage in religious disagreement in the hopes that this yields evidence supporting their positive beliefs. On the question of epistemic norms, given the permissive epistemology espoused by the objector, it is not a foregone conclusion that these will mandate negative beliefs; but even if they do, the believer here too could simply seek additional evidence. So the "all-else-equal" proviso does not particularly help the believer who incurs these consequences avoid the charge of disloyalty.

The first two possible consequences of declining religious disagreement are disloyal by the objector's lights, but not necessarily by mine (more in section 6). In contrast, the third and fourth possible consequences are disloyal by my lights. I assume that they are by the objector's too, even though, as we'll see, they involve *maintaining* one's positive beliefs about God. They are particularly apt to arise for intellectually and emotionally vibrant believers who are passionate to learn about God or to own their faith for themselves.

To see these possible consequences, note that, if a person motivated in this way has a desire to engage in religious disagreement, but also has a competing desire to be loyal to God on the grounds that disagreement is supposedly disloyal, he will experience a cognitive dissonance. Cognitive dissonances are unpleasant (Festinger 1957), in cases even terrifying (Solomon, Greenberg, and Pyszczynski 1991). They strongly dispose our minds to resolve them in favor of one of the conflicting attitudes. Consider, then, a believer who resolves the present dissonance in favor of his desire to be loyal as he understands loyalty. What happens to his desire to engage in religious disagreement—or rather to the passion to learn about God or own his faith that gives rise to this desire?

One possibility is that this passion exits his religious life entirely: he suppresses it or re-directs it toward non-religious interests, such as a relationship or career. Religious apathy is thus the third potential disloyal consequence of declining religious disagreement. Although this person keeps his positive beliefs in theory, his religious passion fades and with it his emotional attitude of association with God. And his religious actions (such as prayer) dwindle entirely or become a matter of rote. If push came to shove he would be indisposed to stick up for God or for his positive beliefs.

The other possibility for the passionate believer—the fourth potential disloyal consequence of declining religious disagreement—is dogmatic belief. The believer in this case *keeps* her religious passion. But instead of investing it in exploratory discourse as she originally wanted to, she invests it in avoiding and even demonizing other viewpoints. That is, she swings toward holding her religious beliefs with strong confidence, and unwaveringly. She either buttresses them with a dogmatic epistemology, or scorns epistemology altogether.

One might think that dogmatic positive belief about God is eminently loyal—it can certainly be motivated by a strong emotional association with him, and seems undeniably to side with him. But in fact it courts serious disloyalty. To see why, note that maintaining dogmatic belief requires rigid cognitive categories that resist change. Our standard means of processing new information is to bring it into something like a reflective equilibrium with our pre-existing cognitive categories. Our categories filter the information, but are standardly not so rigid that it cannot alter them. (Enough information will eventually bring most of us to believe something that we would prefer to remain in denial about.) Not so for the dogmatic believer. Her cognitive categories remain fixed, warping the information she takes in. The result is belief that is apt to be one-sided and simplistic. Such a believer is apt to oversimplify some things and completely misunderstand others.[15]

These oversimplifications and misunderstandings put a dogmatic believer in danger, despite her best intentions, of behaving disloyally. Even though she is motivated by a strong emotional association with God, her actions will often side against him: they will run counter to his will, character, or values. Consider religious believers who promote immoral political, social, or allegedly ethical ends in the tragic name of religious loyalty: aligning with extremist

---

[15] This is so even if her "core" religious beliefs, for example in such-and-such a religious creed, happen to be true (Dormandy 2020b). For core religious beliefs are held in a complex network of auxiliary beliefs, including about how the core beliefs themselves are to be interpreted, what counts as evidence for or against the core beliefs (or a given interpretation), and what the core beliefs (interpreted in a given way) imply about social or ethical matters.

politicians, conducting inquisitions, or oppressing minorities. Or consider Job's companions, who insist that Job must have done something to deserve the massive suffering of losing his children, his possessions, his health, and his assurance of God's love. Their dogmatic beliefs about how God's goodness and justice work cannot accommodate the evident fact of Job's innocence. Due to their cognitive inflexibility, they badly misjudge not only Job's situation, but God himself, who rebukes them on the grounds that they have "not spoken of me what is right" (42:7).

One might object that such behavior is not disloyalty, but rather a problematic form of loyalty—after all, such believers are doing what they think God wants. But recall that loyal conduct amounts to siding with God, not just doing what you mistakenly think sides with God. Conduct that, however motivated, dishonors God and utterly contravenes his values and character sides against him.

We have seen four ways in which declining to engage in religious disagreement, even if you are motivated by an emotional association with God, risks disloyalty, and does so (I suggest) substantially. The first, coming to think poorly of God, and the second, suspecting that your positive beliefs will not withstand scrutiny, are disloyal only by the objector's lights, because they involve negative beliefs about God (or an openness to forming them). They are less likely in any given case to be disloyal by my lights, since I will argue that negative beliefs and openness to forming them are not disloyal as such. The third and fourth possible consequences, keeping your positive beliefs but becoming either apathetic or dogmatic, are disloyal by my lights as well as (presumably) the objector's.

So declining religious disagreement, no less than engaging in it, runs a substantial risk of setting in motion a course of events in which you conduct yourself disloyally. If an action's running such a risk is enough to make it disloyal, then declining religious disagreement, no less than engaging in it, is disloyal. But I take it that this damned-if-you-do, damned-if-you-don't result is absurd. If this is so, then premise 2 (the Substantiality Claim) is false. Merely running a substantial risk of disloyalty is not as such disloyal.

Another way to see this is to construct a parallel argument that both alternative actions, engaging in religious disagreement or declining it, are typically *loyal*. After all, both can be motivated by an emotional association with God, and both have a substantial probability of setting in motion a course of events in which you conduct yourself *loyally*. Engaging in religious disagreement can help the believer better know God and live out his values, or own her faith for herself. Declining religious disagreement can help the believer maintain her positive beliefs about God and thus, dogmatic belief notwithstanding, be motivated to continue living out God's values. Our two alternative actions, because of the loyal consequences they may bring about, thus seem to have an equal right to be called *loyal*.

Of course, there are surely cases in which running a substantial risk of conducting yourself disloyally is itself disloyal. And some surely involve engaging in religious disagreement, whereas others surely involve declining it. But which is the case depends on other factors, such as the psychology of the believer in question, and which alternative actions are available to her. These are matters for case-by-case assessment. Premise 2, the Substantiality Claim, is thus false, and the Argument from Risk is unsound. The most that this argument can establish is that it is *sometimes* disloyal to engage in religious disagreement—just like it is sometimes disloyal to decline to.

I will now argue that the scope of the first "sometimes" is much smaller than the objector thinks. Many of the supposedly disloyal consequences of engaging in disagreement, I will argue, are not disloyal after all. In particular, I will argue that it is not disloyal, at least not as such, to form or be open to forming negative beliefs about God.

6. The Doxastic–Disloyalty Claim Is False

In both arguments we have considered, the Explanation Argument and the Argument from Risk, the Doxastic–Disloyalty Claim does heavy lifting. I will now argue that this claim is false. I will start by showing that it is false for relationships of loyalty between human beings, and will then apply those considerations to relationships of loyalty with God.

6.1 Self-Gaslighting

Suppose that Odysseus is loyal to Calypso, yet Calypso emotionally abuses him. Supposing the Doxastic–Disloyalty Claim is true, then Odysseus has a problem. If he is to know that Calypso is abusive, he must do something that is by his lights disloyal: form a negative belief about her. To the extent that Odysseus is loyal, he will do his best to avoid this. He may avoid negative evidence, or if he notices it, he may explain it away or frame it more positively ("She's having a bad day," "She's just enthusiastic about doing things right," or "It was my fault"). This will not always be a conscious matter of choosing one interpretation over another—it will often be a cognitive habit embedded in emotions. If successful, Odysseus will not believe, or even be disposed to believe, that Calypso is abusive. The Doxastic–Disloyalty Claim recommends cultivating a tendency to overlook problems in a relationship of loyalty, even serious ones. I'll call this the *self-gaslighting problem.*

This problem suffices to reject the Doxastic–Disloyalty Claim. Self-gaslighting perverts what loyalty is all about. Relationships of loyalty provide a context for exchanging and enjoying certain interpersonal goods. They enable the loyal person to receive such things as safety, protection, and a sense of meaning arising from the association with the other party. The object of loyalty for her part receives such things as appreciation, service, or ascriptions of status. The norms of loyalty foster the appropriate transfer of these goods. Self-gaslighting, in contrast, makes you vulnerable to harm. Far from being normative for relationships of loyalty, doxastic partiality—because it promotes self-gaslighting—contravenes these norms.

The doxastic partialist might respond by appealing to the "all else equal" clause in the Doxastic–Disloyalty Claim. Recall that, on both the strong and the epistemological versions of the doxastic-partiality view, this clause exempts you from the charge of disloyalty when you are *psychologically compelled* to believe (or become open to believing) negatively. And recall that, on the epistemological version of the view, you are also exempt when you are *epistemically required* to do so. Surely Calypso's behavior compels Odysseus psychologically to form (or at least be open to forming) negative beliefs about her; and there is surely enough evidence to require him epistemically to do so. The partialist concludes that the Doxastic–Disloyalty Claim can exempt Odysseus from the charge of disloyalty toward Calypso on both of these grounds.

But this response does not work. First, Odysseus is not psychologically compelled to believe (or become open to believing) anything negative about Calypso. On the contrary, because he has loyally cultivated positive belief-forming habits up till now, it is psychologically difficult for him to *not* form (or be disposed toward) positive beliefs about her. The all-else-equal clause that would exempt Odysseus on grounds of doxastic involuntarism never has a chance to kick in.

Second, would epistemic norms exempt Odysseus from the requirement to believe positively of Calypso? If the epistemic norms are internalist, they would not. Why? Because Odysseus will have done his best to believe well of her all along, so his total evidence is apt to strongly support a low probability for negative beliefs, and his long-cultivated belief-forming habits will not easily change his subjective probability distribution. Against this skewed evidential and dispositional backdrop, internalist epistemic norms are not apt to mandate negative belief about Calypso. On the contrary, his misleading evidence is apt to make it reasonable for Odysseus to continue to give her the benefit of the doubt.

The doxastic partialist (at least, of the epistemological persuasion) will fare better with externalist epistemic norms. These are more likely to mandate negative belief for Odysseus, and so exempt him from the requirement to believe positively about Calypso. For such norms would require him to believe in ways that are reliable, and so would be much less forgiving of Odysseus's misleading (internalist) evidence and experiences. Externalist epistemic norms, then, would more likely deliver what the doxastic partialist needs: an exemption for Odysseus from believing positively about Calypso.

In summary, the partialist's appeal to the all-else-equal clause does not work for the strong version of the doxastic-partiality view, which exempts only for psychological compulsion; nor does it work for the epistemological version, as long as the epistemic norms in question are internalist. The only form of the view on which Odysseus might be exempt from positive belief (or dispositions to believe) is an epistemological version positing externalist epistemic norms.

But this exemption does not accomplish much. Even if this version of the partiality view exempts Odysseus in an externalist sense, there is an internalist sense in which he is *not* exempted. Recall that, in Odysseus's skewed doxastic state, recognizing the truth about Calypso's abusive behavior is psychologically difficult, given his loyally cultivated perceptual dispositions and evidence to date. This means that he will be hard-pressed to *recognize* that externalist epistemic norms exempt him from believing positively, because he will be hard-pressed to recognize that his belief-formation vis-à-vis Calypso has been unreliable. (It would have to be a great and serendipitous shock that aligns his perspective with reality.) This means that Odysseus will still *think* that his loyalty mandates positive belief and belief-forming dispositions. So forming or opening himself up to negative beliefs, even if epistemic norms mandate this, *would amount, by his lights, to disloyal conduct.* Even if there is no longer an externalist sense of "ought" on which he ought to believe positively, there is still an internalist one—doing what is loyal from his own perspective. After all, we would rightly think less of his loyalty (at least if we accept the Doxastic–Disloyalty Claim) if he were to do what he thinks violates an important norm of loyalty.

The self-gaslighting problem is thus alive and well, and we can now see that it has two facets. First, obedience to partialist norms of belief will make it psychologically difficult to realize that negative things are true of the object of your loyalty. Second, partialist loyalty itself places internal normative restrictions on any efforts you may make to discover this.

We are in a position to understand the shortcomings of another response that the doxastic partialist might make. This response reminds us that the normative expectation to conduct yourself loyally can itself be cancelled—namely, if the object of loyalty has a negative enough characteristic, such as a tendency to emotionally abuse. Calypso's conduct itself thus absolves Odysseus of any loyalty-based expectation to believe positively about her. But once more, this exemption is of little help. Odysseus will not easily become aware that his relationship with Calypso no longer counts as one of loyalty, because his perspective is stuck where it is—and as long as this is so, he would violate the norms of loyalty by his own lights.

I take self-gaslighting to be an unacceptable consequence of an account of loyalty and disloyalty. Because they follow from the Doxastic–Disloyalty Claim, I take this claim to be false. Forming or being open to forming a negative belief about someone with whom you are in a relationship of loyalty is not, as such, disloyal.

6.2 Epistemically Oriented Loyalty to God

So loyalty does not come with a prescription that mandates doxastic partiality. But from this it does not follow that a modicum of partial belief is not *good*, even if its goodness can be overridden by other factors. The doxastic partialist may still claim that, in a relationship of loyalty, negative belief or openness to forming negative beliefs can still be bad, all else equal, even if not outright disloyal. But I will argue that this milder claim is false too.

I will defend an alternative picture entirely, on which loyalty involves a concern to know what is *true* of the other party, whether positive or negative. We may call this *epistemically oriented loyalty*. A person exhibiting this sort of loyalty abides by truth-conducive epistemic norms when it comes to forming beliefs about the other party. This stands in contrast to partialist loyalty, which (as we saw) involves a concern to believe positively, even if this means violating epistemic norms or at least believing as permissively as they allow. Epistemically oriented loyalty, I contend, is superior to doxastically partial loyalty. This holds too of loyalty to God.

One reason is that epistemically oriented loyalty is more honoring to the other party (Kawall 2013, 359–360). Why? Consider that the person who exhibits partialist loyalty would hold positive beliefs even if the object of loyalty had not merited them. Far from being a compliment, this has something in common with flattery. It is more honoring to be believed great in a way that is sensitive to your demonstrated greatness, so that you might not be believed great otherwise. This holds no less for a perfect God, who is portrayed at least in Jewish and Christian scriptures as keen to list the excellent things that he has done for his people over their history, so that they have faith in him on that basis.

A second reason why epistemically oriented loyalty is superior to partialist loyalty is that the latter, as we have seen, risks promoting certain sorts of misunderstanding about the other party. Self-gaslighting is one example; and even the idea that doxastic partiality is good (as opposed to required) risks promoting misunderstanding. This is not only damaging to you, it does a disservice to the object of loyalty, since in failing to hold her to account, you enable her in persisting as she is. Epistemically oriented loyalty, in contrast, puts you in a better position to perceive negative characteristics and thus to respond constructively (Kawall 2013, 354; Arpaly and Brinkerhoff 2018, 43). Supposing a negative belief about the other party is true, forming (and communicating) it can help her see her own behavior for what it is, perhaps for the first time. This may promote self-reflection, the decision to ask for forgiveness, and further steps toward becoming a better person—things that a loyal person should want for those to whom she is loyal. Forming a negative belief in this spirit can be a way of siding with her: helping her be a better version of herself.

This holds for loyalty to God. For example, the Jewish Scriptures or Old Testament portray people who have special relationships with God, such as Moses or Abraham, talking him down from performing destructive actions. And think of Job, who honestly and openly accuses God of injustice, while continuing to hold up a picture of the just God whom he has always taken himself to worship. Whether or not these passages portray God negatively (an interpretive question that I will not address here), it is striking that these believers do not sycophantically agree that God's actions or intentions are right simply because they are God's. In criticizing God for the sake of what they think is right (indeed what they think is more God-like), they seem to exhibit an epistemically oriented loyalty.

One might think that misunderstanding or mistaken positive beliefs are less of a problem for doxastic partiality when we assume a perfect God, for in this case there are no negative characteristics to come to know about. But the worry applies even with a perfect God. We saw in section 5.1 that doxastic partiality can give rise to dogmatic thought patterns that might prevent a believer from recognizing aspects of God's greatness that do not fit neatly in simplistic categories. We saw the example of Job's companions, and of people who, because of dogmatic misunderstanding, mistakenly pursue harmful projects in God's name. The cognitive flexibility and subtlety promoted by an epistemically oriented loyalty, in contrast, can open one up to new, surprising, discoveries about God—who, especially if he is perfect, has positive characteristics that explode our categories anyway. The dogmatism of Job's companions did not win them a mind-blowing religious experience; Job's epistemically oriented insistence on holding God to account did.

The doxastic partialist may push back. Epistemic norms are often truth-conducive. But evidence can be misleading, and in a relationship of loyalty, a false negative belief is a grave mistake. Imagine believing that your friend is abusing a third party, when it turns out that this is false. Surely a modicum of doxastic partiality, in spite of its other disadvantages, is crucial for avoiding a situation like this. This all the more so in the case of a perfect (or even very good) God. After all, the objector will note, our fallen world contains ample negative evidence about God—against his existence, goodness, and justice. In light of this, the person exhibiting partialist loyalty is more likely to believe truly about him, minor misunderstandings notwithstanding, whereas the person of epistemically oriented loyalty will follow her misleading evidence to form *false* negative beliefs. This means that her beliefs will slander God— and slandering someone you mean to side with is the ultimate disloyalty.

I have two responses. First, we may agree that negative beliefs about those toward whom we are loyal should not, in general, be formed facilely. But the reason is not the bare fact that they are negative. It is rather that, in general, we will usually have seen the better sides of those toward whom we are loyal. This backdrop of positive evidence is apt to make negative beliefs improbable, and to supply ready charitable explanations for negative evidence.[16] But when the evidence is so negative as to overwhelm this background evidence, or there is little background evidence to go on, or when the negative belief supported by the evidence is grave (for example risking bad consequences for third parties), a healthy relationship of loyalty can surely withstand an honest mistake, which is different from slander. This holds all the more if the object of loyalty is a morally perfect or even very good God.

Second, we have said much about what *loyalty* involves, but less about what it takes to be a good *object* of loyalty. And surely a good, indeed deserving,

---

[16] And perhaps there is a high contextual threshold for forming negative beliefs on the basis of negative evidence.

object of loyalty would prefer responsibility to your evidence over obsequious positive belief no matter what. Looking at it this way, for a loyal person to prioritize positive belief over his evidence carries the implicature that the object of loyalty prefers things this way round. And such an implicature, I suggest, dishonors the object of loyalty. A good object of loyalty should see this, all the more so if he is a perfect or even very good God.

I conclude that epistemically oriented loyalty, including toward God, is superior to doxastically partial loyalty.

6.3 Responses to the Arguments for Doxastic Partiality

We are now in a position to respond to the four arguments for doxastic partiality. The first said that believing partially about the object of our loyalty is analogous to treating her partially (Hazlett 2013). But the analogy between beliefs and actions does not work. We have seen that you can better give the other party what she needs if you know about her as she is. In order to treat her partially in a way that will really benefit her, your beliefs must not be partial, but epistemically oriented.

A similar point applies to the second argument. This argument says that relationships of loyalty give rise to normative expectations to commit to the object of our loyalty, including to the goodness of his character (Stroud 2006). But I have argued that if you commit to the person's having a good character, your commitment to *him* may be compromised.

The third argument concerned the supposed phenomenology of relation-ships of loyalty (Stroud 2006; Keller 2004). First, we supposedly feel an impulse to believe well of those to whom we are loyal. I agree that we do, but this is not a guide to the norms of loyalty. I have argued that we can better side with someone by striving to know them as they are. Second, we suppos-edly want those who are loyal to us to believe well of us and be closed to believing badly. I suggest that a healthier way to channel this impulse in a relationship of loyalty is to strive to be the kind of person about whom an epistemically oriented friend could easily believe well.

Finally, the extrinsic argument: that believing positively will strengthen your relationship with the other party, whereas believing negatively will risk weakening it (Stroud 2006). In the religious case this amounts to a strengthening or weakening of faith in God. In response, we have seen that partialist positive belief in God comes with risks of its own, and that epistemically oriented negative belief can be a way of holding God to his own standards, or owning your faith for yourself, and thus siding with him more fully.

6.4 Epistemically Oriented Loyalty and Religious Disagreement

We have established that epistemically oriented religious disagreement can be loyal even by the lights of the doxastic-partiality view. Because we then established that this view is false, new avenues for loyal religious disagreement open. Religious disagreement can be loyal even if it involves negative beliefs about God or an openness to forming them—indeed even because of this. Job is our lode star: his epistemically oriented religious disagreement was with God himself—who took Job seriously enough to respond at length.[17]

For another example, recall the undergraduate (section 5.1) who wanted to own his faith for himself by attending a diverse secular university, but wound up at an insular religious college out of concern to do what he (and his parents) took to be loyal to God. I suggest that attending the secular university and engaging there in religious disagreement (among other things), could have been eminently loyal. And it could have been loyal *precisely because* he would have allowed himself to be open to negative beliefs about God. This is just what he needed to take his faith to the next level. Of course he would have run the risk of weakening or losing it, but this is a risk that he needed to run—precisely because he wanted to maintain and strengthen his emotional attitude of association with God, and continue siding with God all the more decisively thereafter.

7. Conclusion

I have defended epistemically oriented religious disagreement against the worry that it is disloyal. Or at least, against the worry it is disloyal in virtue of involving negative beliefs about God or an openness to forming some. Even assuming that such a doxastic state is disloyal, my response to the Explanation Argument established that there are equally plausible reasons why a believer would engage in religious disagreement. My response to the Argument from Risk established that engaging in disagreement does not risk greater disloyalty

---

[17] However we interpret what God said, it cannot be denied that he took Job seriously.

than declining to engage in it. Doxastic partialists need not fear religious disagreement.

But nor need we—or should we—be doxastic partialists at all. I have also established that negative beliefs about God (or openness to forming some) is not as such disloyal. This enables us to expand my responses to the Explanation Argument and the Argument from Risk. Negative beliefs (or openness to them) can be a perfectly acceptable explanation for a loyal believer's engaging in religious disagreement. And the fact that religious disagreement runs a substantial risk of such a doxastic state is not a problem from the viewpoint of loyalty after all. On the contrary, the best form of loyalty is epistemically oriented: it involves a concern to know the other party as she is, and expresses itself by the assiduous following of truth-conducive epistemic norms.

And one way to express this form of loyalty can be to engage in epistemically oriented religious disagreement. This is not an extraneous addition for believers who simply refuse to make do with the beliefs that they have been given, nor is it a flippant rejection of God's graciously revealed truths. It is an epistemically virtuous way to keep yourself and your religious community from the traps of insularity and groupthink. And it is a way of acknowledging, compatibly with commitment to God and the revelation as your community has received it, God's sovereign freedom to surprise us yet.

In our polarized age, the idea of respectful, open-minded, and epistemically oriented disagreement on matters of ultimate importance may seem out of touch or naïve. But this is yet another reason, beyond the epistemic benefits that it can confer, why it is more important than ever.[18]

References

Anderson, Elizabeth. 1995. "Knowledge, Human Interests, and Objectivity in Feminist Epistemology." *Philosophical Topics* 23: 27–58.

Arpaly, Nomy, and Anna Brinkerhoff. 2018. "Why Epistemic Partiality Is Overrated." *Philosophical Topics* 46: 37–51.

Benton, Matthew A. 2018a. "Pragmatic Encroachment and Theistic Knowledge." In Matthew Benton, John Hawthorne, and Dani Rabinowitz (eds.), *Knowledge, Belief, and God: New Insights in Religious Epistemology*, 267–287. Oxford: Oxford University Press.

---

[18] Many thanks to Matt Benton and Jon Kvanvig for valuable comments.

Benton, Matthew A. 2018b. "God and Interpersonal Knowledge." *Res Philosophica* 95: 421–447.

Buchak, Lara. 2012. "Can It Be Rational to Have Faith?" In Jake Chandler and Victoria Harrison (eds.), *Probability in the Philosophy of Religion*, 225–248. Oxford: Oxford University Press.

Crawford, Lindsay. 2019. "Believing the Best: On Doxastic Partiality in Friendship." *Synthese* 196: 1575–1593.

De Cruz, Helen, and Johan De Smedt. 2013. "The Value of Epistemic Disagreement in Scientific Practice: The Case of Homo Floresiensis." *Studies in History and Philosophy of Science Part A* 44: 169–177.

Dormandy, Katherine. 2018a. "Disagreement from the Religious Margins." *Res Philosophica* 95: 371–395.

Dormandy, Katherine. 2018b. "Does Epistemic Humility Threaten Religious Beliefs?" *Journal of Psychology and Theology* 46: 292–304.

Dormandy, Katherine. 2018c. "Evidence-Seeking as an Expression of Faith." *American Catholic Philosophical Quarterly* 92: 409–428.

Dormandy, Katherine. 2020a. "'In Abundance of Counsellors There Is Victory': Reasoning about Public Policy from a Religious Worldview." In Oliver Wiertz and Peter Jonkers (eds.), *Religious Truth and Identity in an Age of Plurality*, 162–181. London: Routledge.

Dormandy, Katherine. 2020b. "The Epistemic Benefits of Religious Disagreement." *Religious Studies* 56: 390–408.

Festinger, Leon. 1957. *A Theory of Cognitive Dissonance*. Evanston, IL: Row Peterson.

Hawley, Katherine. 2014. "Partiality and Prejudice in Trusting." *Synthese* 191: 2029–2045.

Hazlett, Allan. 2013. *A Luxury of the Understanding*. Oxford: Oxford University Press.

Hazony, Yoram. 2012. *The Philosophy of Hebrew Scripture*. Cambridge: Cambridge University Press.

James, William. 1921. *The Will to Believe, Human Immortality, and Other Essays in Popular Philosophy*. London: Longmans, Green, and Co.

Kawall, Jason. 2013. "Friendship and Epistemic Norms." *Philosophical Studies* 165: 349–370.

Keller, Simon. 2004. "Friendship and Belief." *Philosophical Papers* 33: 329–351.

Keller, Simon. 2007. *The Limits of Loyalty*. Cambridge: Cambridge University Press.

Kelly, Thomas. 2014. "Evidence Can Be Permissive." In Matthias Steup, John Turri, and Erneset Sosa (eds.), *Contemporary Debates in Epistemology*, 298–311. Oxford: Wiley-Blackwell.

Kierkegaard, Søren. 1983. "Fear and Trembling." In Howard V. Hong and Edna H. Hong (eds.), *Fear and Trembling/Repetition*, 1–124. Princeton: Princeton University Press.

Kvanvig, Jonathan L. 2018. *Faith and Humility*. Oxford: Oxford University Press.

Longino, Helen. 1990. *Science as Social Knowledge: Values and Objectivity in Scientific Inquiry*. Princeton: Princeton University Press.

Mugg, Joshua. 2016. "In Defense of the Belief-Plus Model of Propositional Faith." *European Journal for Philosophy of Religion* 8: 201–219.

Plantinga, Alvin. 2000a. "Pluralism: A Defense of Exclusivism." In Kevin Meeker and Philip L. Quinn (eds.), *The Philosophical Challenge of Religious Diversity*, 172–192. Oxford: Oxford University Press.

Plantinga, Alvin. 2000b. *Warranted Christian Belief*. Oxford: Oxford University Press.

Potter, R. Dennis. 2000. "Finitism and the Problem of Evil." *Dialogue: A Journal of Mormon Thought* 33: 83–95.

Solomon, Sheldon, Jeff Greenberg, and Tom Pyszczynski. 1991. "A Terror Management Theory of Social Behavior: The Psychological Functions of Self-Esteem and Cultural Worldviews." *Advances in Experimental Social Psychology* 24: 93–157.

Stroud, Sarah. 2006. "Epistemic Partiality in Friendship." *Ethics* 116: 498–524.

Wettstein, Howard. 2012. *The Significance of Religious Experience*. Oxford: Oxford University Press.

11

Democracy of the Dead? The Relevance of Majority Opinion in Theology

Isaac Choi

1. Introduction

It is commonplace in debates about theological matters that appeals are made to the traditional view of the church on a given question throughout history and across cultures, and this appeal to a dominant majority opinion over time is presented as having a very weighty probative force in favor of that traditional view being true. Roman Catholic and Eastern Orthodox teachings call for deference to such traditional doctrines. Even in Protestant theological circles where tradition is not placed on par with scripture in its authority, such a historical fact about the diachronic consensus (or about the consensus of contemporary experts) is often offered as a very difficult hurdle for minority views to overcome, requiring their cases to be that much stronger. I will argue that while majority opinion is not something to simply dismiss, it should not carry as strong of a weight in theological reasoning as it often is taught or implied to have. For those of us who are not experts on a particular issue, majority opinion and tradition may give us some reason to prefer the majority view, but this reason should be treated as fairly easily defeasible once the relevant arguments and evidence begin to be investigated.

This question about majority opinion in theology naturally connects with the more general social epistemology literature on the place of expertise. When experts disagree, whom should we believe? To address this problem, various indicators—such as credentials, track record, and the number of experts who hold a view—have been suggested as indirect evidence of superior expertise and helpful guides for deciding between experts.[1] I have argued, in contrast to the generally positive opinions of such indicators held by many philosophers and the general public, that indicators are unreliable proxies for expertise and

[1] In a seminal paper on expertise, Goldman (2001) lists and evaluates a number of these indicators.

Isaac Choi, *Democracy of the Dead? The Relevance of Majority Opinion in Theology* In: *Religious Disagreement and Pluralism*. Edited by: Matthew A. Benton and Jonathan L. Kvanvig, Oxford University Press. © Isaac Choi 2021. DOI: 10.1093/oso/9780198849865.003.0011

are often not useful in practice. Because of the serious defeaters involved, I believe that we should be skeptical regarding beliefs based solely on indicators.[2]

In this paper, I will apply my arguments concerning the indicator of numbers to the relevance of majority opinion within theology.[3] I will begin by giving reasons for why Christians in particular might think that the theological consensus should carry so much epistemic weight. I will then offer plausible kinds of scenarios (which have been historically instantiated at various times) where a view became the diachronic and/or synchronic majority view of theological experts for non-truth related reasons. The possibility that such a scenario occurred with a particular theological issue can serve as a potential undercutting defeater for the evidential force of the majority opinion. I will conclude by raising the possibility that the Holy Spirit could underwrite the reliability of the majority, but I will argue that given what we witness in history, both during biblical times and since, it does not seem that the Spirit typically operates in that fashion.

Let us begin with why novel minority views are so often disfavored. Unlike the cultures of modern science and technology, with their celebration of invention and discovery, innovation in theology has not been widely sought or lauded during most of the history of the Christian church. Indeed, wholly new ideas have generally been viewed with suspicion. Cyril of Alexandria, writing around 438, levels this kind of charge against Nestorius:

> Not only does he not welcome the tradition of all the initiates throughout the world (or rather that of all the God-inspired Scriptures), but he even innovates as seems fit to him, and denies that the holy virgin is the Mother of God, and calls her Christ-Mother instead, or Mother-of-the-Man. . . . The mind of the holy scriptures does not admit anything like this. It is rather an invention of a weak and feeble spirit that loves novelty and has no perception of the depth of the mystery.   (Cyril of Alexandria 2000, 52, 88)

A position not having some historical antecedent in theological tradition, especially not having at least some proponents in the patristic era, was seen as a sign of heresy. As a result, proponents of minority views[4] spill

---

[2] For more details, see my paper "The Reliability of Indicators of Expertise" (unpublished).

[3] While I will focus on Christian theology, most of these considerations could be readily applied to the theological epistemology of other religions.

[4] That is, views that are in the minority at the time of the writing of such defenses. As in science, many views that were once held only by a small minority later became dominant, and it is conceivable that many current minority views could eventually or quickly become majority opinion.

considerable ink in attempting to show that there were indeed representatives (or seeds or hints) of their views in scripture or the early church, including theses such as divine passibility, non-twenty-four-hour days of creation, Protestant departures from medieval Catholicism, charismatic continuationism, open theism, annihilationism, universalism, women's ordination, and gay marriage.[5] Indeed, ancient heretical groups (and contemporary sects that mainstream Christianity disavows) employ the same strategy, and they go even further, producing false evidence in the form of pseudepigraphic writings allegedly authored by famous figures in the early church, ranging from the Gospel of Peter to Pseudo-Dionysius the Areopagite, that support their distinctive non-orthodox doctrines.

This highly conservative distrust of new minority opinions is understandable for adherents of any religion that claims to possess revelation from God that should be preserved and passed on, "the faith which was once for all delivered to the saints" (Jude 1:3). If this revelation is genuinely from God, any departure from it might appear to be a bad epistemic move, a falling away from truth and into error. And it may seem sensible to give especially heavy evidential weight to the earliest interpretations of that revelation, by those closest in time, culture, language, and personal relationships to those through whom it came.

2. Diachronic Majority Opinion

In addition to this concern for the pure transmission of original revelation, a second reason for suspicion toward the theologically new—and old positions that have historically been in the minority—is aptly expressed by G. K. Chesterton's metaphor of "the democracy of the dead":

> It is obvious that tradition is only democracy extended through time. . . . The man who quotes some German historian against the tradition of the Catholic Church, for instance, is strictly appealing to aristocracy. . . . Tradition means giving votes to the most obscure of all classes, our ancestors. It is the

---

[5] To give just a few example citations of this widespread phenomenon: Sanders (1994) argues that Justin Martyr, Irenaeus, and Origen conceived of God not determining everything but responding to the libertarian free choices of humans (pp. 73–75) and that Lactantius rejected divine impassibility (p. 76). Kydd (1984) presents passages from early Christian theologians to support his view that the church of the first few centuries was continuationist. And Boswell (1994) argues that there were medieval Christian same-sex liturgies.

democracy of the dead. Tradition refuses to submit to the small and arrogant oligarchy of those who merely happen to be walking about.

(Chesterton 1908, 84–85)

Chesterton is attempting to combat the strong modern preference for the new in all areas of thought, contemporary culture's deep faith in human intellectual progress over time.[6] This partiality is no doubt fueled by the ever-accelerating discoveries of science, which show us how little our distant ancestors knew about how the world operates. Indeed, even our more recent ancestors, our grand parents and great-grandparents, still in living memory, knew far less than we do. One does not have to be a scientific realist to recognize that we are making progress in our understanding of the natural world. At the very least, we have amassed vast libraries of empirical observations in the last several hundred years, even if the anti-realist might deny we have made progress concerning the unobservable.

So when it comes to, say, astronomy or biology, it makes no sense to give equal votes to Ptolemy and Einstein, or count as epistemic peers Aristotle and even an undergraduate student of molecular biology. A democracy cannot hope to be a truth-aimed belief aggregation method if large swathes of voters are ignorant of most or all of the relevant evidence. In fact, it has never been true in any actual society that every citizen is equally well-positioned to make rational and just judgments regarding policy and law and which candidates for office would best implement them. So giving equal votes cannot be based on epistemic equality in the electorate. Instead, democracy is considered the best political compromise by its supporters in part because it makes no presuppositions about who is actually best situated to make the relevant judgments, since different groups will lay claim to that status. And so democracy gives everyone equal say, to not arbitrarily privilege any party's claim of epistemic supremacy over its rivals.

Now, if it were actually clear that a certain group or individual is objectively epistemically best situated, while another group is objectively poorly situated, then oligarchy or monarchy (by a philosopher king, of course) would be far better.[7] And if everyone in a society agreed on the identity of that objectively best situated person or group, then a democracy consisting of those people

---

[6] C. S. Lewis makes a related point with his concept of "chronological snobbery" (Lewis 1955, 207), where one uncritically accepts something because it is modern and rejects a rival view simply because it is old. Thanks to Matthew Benton for reminding me of Lewis's phrase.

[7] This is assuming we are focused on the epistemic justification of democracy. As Jonathan Kvanvig pointed out to me, an epistemically superior oligarchy or monarch might still be morally corrupt and so would not be better for a state.

would turn out to be equivalent to such an oligarchy or monarchy, since every segment of the electorate would defer and vote for the individual(s) universally acknowledged as best. So if Aristotle or Ptolemy were somehow transported to the present, they would no doubt quickly recognize their severe epistemic disadvantage and defer to the contemporary experts, surrendering their votes in making scientific judgments by their own lights (until they have caught up).

Even if Chesterton were to restrict his democracy of the dead to the domain of theology, theologians throughout history have by no means been on equal footing epistemically.[8] The discoveries of earlier manuscripts and papyri of the scriptures, along with the discipline of textual criticism and knowledge of the original languages, give contemporary theologians more accurate biblical sources than their predecessors, especially those who were forced to work with relatively poor translations. More importantly, the many significant archeological and historical discoveries over the last few centuries give scholars a much larger knowledge base to better understand scripture within its linguistic and cultural contexts, as well as to more clearly grasp the theological views and arguments of rival traditions, movements, and denominations throughout Christian history.

Perhaps one might argue that the very earliest Christians were better situated than contemporary Christians, hearing firsthand from Jesus and the apostles and asking them any questions they wished. Yet there is evidence that the first few generations after the apostles were not necessarily in a better epistemic position, given some of their odd beliefs. For example, despite *The Shepherd of Hermas*'s adoptionistic Spirit Christology and ascetic views on sex, it was accepted by many early on as either canonical scripture or quite close to scripture.[9] But even if, for the sake of argument, we ignore early views that were later rejected as heterodox and grant the earliest Christians a special epistemic status, it would still be true that the overwhelming majority of theologians throughout history were at a significant evidential disadvantage relative to both the earliest[10] and latest Christian thinkers. Some had the

---

[8] I will be discussing majorities of theological experts, rather than lay believers (the latter may be what Chesterton had in mind). But if my arguments against the significance of expert majorities are sound, similar arguments against lay majorities should carry even stronger weight.

[9] Origen (early third century) appeals to *Shepherd* approvingly, and yet admits that "some apparently despise" the book (*On First Principles* IV.4, 182). Eusebius later (early fourth century) says that because some rejected *Hermas*, it should not be included in the canon, but he notes that it had sometimes been used in public worship and some of the earliest writers cited it (*The History of the Church* III.3, 66).

[10] As Benton (2006), expanding on Michalson (1979), points out, one aspect of G. E. Lessing's famous "ugly, broad ditch" is Lessing's complaint that being so far removed temporally from the events of the first century makes Christian belief far more difficult for eighteenth-century human beings.

privilege of living shortly after Christ and the apostles, others now benefit from access to twenty-first-century scholarship, but most had neither advantage—and yet they would have the bulk of the votes in a democracy of the dead.

A different response to my argument might be that despite the major advances in knowledge over the last several centuries, present-day theological experts are afflicted with ideological and philosophical biases that distort their pursuit of the truth. Many theologians have a fallacious bias against the possibility of miracles,[11] which negatively affects their historical and theological conclusions, while others are heavily influenced in their theological presuppositions and methodology by a secular philosophical school, such as Hegelianism, existentialism, or postmodernism. Still others exhibit an unquestioning allegiance to every claim of their own denominational tradition. However, it is also true that theologians of the past were likewise affected by other non-Christian philosophies, assumptions, and misleading evidence. For example, the works of Pseudo-Dionysius the Areopagite were written around the turn of the sixth century and claimed to be the first-century writings of Dionysius, an Athenian convert of the apostle Paul mentioned in Acts 17:34.[12] Widely believed to be genuine until the Renaissance and even into the modern era in some circles, the apophatic Neoplatonism of Pseudo-Dionysius was highly influential among medieval theologians, who considered his views only one step removed from the apostle's teaching, and it thus distorted the development of theology for over a millennium. Even those who have more of a favorable opinion of negative theology and Proclus would admit that the effects of Pseudo-Dionysius on the development of theology were disproportionate, directly resulting from its false self-attribution.

Whether earlier or later theological biases were more detrimental overall is probably an impossible question to answer. Perhaps the best we can do is take things case by case, examining which particular doctrines and areas of theology would be most affected by a given bias.[13] But for Chesterton's democracy of the dead to generally hold in theology, contemporary biases would have to be so much worse than the biases of past ages so as to balance out the significantly better evidential situation of contemporary scholars. Even if such a case could be made, an unfortunate consequence of any such downward

---

[11] See Earman (2000) for a critical analysis of Hume's influential argument against miracle testimony.

[12] For more on Pseudo-Dionysius, see Corrigan and Harrington (2019).

[13] Of course, even here, such an examination would be hobbled by our ignorance of our contemporary blind spots, those biases that we (and possibly even our most perceptive critics) do not yet recognize in ourselves.

leveling across the board would be that theologians of *all* ages would end up being in poor epistemic states, making all of their votes far less significant. Why should anyone take seriously the majority opinion of a group of largely unreliable thinkers?

Furthermore, with regard to the epistemic weight put on the original revelation and the interpretations of that revelation in the earliest years of the church, unless those early interpretations were wholly correct (which seems unlikely given the diversity of early views and the opinions in *Hermas* and elsewhere that would later be deemed heterodox), some error was mixed into those views. Yet those false beliefs were treated by later theologians—as a result of the understandably conservative mindset I described in the introduction—with the same deference and weight as the truth that was present. Many today charge early theologians of uncritically importing Hellenistic philosophical ideas and values they absorbed during their pre-Christian education.[14] Other times, falsehoods creep into the community's views unnoticed, as in the case of Pseudo-Dionysius, either accidentally or intentionally. Both kinds of errors can become highly influential as a result of the social epistemological phenomenon of information cascades. In information cascades, people observe the past decisions that others have made and defer to them, or they at least place a heavy evidential weight on those earlier judgments.[15] This strategy has a similar rationale to deferring to experts in general: someone who has only begun to think about a question may look to the final judgments of people who have spent much more time on the topic. As time goes on, the majority becomes larger and the evidential weight seems to get stronger, as many people in each generation decide to agree with their predecessors. But in a cascade, this repeated deference has little to do with independent thought and research, making this diachronic majority far less significant than it may appear. So the same mechanism intended to preserve important theological truths over time gives falsehoods a chance to become dominant and entrenched; it allows tares to grow strong among the wheat.[16]

---

[14] As one example, John Sanders (1994) appeals to this Greek philosophical influence as central to his error theory as to why Christian theology has historically been committed to an immutable and impassible God, and not to the open God he prefers and claims scripture reveals.

[15] The concept comes from behavioral economics. See Sunstein (2006, 200–202) and Sunstein (2005) for more on cascades and their negative epistemic effects.

[16] In his commentary on Jesus' parable of the wheat and the weeds in Matthew's gospel, Origen interprets the weeds as "bad" or "evil opinions" sown by the devil alongside "wholesome words" (Origen 1896, 414).

So Chesterton's appeal to tradition, if it is construed as the total majority opinion of experts or laypeople throughout history, runs into serious problems and is not nearly as strong of a consideration as he believes it is.

3. Synchronic Majority Opinion

What if we shift from Chesterton's democracy of the dead to a democracy of the living, from diachronic majority opinion to synchronic majority opinion? This could eliminate the historical disparity resulting from recently discovered evidence, but there are still several serious problems with polling contemporary experts. The epistemic justification of democracy[17] rests on the premise that it is more likely that the majority opinion of a large group is right than the belief of an individual or the views of a small oligarchic group. To support this premise, appeals have been made to Condorcet's jury theorem, which states that if each individual in a group is at least slightly more likely to believe the truth than not, then the larger the group, the higher the probability that the majority will be correct, with this probability approaching 1 as the group size increases. However, the theorem also requires that the individuals' beliefs be probabilistically independent of each other, which is unrealistic given the countless influences that produce probabilistic dependence (Goldman 1999, 319). This is especially the case in fields like theology, where thinkers are almost always following and reacting to each other and their predecessors.

Instead of relying on Condorcet's theorem, Alvin Goldman presents a Bayesian analysis of when two experts believing a hypothesis H should count as stronger evidence for H than a single expert's belief (Goldman 2001, 99–102). He concludes that what is required is weaker than the independence the jury theorem requires; expert Y's route to coming to a belief can depend on expert X's route but Y must employ at least some independent checks or sources, so that Y is not merely parroting X's conclusions. While Goldman thinks that in many cases it is difficult to know whether this condition obtains, he is cautiously optimistic regarding scientists and their independent checking of each other's results. However, I will argue that even if a group of experts were to meet Goldman's weaker condition, a majority of such a group can (and often does) come to agree on a view for many reasons unrelated to that view's truth. Among them, I will discuss ignorance of

---

[17] At least for democracies where there are not large numbers of citizens who are especially epistemically disadvantaged (for whatever reason), as I discussed in the previous section.

minority arguments, biases, selection effects, and the difficulty of choosing who gets to vote. As I mentioned earlier, these are potential undercutting defeaters for the epistemic significance of a view's majority status.

3.1 Ignorance of Minority Arguments

The majority may be unaware of an important argument or piece of evidence that plays a crucial role in the minority's case. A discovery may not have been widely disseminated yet, or perhaps the majority experts are aware of this evidence but ignore or downplay its significance. A disturbing example is found in a debate among physicians over whether symptoms traditionally associated with shaken-baby syndrome can sometimes result from a different condition entirely, which could exonerate some caregivers convicted of killing infants (Bazelon 2011, 33–35). Patrick Barnes, a pediatric radiologist who had co-written a chapter on shaken-baby syndrome for a textbook, was serving as an expert witness for the prosecution in a shaken-baby trial. Listening to the defense's experts raised doubts. He said, "I'd been in lockstep with the child-abuse establishment for 20 years. For the first time, I saw that there were well-qualified experts on the other side giving opinions I'd never heard, that I knew nothing about." Barnes was considered an authority on the topic, having written a textbook chapter, and yet he had never even heard of the opposition's arguments. Once he did hear them, they eventually convinced him. This illustrates how insular even the best-informed members of a majority can be. And the larger the majority, the more likely such ignorance is present, since the minority appears insignificant, worthy to be ignored—after all, one might reason, if they did have any good arguments, why do so few hold their view? But this assumes that most of the experts know the minority's case and have fairly considered it.

This assumption is often false, and in the contemporary theological scene, it is especially exacerbated by its fragmentation and tribalism. This fragmentation existed even before the big schisms within Christianity, with Latin-speaking Western theologians unable to read Eastern theologians who wrote in Greek, but it has accelerated in recent centuries. Few Catholics attend Protestant seminaries, few theological liberals choose to enroll in conservative schools, and vice versa. It is rare that seminarians and doctoral students get sustained exposure to the strongest arguments for theological perspectives that are very different from their own, and many scholars exclusively read and write for others within their own tribe and perhaps one or two neighboring tribes. This is partly to avoid intractable arguments about fundamental issues, where one has little hope of convincing the other side. But it is also a result of the enormous amount of scholarship regarding other theological traditions that has been produced—no one can hope to master all of it, and so one might prefer to stay within one's specialization and tradition.

3.2 Bias, Pressure, and Selection Effects

I have already mentioned some examples of biases that have afflicted theologians past and present, with the importing of non-Christian cultural and philosophical premises into their reasoning processes. In addition to those kinds of biases, personal conflicts of interest and cognitive biases can be quite effective in rejecting the views of others. Once a thinker has come to a conclusion and has invested time and effort in promoting and defending it, they will not easily change their mind. For instance, the theory that peptic ulcers are caused by the bacterium *Helicobacter pylori* (and not stress or excessive acid) was long resisted by physicians despite the strength of the scientific evidence that convinced many researchers (Thagard 1998). Concern over remaining "respectable" in the eyes of peers in the guild and not drawing their scorn helps preserve the status quo.

There are also institutional pressures on theologians. Historically, there were the well-known sins of Constantinian Christianity, including the Medieval Inquisition and the Magisterial Reformers using the power of the state to enforce theological conformity, sometimes upon pain of death (with Anabaptists, Quakers, and other dissenters protesting). But even with contemporary freedom of religion and separation of church and state, theologians' employers, churches, and denominations will often require them to agree with and teach specific doctrines. On the other side, secular and religiously unaffiliated universities also have their own shibboleths and red lines that cannot be crossed if one wants to gain or retain tenure in theology or religious studies. The major social costs and uncertainties involved with finding a new religious community or employer (especially in a difficult academic job market) serve as conscious or unconscious motivation to stay within the acceptable range of views on those doctrines, even without the threat of external punishment.

These pressures, together with existing institutional structures, can produce distorting selection effects in the number of theologians who side with one view. How many experts there are that hold a certain view depends on how many get educated and hired that hold that view, which in turn depends largely on how many academic institutions teach that view and how many organizations would offer jobs to subscribers of that view. The numbers of physicians who graduate each year with M.D.s and D.O.s will be dictated by how many medical schools of each tradition (allopathic vs. osteopathic) exist and how many students they admit, not how each tradition relates to the medical truth. So it would be a mistake to believe that the ratio of M.D.s to D.O.s indicates which tradition is closer to the truth. Similarly, the numbers of Ph.D.s and professors who hold to a particular theological tradition are heavily influenced by the number of institutions who train and hire scholars of that tradition. And the numbers of institutions various theological traditions have seem very unlikely to correlate with how correct each tradition's views are. Instead, it seems far more likely to be a result of irrelevant sociological factors, such as the relative size and wealth of each tradition, along with how much it values theological education.

3.3 Who Gets to Vote?

This brings us to a fundamental problem with numbers as an indicator of expertise. Appealing to numbers requires at least an implicit decision about whom to include as an expert when counting heads. We would not want to include people who have insufficient relevant expertise to make an informed, reasoned judgment. Nor would we want to exclude those who do have genuine expertise in the area. But if we are unsure which people or groups have the necessary expertise, then how can we choose what group to poll?

Consider three rival traditions of medicine: Western, Eastern, and shamanist. Do we only poll Western physicians concerning the proper treatment of a particular illness? This presupposes which camp is right before we begin to count. Should we then poll practitioners of all three traditions? If there turn out to be many more shamans in the world than Western doctors, does this mean that the shamans have greater expertise and are more likely to be right simply because of this contingent historical fact?

The application to theological traditions should be obvious. Most Catholic, Protestant, and Orthodox theologians would not give votes to theologians who subscribed to Mormonism or Arianism (or its modern-day counterpart, Jehovah's Witnesses). Even within Trinitarian Christianity, there are many denominations that view other Trinitarian sub-traditions as unqualified to come to reliable theological conclusions because of what they perceive as seriously faulty methodology or critically false doctrines. Deciding who gets to vote seems to require in many cases knowing in advance who is right, or at least who is very likely to get it right. Since we typically do not know in advance who is right, we are in effect choosing our pool of expert voters out of ignorance. If we give the vote to too many, the genuine expertise in the pool becomes severely diluted by including large groups that lack it, while overly restricting the vote results in undercounting the actual experts or leaving them out entirely. Either error can easily result in the majority opinions of such pools being mistaken.

4. The Internal Testimony of the Holy Spirit

Given all these possible confounding variables—ignorance of minority arguments, biases, selection effects, and mistaken choices of whose opinions to count—it seems that the proportion of experts who hold a particular view cannot serve as a strong indicator of where the truth lies. But perhaps we can rescue Chesterton's democracy of the dead by appealing to a different source of true beliefs unavailable to experts in other fields: the internal testimony of the Holy Spirit. After all, Jesus promised his disciples, "When the Spirit of truth comes, he will guide you into all the truth" (John 16:13). Playing a role in both Aquinas and Calvin's religious epistemologies, the testimony of the Spirit is central to Alvin Plantinga's views on the warrant for Christian belief, in causing Christians to come to believe and have confidence in the "great truths of the gospel" (2000, 245). If the majority of the followers of Jesus throughout history turned out to be wrong on a theological doctrine, it might seem that the Spirit has been doing a poor job of guiding them into all truth. So Chesterton could appeal to this role of the Spirit to bolster the reliability of believers throughout history and give supernatural assistance to majority opinion in theology.

Yet by the lights of most theologians, the history of the church is replete with examples of moments when most if not all believers were wrong on important theological questions, and that these errors had been entrenched for most or all of church history before that point in time. Here are a number of positions that were at one point non-existent or tiny minority views but later became widely or virtually universally held: Gentiles not needing to become Jews to be Christians, the Trinitarian and Christological views promulgated at the ecumenical councils of Nicea and Chalcedon (vs. Arianism, which during some periods seemed dominant), Anselm's theory of the atonement, priestly celibacy (and its rejection), justification by faith, and continuationism regarding spiritual gifts. No Christians would agree that all of these were good developments that were closer to the truth (especially given that priestly celibacy and its negation are both in this list), but each is viewed by some significant group of theologians as progress made in theological understanding. I would venture to say that for most Christians, at least three of these views in this list would fall in this positive categorization (the first two being not needing to become Jews and the Nicean/Chalcedonian view of the nature of God).

Most distinctive doctrines (sometimes called doctrinal distinctives)—views that characterize and are unique to a given denomination or sub-branch of Christianity—are minority views relative to the rest of the faith, usually in both synchronic and diachronic senses. So most denominations believe in some views that they think the majority of Christians are wrong about. If any denomination is correct with regard to a distinctive doctrine it holds, then it is a fact that the majority of Christians throughout history have held to an incorrect (or at best very partial) understanding of the truth in that area.[18]

Even the apostles, presumably the best positioned epistemically to know and understand the truth, often held wildly incorrect beliefs. Despite the fact that the Spirit was actively revealing truth to the disciples during Jesus' ministry (after Peter's confession of Christ in Matthew 16:16–17, Jesus says, "flesh and blood has not revealed this to you, but my Father in heaven."), they were clearly wrong concerning the mission and purpose of that ministry: "But they understood nothing about all these things; in fact, what he said was hidden from them, and they did not grasp what was said" (Luke 18:34). They were so captivated by their culture's prevailing conception and anticipation of a political Messiah that even after the resurrection, they ask him when he will deliver the nation from the Romans (Acts 1:6).

Though the coming of the Spirit in fullness on Pentecost does give much greater understanding to the apostles, they still persist in errors or lack of knowledge in important areas, and it takes time for their understanding to

---

[18] Perhaps partisans of a very exclusive tradition of Christianity might claim that everyone outside that tradition is not a genuine Christian or is sub-par in some way (because they do not actually have the Holy Spirit, or they do not read the Bible properly, or they are ignoring the authority of the magisterium, or . . .), so in fact, the majority of *true* Christians throughout history have agreed with their denominational distinctives. This seems to me a case of the No True Scotsman fallacy, gerrymandering the set of true experts so that they all happen to agree with the partisan. It is also a logically futile move, since the appeal to the majority opinion of that narrow, specific tradition can then have motivating force only to those already within that tradition and accepting of its claims. If a certain group claims to be the only true church, then an appeal to a majority opinion of just that group's theologians will not motivate anyone outside that group to agree. Such an argument circularly presupposes the truth of the group's claim to being the only true church.

grow and unfold. The church goes through struggles over whether Gentile believers have to become Jews, with Paul vehemently disagreeing with Peter on that topic (Acts 15; Galatians 2:11–16). In their letters, both Peter and Paul admit that their theological understanding is partial (1 Corinthians 13:12; 2 Peter 3:16), and there is a sense that they did not fully comprehend what they were writing; perhaps they knew at some level that they were transmitting things for future generations to more fully grasp (along the lines of their view of the prophets of past generations; see 1 Peter 1:10–12).

The model of gradually increasing understanding of revelation over the centuries since Jesus' time fits well with progressive revelation during the timespan of the biblical narratives themselves. Jesus' teaching on divorce is more stringent than Moses', and he tells his hearers that Moses was more lenient because of their "hardness of heart" (Matthew 19:8). Moses' hearers could not bear to hear the full teaching on marriage and divorce, while Jesus judges that conditions have changed (or are about to with the imminent appearance of the kingdom of God and the outpouring of the Spirit), and his disciples could now receive it. In a similar way, during the Last Supper, Jesus tells his disciples that they still lack many truths they need to know for similar reasons (providing some important context for the portion I quoted earlier): "I still have many things to say to you, but you cannot bear them now. When the Spirit of truth comes, he will guide you into all the truth" (John 16:12–13). Into "all the truth," yes, but it seems unlikely that the disciples or the church would receive (or be able to bear to hear) all that truth at one moment, in a single flash of insight. Even if one affirms that the canon of scripture is now closed and progressive revelation finished, there is still room for a progressive understanding and drawing out of implications of that revelation, led by the Holy Spirit. The seed of scripture may be planted, but its growth into a mature tree, with its flowering and fruiting, continues over centuries.

The Holy Spirit does not seem to be in a great hurry to correct all of the church's theological errors and misunderstandings. How then should we understand the epistemic role of the Spirit? Here is a proposal: God is most interested in people coming to have saving faith. Believing a set of propositional truths clearly is not sufficient for saving faith—after all, according to James, even the demons believe the relevant truths. Nevertheless, on most Christian views of soteriology, it is necessary to believe some very minimal set of truths; for example, someone might claim that salvation requires some level of conviction that God exists, sin is real and I cannot deal with it on my own, and Jesus died for our sins. Once the Spirit has led a person to believe whatever is necessary to be saved (let us call these the essential beliefs),[19] God is in no rush to fix all their other false beliefs in this life (and the same would go for the church over time). After all, once a person is saved, there is an eternity of time to correct and properly educate.

Perhaps God deals with our non-essential theological errors in a patient manner, similar to the gentle way he works for our sanctification: God typically deals with one or two areas of sin at a time; if we were confronted simultaneously with all the ways we fall short morally, we would be over-whelmed and likely give up in despair. Or perhaps because I would strongly resist accepting certain truths that are unpalatable or even unbearable by my current lights (just as my deepest and most entrenched sinful habits may most resist correction and change), God chooses not to overpower me and instead works first in other areas where he knows I will be less resistant. Whatever the reason, God's Spirit of love usually teaches and corrects us gently, usually one moral or theological truth at a time. And similar considerations regarding our potential despair and resistance and the Spirit's patience and gentleness apply to groups, churches, and denominations.

Because this corrective process in the church may take centuries, even millennia, there is no guarantee or even a moderately high probability, even with the internal activity of the Holy Spirit, that the majority opinion of the church at a moment or over its history until now on a particular non-essential theological question will be the correct one. Now, we are not sure how far the borders of the set of salvifically essential truths extend, so if there is some uncertainty over whether a given question is essential, we may want to pay more careful attention to the diachronic majority opinion on that question. But for most controversial theological questions, such as models of foreknowl-edge and free will, or church polity, or evolution and the age of the earth, or even whether certain actions are sinful or permitted, these questions seem far

---

[19] I give this particular minimal set of beliefs merely as an example, and I am not giving an argument here that it is the actual set of essential beliefs. I take it as a summary of the core gospel message of the early sermons in the book of Acts and what Paul says is the core of his preaching in 1 Cor. 15:3–7 (thanks to an audience member at the SCP conference, where an earlier version of this paper was presented, for reminding me of Acts sermons). A slightly larger set could be produced by taking the intersection of the contents of the early creeds that are held by virtually all branches of the church. Neither set entails very much about where the rest of theology should land.

If a form of soteriological inclusivism is true, the set of essential beliefs might be even smaller, perhaps just that some kind of higher power exists and I need rescue from my moral faults. For the universalist, even if the set of presently held beliefs that are necessary is empty, someone could not be in a good relationship with God in the afterlife without at some point coming to believe (perhaps at some point postmortem) some set of essential beliefs about God's reality and character. If a more liberal inclusivism or universalism turns out to be true, then the Spirit would have even less reason to be in a rush to correct our theological errors in this life.

from being essential in this sense, and so we should not have a strong preference for the majority opinions regarding such issues solely on the basis of their being held by the synchronic and/or diachronic majority.

This is not to say that we should flippantly ignore majority opinion or casually discard the strong consensus of the church over time. In her formulation of a *Consensus Gentium* argument for the existence of God, Linda Zagzebski (2011) appeals to our self-trust and symmetry considerations in order to urge us to trust others' intellectual abilities and conscientiousness. In a similar line of argument, Thomas Kelly points out that we often give other people's beliefs weight because we believe they are "generally competent interpreters of their evidence and experience" (2011, 139). If we believe that theologians throughout history, despite their biases and incomplete evidence, still had a good deal of evidence and many of them experienced at least some internal testimony of the Spirit, we cannot completely disregard their beliefs. It is possible that the Spirit did lead them into truth in this area, and perhaps there were good truth-related reasons why so many thinkers accepted a given view—certainly they themselves thought that they had such compelling reasons. Because of the potential defeaters of biases, selection effects, and social pressures, the indicator of numbers does not help us in determining whether there actually were good reasons for a given majority view. We can only know that once we have done our homework and carefully evaluated the evidence and arguments that these theologians relied on in making their cases, as well as the counterarguments of their minority critics, and the continuing debates to the present day. Who won those debates in the sense of which view became more popular among experts may have partially resulted from psychological and sociological factors unrelated to the view's truth, but the debates are still useful to us in furnishing us the strongest considerations and evidence put forward by all sides, the material that we can sift through and weigh in coming to our own conclusions.

This can be a massive scholarly task, and obviously no one, not even the professional theologian, can do this for every question, or at least to the same level of detail. So in considering a theological question, I should have some intellectual humility and be somewhat agnostic about topics where I have not done much research, perhaps with a leaning toward the historically majority view, but a leaning that I consider fairly easily defeasible once the evidence is engaged. In those areas where I have done some of the homework, but have not thoroughly investigated the arguments, I may have somewhat more firmly held beliefs, but I should still hold to my current conclusions somewhat tentatively, to a lesser level of confidence than the typical theological disputant, who can so easily fall into becoming a hostile polemicist. This kind of intellectually humble stance, of having convictions while being keenly aware of one's own intellectual limitations and possible biases, if widely held, would be a community blessing in how we treat those who disagree with us. It would be an approach that would be loving and winsome to believers and non-believers alike.[20]

References

Bazelon, Emily. 2011. "Shaken-Baby Syndrome Faces New Questions in Court." *The New York Times Magazine*, February 6, MM30-37, 44–47.

Benton, Matthew A. 2006. "The Modal Gap: The Objective Problem of Lessing's Ditch(es) and Kierkegaard's Subjective Reply." *Religious Studies* 42: 27–44.

Boswell, John. 1994. *Same-Sex Unions in Premodern Europe*. New York: Villard Books.

Chesterton, G. K. 1908. *Orthodoxy*. London: John Lane.

Corrigan, Kevin, and L. Michael Harrington. 2019. "Pseudo-Dionysius the Areopagite." In *The Stanford Encyclopedia of Philosophy*, ed. Edward N. Zalta, Summer 2019 edition. https://plato.stanford.edu/archives/sum2019/entries/pseudo-dionysius-areopagite/

Cyril of Alexandria. 2000. *On the Unity of Christ*. Trans. J. A. McGuckin. Crestwood, NY: St. Vladimir's Seminary Press.

Earman, John. 2000. *Hume's Abject Failure: The Argument against Miracles*. Oxford: Oxford University Press.

Eusebius of Caesarea. 1989. *The History of the Church from Christ to Constantine*. Trans. G. A. Williamson. London: Penguin Books.

Goldman, Alvin I. 1999. *Knowledge in a Social World*. Oxford: Clarendon Press.

Goldman, Alvin I. 2001. "Experts: Which Ones Should You Trust?" *Philosophy and Phenomenological Research* 63: 85–110.

Kelly, Thomas. 2011. "Consensus Gentium: Reflections on the 'Common Consent' Argument for the Existence of God." In Kelly James Clark and Raymond J. VanArragon (eds.), *Evidence and Religious Belief*, 135–156. Oxford: Oxford University Press.

[20] My gratitude to Matthew Benton, Jonathan Kvanvig, Ross McCullough, and Alvin Plantinga for their perceptive comments and suggestions on earlier versions of this paper. Thanks also to the audience at a Society of Christian Philosophers conference for helpful discussion and encouragement when I first presented the paper's core argument. This publication was made possible in part through the support of a grant from the John Templeton Foundation. The opinions expressed in this publication are those of the author and do not necessarily reflect the views of the John Templeton Foundation.

Kydd, Ronald A. 1984. *Charismatic Gifts in the Early Church: An Exploration into the Gifts of the Spirit During the First Three Centuries of the Christian Church.* Peabody, Mass.: Hendrickson Publishers.

Lewis, C. S. 1955. *Surprised by Joy: The Shape of My Early Life.* New York: Harcourt, Brace & World.

Michalson, Gordon E. 1979. "Lessing, Kierkegaard, and the 'Ugly Ditch': A Reexamination." *The Journal of Religion* 59: 324–334.

Origen. 1896. "Commentary on the Gospel of Matthew." In Allan Menzies (ed.), *The Ante-Nicene Fathers*, Vol. 9. Edinburgh: T&T Clark.

Origen. 1979. *Origen: An Exhortation to Martyrdom, Prayer, and Selected Works.* Trans. R. A. Greer. New York: Paulist Press.

Plantinga, Alvin. 2000. *Warranted Christian Belief.* Oxford: Oxford University Press.

Sanders, John. 1994. "Historical Considerations." In Clark Pinnock et al. (eds.), *The Openness of God: A Biblical Challenge to the Traditional Understanding of God*, 59–100. Downers Grove, Ill.: InterVarsity Press.

Sunstein, Cass R. 2005. *Why Societies Need Dissent.* Rev. edn. Cambridge, Mass.: Harvard University Press.

Sunstein, Cass R. 2006. "Deliberating Groups versus Prediction Markets (or Hayek's Challenge to Habermas)." *Episteme* 3: 192–213.

Thagard, Paul. 1998. "Ulcers and Bacteria I: Discovery and Acceptance." *Studies in History and Philosophy of Science Part C* 29: 107–136.

Zagzebski, Linda. 2011. "Epistemic Self-Trust and the Consensus Gentium Argument." In Kelly James Clark and Raymond J. VanArragon (eds.), *Evidence and Religious Belief*, 22–36. Oxford: Oxford University Press.

Index

For the benefit of digital users, indexed terms that span two pages (e.g., 52–53) may, on occasion, appear on only one of those pages.

absolutism 217, 223
Adams, Marilyn 132
affirmation 173
agent partiality 190–1
agnosticism 14–15, 28, 79–80, 86–7
akrasia, epistemic 160n.32
al-Ghazālī 18
Alston, William 14–16, 16n.38, 29n.61, 68n.6, 93–4
Anderson, Charity 8n.17, 21n.50
annihilationism 272–3
anonymous Christians 22n.54, 220–4
apologetics 21n.51, 28–9, 142–3
apologetics, sledgehammer 146–52
Aquinas, Thomas 146–7, 164–5, 282
Argument from Risk 253–60
Aristotelian mean 150–1
atheism 14–17, 24n.55, 28–9, 79–80, 86
Audi, Robert 2nn.1,2
Axtell, Guy 14n.32, 20n.46

bad prospects 66
Baehr, Jason 150–1
Baker-Hytch, Max 9n.19, 16, 22n.52, 69n.8
Ballantyne, Nathan 150n.14
Barnes, Patrick 279
basic beliefs 67–8
Basinger, David 14n.32, 18n.42
Battaly, Heather 150–1
Bayes Theorem 185
Bayesianism 11, 18n.41, 180
Bazelon, Emily 279
belief 1–4
belief forming methods, safe 20n.45
belief polarization 13–14
belief, contingency of 15–20
Benton, Matthew 2n.3, 8n.17, 9nn.19,20, 16n.37, 24n.55, 51n.20, 69n.8, 241n.2

Bergmann, Michael 69n.8, 73–80, 93n.4
Blanchard, Joshua 28
Bogardus, Thomas 18n.41, 20n.45, 24n.55, 91, 94n.5, 103
Buchak, Lara 2n.1, 251n.13
Buddhism 202–3, 210–11
Byrne, Peter 218–19

calibrationism 186n.8
Callahan, Laura Frances 26–7
Calvin, John 134, 282
Calvinism 222n.4
Cameron, Kirk 156
candidate self 134–5
Chalcedon, council of 282–3
charismatic continuationism 272–3
Chesterton, G.K. 31, 273–5, 278, 282
Chignell, Andrew 147n.5, 228–9
Choi, Isaac 31
Choo, Frederick 94
Christensen, David 2n.4, 3n.5, 4n.9, 5n.10, 43–4, 92, 95, 95n.7
Christianity 22, 30–1
Christianity, Holy Spirit 31, 272, 282–7
Clark, Kelly 146, 148–9, 165
Cohen, Stewart 4n.9
Conciliationism 4–7, 9–11, 13–15, 17–18, 24–5, 27, 103–4, 108–10, 115–16, 120, 138–9, 180
Conciliationism, strong 180–201
conditionalization 181
Condorcet jury theorem 278–9
confirmation 75
common consent/Consensus Gentium arguments 25–6, 286
conversion 16–17, 20, 28, 127–8, 131n.3, 133–4, 136–9, 169, 172–3
Craig, William Lane 170–1

credence function 181
credences 3–4, 6, 181–93, 203–8
cumulative case argument 166–7
Cyril of Alexandria 272

Dawkins, Richard 50n.19, 171–2
De Cruz, Helen 14n.32, 20n.46, 93n.4, 111n.3, 113n.7, 131n.3, 133n.10, 137n.16, 138n.18
de Ridder, Jeroen 195n.18
debunking arguments 8–9, 17–21
defeater/defeat 9, 17–18, 24, 67n.4, 68–70
defeater, epistemic 8n.17
defeater, normative 9n.20, 69n.10
defeater, rebutting 67n.4
defeater, undercutting 67
defeater, undermining 67n.4
defeating doubt 67
democracy of the dead 31, 273–8, 282
DePoe, John 94n.5
Descartes, Rene 18–19
disloyalty 30–1, 243, see also loyalty
disloyalty of difference 245
disloyalty of valence 245
divine hiddenness 17–18, 21–2, 28–9, 142–3, 152, 157–8, 168–9
dogmatism 138–9
Dormandy, Katherine 30–1, 93n.4
doxastic disloyalty 239, 244–50
doxastic involuntarism 248
doxastic partiality 30–1, 242
doxastic voluntarism 257
Dumsday, Travis 22n.52
Dunaway, Billy 16n.37

Edwards, Jonathan 134
Elga, Adam 4n.9, 10n.21, 92, 104
Elgin, Catherine 48–9
epistemic norms 261–2
epistemic permissibility 125
epistemic principles 115–17
equal weight view 4, 10–11, 18n.41, 93–4
eschatology 155–7, 160
etiology of religious belief 8–9, 80–6
evangelism 155–6
evidence one does not possess 150
evidence, conclusive 147–8
evidence, double-counting 10–11

evidence, experiential 118–24, 150
evidence, first-order 109–10
evidence, higher-order 6–10, 11n.23, 25–6, 70, 109–10, 128–9
evidence, in religion 15–17, 27–8
evidence, incommunicable 97–8
evidence, objective 75–7
evidence, overriding 150
evidence, private 15–16, 71–2
evidence, publicly available 15–16
evidence, total 71–2
evidentialism 115, 117
exclusivism 22, 24–5, 30, 217–20, 223, 225–7, 234
Explanation Argument 250–3
externalist epistemology 13n.29, 67–8, 195–6

faith 1–2, 2n.1, 30, 113, 173, 227–8, 231–6
Faulkner, Paul 2n.1
Feldman, Richard 2n.4, 3n.6, 5n.11, 7–9, 15n.35, 18n.41, 27–8, 43–4, 68n.7, 91n.1, 152–3
Ferrari, Filippo 2n.4
Fitelson, Branden 7n.16
Flew, Antony 131n.3
Foley, Richard 55–6, 56n.27
Frances, Bryan 2n.4, 111n.4, 119n.13
Frege, Gottlob 199–200

Garber, Daniel 139–40
generality problem for reliabilism 69–70
Goldberg, Sanford 9–10, 16n.39, 27
Goldman, Alvin 96–8, 278–9
Greco, John 9n.19
Green, Adam 21n.50
Grimm, Stephen 47n.14
Gutting, Gary 14

Hájek, Alan 3n.7
Harris, Sam 171
Hawley, Katherine 248–9
Hawthorne, John 9n.19, 12–13, 16n.37, 24n.55, 53n.23
Hazlett, Allan 247n.7
hell, problem of 152, 156
Hick, John 14, 23–4, 217, 224
hope 173, 228–30
Horowitz, Sophie 6

Howard-Snyder, Daniel 2n.1, 150–1
humility, epistemic 17–18, 28–9, 142, 145,
    150–2, 162–4, 167
humility, intellectual 286–7
humility, Kantian 235

inclusivism 22–5, 22n.54, 30, 220, 223,
    225–7, 233–4, 285n.19
internalist epistemology 13n.29, 195–6
irrelevant influences 18–21, 24, 80–1
Isaacs, Yoaav 24n.55
Islam 14–15, 21n.49, 22nn.53,54, 144

James, William 13n.29, 16n.38, 133–4,
    135n.13
Judaism 22, 144, 263–4
justification 82–3, 109
justification, degree of 115
justification, partisan 29–30
justified belief 65

Kawall, Jason 248–9
Keller, Lorraine Juliano 51n.20
Keller, Simon 242–4
Kelly, Thomas 3n.6, 8n.17, 10–14, 14n.32,
    25, 43–4, 174–5, 286
King, Nathan 4n.9, 14n.32, 18n.41, 21n.51,
    28–9, 65n.2, 92, 97n.9
knockdown arguments 142–3
knowledge 1–2, 8n.17, 12–13, 16, 19,
    20n.45, 24
knowledge disagreement norm 12–13
Kopec, Matthew 5n.11
Korman, Daniel 19n.44
Kraft, James 14n.32, 18n.42, 93n.4
Kvanvig, Jonathan 2n.1, 7n.15,
    22n.54, 30, 46n.10, 47n.13, 149n.13,
    151n.19, 250

Lackey, Jennifer 2n.4, 9n.20, 16, 17n.40,
    69n.10, 87n.31, 92
Lasonen-Aarnio, Maria 9n.19, 11,
    69n.8
Law of Total Probability 185
Lepper, Mark 13n.30
Lewis, C.S. 274n.6
Lewis, David 147
Limited Atonement 222n.4
Lord, Charles 13n.30

Lougheed, Kirk 93–4, 94n.5
loyalty, epistemically oriented 30–1,
    239–40, 242–4, see also disloyalty
loyalty, norms of 243–4
luminosity 12n.28

Machuca, Diego 2n.4
MacIntyre, Alasdair 16
Mackie, J.L. 2n.2
majority opinion, diachronic 31, 271–8,
    283, 285–6
majority opinion, synchronic 31, 272,
    278–82
Marie of the Incarnation 213–14
Marsh, Jason 21n.51
Marsh, Jon 21n.51
Martin, C.B. 16n.38
Matheson, Jonathan 2n.4, 4n.9, 91n.1
McGinnis, Jon 21n.49
McGrath, Sarah 52n.21
McGrew, Lydia 167
McGrew, Timothy 167
McKaughn, Daniel 2n.1
McNabb, Tyler 29n.61
Meister, Chad 14n.32
mental math case 2–4
metaethics 219
Mill, J.S. 19n.43
Monty Hall Problem 188, 196–9
moral testimony 47
moral understanding 26–7
Moreland, J.P. 170
Moser, Paul 132–4
Murphy, Nancey 42n.3
Murray, Michael 146, 148

new evil demon problem 196n.19
Nicea, council of 282–3
non-conciliatory views of
    disagreement 102–3, see also Steadfasters

open theism 272–3
Origen 275n.9

partisan justification 29–30, 192–201
Pascal, Blaise 131–2, 134, 139, 166–7
Paul, L.A. 28
Pedersen, Nikolaj 2n.4
peer disagreement 71–4, 128, 143n.1

peer, epistemic 3n.6, 4, 16–17, 73–4, 109–10

peers, evidential 122–3

perception 15–16, 19n.44

Pereboom, Derk 147n.5

permissive 142–4, 152–8, 169–73

permissivism, epistemic 5–6, 27–9, 65, 80–6, 153–5, 158, 174–5

Pittard, John 10n.21, 14n.32, 16–17, 29–30, 94–5, 95n.7, 99–100

Plantinga, Alvin 14, 24, 29n.61, 68n.6, 68n.7, 73–4, 93–4, 134, 164–5, 231, 248n.9, 282

pluralism 17–18, 23–6, 28, 30, 217–20, 223, 225–7, 233–4

pluralism, abductive 23–6

pluralism, anti-realist 23–4

preface paradox 54–7

Pritchard, Duncan 47n.13

probability 75, 82–3

Proper Functionalism 67–8

Pseudo-Dionysius the Areopagite 276

Quine, W.V.O. 42n.3

Quinn, Philip 18n.42

Rabinowitz, Dani 16n.37

Rahner, Karl 22n.54, 30, 220–4

rational belief 65

rational demotion 74, 80, 86

Rational Independence 83–4

rational insight 29–30

Rationalism 207–14

Rea, Michael 21n.50

reasons partiality 190–1

Reformed epistemology 29–30, 211–12

Reining, Stefan 92–4

relativism 30, 217, 223

Reliabilism 67–8

religious agreement 15, 25–6

religious belief 66–7

religious disagreement 14–26

religious disagreement, distinctive 27–8, 91–6, 98–100, 108, 114–16

religious disagreement, extra-religious 14–15, 17, 18n.41, 25n.56

religious disagreement, inter-religious 14–15, 17, 25–6

religious disagreement, intra-religious 14–15, 31

religious diversity 15n.34, 18–24

religious experience 15–17, 27–8, 118–23

religious truth 22–6, 30, 201, 217–20

religious understanding 26–7, 41–3, 48–51

Rice, Rebekah 2n.1

Rosen, Gideon 14

Rosenberg, Alex 100

Ross, Lee 13n.30

Roush, Sherilee 160n.32

Rowland, Richard 2n.2

salvation/redemption 22–4, 30

Schellenberg, J.L. 21, 132n.7, 157, 157n.28

Schoenfield, Miriam 5–6, 81–6, 193n.15

Scott, Kyle 41n.1

seemings, theistic 75–6

self-defeat 145

self-disagreement 136–40

self-gaslighting 260–3

sensus divinitatis 134–6

set theory 199–200

Shah, Nishi 62n.34

Shepherd of Hermas 275–7

Simpson, Thomas 2n.1

skepticism 65

skepticism, religious 16–18, 16n.37, 27–8

Sosa, Ernest 16n.39, 20n.45

soteriology 228–9, 284–5

Spurgeon, Charles 155

Srinivasan, Amia 8n.18, 9n.19, 13–14, 53n.23

Staffel, Julia 3n.7

Stanford, Kyle 149n.13

Steadfasters 11–13, 24–5, 27

Strong Impartiality 186–7, 190–1, 193–201

Stump, Eleonore 21n.50

Swinburne, Richard 15–16, 164–5

testimony 15–16, 26–7, 118

theism 14–16, 15n.33, 21–2, 22n.53, 24, 28–31, 75, 79–80, 85–7, 130–1, 144, 149–50, 205–6, 210

theology, diversity of opinion 31, 271–3

Thurow, Joshua 18n.41

Titelbaum, Michael 5n.11, 12n.25

transformative experience 27–8, 93n.4,
    127–31, 136–40
Truth Independence 83–4
Turnbull, Margaret Greta 27, 98n.12

Ullian, Joseph 42n.3
underdetermination 148–9
underdetermination, contrastive 149
underdetermination, holist 149
understanding 41–2, 45–8
Uniqueness thesis 5–6, 8–9, 11, 28–9, 81,
    153, 174–5
universalism 168, 272–3, 285n.19

van Inwagen, Peter 12n.25, 14, 94n.5, 147
Vavova, Katia 2n.2, 8n.18, 19–20

Velleman, David 62n.34
veridicality 76

Wager argument 139
Warfield, Ted 2n.4
Weatherson, Brian 10, 12n.25
Weisberg, Jonathan 11n.22
Whitcomb, Dennis 150–1
White, Roger 5–6, 8n.18, 15n.34, 19n.44,
    70, 80n.27, 154, 174, 208n.32
Wiebe, Philip 93–4
Williamson, Timothy 12n.28, 20n.45,
    69n.8
Wolterstorff, Nicholas 29n.61

Zagzebski, Linda 16, 25n.57, 286